SUNDAY BUSINESS

MILLENNIUM EDITION

Dear diner,

We at Sunday Business are delighted to offer
our loyal and fast-growing readership this
special millennium edition of the world-famous
Zagat guide to 1,200 London restaurants.
Like Sunday Business, Zagat prides itself on
being readable and authoritative. Together
we cut a path through life's clutter to bring
you accessible, accurate information, enabling
readers to make the right decisions.
A top-notch guide for a high-class newspaper.
A perfect match for the year 2000.

Best wishes,

JEFF RANDALL, EDITOR

D0813702

ZAGATSURVEY®

2000

LONDON
RESTAURANTS

Edited and coordinated by
Sholto Douglas-Home
and Susan Kessler

Published and distributed by
ZAGAT SURVEY, LLC
4 Columbus Circle
New York, New York 10019
Tel: 212 977 6000
E-mail: zagat@zagatsurvey.com
Web site: zagat.com

Acknowledgments

Gilian Annesly, Jane and Stephen Barclay, Deborah Bennett, Karen Bonham, Robert Brunck, Caroline Clegg, Ricki Conway, Alex Douglas-Home, Amanda Fox, Polly Greene, Michael and Sandra Howard, Barbara Illias, Larry Kessler, Le Cordon Bleu, Pamela and Michael Lester, Jenny Linford, Annie McIsaac, Jeremy Miles, Ben and Sheila Miller, Zoe Miller, Jean Oddy, Emmy Reyes, Natasha Robinson, Anne Semmes, Clare Sievers, Alexandra Spezzotti, Rebecca Stephenson, Annie Tobin, Karenza Townend, Peter Vogl, Giles Webster, Susan Weingarten and Beverley Wilson.

Contents

Starters

Here are the results of our *2000 London Restaurant Survey* covering almost 1,200 restaurants in the London area, including nearly 50 favourites outside the capital.

By regularly surveying large numbers of local restaurant-goers, we think we have achieved a uniquely current and reliable guide. We hope you agree. More than 2,700 people participated. Since the participants dined out an average of 2.45 times per week, this *Survey* is based on about 344,000 meals per year.

We want to thank each of our participants. They are a widely diverse group in all respects but one – they are food lovers all. This book is really "theirs."

Of the surveyors, 48% are women, 52% are men; the breakdown by age is 21% in their 20s, 34% in their 30s, 22% in their 40s, 16% in their 50s and 7% in their 60s or above.

To help guide our readers to London's best meals and best buys, we have prepared a number of lists. See, for example, London's Most Popular Restaurants (page 12), Top Ratings (pages 13–18) and Best Buys (pages 19–20). On the assumption that most people want a quick fix on the places at which they are considering eating, we have tried to be concise and to provide handy indexes.

We are particularly grateful to our editors/coordinators: Sholto Douglas-Home, a London restaurant critic for 13 years, and Susan Kessler, Managing Director of Zagat Survey in the UK and a cookbook author and freelance writer for publications in the UK and US.

We invite you to be a reviewer in our next *Survey*. To do so, simply send a stamped, self-addressed, business-size envelope to ZAGAT SURVEY, Suite 568, 28 Old Brompton Rd, London, SW7 3SS, or 4 Columbus Circle, New York, NY 10019, so that we will be able to contact you. Each participant will receive a free copy of the next *London Restaurant Survey* when it is published.

Your comments, suggestions and even criticisms of this *Survey* are also solicited. There is always room for improvement with your help.

New York, New York   Nina and Tim Zagat
26 August, 1999

What's New

Welcome to the fourth edition of the *Zagat London Restaurant Survey* (and, of course, the first of the new millennium), which includes feedback from over 2,700 participants on almost 1,200 restaurants, including nearly 50 favourites outside London. All our participants are restaurant enthusiasts, eating out an average of 2.45 times a week and visiting the places they voted on an average of 8.9 times a year.

The results of this year's *Survey* paint an interesting picture after last year's game of musical chairs at the highest echelons of London's culinary scene, i.e. the relocation of La Tante Claire, Gordon Ramsay striking out on his own and The Belgo Group purchasing The Ivy and Le Caprice, among others.

In the Top Food rankings, Le Manoir aux Quat'Saisons in Oxfordshire moved from No. 2 in 1999 to pole position in 2000, with the former leader, La Tante Claire, sliding down to 9th – suggesting that its move to The Berkeley Hotel has not been to everyone's satisfaction. Meanwhile, Gordon Ramsay's year out of the ratings (due to his leaving Aubergine to set up on his own) has been short-lived, with his eponymous restaurant making a storming debut in the No. 2 spot – making it No. 1 within London.

In the Popularity stakes, The Ivy and Le Caprice are clearly doing well under new owners the Belgo Group as the siblings now rank as London's two Most Popular restaurants (with The Ivy retaining its first-place title from last year and Le Caprice moving up from 3rd). La Tante Claire, meanwhile, fell from second Most Popular last year to 17th this year. Other major moves: Nobu rose to 4th (from 7th last year) and The Square broke into the Top 10 for the first time at No. 6 (up from 15th), whilst Gordon Ramsay and Mirabelle both entered the Top 10 in their first rated years, placing 9th and 10th respectively. Major moves in the opposite direction: Blue Elephant (from 6th down to 12th), Le Pont de la Tour (11th to 18th) and Quaglino's (10th down to 20th).

The entry of The Square and Gordon Ramsay into London's Top 10 Most Popular rankings offers convincing evidence that there's still a demand for 'fancier food', despite the hot debate in the industry over whether Londoners' palates are 'dumbing-down' the standard of cooking in the capital. The issue has been bubbling away since respected chef Garry Hollihead left Morton's, claiming his diners were not interested in 'serious food' and just wanted to be in and out in an hour. There may be some truth in this, but that isn't necessarily a bad thing for the industry. Londoners' dining patterns have changed to such an extent that casual eating out is becoming as much a way of life in London as it is in New

6

York, hence restaurateurs have seen a boom in everyday dining. And as the Top 10 Most Popular ranking proves, top-end restaurants offering special occasion dining are also faring well.

As in years past, the industry's biggest shortcoming is the quality of service, with surveyors frequently citing "slow" or generally "poor" service. However, the quality of the cooking remains a more important factor, with 89% of respondents claiming, not surprisingly, that the most important element in their appraisal of a restaurant is food.

Other interesting results: the average cost per-meal was £28.86; surveyors report tipping an average of 11.8%; 71% believe men are treated better in restaurants (52% of the surveyors were men); and 66% 'always' have wine with a meal versus 30% who 'sometimes' do. When asked where they would like to dine on millennium night, many surveyors answered 'at home' – no doubt reflecting wariness of inflated costs on millennium eve. As for restaurants, a frequently named millennium venue was Oxo Tower, aided no doubt by all the festivities planned along the Thames.

So what does the future of London dining look like as we head into the new millennium? It is something of a curate's egg. There are restaurants enjoying boom times, with double sittings, waiting lists and high profits, whilst many others are finding the going tough, with slow lunchtime traffic, squeezed margins and skilled staff becoming ever more difficult to find and keep. Even so, the determination of seasoned restaurateurs to open new ventures appears undiminished. Coming soon: FireBird, a glossy Russian in Mayfair; Isola, a sophisticated Knightsbridge Italian from Oliver Peyton; The Site, Paul Merrett's interesting newcomer in Tower Street; Smith's, from John Torode, near Smithfield Market; and a new venture from Terence Conran in his handsome Great Eastern Hotel in Bishopsgate.

Takeover activity also continues: the team behind Avenue and Circus are taking over the established trio of The Brackenbury, Kensington Place and Launceston Place; Matthew Freud and Damien Hirst (Pharmacy) are in merger talks with the Montana group (Canyon, Dakota, Idaho, Montana); and the Searcy/Richard Corrigan team is moving in on English Garden.

This hive of activity from respected names is as good an omen for the future as any – and as always, we'd love to hear what you think about their efforts. So if you are not already a contributor, please register your interest in becoming a reviewer for the *2001 Zagat London Survey*. Here's wishing you many enjoyable meals throughout 2000.

Kensington, London   Sholto Douglas-Home
26 August, 1999

Key to Ratings/Symbols

This sample entry identifies the various types of information contained in your Zagat Survey.

(1) Restaurant Name, Address, Tube Stop & Phone Number

(2) Hours & Credit Cards

(3) ZAGAT Ratings

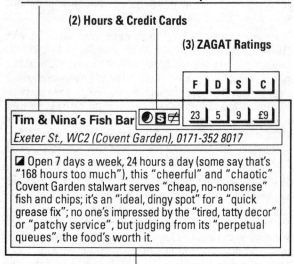

F	D	S	C
23	5	9	£9

Tim & Nina's Fish Bar ◑ S ⌿
Exeter St., WC2 (Covent Garden), 0171-352 8017

☑ Open 7 days a week, 24 hours a day (some say that's "168 hours too much"), this "cheerful" and "chaotic" Covent Garden stalwart serves "cheap, no-nonsense" fish and chips; it's an "ideal, dingy spot" for a "quick grease fix"; no one's impressed by the "tired, tatty decor" or "patchy service", but judging from its "perpetual queues", the food's worth it.

(4) Surveyors' Commentary

The names of restaurants with the highest overall ratings and greatest popularity are printed in **CAPITAL LETTERS**. Address and phone numbers are printed in *italics*. **PLEASE NOTE:** the UK telephone system is being reorganised. As from 22nd April 2000, all numbers that now begin with 0171 will begin instead with (020)-7, and all numbers that now begin with 0181 will begin instead with (020)-8.

(2) Hours & Credit Cards

After each restaurant name you will find the following courtesy information:

◑ .... *serving after 11 PM*

S .... *open on Sunday*

⌿ .... *no credit cards accepted*

(3) ZAGAT Ratings

Food, **Decor** and **Service** are each rated on a scale of **0** to **30**:

F	D	S	C

F .... *Food*
D .... *Decor*
S .... *Service*
C .... *Cost*

23	5	9	£9

0 - 9	....	*poor to fair*
10 - 15	....	*fair to good*
16 - 19	....	*good to very good*
20 - 25	....	*very good to excellent*
26 - 30	....	*extraordinary to perfection*

▽ 23	5	9	£9

▽ .... *Low number of votes/less reliable*

The **Cost (C)** column reflects the estimated price of a dinner with one drink and service. Lunch may cost up to 25% less.

A restaurant listed without ratings is either an important **newcomer** or a popular **write-in**. The estimated cost, with one drink and service, is indicated by the following symbols.

–	–	–	VE

I .... *£15 and below*
M .... *£16 to £25*
E .... *£26 to £35*
VE .... *£36 or more*

(4) Surveyors' Commentary

Surveyors' comments are summarised, with literal comments shown in quotation marks. The following symbols indicate whether responses were mixed or uniform.

▨ .... *mixed*
■ .... *uniform*

London's Most Popular

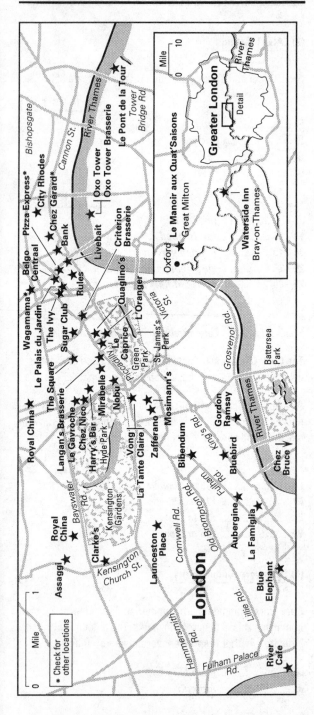

Greater London

- River Thames
- Tower Bridge Rd.
- Mile 0 10
- Detail
- Le Manoir aux Quat'Saisons — Great Milton
- Oxford
- Waterside Inn — Bray-on-Thames

London map

- River Thames
- Bishopsgate
- Cannon St.
- Le Pont de la Tour
- Oxo Tower
- Oxo Tower Brasserie
- City Rhodes
- Pizza Express*
- Chez Gerard*
- Bank
- Belgo Centraal
- Criterion Brasserie
- Livebait
- Quaglino's
- Wagamama
- Rules
- The Ivy
- Le Palais du Jardin
- Sugar Club
- L'Oranger
- Le Caprice
- Victoria St.
- St. James's Park
- Green Park
- Piccadilly
- The Square
- Langan's Brasserie
- Le Gavroche
- Chez Nico
- Mirabelle
- Nobu
- Royal China
- Harry's Bar
- Hyde Park
- Vong
- Mosimann's
- Grosvenor Rd.
- Battersea Park
- Zafferano
- La Tante Claire
- Bibendum
- Gordon Ramsay
- King's Rd.
- Bluebird
- Chez Bruce
- River Thames
- Royal China
- Bayswater Rd.
- Kensington Gardens
- Clarke's
- Launceston Place
- Kensington Church St.
- Cromwell Rd.
- Old Brompton Rd.
- Aubergine
- La Famiglia
- Blue Elephant
- Fulham Rd.
- Lillie Rd.
- Assaggi
- Mile 0 1
- * Check for other locations
- Hammersmith Rd.
- Fulham Palace Rd.
- River Cafe
- London

10

Outside London

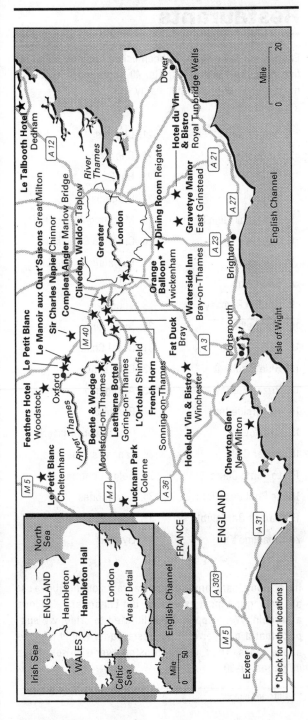

Le Talbooth Hotel Dedham

Hotel du Vin & Bistro Royal Tunbridge Wells

River Thames

Le Manoir aux Quat'Saisons Great Milton

Sir Charles Napier Chinnor

Compleat Angler Marlow Bridge

Cliveden, Waldo's Taplow

Greater London

Dining Room Reigate

Gravetye Manor East Grinstead

Orange Balloon*

Waterside Inn Bray-on-Thames

Twickenham

Brighton

English Channel

Isle of Wight

Portsmouth

Feathers Hotel Woodstock

Le Petit Blanc

Fat Duck Bray

French Horn Sonning-on-Thames

L'Ortolan Shinfield

Beetle & Wedge Moulsford-on-Thames

Leatherne Bottel Goring-on-Thames

Oxford

Hotel du Vin & Bistro Winchester

Chewton Glen New Milton

Le Petit Blanc Cheltenham

Lucknam Park Colerne

River Thames

ENGLAND

Dover

Area of Detail

North Sea

ENGLAND

Hambleton

Hambleton Hall

WALES

London

FRANCE

Irish Sea

Celtic Sea

English Channel

Exeter

* Check for other locations

11

Most Popular Restaurants

Each of our reviewers has been asked to name his or her five favourite restaurants. The 40 spots most frequently named, in order of their popularity, are:

1. Ivy	21. Clarke's
2. Le Caprice	22. Chez Nico
3. River Cafe	23. Bank
4. Nobu	24. Wagamama
5. Le Manoir/Quat'Saisons†	25. Mosimann's (club)
6. Square	26. Criterion Brasserie
7. Zafferano	27. Le Palais du Jardin
8. Bibendum	28. Rules
9. Gordon Ramsay	29. Vong
10. Mirabelle	30. Aubergine
11. Le Gavroche	31. Royal China
12. Blue Elephant	32. Chez Bruce
13. Pizza Express	33. Assaggi
14. Waterside Inn†	34. Bluebird
15. Oxo Tower	35. Oxo Tower Brasserie
16. Sugar Club	36. Langan's Brasserie
17. La Tante Claire	37. Belgo Centraal
18. Le Pont de la Tour	38. City Rhodes
19. Harry's Bar (club)	39. Chez Gérard
20. Quaglino's	40. Livebait

It's obvious that many of the restaurants on the above list are among the most expensive, but Londoners also love a bargain. Were popularity calibrated to price, we suspect that a number of other restaurants would join the above ranks. Thus, we have listed over 170 Best Buys on pages 19–20.

† Outside London.

Top Ratings*

Top 40 Food Ranking

28 Le Manoir/Quat'Saisons†
27 Gordon Ramsay
    Le Gavroche
    Waterside Inn†
    Chewton Glen Hotel†
    Capital
26 Nobu
    Square
    La Tante Claire
    Chez Nico
    Oak Room MPW
    L'Ortolan†
25 Chez Bruce
    Zafferano
    Mosimann's (club)
    Aubergine
    Pied-à-Terre
    Hambleton Hall†
    Clarke's
    Halkin, Stefano Cavallini

    Club Gascon
    Monsieur Max**
    River Cafe
    Connaught Hotel
    Assaggi
    Cafe Japan
    Ivy
    Royal China
24 Harry's Bar (club)
    Pizza Metro
    Le Caprice
    Mark's Club (club)
    Rasa
    Richard Corrigan
    City Rhodes
    Kai
    Gravetye Manor†
    Cliveden, Waldo's†
    Dining Room†**
    Caviar Kaspia

Top Spots by Cuisine

Breakfast††
20 Bank
19 Villandry
18 Nicole's
    Cafe at Sotheby's
17 Simpson's in The Strand

British (Modern)
25 Chez Bruce
    Clarke's
24 Richard Corrigan
    City Rhodes
    Leith's

British (Traditional)
25 Connaught Hotel
23 Savoy Grill
    Dorchester, Grill Room
    Wilton's
22 Guinea

Brunch
24 Le Caprice
21 Café Milan
20 Lola's
19 Dakota
    Villandry

Cafes
21 Café Milan
20 Bibendum Oyster Bar
    Patisserie Valerie
18 Cafe at Sotheby's
    Fifth Floor Cafe

Cheeseboard
27 Gordon Ramsay
26 Square
    La Tante Claire
    Chez Nico
    Oak Room MPW

---

*   Excluding restaurants with low voting.
†   Outside London.
** Tied with the restaurant listed directly above it.
†† Other than hotels.

Top Food

Chinese
- **25** Royal China
- **24** Kai
- **23** Dorchester, Oriental
  Mao Tai
- **22** Zen Garden

Chophouses
- **22** Guinea
- **21** Quality Chop House
- **20** Gaucho Grill
  El Gaucho
- **18** Butlers Wharf

Eclectic/International
- **23** Bibendum
  Four Seasons, Lanes
- **22** Savoy River Rest.
  Blakes Hotel
- **21** Lanesborough Conservatory

Fish 'n' Chips
- **22** Two Brothers Fish
- **21** Sweetings
- **20** Rudland & Stubbs
- **19** Upper St. Fish Shop
- **17** Seashell

French (Classic)
- **27** Le Gavroche
- **26** La Tante Claire
  Chez Nico
  Oak Room MPW
- **25** Monsieur Max

French (New)
- **27** Gordon Ramsay
  Capital
- **26** Square
- **25** Aubergine
  Pied-à-Terre

Greek
- **20** Halepi
- **19** Daphne
  Lemonia
- **18** Greek Valley
- **17** Kalamaras Micro

Hotel Dining
- **27** Capital/Capital Hotel
- **26** Nobu/Metropolitan Hotel
  La Tante Claire/Berkeley
  Chez Nico/Grosvenor Hse.
  Oak Room MPW/Le Meridien

Indian/Pakistani
- **24** Rasa
- **23** Tamarind
  Vama
  Salloos (Pakistani)
- **21** Lahore Kebab (Pakistani)

In-Store Eating
- **22** Books for Cooks
- **21** Fifth Floor
- **18** Nicole's
  Bluebird
  Cafe at Sotheby's

Italian
- **25** Zafferano
  Halkin, Stefano Cavallini
  River Cafe
  Assaggi
- **23** Tentazioni

Japanese
- **26** Nobu
- **25** Cafe Japan
- **23** Suntory
  Tatsuso
  Miyama

Lunch Spots
- **26** Nobu
  Square
- **25** Zafferano
  Ivy
- **23** Mirabelle

Mediterranean
- **22** Moro
  Eagle
- **21** Olivo
- **20** Snows on the Green
- **19** Oxo Tower Brasserie

Mexican/Tex-Mex/SW
- **20** Montana
- **19** Dakota
  Canyon
- **16** Café Pacifico
  Navajo Joe

Middle Eastern
- **23** Al Sultan
- **21** Maroush
  Phoenicia
- **20** Fakhreldine
  Al Hamra

Top Food

Modern European

25 Ivy
24 Le Caprice
23 Frith Street
22 Le Pont de la Tour
21 Gresslin's

Newcomers/Rated

25 Club Gascon
23 Frith Street
    Four Seasons, Lanes
22 J. Sheekey
21 Floriana

Newcomers/Unrated

    Fish!
    Glasshouse
    Idaho
    Prism
    Zaika

North American

18 Christopher's
17 Wolfe's
    Blues Bistro & Bar
    Joe Allen
16 Arkansas Cafe

Offbeat

25 Club Gascon
22 Books for Cooks
21 Birdcage
17 Belgo Noord
    Pharmacy

Olde England

25 Connaught Hotel (1897)
23 Wilton's (1742)
    Claridge's Rest. (1898)
21 Sweetings (1889)
20 Rules (1798)

Outdoor

25 River Cafe
23 Mirabelle
22 Le Pont de la Tour
20 La Famiglia
18 Coq d'Argent

People-Watching

26 Nobu
25 Ivy
24 Le Caprice
19 San Lorenzo
17 Pharmacy

Pizza

24 Pizza Metro
21 Eco
    Pizzeria Castello
20 Oliveto
19 Red Pepper

Private Clubs (Members Only)

25 Mosimann's
24 Harry's Bar
    Mark's Club
21 Monte's
20 Annabel's

Private Rooms

26 Square
25 Connaught Hotel
23 Dorchester, Oriental
    Mirabelle
19 Sartoria

Pub Dining

22 Eagle
21 Churchill Arms
20 Duke of Cambridge (SW11)
19 Peasant
    Chelsea Ram

Rooms with a View

26 Nobu
22 Le Pont de la Tour
20 Oxo Tower
18 Coq d'Argent
17 Putney Bridge

Seafood

23 Wilton's
22 Jason's
    Pescatori
21 Sweetings
    One-O-One

Spanish

20 Gaudi
19 El Blason
18 Cambio de Tercio
17 Meson Don Felipe
16 La Mancha

Sunday Lunch/Town

25 Chez Bruce
    River Cafe
    Assaggi
    Ivy
21 Greenhouse

Top Food

Sunday Lunch/Country
- **28** Le Manoir/Quat'Saisons
- **27** Chewton Glen Hotel
- **26** L'Ortolan
- **23** Fat Duck
- Beetle & Wedge

Tasting Menus
- **27** Gordon Ramsay
- **26** Nobu
- Square
- Oak Room MPW
- **25** Club Gascon

Tea
- Brown's Hotel
- Capital Hotel
- Lanesborough Hotel
- Ritz Hotel
- Savoy Hotel

Thai
- **23** Vong
- **22** Blue Elephant
- **21** Patara
- Bangkok
- Thai on the River

Theatre District
- **23** Frith Street
- **22** J. Sheekey
- **20** Bank
- Criterion Brasserie
- **18** Christopher's

Vegetarian
- **24** Rasa
- **23** Gate
- **19** Blah! Blah! Blah!
- Mandeer
- Rani

Wild Cards
- **23** Sugar Club/Pacific Fusion
- **22** Moro/Moorish-Med.
- **21** bali sugar/Japan.–S. Amer.
- I-Thai/Italian-Thai
- **19** Silks & Spice/Thai-Malay.

Wine Bars
- **19** Bleeding Heart
- **18** L'Estaminet
- Crescent
- **17** Ebury Wine Bar
- **16** Le Metro

Top Spots by Area

Belgravia/Chelsea/South Kensington/Knightsbridge
- **27** Gordon Ramsay
- Capital
- **26** La Tante Claire
- **25** Zafferano
- Aubergine

City/Clerkenwell
- **25** Club Gascon
- **24** City Rhodes
- **23** Tatsuso
- **22** Moro
- Maison Novelli

Covent Garden/Soho
- **25** Ivy
- **24** Richard Corrigan
- **23** Sugar Club
- Savoy Grill
- Frith Street

Kensington/Notting Hill
- **25** Clarke's
- Assaggi
- **24** Leith's
- **23** Room at Halcyon
- **21** bali sugar

Mayfair/Piccadilly
- **27** Le Gavroche
- **26** Nobu
- Square
- Chez Nico
- Oak Room MPW

Trips to the Country
- **28** Le Manoir/Quat'Saisons/
  Great Milton
- **27** Waterside Inn/
  Bray-on-Thames
- Chewton Glen Hotel/
  New Milton
- **26** L'Ortolan/
  Shinfield
- **25** Hambleton Hall/
  Hambleton

Top 40 Decor Ranking

27 Ritz Restaurant

26 Le Manoir/Quat'Saisons†
Mosimann's (club)
Amberley Castle†
Mark's Club (club)
Cliveden, Waldo's†

25 Sàrastro
Criterion Brasserie
Hartwell House†
Hambleton Hall†
Chewton Glen Hotel†

24 Lanesborough Conservatory
I-Thai
Graveteye Manor†
Blue Elephant
Momo
Waterside Inn†
Oxo Tower
La Porte des Indes

23 Windows on the World

Annabel's (club)
Savoy River Rest.
Capital
Floriana*
Harry's Bar (club)
Connaught Hotel
Dorchester, Grill Room
Blakes Hotel
Lucknam Park†
Bibendum
Ivy
Pasha (SW7)
Oxo Tower Brasserie
Buckland Manor†
Oak Room MPW

22 Halkin, Stefano Cavallini
Rainforest Cafe
Rules
Odin's
Le Pont de la Tour

Outdoor

Admiral Codrington
Al Hamra
Belair House
Belvedere
Canyon
Coq d'Argent
Dan's
Daphne's

La Famiglia
Le Pont de la Tour
Mirabelle
Oxo Tower
Ransome's Dock
Ritz Restaurant
River Cafe
Room at Halcyon

Romantic

Andrew Edmunds
Belvedere
Blakes Hotel
Claridge's Rest.
Gordon Ramsay
Julie's
La Poule au Pot
Launceston Place

Le Gavroche
Mirabelle
Odin's
Pétrus
Prism
Richard Corrigan
Ritz Restaurant
Snows on the Green

---

† Outside London.
* Tied with the restaurant listed directly above it.

Rooms

Avenue
Bluebird
Capital
Connaught Hotel
Criterion Brasserie
Ivy
Lanesborough Conservatory
Mirabelle

Momo
Oak Room MPW
Pharmacy
Quaglino's
Ritz Restaurant
Square
Tate Gallery
Titanic

Views

Belair House
Belvedere
Blue Print Cafe
Canteen
Canyon
Coq d'Argent
County Hall
Le Pont de la Tour

Nobu
Oxo Tower
Park Restaurant
People's Palace
Putney Bridge
Tenth
Thai on the River
Windows on the World

Top 40 Service Ranking

27 Mark's Club (club)
26 Le Manoir/Quat'Saisons†
Le Gavroche
Chewton Glen Hotel†
Waterside Inn†
25 Capital
Connaught Hotel
Gordon Ramsay
Harry's Bar (club)
Mosimann's (club)
Cliveden, Waldo's†
Gravetye Manor†
Hambleton Hall†
24 Dorchester, Grill Room
La Tante Claire
Square
Buckland Manor†
Lucknam Park†
Claridge's Rest.
Hartwell House†

Wilton's
Ritz Restaurant
Le Soufflé
23 Ivy
Savoy Grill
Dorchester, Oriental
Annabel's (club)
Chez Nico
Le Caprice
Halkin, Stefano Cavallini
Oslo Court
Oak Room MPW
Goring Dining Room
L'Ortolan†
Clarke's
Room at Halcyon
Aubergine
Savoy River Rest.
755
Upstairs at The Savoy*

---

† Outside London.
* Tied with the restaurant listed directly above it.

Best Buys

This list reflects the best dining values in our *Survey*. It is produced by dividing the cost of a meal into the combined ratings for food, decor and service.

1. Soup Opera
2. Starbucks/Seattle Coffee
3. Coffee Republic
4. Maison Bertaux
5. Aroma
6. Caffè Nero
7. Food for Thought
8. Churchill Arms
9. Tom's Delicatessen
10. Place Below
11. Cranks
12. Books for Cooks
13. Patisserie Valerie
14. Wagamama
15. Pollo Bar
16. Pizzeria Castello
17. Troubadour
18. Pizza Express
19. Ed's Easy Diner
20. Mildreds
21. Duke of Cambridge (SW11)
22. Pepper Tree
23. Jenny Lo's Tea House
24. Ask Pizza
25. Viet Hoa
26. Nautilus Fish
27. Eco
28. Little Bay
29. Ravi Shankar
30. Waxy O'Connor's Pub
31. DKNY Bar
32. Film Café
33. Lahore Kebab House
34. Satsuma
35. Alounak
36. Chelsea Kitchen
37. Two Brothers Fish
38. Gate
39. Arkansas Cafe
40. Fox & Anchor
41. Condotti
42. Blah! Blah! Blah!
43. Costa's Grill
44. Chelsea Bun
45. Upper St. Fish Shop
46. Fatboy's Cafe
47. Prince Bonaparte
48. Eagle
49. Mandeer
50. Buona Sera
51. New Culture Revolution
52. Chutney's
53. Rasa
54. Luigi's Delicatessen
55. Pizza Metro
56. Havelock Tavern
57. Honest Cabbage
58. Adams Cafe
59. Sofra
60. All Bar One
61. Rotisserie Jules
62. Pizza The Action
63. Anglesea Arms
64. Marine Ices
65. Greek Valley
66. Sporting Page
67. Cantaloupe Bar & Grill
68. Ben's Thai
69. Tokyo Diner
70. Great Nepalese
71. Wok Wok
72. Cafe Japan
73. Pizza on the Park
74. Japanese Canteen
75. Belgo Noord
76. Balans West
77. Lee Fook
78. Kulu Kulu Sushi
79. Rainforest Cafe
80. Hi Sushi

Additional Good Values
(A bit more expensive, but worth every penny)

Andrew Edmunds
Arancia
Balans
Bangkok
Bengal Trader
Bertorelli's Cafe Italian
Bibendum Oyster Bar
Blue Jade
Bombay Bicycle Club
Cafe at Sotheby's
Café Delancey
Cafe des Arts
Café Milan
Café Pacifico
Cafe Spice Namaste
Calzone
Camden Brasserie
Chelsea Ram
Chez Gérard
Chiang Mai
Chuen Cheng Ku
Cookhouse
Côte à Côte
Crescent
Daphne
Efes Kebab House
El Gaucho
Elistano
Engineer
Enterprise
Esarn Kheaw
Feng Shang Floating
ffiona's
Fifth Floor Cafe
Fortnum's Fountain
Four Seasons Chinese
Geale's
Golden Dragon
Gopal's of Soho
Green Cottage
Hard Rock Cafe
Harrods
Havana
itsu
Jen
Jin Kichi

Joy King Lau
Khan's
Lansdowne
Lavender
Lemonia
Made in Italy
Ma Goa
Maggiore's
Malabar
Malabar Junction
Mandola Café
Maroush
Melati
Min's
Noor Jahan
Noto
Oliveto
Osteria Basilico
Patara
Picasso
Pitcher & Piano
Pizza Pomodoro
PJ's Bar & Grill
Planet Hollywood
Poons
Purple Sage
Queens
Randall & Aubin
Rani
Red Pepper
Reynier Wine Library
Royal China
Seashell
Silks & Spice
Solly's
Spighetta
Sticky Fingers
Tandoori Lane
Tate Gallery
Tui
Veronica's
Vingt-Quatre
Westbourne
Yo! Sushi
Yum Yum Thai
Zamoyski

Alphabetical Directory of Restaurants

London

| F | D | S | C |

Abingdon, The S
17 | 15 | 16 | £25

54 Abingdon Rd., W8 (Earl's Court/High St. Kensington), 0171-937 3339

■ "Solid on all fronts" is the consensus on this "friendly", "quaint" Kensington pub conversion (owned by Capital Radio) known for "decent", "steady" Modern French food that's "good value" to some, but "a tad expensive" to others; "media types" and "local lushes" are so enamoured of the "great bar area" that it can get "uncomfortably full."

Adams Cafe S
16 | 8 | 16 | £15

77 Askew Rd., W12 (Ravenscourt Park/Shepherd's Bush), 0181-743 0572

■ This "cheap, cheerful" Shepherd's Bush venue makes a "remarkable evening transition" from a "greasy" local cafe into a "cosy", "family-run house" serving "very reliable", "wholesome" Tunisian-Moroccan dishes from an "interesting" if "small menu."

Admiral Codrington, The ●S
_ | _ | _ | E

17 Mossop St., SW3 (South Kensington), 0171-581 0005

A major transformation of this landmark Chelsea pub spruced up the bar and added an airy, narrow restaurant at the rear showcasing the talents of Stephen Terry (consultant chef) and Nina Campbell (interior design); the upshot: a polished newcomer with straightforward Modern British fare, well-priced wines and a retractable glass roof for instant alfresco dining.

Alastair Little ●
22 | 13 | 19 | £36

49 Frith St., W1 (Tottenham Court Rd.), 0171-734 5183

◪ The "clinical" atmosphere of this "austere" Soho eaterie is "perversely gratifying" to some, whilst others claim it "sucks the emotion from food", yet the "uncomplicated" Modern British cooking featuring "high-quality ingredients" "hits the spot" for most; however, price is as much a bugbear as the decor: "a little style, but a lotta dosh."

Alastair Little at Lancaster Rd.
20 | 13 | 17 | £32

136A Lancaster Rd., W11 (Ladbroke Grove), 0171-243 2220

◪ "A neighbourhood bistro for the Notting Hill mob" that draws a mixed response, with some praising Alastair Little's "lovely touch" and "excellent food" and others finding it "overpriced" and "not quite up to expectations"; the setting is "cramped" and "unrelaxing" but offers one bonus: "enjoyed the conversation of all our neighbours."

Alba 17 | 11 | 17 | £24
107 Whitecross St., EC1 (Barbican/Moorgate), 0171-588 1798
■ "Decent for a quick lunch" of "genuine Piedmontese" cooking from a "good value", "consistent" Modern Italian menu that's "cooked by, served by, and often to, Italians"; it's "convenient for the Barbican", but expect "many lawyers" and "decor as drab as Turin."

Al Bustan [S] 19 | 15 | 18 | £28
27 Motcomb St., SW1 (Knightsbridge), 0171-235 8277
■ "Nothing is too much trouble" at this "friendly" Lebanese on the Knightsbridge-Belgravia border serving "great fresh food" of "consistent quality"; some feel the place is "let down by a lack of ambience", but there's always "good takeout": "my dogs are addicted to my leftovers."

Alfred ◐ 18 | 11 | 15 | £24
245 Shaftesbury Ave., WC2 (Tottenham Court Rd.), 0171-240 2566
◪ The "spartan interior" with its "Formica-table canteen atmosphere" puts off some, but not those who say the "good, basic" English cooking is "like going home to mother" and "good value" for "the area" (the top of Shaftesbury Avenue); some go just for the cider selection and "interesting beer cocktails."

Al Hamra ◐ [S] 20 | 14 | 16 | £30
31-33 Shepherd Mkt., W1 (Green Park), 0171-493 1954
■ A "stalwart for business diners" in Shepherd Market, this Lebanese offers "authentic", "continuously good food", including "nice veggie choices" and "excellent meze"; although some claim "prices have risen" and lament "slow service", most enjoy the chance "to eat alfresco in warm weather."

alistair Greig's Grill ◐ [S] ▽ 19 | 15 | 19 | £40
26 Bruton Pl., W1 (Bond St./Green Park), 0171-629 5613
■ There's "a unique atmosphere" at this "great chophouse" in a Mayfair mews; a true carnivore's den, it's a bit of a "men's joint", offering a traditional British menu of grilled meat and fish, supported by a 100-strong wine list.

All Bar One 12 | 13 | 12 | £14
19 Henrietta St., WC2 (Covent Garden), 0171-557 7941 [S]
48 Leicester Sq., WC2 (Leicester Sq.), 0171-747 9921 [S]
126-128 Notting Hill Gate, W11 (Notting Hill Gate), 0171-313 9362 [S]
289-293 Regent St., W1 (Oxford Circus), 0171-467 9901 [S]
7-9 Paddington St., W1 (Baker St.), 0171-487 0071 [S]
587-591 Fulham Rd., SW6 (Fulham Broadway), 0171-471 0611 [S]
311-313 Fulham Rd., SW1 (Fulham Broadway), 0171-349 1751 [S]
1 Liverpool Rd., N1 (Angel), 0171-843 0021 [S]
44-46 Ludgate Hill, EC4 (St. Paul's), 0171-653 9901 [S]
(Continues)

All Bar One (Cont.)
93A Charterhouse St., EC1 (Farringdon), 0171-553 9391
42 MacKenzie Walk, E14 (Canary Wharf), 0171-513 0911
Additional locations throughout London.
◪ "Been to one, been to all" – this "dependable" Modern British chain makes a "good meeting place" that's a "nice alternative to a pub", but it "can be noisy and hideously crowded" with an "office party atmosphere"; although it's "more a youngsters' bar than a restaurant", most rate it "acceptable for a quick meal"; N.B. no children allowed.

Alounak ◐ [S] 18 | 11 | 14 | £15
44 Westbourne Grove, W2 (Bayswater), 0171-229 4158
10 Russell Gardens, W14 (Kensington/Olympia), 0171-603 1130
■ A pair of "low-key" eateries in Olympia and Westbourne Grove serving "good, informal Persian food" that's called "authentic" and "well prepared" (although to a few it "all tastes a bit similar"); "no corkage" fee on BYO (wine only) ensures that this "busy, buzzing" duo offers "great value."

Al San Vincenzo 22 | 13 | 16 | £37
30 Connaught St., W2 (Marble Arch), 0171-262 9623
◪ Admirers point to "almost perfect", "high-quality" cooking at this "small", "romantic" Bayswater Italian with "friendly", "family" service, whilst others consider it "unreasonably expensive" and suffering from "an atmosphere bypass"; N.B. the food rating continues to climb, supporting fans.

Al Sultan ◐ [S] 23 | 14 | 20 | £31
51-52 Hertford St., W1 (Green Park/Hyde Park Corner), 0171-408 1155
■ This "comfortable" Shepherd Market Lebanese with "light, crisp decor" is good for "a large crowd", offering music, "slick service" and outside tables; although most find the food "superb" (some dub it the "best Middle Eastern in London"), a few wags think it's "time to re-whip the houmous" – but they're soundly outvoted.

Amandier – | – | – | E
26 Sussex Pl., W2 (Lancaster Gate), 0171-262 6073
Daniel Gobet (ex La Ciboulette) is chef-owner of this stylish new arrival near Lancaster Gate that boasts accomplished, Provençal-inspired Modern French cooking and a healthy selection of regional French wines; whilst pricier than its basement sibling (Bistro Daniel), it's usually more tranquil and a "real treat" according to early visitors.

Andrew Edmunds [S] 20 | 17 | 17 | £26
46 Lexington St., W1 (Oxford Circus), 0171-437 5708
◪ A Soho haunt "for bohemian romantics" that's "a bit scruffy" (some say "quaint") and "cramped" (some say "cosy"), with "dripping candles" and "gothic surroundings"; the "interesting" Eclectic menu is "dependable" rather than "innovative", and there's a "well-chosen wine list."

Anglesea Arms 🅂   17 | 15 | 12 | £17
35 Wingate Rd., W6 (Goldhawk Rd./Ravenscourt Park),
0181-749 1291
◼ The "slowest service in London" complain many, but
they come anyway to this Sheperd's Bush restaurant for
"first-rate" Modern British pub cooking that's "lovely
once you get it" as well as being "fantastic value";
even though it's "always busy", it retains a "wonderful,
relaxed" atmosphere with "loads of character" and
"great outdoor seating" in summer.

Annabel's 🌓   20 | 23 | 23 | £60
Private club; inquiries: 0171-629 1096
◪ Many surveyors consider this "timeless and elegant"
Mayfair venue to be the "classiest [private] club in
London", citing its "great ambience", "attentive service"
and "excellent" classic European fare; doubters claim
it's "had its day" and is "for diners with more money than
sense", but most agree that for a "glamorous", "glitzy"
night out, it's hard to top.

Anna's Place ⇗   19 | 17 | 20 | £27
90 Mildmay Park, N1 (Angel/Highbury & Islington),
0171-249 9379
◪ Though the name remains the same, former owner Anna
Hegarty sold out to the chefs two years ago and there's
now a split vote as to whether this "cosy, enjoyable"
Islingtonian with a "varied" Scandinavian menu "offers
the same great cooking" or has "gone downhill"; either
way, "service remains excellent" and the "pretty paved
courtyard" has its advocates.

Apprentice, The   16 | 13 | 13 | £22
Butlers Wharf Chef School, Cardamon Bldg., 31 Shad
Thames, SE1 (London Bridge/Tower Hill), 0171-234 0254
◪ "Keep practising" suggest those who are less than
impressed by "hit-and-miss service" from trainees who
nevertheless "try very hard" at this culinary training
ground (affiliated with the Butlers Wharf Chef School)
near Tower Bridge; if some claim that the setting is "lacking
in atmosphere", fans say the "good value" Modern British
cooking sometimes "puts the professionals to shame."

Aquarium   16 | 16 | 13 | £28
Ivory House, St. Katharine's Dock, E1 (Tower Hill),
0171-480 6116
◪ All agree the "scenery at St. Katharine's Dock" is
"wonderful" ("a haven amongst commuter madness"),
but there's otherwise little consensus over this new
seafooder, with some finding it "very snooty" and rather
"overhyped", and others reporting "fresh", "superbly
cooked" fish enhanced by the "peaceful" marina setting.

Arancia ▽ 23 | 12 | 19 | £23
Battersea Arts Centre, Old Town Hall, Lavender Hill, SW11 (Clapham Junction), 0171-228 2286
52 Southwark Park Rd., SE16 (Bermondsey), 0171-394 1751
■ It "feels like having dinner at somebody's home" at this "earthy" Bermondsey spot serving "typically hearty Italian peasant food" like "grandmother would make" at "very reasonable" prices; a sibling venue in the Battersea Arts Centre is a cafe by day and a small restaurant at night.

Arcadia [S] 17 | 16 | 18 | £29
35 Kensington High St., W8 (High St. Kensington), 0171-937 4294
◪ The "intimate atmosphere is punctuated by the loud squawking of the resident parrots" at this "fun" Kensington local with "character", where "good" International cooking and "professional service" are appreciated by regulars; critics feel it "needs a revamp" and growl "the parrots can make diners crazy."

Archduke, The 14 | 14 | 13 | £18
Concert Hall Approach, South Bank, SE1 (Waterloo), 0171-928 9370
◪ "Proximity to the Royal Festival Hall is the main virtue" of this "quick, efficient" Eclectic serving "average" but "wholesome" fare "under the arches" of a railway line; some also enjoy the "cheerful, relaxed" ambience, but the more critical think it looks "so dull and '80s" and "doesn't fulfil its potential."

ArdRí at the O'Conor Don ▽ 15 | 11 | 14 | £22
88 Marylebone Ln., W1 (Baker St./Bond St.), 0171-935 9311
◪ Boosters enjoy the "1950s country hotel decor" and "wonderful atmosphere" of this dining room serving "heavy, homely" Irish food and oysters above a crowded Marylebone pub; but detractors claim it's all rather "bland" and a "poor attempt" at creating an "Irishy" experience.

Arkansas Cafe [S] 16 | 8 | 17 | £14
Unit 12, Old Spitalfields Market, E1 (Liverpool St.), 0171-377 6999
■ This "novelty" lunch-only cafe near Spitalfields Market is a "carnivore's delight", serving "simple", "authentic" American barbecue at a "fair price" in "homespun, basic" surroundings – including "uncomfortable seating."

Aroma [S] 11 | 13 | 11 | £9
37 Bedford St., WC2 (Charing Cross/Covent Garden), 0171-836 8816
125 The Strand, WC2 (Charing Cross), 0171-836 8852
1B Dean St., W1 (Tottenham Court Rd.), 0171-287 1633
168 Piccadilly, W1 (Green Park/Piccadilly Circus), 0171-495 6945
273 Regent St., W1 (Oxford Circus), 0171-495 4911

Aroma (Cont.)
187 Tottenham Court Rd., W1 (Tottenham Court Rd.),
0171-637 3346
132 Brompton Rd., SW3 (Knightsbridge), 0171-581 9920
Royal Festival Hall, SE1 (Embankment/Waterloo), 0171-928 0622
60 Fleet St., EC4 (Chancery Ln.), 0171-583 5959
Additional locations throughout London.

■ In addition to the caffeine, "the colour scheme wakes you up" at these "bright", "loud" coffee shops recently taken over by McDonald's, where the coffee has as many friends ("flavourful") as enemies ("run-of-the-mill"); but they're "efficient" and "good value" for a "quick snack."

Aroma Chinese Restaurant ●S 16 | 13 | 15 | £19
11 Gerrard St., W1 (Leicester Sq.), 0171-439 2720
118-120 Shaftesbury Ave., W1 (Leicester Sq./
Tottenham Court Rd.), 0171-437 0377

◪ The "crowded" Chinatown original has been joined by a twin on Shaftesbury Avenue, both preparing "excellent" multiregional Chinese fare; but whilst some praise them as "friendly", a few sniff "success has gone to their heads"; N.B. not to be confused with the same-name coffee chain.

Asia de Cuba ●S – | – | – | VE
St. Martin's Ln. Hotel, 45 St. Martin's Ln., WC2 (Leicester Sq.),
0171-300 5588

Due to open at press time, this elegant dining room in Ian Schrager's flashy, modern new Theatreland hotel will introduce Londoners to the same exciting Asian-Cuban fusion fare that's been a hit in his New York and Los Angeles restaurants of the same name; the hotel also has a more casual brasserie (Saint M) and a trendy bar.

Ask Pizza ●S 15 | 15 | 15 | £14
145 Notting Hill Gate, W11 (Notting Hill Gate), 0171-792 9942
222 Kensington High St., W8 (High St. Kensington),
0171-937 5540
219-221 Chiswick High Rd., W4 (Turnham Green), 0181-742 1323
121-125 Park St., W1 (Marble Arch), 0171-495 7760
48 Grafton Way, W1 (Warren St.), 0171-388 8108
1 Gloucester Arcade, SW7 (Gloucester Rd.), 0171-835 0840
345 Fulham Palace Rd., SW6 (Hammersmith/Putney Bridge),
0171-371 0392
300 King's Rd., SW3 (Sloane Sq.), 0171-349 9123
160-162 Victoria St., SW1 (St. James's Park/Victoria),
0171-630 8228
216 Haverstock Hill, NW3 (Belsize Park/Chalk Farm),
0171-433 3896
Additional locations throughout London.

■ "As Italian as a bulldog, but a great place nonetheless" sums up the majority's reaction to this "clean-cut", "lively" chain offering a "decent" pizza/pasta/salad menu at a "fair price" with "attentive service"; they "fit a busy lifestyle" but some say they're "a wee bit boring" and the "quality varies."

ASSAGGI [S] 25 18 22 £35
39 Chepstow Pl., W2 (Notting Hill Gate), 0171-792 5501
◪ Whether it's "worth the aggro" to get a table on "a month's waiting list" is a moot point with some ("overhyped, overpriced"), but most applaud this "charming" eaterie near Notting Hill where "deliciously authentic" Italian fare and "effusive service" add up to "a perfection you don't expect."

Atlantic Bar & Grill ◐ [S] 16 20 13 £35
20 Glasshouse St., W1 (Piccadilly Circus), 0171-734 4888
◪ "On the out" is how foes describe this "big cave" under Piccadilly Circus, citing an "annoying door policy", "variable" Modern British food, "haphazard service" and "people on the pull"; allies, however, enjoy the "funky", "lively atmosphere" that's "great fun for a night out" with "good people-watching" – just "don't take granny."

Atrium 15 17 15 £29
4 Millbank, SW1 (Westminster), 0171-233 0032
◪ The location inside a Westminster office block has its backers ("spacious", "bright") and bashers ("soulless") and opinions on the Traditional British fare also vary ("excellent" vs. "overpriced" and "disappointing"), but you may "spot a politician" here, since "in a restaurant wasteland", it's "ok for business" and "people-watching."

AUBERGINE 25 21 23 £56
11 Park Walk, SW10 (Gloucester Rd./South Kensington), 0171-352 3449
◪ "Trying to reach the same standards as Gordon Ramsay" is a tall order, but new chef William Drabble is judged by many a "credible successor", thanks to "superb", "refined" Contemporary French cooking that's "well presented" and "worth it on a special occasion"; however, the jury is still out amongst some who note "patchy service" and think this fabled Chelsea venue "has lost much of its charm."

Avenue Restaurant & Bar ◐ [S] 18 19 16 £36
7-9 St. James's St., SW1 (Green Park), 0171-321 2111
◪ "Sleek room, sleek food" is what fans find at this "trendy" St. James's hangout where "beautiful people" "socialise and feel glamorous"; critics claim the "expensive" Modern British fare "is not as impressive as the decor" and further cite "slow service", but concede it's "ok in small doses."

Axis ◐ 18 18 19 £41
One Aldwych, 1 Aldwych, WC2 (Covent Garden/Holborn), 0171-300 0300
◪ This "very Manhattan", "clubby" Eclectic–Modern British eaterie in the basement of an impressive new Strand hotel polarises diners, with some rating it an "excellent newcomer" with "stylish food and surroundings" and others disdaining "style over substance" and finding it "overpriced"; no one argues that it's become a "place to see or be seen."

Aykoku-Kaku   19 | 9 | 15 | £28 |
Bucklersbury House, 9 Walbrook, EC4 (Bank), 0171-236 9020
◪ A "good, basic Japanese in the City" that's become something of "an institution", offering "excellent dishes" such as "fine teppanyaki" and sushi served in a "staid" (even "cold") setting; it's a "reliable" business option, with two private rooms suitable for hush-hush deal-making.

Babe Ruth's S   12 | 14 | 14 | £19 |
O₂ Ctr., 255 Finchley Rd., NW3 (Finchley Rd.), 0171-433 3388
172-176 The Highway, E1 (Shadwell DLR), 0171-481 8181
■ These "cheerful" sports bars in Finchley (in a vast leisure centre) and Wapping (with basketball court) are "great for kids" or an "office party" thanks to "hearty" American food, "loads of TVs" and "plenty of things to do when not eating."

Back to Basics   ▽ 25 | 19 | 22 | £24 |
21A Foley St., W1 (Oxford Circus), 0171-436 2181
■ An "extensive selection of imaginative fish dishes" from a reasonably priced Mediterranean menu is the draw at this "simple, almost rustic" Fitzrovian restaurant – but "get there early as they run out"; there's alfresco dining too.

Balans ◑S   16 | 12 | 16 | £19 |
60 Old Compton St., W1 (Leicester Sq./Piccadilly Circus), 0171-437 5212
■ "Always buzzing" "day and night" (closes at 5 AM), this "nice, cheap place to meet and eat" in Soho attracts a "trendy, gay crowd"; the Eclectic fare is "well intentioned" and "reliable" but leaves some unmoved: "hang out there by all means, but you wouldn't really go for the food."

Balans Knightsbridge S   – | – | – | M |
239 Brompton Rd., SW3 (Knightsbridge), 0171-584 0070
The newest Balans, which opened post-*Survey*, is a casual, cafe-style spot in Knightsbridge offering Eclectic fare similar to that served at its Soho and Earl's Court siblings, but with less of their gay bonhomie; it offers all-day dining plus a few outside tables overlooking the Brompton Oratory.

Balans West ◑S   15 | 15 | 17 | £19 |
239 Old Brompton Rd., SW5 (Earl's Court), 0171-244 8838
■ "Less manic" and "brighter" than its Soho sibling, this Earl's Court Eclectic gets "very gay and lively in the evenings" and is also a "great brunch spot" thanks to "eggs Benedict to die for"; "friendly" service is appreciated.

bali sugar S   21 | 18 | 19 | £36 |
33A All Saints Rd., W11 (Westbourne Park), 0171-221 4477
◪ This "serene" successor to (and sibling of) the Sugar Club (which relocated a year ago from Portobello to the West End) remains "a good neighbourhood place", though some think it "has the potential to be much better"; the "surprising" Eclectic menu offers a "twist of its own", drawing on influences from Japan and South America.

Bam-Bou ◑ | – | – | – | E |
1 Percy St., W1 (Tottenham Court Rd.), 0171-323 9130
Mogens Tholstrup's trio of eateries (Daphne's, Pasha, The
Collection) may have been absorbed by the Belgo Group, but
that hasn't dulled his appetite for expansion: he's taken over
Fitzrovia's short-lived No. 1 Cigar Club (previously the White
Tower) and reopened it as a French-Vietnamese restaurant
with an interesting menu and French colonial–style decor.

Bangkok | 21 | 10 | 17 | £24 |
9 Bute St., SW7 (South Kensington), 0171-584 8529
■ "Top Thai tucker" say those who overlook "basic"
surroundings and "slow service" on busy nights to sample
"simple, delicious" cooking from an "excellent small menu"
at this long-established South Kensington eaterie; "low
prices" are a plus and there's "more atmosphere than
one would expect from the decor", especially now that the
restaurant opens onto the pavement on warm days.

BANK RESTAURANT ◑ **S** | 20 | 19 | 17 | £35 |
1 Kingsway, WC2 (Holborn), 0171-379 9797
☑ The "interior design appeals to the eye, but not the ear" at
this "cool, sophisticated" Aldwych New French with "glass
shards hanging from the ceiling"; if many find it "unrelaxing"
("very noisy", "speedy service"), at least the "consistent,
interesting" cooking is "a safe place to put your money"
and the "useful" location between the City and West End
makes it "good after theatre" or for breakfast.

Bar Bourse | 16 | 16 | 17 | £25 |
67 Queen St., EC4 (Cannon St.), 0171-248 2200
■ Something of a "City favourite" amongst a "young,
trendy" crowd that enjoys "good" Modern European fare in
a "pleasant" L-shaped basement setting, which sometimes
resembles a "scrum" at lunch – hence service can be "a
little slow"; in the evenings, the place turns into a "loud"
bar with a long cocktail list.

Barcelona Tapas Bar **S** | 15 | 11 | 12 | £17 |
481 Lordship Ln., SE22 (Dulwich B.R.), 0181-693 5111 ◑
15 St. Botolph St., EC3 (Aldgate/Liverpool St.), 0171-377 5222
1 Bell Ln., E1 (Aldgate East/Liverpool St.), 0171-247 7014
■ A trio of "loud, small" tapas bars in the City and out in
Dulwich serving "relatively inexpensive, authentic" Spanish
cooking to a "casual" crowd that often appears more
interested in the "happy hours" than the "traditional
paella" and "super tapas."

Bar Madrid ◑ | 9 | 10 | 9 | £18 |
4 Winsley St., W1 (Oxford Circus), 0171-436 4649
■ "More tap-arse than tapas": "food is not the main
attraction" at this "dark", "lively" Spaniard off Oxford Street
as most go for "a bit of midweek boogie" and to "watch
some sexy lambada"; it's "great if you're 21."

Bayee House ⬡   ▽ 18 | 14 | 18 | £27
100 Upper Richmond Rd., SW15 (East Putney), 0181-789 3161
Bayee Village ⬡
24 High St., SW19 (Wimbledon), 0181-947 3533
■ This "excellent local Chinese" in Putney (with a larger Wimbledon sibling) is "too pricey" and subdued for some, but that doesn't deter others from enjoying "consistent quality without the hassle of getting to Chinatown."

Beach Blanket Babylon ⬡   13 | 22 | 13 | £26
45 Ledbury Rd., W11 (Notting Hill Gate), 0171-229 2907
◪ The "mysterious", "bizarre" decor ("a mix between a monastery and a prison") gives this "candlelit dungeon discovery" near Notting Hill "great bohemian atmosphere", but most think the surroundings "overshadow" the "limited" Mediterranean menu ("average", "overpriced for what you get"); the "cool singles crowd" that flocks here tends to "stick to the drinks."

Bedlington Cafe ⬡⊟   18 | 3 | 11 | £16
24 Fauconberg Rd., W4 (Gunnersbury), 0181-994 1965
◪ This glass-fronted "hangout" in a quiet Chiswick street operates as a "truckers' cafe" during the day and serves "great Thai food" in the evenings; fans say it's "still fun" and enjoy the BYO, but others find it "too squashed" and "basic."

Beiteddine ◑⬡   19 | 11 | 18 | £32
8 Harriet St., SW1 (Knightsbridge/Sloane Sq.), 0171-235 3969
■ "Considered one of the best Lebanese by Lebanese people", this "small", "reliable" Knightsbridge eaterie is a good place to "let the staff do the meze ordering for you"; it's also "great for takeaway."

Belair House ⬡   17 | 19 | 17 | £36
Gallery Rd., Dulwich Village, SE21 (West Dulwich B.R.), 0181-299 9788
◪ Despite a setting in a "gorgeous" Dulwich building with "beautiful views over the grounds", many are dissatisfied by the "overpriced" Modern British–French cooking "with ideas above its station" and "stuffy" ambience at this out-of-the-way eaterie; still, some consider it a "haven" that's "very convenient for lunch when visiting Dulwich art gallery."

Belgo Centraal ◑⬡   16 | 16 | 15 | £21
50 Earlham St., WC2 (Covent Garden), 0171-813 2233
◪ "Bigger mussels than Jean-Claude Van Damme" dominate the "skillfully limited" Belgian menu (pumped up with "good frites" and an "infinite choice of beers") at this "chaotic", "noisy" subterranean Soho spot with "fascinating industrial chic decor"; it's "great if you're in the mood" and "don't mind eating with strangers" at communal tables, but "don't try muscling in without a reservation."

Belgo Noord ◐ [S] 17 | 18 | 16 | £21

72 Chalk Farm Rd., NW1 (Chalk Farm), 0171-267 0718

◪ For a "noisy way to enjoy mussels and beer", try this "stark" Camden venue with a "great party atmosphere" (though "quieter than Centraal") and "basic Belgian nosh"; those who tire of the "bizarre architecture", "waiters dressed as monks" and general "bedlam" sigh it's "not habit-forming", but the main concern for others is that it's "far too easy to get carried away on the endless beer menu."

Belgo Zuid ◐ [S] – | – | – | M

124 Ladbroke Grove, W11 (Ladbroke Grove), 0181-982 8400

Belgo's latest branch opened with a flourish in a dramatically converted dance hall in Ladbroke Grove, featuring their signature moules-frites dishes (prepared 10 ways) but also adding seafood and vegetarian choices; numerous, novel Belgian brews keep the panoramic bar buzzing.

Belvedere, The [S] 17 | 20 | 17 | £34

Holland House, off Abbotsbury Rd., W8 (Holland Park), 0171-602 1238

■ "Peacocks calling" in the surrounding greenery "add to the attraction" of this "magical" spot inside Holland Park, with "well-spaced" tables spread over three levels and "simple", "consistent" Modern British cooking; a few report "slow service" and suggest the "food doesn't do justice to the location", but for most it's "peaceful in winter, magnificent in summer" (and "great for Sunday lunch").

Bengal Clipper ◐ [S] 19 | 18 | 17 | £27

Butlers Wharf, 11-12 Cardamon Bldg., 31 Shad Thames, SE1 (London Bridge/Tower Hill), 0171-357 9001

◪ It's a bit "out of the way" near Tower Bridge, but this "airy" Indian with a pianist has a "good" menu featuring "great curry"; although a few caution it's a "bit expensive" and "nothing to shout about", no one knocks the "excellent value Sunday buffet for those with unlimited appetites."

Bengal Trader ◐ ▽ 20 | 17 | 19 | £21

44 Artillery Ln., E1 (Liverpool St.), 0171-375 0072

■ Off to an auspicious start, this "refreshingly different" Spitalfields sibling to Bengal Clipper is "well laid-out" and offers "very good Indian food " at "decent prices"; it's considered "one of the better places to do lunch in the City."

Benihana [S] 18 | 16 | 18 | £31

37 Sackville St., W1 (Green Park/Piccadilly Circus), 0171-494 2525
77 King's Rd., SW3 (Sloane Sq.), 0171-376 7799
100 Avenue Rd., NW3 (Swiss Cottage), 0171-586 9508

■ "Chop, chop, sizzle, sizzle" – the "novelty value" of watching "clever" chefs at work makes "great theatre" and draws many to this "Americanised Japanese" chain, despite claims that the settings are "a bit soulless" and the food "expensive, unless you take advantage" of special offers.

Ben's Thai 19 | 11 | 14 | £17

48 Red Lion St., WC1 (Holborn), 0171-404 9991

◪ To admirers, "good, reliable Thai food" served in "pub surroundings" makes this "a must if you live in Maida Vale", especially given "great bargain" prices ("always a tenner a head!"), but a few are less enthused, insisting the "very Anglicised" fare is "overrated"; despite the doubters, it's a popular "local takeaway."

Bentley's ◐ [S] 20 | 18 | 18 | £35

11-15 Swallow St., W1 (Piccadilly Circus), 0171-734 4756

■ A "grown-up restaurant" of "polished traditionalism" that's "convenient" for Piccadilly and feels "like an old slipper" ("old-fashioned but comfortable"); as well as the "satisfying", "reliable" British seafood menu, there's an "excellent clubby atmosphere" – all of which "you pay for."

Beotys ◐ 17 | 13 | 19 | £31

79 St. Martin's Ln., WC2 (Leicester Sq.), 0171-836 8768

■ This "fun", simple Greek stalwart in Theatreland has "a very friendly atmosphere" and offers "good" standards ("the lamb falls off the bone") from a menu that includes some Cypriot and French dishes; "who says old-fashioned courtesy doesn't exist anymore? – it does at Beotys."

Bertorelli's ◐ 17 | 15 | 16 | £27

44A Floral St., WC2 (Covent Garden), 0171-836 3969

■ "Jolly" Covent Garden Italian that's "seen better days" but remains "excellent for pre-opera" and a "reliable standby" for a "relaxed" lunch or "after-work" meeting place; cooking of "consistent quality" at a "fair price" gets a thumbs-up from most.

Bertorelli's Cafe Italian 18 | 17 | 17 | £23

19-23 Charlotte St., W1 (Goodge St./Tottenham Court Rd.), 0171-636 4174

◪ Bertorelli's "clean, efficient" bi-level Fitzrovian sibling has a "good buzz" and strikes many as a "fun spot for a decent meal" of "sound" Italian food; others claim it's "not as good as it used to be", but few knock the "reasonable prices."

BIBENDUM ◐ [S] 23 | 23 | 21 | £48

Michelin House, 81 Fulham Rd., SW3 (South Kensington), 0171-581 5817

■ "Hanging on well" is the consensus on Brompton Cross' "great restaurant in the classical sense", a "No. 1 standby to impress" thanks to its "perfect setting" in a handsome art deco building and Matthew Harris' "first-class, imaginative" French-Eclectic cooking that's "expensive but worth every penny"; though there's debate over service ("snooty" vs. "attentive") and a few insist the fare's "overrated", there's little doubt this is a "grown-up" "special occasion spot."

Bibendum Oyster Bar [S] 20 | 18 | 17 | £28

Michelin House, 81 Fulham Rd., SW3 (South Kensington), 0171-589 1480

■ A "quick version of Bibendum" on the street level of its big brother's Brompton Cross building, with art deco architecture that "still charms"; "sparkling fresh" seafood makes it popular with a "chic SW3 clientele" as a "great lunch or light supper" place, even if it is "pricey."

Bice 17 | 15 | 17 | £36

13 Albemarle St., W1 (Green Park/Piccadilly Circus), 0171-409 1011

◪ "Not close to NY or Milan counterparts" judge globe-trotting visitors to this "professional" Italian in a Mayfair basement that attracts its share of "company credit cards" and "beautiful people"; the "nouveau Italian" cooking divides opinions: "excellent all-round" vs. "more show than tell", but all concur it's "a tad overpriced."

Bierodrome ◐ [S] – | – | – | M

173-174 Upper St., N1 (Highbury & Islington), 0171-226 5835

The Belgo group has expanded into Islington with this bar-only venue featuring heavily stylised decor and over 200 Belgian beers, including rare vintages and Nebuchadnezzars; the menu of bar snacks is short and dominated by the trademark Belgo specialty, mussels and frites.

Big Chef, The (CLOSED) 19 | 15 | 16 | £35

(fka MPW)

Cabot Pl. East, 2nd fl., E14 (Canary Wharf), 0171-513 0513

◪ The name change and chef departure suggest things are not necessarily going to plan at Marco Pierre White's Canary Wharf New French; that said, some consider it a local "saviour" supplying the "best food in a soulless area" (including "a steal" of a set lunch), but foes charge it with "taking advantage of its monopoly position"; N.B. the chef change may not be reflected in the food rating.

Big Easy ◐ [S] 12 | 12 | 14 | £19

332-334 King's Rd., SW3 (Sloane Sq.), 0171-352 4071

■ Most "suited to those seeking manic Americana", this "fun" King's Road eaterie serves "massive portions" of "good all-American food" and is "great for kids" as "they eat for free – one per adult", whilst catering to grown-ups with live music in the evenings; "what it does, it does well."

Birdcage ◐ 21 | 22 | 20 | £35

110 Whitfield St., W1 (Goodge St./Warren St.), 0171-323 9655

◪ "Very novel", this "tiny" Fitzrovian newcomer can be "excellent fun" say fans of its "stunningly inventive" Thai-French fusion fare and "beautiful but bizarre" setting, yet critics think its "studied eccentricity" and "gimmicks" ("menu folded into origami and delivered in a cage") are "OTT" – "amusing and trendy, but for how long?"

Bistro Daniel [S] – | – | – | M

26 Sussex Pl., W2 (Lancaster Gate), 0171-262 6073
Amandier's cosy, unpretentious cellar sibling near Lancaster Gate is a traditional bistro-style spot where simple Provençal cooking and well-priced regional wines attract a jolly local crowd; Daniel Gobet's touch is as evident in the cooking here as in his pricier flagship eaterie upstairs.

Bistrorganic [S] – | – | – | E

(fka Woz)
46 Goldborne Rd., W10 (Ladbroke Grove/Westbourne Park), 0181-968 2200
Antony Worrall Thompson has revamped Woz, his set-menu concept near Portobello Road, into this à la carte Mediterranean emphasising organic food, wines and beers; fans of AWT hope it will provide as exciting a "culinary adventure" as they previously enjoyed here.

Bistrot 190 ◐[S] 16 | 16 | 15 | £28

190 Queen's Gate, SW7 (Gloucester Rd./High St. Kensington), 0171-581 5666
■ A "colourful", "lively" Kensington bistro/club that's popular more for its proximity to the Royal Albert Hall and "noisy", "trendy" bar than for its "reasonable" but "undistinguished" Modern British–French food; members get priority over nonmembers on bistro reservations and can stay at the bar until 1 AM.

Bistrot 2 Riverside [S] 16 | 17 | 16 | £29

Oxo Tower Wharf, Barge House St., 2nd fl., SE1 (Blackfriars/Waterloo), 0171-401 8200
■ There's "a better view of the Thames than up top" at Oxo Tower ("not a bad standby for the inevitable table turn-down from [Oxo] above") as well as an "arty feel" to this South Bank "oasis", and the "innovative" Modern British cooking is "much better" than it has to be given the surroundings; it's "not for a quiet two-and-two, but good for big parties."

Black Truffle [S] – | – | – | M

40 Chalcot Rd., NW1 (Primrose Hill B.R.), 0171-483 0077
Adding another colour to the palette of the team behind Green Olive, Red Pepper et al., this attractive, split-level Primrose Hill restaurant/bar, due to open at press time, will offer a moderately priced prix fixe menu featuring Southern French and Northern Italian cooking; given the group's track record, the outlook is encouraging.

Blah! Blah! Blah! 🚫 19 | 12 | 16 | £17

78 Goldhawk Rd., W12 (Goldhawk Rd.), 0181-746 1337
■ The "decor is a bit off-putting, but the food is excellent" at this "hippie-style" Vegetarian in Shepherd's Bush serving "interesting", "imaginative" food that "doesn't feel too heavy" (though a few see a "need to vary the menu"); remember to "bring your own booze."

Blakes — — — E
31 Jamestown Rd., NW1 (Camden Town), 0171-482 2959
In a "funky" space above a "bustling" pub conversion is this "buzzy", high-ceilinged dining room with "eclectic decor", "very friendly" service and "high-quality" Eclectic cooking that seems to satisfy a local "bohemian" crowd; a Clerkenwell sibling is scheduled to open in autumn '99.

Blakes Hotel ◑S 22 23 20 £55
Blakes Hotel, 33 Roland Gardens, SW7 (Gloucester Rd./ South Kensington), 0171-370 6701
■ A "guaranteed seduction spot", the "absurdly dark", "sexy" dining room at this "discreet" South Kensington hotel is a "romantic" showcase for Neville Campbell's "divine" Thai-accented Eclectic cooking backed up by "very good service"; outvoted critics suggest the place is "past its sell-by date" and find prices "exorbitant", but most are resigned to paying a "fantastic price" for "fantastic quality."

Bleeding Heart Restaurant 19 17 17 £30
Bleeding Heart Yard, Greville St., EC1 (Farringdon), 0171-242 2056
Bleeding Heart Tavern
Bleeding Heart Yard, 19 Greville St., EC1 (Farringdon), 0171-404 0333
■ This "quaint", "relatively unknown" cellar "tucked away in a back street" near Farringdon offers an "excellent" albeit "expensive" Contemporary French menu and "one of the best wine lists" around; "whether for a business lunch or romance", admirers call it a "terrific find", complete with outside tables in summer; N.B. they've opened a new tavern on a corner of Bleeding Heart Yard offering a grill menu.

Bloom's ◑S 15 8 11 £19
130 Golders Green Rd., NW11 (Golders Green), 0181-455 1338
☑ Golders Green delicatessen serving "good, old-fashioned, high-cholesterol Jewish cooking" in "noisy", "'50s time warp" surroundings (the "dated decor is so bad it is seriously cool"); it's certainly "unique", but many suggest "it can do better", especially in terms of "rushed" service from staffers who "wait for you to put the last mouthful in."

Bluebird ◑S 18 20 16 £35
350 King's Rd., SW3 (Sloane Sq.), 0171-559 1000
☑ The "superb architecture" of Sir Terence Conran's "chic", "buzzing" Chelsea "feeding parlour" – a shopping/dining emporium – is praised more readily than the "average" Modern British menu at "designer prices" or the "patchy service"; although fans chirp about "lovely" meals including a kid-friendly Sunday brunch, others suggest "Conran alter the formula before we get bored"; a large private room looks down on the main dining area.

BLUE ELEPHANT ●S   22 | 24 | 20 | £35
4-6 Fulham Broadway, SW6 (Fulham Broadway), 0171-385 6595
■ "How Disney would do" Thai: the "surreal", "spectacular" interior of this "jungle in the middle of Fulham" is "like stepping into a fairy-tale setting" (which may explain "high prices") and provides a fitting showcase for "excellent", "flavoursome" Thai cooking; although some think the "extraordinary atmosphere" outshines the kitchen, most insist that "even without all the bells and whistles, you'd still have some darn good food."

Blue Jade   ▽ 19 | 13 | 16 | £24
44 Hugh St., SW1 (Victoria), 0171-828 0321
◪ This "no-frills" Pimlico Thai "lacks personality", but fans say it makes up for it with "tasty", "affordable" dining; the less enthused claim it "varies wildly from night to night."

Blue Legume S⊭   ▽ 17 | 15 | 15 | £13
101 Stoke Newington Church St., N16 (Manor House/Stoke Newington B.R.), 0171-923 1303
■ "Who wants a vegetarian fry-up?" – the "trendy" veggie-lovers who flock to this Stoke Newington cafe, attracted by "tasty" Eclectic-Vegetarian fare and "divine pressed juices"; the fact that it's "great value" also helps.

Blue Print Cafe S   20 | 20 | 17 | £32
Design Museum, Butlers Wharf, SE1 (London Bridge/Tower Hill), 0171-378 7031
◪ The "amazing view of the Thames" adds to the "airy feel" of Terence Conran's Design Museum venue, but whilst the Eclectic food is generally regarded as "good", it's also said to "have its ups and downs"; in any case, the atmosphere is "excellent" and despite being "glassed-in" ("a great mistake" to some), the terrace is "superb."

Blues Bistro & Bar ●   17 | 16 | 16 | £24
42-43 Dean St., W1 (Piccadilly Circus/Tottenham Court Rd.), 0171-494 1966
■ A young Soho crowd "feels very at home" at this stylish yet "unpretentious" bistro/bar serving "safe, reliable" East Coast American food; it's "a good bet" as a "great lunch place" or for a "nice evening out."

Boardwalk ●   11 | 12 | 11 | £20
18 Greek St., W1 (Leicester Sq./Tottenham Court Rd.), 0171-287 2051
◪ This bubbling Soho venue with "bouncers" in the evening is "loads of fun" for "a group night out" thanks to a "very good value" happy hour, but as for the "uninspiring" Cajun-American food, there's a feeling "they should concentrate on the bar – it's as if the chef already has."

Boisdale ⚫🅂   18 | 16 | 17 | £30
15 Eccleston St., SW1 (Victoria), 0171-730 6922
■ It's "like taking a step back in time" at this "club-like" eaterie on the Belgravia-Victoria border; as "comfortable as an old shoe", it has a "quirky" Traditional British menu with a strong Scottish emphasis offering "robust tucker" ("love the haggis") complemented by an "exceptional" wine list; a new late-night offshoot has opened next door with an eight-metre zinc cocktail bar, live jazz (Monday–Saturday) and a selection of over 100 Cuban cigars.

Bombay Bicycle Club   21 | 17 | 18 | £23
95 Nightingale Ln., SW12 (Clapham South), 0181-673 6217
■ Though a bit "off the beaten path" in Clapham, this "refined", "colonial" Indian wins many admirers for its "above-average", "fresh-tasting" cooking, especially the "good" curries that are "always very hot"; "unassuming", "attentive" service is also appreciated.

Bombay Brasserie ⚫🅂   19 | 20 | 18 | £32
Courtfield Rd., SW7 (Gloucester Rd.), 0171-370 4040
☑ A sense of "fading grandeur" lends a "wonderful atmosphere" to this "comfortable" South Kensington Indian (cynics suggest "a face-lift"), but whilst the "pretty conservatory" is admired, the cooking splits voters: fans say it's "consistent" and "a real taste of India", but others label it "uninspiring" and catering to "European taste buds."

Bonjour Vietnam 🅂   14 | 11 | 13 | £21
593-599 Fulham Rd., SW6 (Fulham Broadway), 0171-385 7603
■ Diners are "never left hungry" at this "eat as much as you can" Asian on Fulham Broadway that's "cheap, but not particularly cheerful"; it's "good to go with a group to sample all the different dishes" – although one wag claims it all "tastes the same."

Books for Cooks   22 | 15 | 18 | £16
4 Blenheim Crescent, W11 (Ladbroke Grove/Notting Hill Gate), 0171-221 1992
■ A "microsize bookshop with a mini kitchen/dining area", this "unusual, cramped and chaotic" store-cum-kitchen near Ladbroke Grove is "a must for foodaholics" in search of an "excellent range of cookbooks" plus "well-cooked" Eclectic fare served by "friendly" staff; it's a "fun place to meet or bring friends" or take cooking classes.

Brackenbury, The 🅂   21 | 14 | 18 | £28
129 Brackenbury Rd., W6 (Goldhawk Rd.), 0181-748 0107
☑ Though critics feel that this "unpretentious", "cramped" British-Eclectic eaterie in Shepherd's Bush has "lost its sparkle", fans rally to its defence, calling it a "gem" that "perks up the neighbourhood" with its "interesting" menu, "reasonable prices" and "friendly" attitude; N.B. it was recently acquired by the team behind Circus and Avenue.

Bradley's 🟥   20 | 16 | 18 | £32
25 Winchester Rd., NW3 (Swiss Cottage), 0171-722 3457
◪ A "comfortable" Swiss Cottage "standby" that's "hidden away, but worth the search", serving "bistro-style" Modern British food in a "discreet atmosphere" with an "interesting wine list" ("no French, only New World"); to a minority, though, it's "a little pricey" and "resting on its laurels."

Brady's ⊟   ▽ 21 | 9 | 13 | £15
513 Old York Rd., SW18 (Wandsworth Town B.R.), 0181-877 9599
◼ "Huge fish 'n' chips" and other "good" seafood draw diners to this "busy, local" Wandsworth joint that's "posh for a chippy, but still needs a coat of paint."

Brasserie Rocque   16 | 15 | 15 | £29
37 Broadgate Circle, EC2 (Liverpool St.), 0171-638 7919
◼ "Good for a business lunch, maybe too stuffy for pleasure" opine patrons of this "busy" Broadgate "haunt" that's sometimes "too full to be enjoyable" (especially "on a sunny Friday" when outside tables entice more customers); there's "good" if "not cheap" Eclectic fare in the restaurant and more reasonably priced "bar snacks" in the brasserie.

Brasserie St. Quentin 🟥   17 | 16 | 17 | £31
243 Brompton Rd., SW3 (Knightsbridge/South Kensington), 0171-589 8005
◪ "Excellent" brasserie fare, "crisply starched white tablecloths" and a "lively" ambience that "could be in a favourite arrondissement of Paris" have won a following for this "underrated" "French standby" in Knightsbridge; although a few find it "boring" and "pricey" (except for the £10 pre-theatre menu), most happily "keep going back."

Break for the Border   9 | 11 | 10 | £20
5 Goslett Yard, WC2 (Tottenham Court Rd.), 0171-437 8595
8 Argyll St., W1 (Oxford Circus), 0171-734 5776
◼ "When all that matters is drinking, dancing and something to fill your stomach", this pair of "dark", "brash" Tex-Mexers with "mad tequila girls" are "good fun" ("they let you throw food"); eating is "not the reason for going" – "no way, Jose."

Brinkley's ◗🟥   14 | 13 | 15 | £27
47 Hollywood Rd., SW10 (Earl's Court), 0171-351 1683
◼ "Good Sloaney fun" is what most diners find at this "very Chelsea" local eatery with a "basic menu" of British-International food and "good service"; the "great selection" of "cheap wine" and a covered garden add appeal.

Brompton Bay 🟥   ▽ 20 | 22 | 19 | £34
96 Draycott Ave., SW3 (South Kensington), 0171-225 2500
◼ Few surveyors commented on this "very nice new place" with "superb" decor in the Brompton Cross restaurant hotbed, but those who know it give encouraging marks to the Modern European fare of David Massey, a "chef who knows his stuff"; "could be good" say hopefuls.

Brown's Hotel, 1837 S   20 | 20 | 21 | £41 |
Brown's Hotel, 32 Albemarle St., W1 (Green Park), 0171-408 1837
■ "As snug as the chairman's wallet" is how some describe
the "men's club" ambience at this "elegant" wood-panelled
Mayfair hotel dining room with "expensive but impressive"
Modern French cooking and a "fantastic wine list" overseen
by "brilliant sommelier" John Gilchrist; a few critics point
to "fussy" food that's "not quite up to the prices", but they're
outvoted; N.B. the hotel drawing room is "wonderful for
tea", with fireplaces and "comfortable armchairs."

Browns Restaurant   16 | 16 | 15 | £22 |
82-84 St. Martin's Ln., WC2 (Leicester Sq.), 0171-497 5050 ◐ S
47 Maddox St., W1 (Oxford Circus), 0171-491 4565
201 Castlenau Row, SW13 (Hammersmith), 0181-748 4486 S
114 Draycott Ave., SW3 (South Kensington), 0171-584 5359 S
■ This chain of "relaxed", "colonial"-style brasseries serves
"inexpensive" International–Modern British fare that's "jolly
wholesome" even if it leaves "no lasting impression"; they're
"good meeting points" with the benefit of "pre-theatre
deals" for under £10 at the Theatreland venue.

Buchan's S   19 | 16 | 18 | £24 |
62-64 Battersea Bridge Rd., SW11 (Sloane Sq.), 0171-228 0888
■ There's a "lovely atmosphere" ("like dining with family")
and "Scottish fayre" that's "always at least good and
sometimes excellent" at this "cheerful" Battersea restaurant/
bar; reasonable prices and "helpful" service are pluses.

Builders Arms, The S   – | – | – | M |
*13 Britten St., SW3 (Sloane Sq./South Kensington),
0171-349 9040*
From the same stable as Duke of Cambridge and The Queens
comes this new, airy gastropub in a pretty Chelsea street
off King's Road, serving well-priced, well-pitched Modern
European fare in a comfortable, country-style dining area.

Buona Sera ◐   18 | 14 | 17 | £18 |
43 Drury Ln., WC2 (Covent Garden), 0171-836 8296
*22 Northcote Rd., SW11 (Clapham Junction B.R.),
0171-228 9925 S*
☑ "So full of life" it "always gives you a lift" say fans of this
"family restaurant" in Battersea offering "simple but tasty"
Italian fare including "huge pizzas"; the less enthused claim
it "used to be good" but is "now too noisy, with Hooray
Henrys being obnoxious"; there's a new Covent Garden site.

Buona Sera at the Jam ◐ S   12 | 14 | 12 | £18 |
289A King's Rd., SW3 (Sloane Sq.), 0171-352 8827
☑ Although it's "uncomfortable for adults", kids "adore"
the "mezzanine bunk bed" eating booths at this "funky"
King's Road Italian with a "lively" ambience and "consistent,
good value" cooking; those who find it "a bit spartan" and
"squashy" say "buona sera – as in goodbye!"

Busabong Too 🅂   19 | 16 | 18 | £27
*1A Langton St., SW10 (Fulham Broadway/Sloane Sq.),
0171-352 7414*

■ "Steady" is the consensus on this "good local Thai" on
two floors of a World's End townhouse, where "reliable"
fare is "politely served"; regulars say it's "fun to sit
upstairs" (request when booking) with pillow seating.

Busabong Tree 🌑🅂   19 | 16 | 18 | £28
*112 Cheyne Walk, SW10 (Fulham Broadway/Sloane Sq.),
0171-352 7534*

☑ "Busabong on down" suggest boosters of this "good
local Thai" on the Chelsea Embankment where you "can
usually get a table at the last minute" and enjoy a "beautiful
combination of food and service"; a recent renovation
should please those who find it "stuck in the '70s."

Bu-San 🌑🅂   ▽ 18 | 6 | 15 | £22
43 Holloway Rd., N7 (Highbury & Islington), 0171-607 8264

■ Though the decor leaves something to be desired, a
"good social atmosphere" and "warm, friendly service"
earn praise for this Highbury Korean, as does its "unusual
food" (including what some call the "best salmon sashimi in
town") made with "always fresh ingredients"; enthusiasts
recommend it for "simple", "good value" meals.

Butlers Wharf Chop House 🅂   18 | 17 | 17 | £33
*Butlers Wharf Bldg., 36E Shad Thames, SE1 (London Bridge/
Tower Hill), 0171-403 3403*

☑ Most agree that the "beautiful location" of this early
Conran creation offers the "very best view of Tower Bridge",
but there's less unity when it comes to the Traditional
British cuisine, with some extolling "authentic" "comfort
food at its best" ("great meat", "excellent wine list") and
others yawning over "unmemorable" cooking that's "not
as special as the prices."

Byron's 🅂   20 | 18 | 18 | £28
3A Downshire Hill, NW3 (Hampstead), 0171-435 3544

☑ "Sometimes inspired, sometimes tired" is the reaction to
the "hit-or-miss menu" of "creative" Modern British cooking
at this "elegant" Hampstead townhouse; still, solid ratings
suggest it hits more than it misses, and there's a "beautiful
wine list", courteous service and a popular Sunday brunch.

Cactus Blue 🌑🅂   14 | 17 | 14 | £24
86 Fulham Rd., SW3 (South Kensington), 0171-823 7858

☑ Aficionados of this "amusing" Chelsea haunt praise
its "innovative", "true campfire" American Southwestern
cooking, whilst critics say "they try hard" but the results are
"rather insipid"; still, even if it's "not the best food in town",
the place is "always fun and lively", with "fab margaritas"
and "cute theme decor" that make it "popular for parties."

Cafe at Sotheby's
18 | 16 | 18 | £23 |
34-35 New Bond St., W1 (Bond St.), 0171-293 5077

☑ An "oasis of peace" in an "elegant" Bond Street auction house that's a "delightful place to lunch with mother" and "convenient" for breakfast or tea; most are content with its "good quality", if somewhat "pricey", Modern British menu, although some suggest that it's the setting that "gives an ordinary lunch a touch of class"; N.B. closed evenings.

Café Boheme ◑ⓢ
15 | 15 | 14 | £19 |
13-17 Old Compton St., W1 (Leicester Sq./Piccadilly Circus), 0171-734 0623

■ "Bohemian is the word" for Soho's "cosy, cosmopolitan" French bistro with a "wonderfully old, shabby interior" that gets "far too crowded" for some ("worth taking earplugs"); some find the cooking "surprisingly good" whilst others say it "needs more attention", but all agree it's a "cool" place to "sit and watch the world go by."

Café Delancey ◑ⓢ
16 | 15 | 15 | £20 |
3 Delancey St., NW1 (Camden Town), 0171-387 1985

☑ This "rambling" Camden "institution" serves "homely", "dependable" French fare at "moderate prices" and is considered "great for Sunday lunch" or just a "relaxing" meal; a few find it "boring" and "formulaic", but even they concede it's "pleasant" "when you have no place to go."

Café dell'Ugo
15 | 13 | 13 | £25 |
56-58 Tooley St., SE1 (London Bridge), 0171-407 6001

☑ It's "good for business lunches" and has a "great bar scene" in the evenings, yet this Mediterranean under the railway arches near London Bridge doesn't quite please everyone; whilst some call it an "efficient food factory" and applaud the presence of "new ideas" on the menu, others feel its "mix and match of food styles" yields "so-so" results.

Cafe de Paris ◑
14 | 19 | 13 | £35 |
3 Coventry St., W1 (Leicester Sq.), 0171-734 7700

■ "Decadent and sexy", this private Piccadilly nightclub allows nonmembers to make dinner reservations in the balcony restaurant and "pay for the view" of those dancing below; critics find the Modern British fare "overpriced and overrated" and claim "the club is losing its crowd", but defenders focus on the "nice atmosphere" and call it "good for special occasions."

Café des Amis du Vin ◑
15 | 14 | 14 | £25 |
11-14 Hanover Pl., WC2 (Covent Garden), 0171-379 3444

☑ The new decor at this Covent Garden stalwart is playing to mixed reviews: some say it has "improved" the place "beyond all recognition", whilst others think it's "lost some of its atmosphere"; either way, most appreciate the "reliable" French brasserie fare, "fast service" ("useful for Royal Opera snacks") and "fun" downstairs wine bar.

Cafe des Arts ● S | 17 | 17 | 17 | £22 |
82 Hampstead High St., NW3 (Hampstead), 0171-435 3608
■ It may be a bit "twee", but most consider this Hampstead cafe "perfect for a twosome", with "imaginative" New French–Med food and a "relaxed" feel; even those who knock "fake French" fare say it's "ok for a basic meal."

Café Fish ● S | 18 | 14 | 16 | £26 |
36-40 Rupert St., W1 (Piccadilly Circus), 0171-287 8989
☑ "The new venue improves it" say many about this "jolly", "clean-tiled" Soho seafooder that moved from its longtime Panton Street home over a year ago; the few who feel it "lost some ambience" and grumble about "hit-and-miss" cooking and "cramped" quarters are outvoted by those who praise its "simple", "mouthwatering" fare and call it an "essential" lunch stop and "perfect after the theatre."

Café Flo ● S | 14 | 14 | 13 | £20 |
51 St. Martin's Ln., WC2 (Leicester Sq.), 0171-836 8289
127 Kensington Church St., W8 (Notting Hill Gate), 0171-727 8142
103 Wardour St., W1 (Leicester Sq./Piccadilly Circus), 0171-734 0581
13 Thayer St., W1 (Bond St.), 0171-935 5023
676 Fulham Rd., SW6 (Parsons Green), 0171-371 9673
89 Sloane Ave., SW3 (South Kensington), 0171-225 1048
11 Haymarket, SW1 (Piccadilly Circus), 0171-976 1313
334 Upper St., N1 (Angel/Highbury & Islington), 0171-226 7916
38-40 Ludgate Hill, EC4 (St. Paul's), 0171-329 3900
149 Kew Rd., Kew (Richmond), 0181-940 8298
Additional locations throughout London.
☑ "You know what you're getting" and it's usually "decent" at this "Franglais bistro" chain that's "nothing special" but "good for a cheap, uncomplicated meal" in "bright" if "characterless" environs; "went with low expectations and was pleasantly surprised" says one convert.

CAFE JAPAN S | 25 | 9 | 20 | £21 |
626 Finchley Rd., NW11 (Golders Green), 0181-455 6854
■ "Truly an art form" is how fans describe the "authentic" sushi served at this Finchley spot, which some consider the "best value for Japanese food in London"; praise also goes to the "friendliest service" and "good atmosphere", and though it's not much to look at, "who goes there for decor?"

Cafe Lazeez | 16 | 15 | 16 | £24 |
93-95 Old Brompton Rd., SW7 (South Kensington), 0171-581 9993 ● S
88 St. John St., EC1 (Farringdon), 0171-253 2224
☑ A pair of "trendy" Indians (in South Kensington and the City) known for their "upmarket", "modern approach" to Indian cuisine; most call it a "great concept" and praise "excellent food" served in "fresh surroundings", but a few dissenters find it "confused" and "average"; the South Ken branch has "good" live jazz at weekends.

Cafe Med ❶S   15 16 15 £23
184A Kensington Park Rd., W11 (Notting Hill Gate),
0171-221 1150
21 Loudoun Rd., W8 (St. John's Wood), 0171-625 1222
320 Goldhawk Rd., W6 (Stamford Brook), 0181-741 1994
22 Dean St., W1 (Tottenham Court Rd.),
0171-287 9007
2 Hollywood Rd., SW10 (Earl's Court),
0171-823 3355
2 Northside, Wandsworth Common, SW18
(Clapham Junction B.R.), 0171-228 0914
370 St. John St., EC1 (Angel), 0171-278 1199
◪ "Slightly offbeat" and "bohemian" in character, this
chain of Mediterranean cafes serves "reliable" if rather
"pedestrian" fare and generally earns more compliments
("healthy portions", "great cafe atmosphere", "good
value") than complaints ("nothing to inspire", "uppity
service"); most would agree it's "useful as a local" as
there's "no stress" and "great fries."

Café Milan S   21 19 18 £26
312-314 King's Rd., SW3 (Sloane Sq.), 0171-351 0101
◪ At this "stylish", "cool" newcomer in an "excellent
location" on King's Road, some find "authentic", "fresh
Italian cooking" that's "different in an interesting way"
whilst others report "disappointing food" and "slow
service", but judging by the ratings, most feel it's making
a "good start"; besides the restaurant, there's a "great
antipasti bar" and a retail shop.

Café Pacifico ❶S   16 14 14 £21
5 Langley St., WC2 (Covent Garden), 0171-379 7728
■ "The closest you can get to authentic Mexican food
and drinks" say supporters who praise the "yummy"
cooking and "terrific margaritas" at this "very casual",
bustling Covent Garden venue; though often "noisy" and
"crowded", it has an "excellent atmosphere for parties"
and is "cheap" to boot.

Cafe Rouge   12 13 12 £18
34 Wellington St., WC2 (Covent Garden), 0171-836 0998 S
158 Fulham Palace Rd., W6 (Hammersmith),0181-741 5037 S
98-100 Shepherd's Bush Rd., W6 (Shepherd's Bush),
0171-602 7732 S
227-229 Chiswick High Rd., W4 (Chiswick Park),
0181-742 7447 S
31 Kensington Park Rd., W11 (Ladbroke Grove),
0171-221 4449 S
15 Frith St., W1 (Tottenham Court Rd.), 0171-437 4307 S
102 Old Brompton Rd., SW7 (South Kensington),
0171-373 2403 S
27-31 Basil St., SW3 (Knightsbridge), 0171-584 2345 S
390 King's Rd., SW3 (Sloane Sq.), 0171-352 2226 S

Cafe Rouge (Cont.)
*120 St. John's Wood High St., NW8 (St. John's Wood),
0171-722 8366* S
*29-35 McKenzie Walk, E14 (Canary Wharf), 0171-537 9696
Additional locations throughout London.*
◪ "A reliable choice" for a "quick shopping lunch" or a meal with "the kids" when all that's wanted is "basic" (some say "dumbed-down") French bistro food at "prices that won't leave the bank balance in the rouge"; critics knock "gloomy decor" and "slow" service and say quality can be "potluck depending on the location."

Cafe Spice Namaste   21 | 19 | 18 | £26
*247 Lavender Hill, SW11 (Clapham Junction B.R.),
0171-738 1717* ●S
16 Prescot St., E1 (Aldgate/Tower Hill), 0171-488 9242
■ The "only problem is location" (City or Battersea) for these "refreshingly different", "upmarket Indians" with "funky decor", an "innovative" menu and "classy presentations"; a few critics snipe that they're "overpriced" for "trendiness with no substance", but they are overruled by fans who "wish it were close to home or a tube."

Caffè Nero   S⊠   15 | 12 | 13 | £10
*Unit 1, 65-72 The Strand, WC2 (Charing Cross/Covent Garden),
0171-930 8483
2 Lancaster Pl., WC2 (Covent Garden), 0171-836 6346
29 Southampton St., WC2 (Covent Garden),
0171-240 3433
79 Tottenham Court Rd., W1 (Goodge St.), 0171-580 3885
62 Brewer St., W1 (Piccadilly Circus), 0171-437 1497
225 Regent St., W1 (Oxford Circus), 0171-491 0763
43 Frith St., W1 (Piccadilly Circus), 0171-434 3887* ●
*66 Old Brompton Rd., SW7 (South Kensington),
0171-589 1760
1 Hampstead High St., NW3 (Hampstead),
0171-431 5958
Unit 1, Winchester House, EC2 (Liverpool St.), 0171-588 6001
Additional locations throughout London.*
◪ "No awards" are likely to go to these "typical cappuccino joints", but they offer a "good choice of hot snacks" and pizzas from an Italian-accented menu that's "ok for an everyday lunch" (or breakfast – no dinner); staunch fans even rate it "best of its type", praising "decent sandwiches" and "excellent hot chocolate", if not seating that some suggest was "clearly intended to discourage loiterers."

Calzone   S   14 | 10 | 13 | £16
*2A-2B Kensington Park Rd., W11 (Notting Hill Gate),
0171-243 2003* ●
*352 King's Rd., SW3 (Sloane Sq./South Kensington),
0171-352 9790*
(Continues)

Calzone (Cont.)
335 Fulham Rd., SW10 (South Kensington), 0171-352 9797 ◐
66 Heath St., NW3 (Hampstead), 0171-794 6775 ◐
35 Upper St., N1 (Angel), 0171-359 9191

▨ "If you like your pizza thin and crusty, go for it" urge fans of this "noisy" chain, praising its "tasty" pizzas and other Italian fare; a few critics think they have "ideas above their station" and no one is wowed by the decor, but they fill the bill in "a 'let's just grab lunch' situation."

Cambio de Tercio ◐Ⓢ　　　18 | 16 | 18 | £31
163 Old Brompton Rd., SW5 (Gloucester Rd.), 0171-244 8970

▨ To supporters, this "small" South Ken Spaniard "gets better and better", offering "spicy" food in a "lovely atmosphere"; the praise isn't quite unanimous ("overrated", "surprisingly expensive"), but most enjoy its "authentic delights" – "pity it's sometimes rather empty" say regulars.

Camden Brasserie ◐Ⓢ　　　17 | 15 | 17 | £23
216 Camden High St., NW1 (Camden Town/Chalk Farm),
0171-482 2114

▪ "Gets no better, gets no worse" is how some appraise this "consistent" Camden brasserie serving "reasonable" Mediterranean staples "enlivened by specials"; some feel it "could do with more variation", but it's "a splash of taste" in the area and appreciated for its "willing" service.

Cantaloupe Bar & Grill ◐Ⓢ　　　19 | 16 | 15 | £20
35 Charlotte Rd., EC2 (Old St.), 0171-613 4411

▪ "Don't take grandma" to this "funky" restaurant/bar in "up-and-coming" Shoreditch with "industrial decor" and a crowd that's "full of suits" ("avoid Friday nights"); most are "pleasantly surprised" by the Mediterranean food and "quick" service, which makes it good for business lunches.

Canteen, The　　　　　　　21 | 19 | 18 | £39
Harbour Yard, Chelsea Harbour, SW10 (Earl's Court/
Fulham Broadway), 0171-351 7330

▨ The location is a bit "out of the way" in Chelsea Harbour, but it's "a joy to be surrounded by yachts" and Michael Caine's restaurant draws a "bubbling" crowd with Raymond Brown's "thoroughly reliable" New French–Med fare; if a few feel this "formal" venue is pricey and a bit "tired", most say it's "still a good standby" for a "civilised" meal.

Cantina del Ponte Ⓢ　　　　17 | 16 | 14 | £30
Butlers Wharf Bldg., 36C Shad Thames, SE1 (London Bridge/
Tower Hill), 0171-403 5403

▨ The "decor's nothing special", but the "excellent views" of Tower Bridge are universally admired at this Terence Conran eaterie, something that cannot be said of the Mediterranean cooking, which some find "very good" and "underrated" and others label "disappointing"; still, it's one of the "nicer" spots to "cater to kids" and you "can't go wrong" seated outside.

Cantinetta Venegazzu ◐ S   ▽ 15 | 14 | 17 | £26
31-32 Battersea Sq., SW11 (Clapham Junction B.R.),
0171-978 5395
■ It's "too cramped" inside for some, but there's "great outdoor eating when the weather is nice" at this "well-run Italian" in Battersea offering an "interesting, frequently changing menu" of Venetian specialties plus "good service"; a few consider the "food not good enough for the money."

Canyon Restaurant & Bar S   19 | 22 | 17 | £32
Riverside, near Richmond Bridge, Richmond (Richmond),
0181-948 2944
■ "At last the suburbs are catching up with central London" cheer admirers of this "impressive", "stylish" Richmond newcomer in a riverside setting that's "perfect" if "a bit difficult to find"; from the team behind Dakota and Montana, it's winning early acclaim for its "very good" American Southwestern cooking and "jolly service", though some find it "too loud", especially at tables near the bar.

Capital Radio Cafe ◐ S   11 | 13 | 12 | £17
19-20 Leicester Sq., WC2 (Leicester Sq.), 0171-484 8888
O₂ Ctr., 255 Finchley Rd., NW3 (Finchley Rd.), 0171-435 9685
☑ "Let's face it, nobody expects gourmet food" in a "buzzing" Leicester Square cafe that looks like a *"Blue Peter"* TV set with Capital Radio "DJs playing tunes", but it's "fun for kids" and "teen outings"; expect "generous portions" of "average", American-style burger fare, an "excellent choice of nonalcoholic and alcoholic drinks" and service that varies from "slow" to "rushed"; there's a new branch in the O₂ leisure center.

CAPITAL RESTAURANT ◐ S   27 | 23 | 25 | £56
Capital Hotel, 22-24 Basil St., SW3 (Knightsbridge),
0171-589 5171
■ This "wonderfully calm", "very formal" Knightsbridge hotel dining room strikes some as "the only place to hold important meetings" (and "abuse your expense account"), but the departure of celebrated chef Philip Britten means that Eric Chavot now has the task of maintaining the kitchen's lofty reputation; admirers expect it to continue offering "first-class" New French fare as part of an overall "outstanding dining experience."

Caraffini ◐   19 | 15 | 19 | £33
61-63 Lower Sloane St., SW1 (Sloane Sq.), 0171-259 0235
☑ The decor may be "rather bland", but this "energetic", "upmarket" eaterie near Sloane Square is considered a "reliable" option for "typical Italian" cooking; some report "unconcerned service" and "intolerable noise" when the place gets "too busy to cope", but fans retort "who would want them to change?"

Caravaggio 19 18 16 £34
107-112 Leadenhall St., EC3 (Bank/Monument), 0171-626 6206
■ "Fine food in a fine setting" is what most find at this "buzzy" (especially "at lunchtime"), "City-slick restaurant in a former bank" near Lloyds; it boasts "modern decor" and a "diverse" menu of "consistently good Italian" dishes, and if some feel "the high-quality food is spoilt by poor service", a "superb wine list" helps compensate.

Casale Franco ◐ [S] 17 16 14 £25
134-137 Upper St., N1 (Angel/Highbury & Islington), 0171-226 8994
◪ Critics suggest that an "attempted move upmarket has failed", but most seem content with the "decent, authentic Italian" fare offered at this "cramped" Islingtonian; assets include "great pizza" and a popular summer courtyard that's "well worth trying even on a busy Friday or Saturday night."

Cave ▽ 24 20 20 £40
Caviar House, 161 Piccadilly, W1 (Green Park), 0171-409 0445
◪ This glass-fronted Piccadilly seafooder in a caviar retail store serves "pleasant" French-accented cooking with, predictably, a wide selection of caviar ("you must try vodka and beluga caviar" urge bon vivants); some consider it "overpriced for such a casual place" (though there is a £22.50 set lunch menu), but on the plus side the attitude is "not at all pretentious."

Caviar Kaspia ◐ 24 20 22 £57
18-18A Bruton Pl., W1 (Bond St./Green Park), 0171-493 2612
■ "Being taken here is the ultimate treat" enthuse admirers of the "wonderful" Franco-Russian food and "wonderful service" ("no complaints") at this old-world Mayfair caviar specialist – the "best in London" according to partisans; it's "primarily a lunch spot" but also "terrific for a first-class romantic dinner" – "if you can afford it."

Cecconi's ◐ 21 15 21 £50
5A Burlington Gardens, W1 (Green Park), 0171-434 1509
◪ Sit "among titans of industry" at this "long-standing Italian" off Bond Street that feels "more like a club than a restaurant"; whilst some call it a "frightfully expensive" "time warp" for "jet setters looking to impress", others insist it's "still one of the best" places "to be pampered" with "good, old-fashioned" cooking and "excellent service."

Chapel, The [S] 18 14 12 £20
48 Chapel St., NW1 (Edgware Rd.), 0171-402 9220
■ This "pleasant" Edgware "local" with a lovely terrace is "a pain to get to" but worth the effort since it "answers prayers for an affordable wine bar with decent nosh" in the form of Modern British–Med fare; a few hard-to-please types say the "menu sometimes fails to tempt", but even they enjoy the "nice atmosphere."

Chapter Two S   ▽ 23 | 21 | 21 | £33
43-45 Montpelier Vale, SE3 (Blackheath), 0181-333 2666
◪ In "picturesque" Blackheath, this newcomer (a sibling of Chapter One in Kent) serves "superb" Modern European fare in a "simple setting" with a "nice ambience"; despite disagreement as to whether it's "good value" or "very pricey", most give it a thumbs-up: "great start all-round."

Charco's   17 | 16 | 17 | £28
1 Bray Pl., SW3 (Sloane Sq.), 0171-584 0765
◼ It may look "rather austere", but this "underrated local Chelsea restaurant" just off King's Road offers "light, elegant" Modern British fare and a "bargain" £9.50 set menu at midday and pre-theatre; "friendly staff" is another reason why it's popular with "ladies who lunch."

Che ◑   19 | 20 | 19 | £41
23 St. James's St., SW1 (Green Park), 0171-747 9380
◪ This "interesting" newcomer with an unusual layout (the airy, spacious room is entered via an escalator) and "fab views" over St. James's has friends who praise its "attentive service" and James Kirby's "varied" Eclectic cuisine, but also critics who suggest the cooking "lacks consistency"; draws include a "trendy bar", spectacular wine list and cigar room that's "the place to light up."

Cheers Restaurant & Bar S   12 | 14 | 12 | £18
72 Regent St., W1 (Piccadilly Circus), 0171-494 3322
◪ "Good TV shows don't make good restaurants" is the lesson some draw from this "busy", "friendly" Piccadilly theme bar where "*Cheers* episodes are played" on giant TV screens; still, the "limited" American-style menu is "good for a quick lunch" and if it lacks "innovation", that's hardly what most are looking for here.

Chelsea Bun S   14 | 9 | 12 | £13
*70 Battersea Bridge Rd., SW11 (Clapham Junction B.R./
Sloane Sq.), 0171-738 9009*
Limerston St., SW10 (Earl's Court), 0171-352 3635
◪ For "a big breakfast to set you up for the day" or a "cheap, cheerful" homestyle lunch or dinner, these "dingy" diners in Chelsea and Battersea are "acceptable options"; some grumble about "irritating", "badly organised" service, but few would deny they're good "post-hangover hangouts."

Chelsea Kitchen ◑ S ⇴   12 | 8 | 13 | £11
98 King's Rd., SW3 (Sloane Sq.), 0171-589 1330
◼ "Long may it live" enthuse devotees of this "scruffy", "unpretentious canteen" in the "heart of Chelsea" serving "basic school food" at "ridiculously cheap" prices; filled with "interesting characters", it's "endlessly entertaining" and perfect when "you just need a good greasy spoon."

Chelsea Ram S   19 | 15 | 14 | £21
32 Burnaby St., SW10 (Earl's Court/Fulham Broadway),
0171-351 4008
⬛ A "nice gastropub" in Chelsea that's "full of character",
attracting a "young" crowd with its "relaxed" atmosphere
and "ever-changing", "good value" British menu that's
"much more than pub grub"; it's "the perfect local", save
for two niggles: "cigarette smoke" and no reserving – "if
only you could rely on getting a table."

Cheng-Du ◑S   ▽ 20 | 15 | 17 | £24
9 Parkway, NW1 (Camden Town), 0171-485 8058
⬛ It's "not particularly memorable", but this low-key Chinese
in Camden Town serves "really good Szechuan" cooking
that's "great value" – "and they deliver!"

CHEZ BRUCE S   25 | 19 | 21 | £36
Wandsworth Common, 2 Bellevue Rd., SW17 (Balham),
0181-672 0114
⬛ "It doesn't get much better" say fans of this "buzzy"
Wandsworth "secret" that locals "can no longer keep to
themselves", where Bruce Poole "never disappoints" with
"stunning, lovingly prepared" Modern British–French fare
at "excellent prices"; a few find it "cramped" and feel the
"decor lets the food down", ditto service that's "a little
slow", but most judge it "a very pleasant experience overall."

Chez Gérard   18 | 16 | 16 | £28
119 Chancery Ln., WC2 (Chancery Ln.), 0171-405 0290
Opera Terrace, The Market, 45 East Terrace, 1st fl., WC2
(Covent Garden), 0171-379 0666 ◑S
8 Charlotte St., W1 (Goodge St.), 0171-636 4975 ◑S
31 Dover St., W1 (Green Park), 0171-499 8171 ◑S
3 Yeoman's Row, SW3 (Knightsbridge/South Kensington),
0171-581 8377 ◑S
14 Trinity Sq., EC3 (Tower Hill), 0171-480 5500
64 Bishopsgate, EC2 (Bank/Liverpool St.), 0171-588 1200
84-86 Rosebery Ave., EC1 (Angel), 0171-833 1515
⬛ "By keeping it simple they keep it good" is how some
analyse the "winning formula" behind this "lighthearted"
French brasserie chain in "handy locations" around London;
its "unfussy", "honest" bistro food really "hits the spot for
carnivores" thanks to "delicious" steak frites, and if some
report "occasional glitches" and "brittle service", others
say it's a "consistent player" and "good for a business lunch."

Chez Liline   ▽ 22 | 9 | 15 | £31
101 Stroud Green Rd., N4 (Finsbury Park), 0171-263 6550
⬛ Fans say it's "worth living in Finsbury" to be near this
"unpretentious" seafooder "with a difference", offering
"uncomplicated, gutsy" Mauritian dishes showcasing "great
fish" from the adjacent fish shop (same owners); the staffers
are "great", if sometimes "slow", but the setting is "terribly
cramped" and some find it "expensive for the area."

Chez Max 24 14 22 £35

168 Ifield Rd., SW10 (Earl's Court/West Brompton), 0171-835 0874

■ This "cramped basement" on the Chelsea-Fulham border gets "hot and cosy" and some report "uncomfortable seats", but most consider it "a treat" thanks to "always excellent" French food marked by "strong flavours" and "imaginative combinations", as well as a "welcoming" (or is it "OTT"?) host; one regular pleads: "please write a bad review so it doesn't get any more crowded."

Chez Moi 21 18 21 £39

1 Addison Ave., W11 (Holland Park), 0171-603 8267

◪ Opinion is mixed on this "sedate, civilised" Holland Park veteran that's been around since the '60s: to some, it's a "dinosaur" with an "unexciting" menu that "rarely changes" and a "boring" ambience that makes you "feel you should be silent", but others enjoy its "consistently good" French-International fare, "warm welcome" and "accommodating" service; either way, it's "wonderful for illicit dining."

CHEZ NICO 26 21 23 £56

Grosvenor House Hotel, 90 Park Ln., W1 (Marble Arch), 0171-409 1290

◪ "You know you're in heaven when you've had your first taste" of Nico Ladenis' "exquisite" Classic French fare ("so good we almost swallowed our tongues") at this "polished" if "slightly old-fashioned" Mayfair hotel dining room; some find it "intimidating" with high prices and "too many waiters circling", but to most, it's "the ultimate overindulgence" complete with "politician-gazing."

Chiang Mai [S] 20 11 14 £24

48 Frith St., W1 (Leicester Sq./Tottenham Court Rd.), 0171-437 7444

■ The decor may "have seen better days", but this friendly Thai is "still a worthy survivor in the restaurant jungle of Soho", offering "excellent", "unusual dishes" from an "authentic", "good value" menu; it's a place to "enjoy good food while reminiscing about that holiday in the Far East."

Chicago Rib Shack ☾ [S] 14 14 15 £21

1 Raphael St., SW7 (Knightsbridge), 0171-581 5595

◪ Vegetarians are advised to "stay away" from this "lively" American in Knightsbridge dishing up "huge portions" of barbecue fare that some rate "good" ("love the ribs", the "onion loaf is to die for") and others "average"; either way, it's fine for kids or adults in the mood for "a mega blowout."

China Blues [S] ▽ 17 16 15 £21

29 Parkway, NW1 (Camden Town), 0171-482 3940

◪ Whilst some find "nothing special about the food" at this glass-fronted, multiregional Camden Chinese, it's considered a "great retreat for a romantic night" out, with "pleasant" live music on some nights that creates a "lovely" ambience.

China City ⏺🅂   18 | 13 | 14 | £19
25A Lisle St., WC2 (Leicester Sq.), 0171-734 3388
■ This "busy" Soho Chinese offers "dependable dim sum" and other "good value" fare in an "excellent environment."

China Jazz ⏺   18 | 18 | 16 | £31
12 Berkeley Sq., W1 (Green Park), 0171-499 9933
☑ Sibling to China Blues, this Berkeley Square newcomer wins praise for its "quality" Chinese food, "excellent decor" and live jazz, but a few dissenters report "mediocre", "overpriced" fare and say it's "unfortunate if you don't like the singer" performing that night; N.B. changes may be on the horizon now that it's in receivership.

Chinon   23 | 13 | 14 | £36
23 Richmond Way, W14 (Olympia/Shepherd's Bush), 0171-602 4082
■ This "low-key" Shepherd's Bush eaterie behind Olympia "never ceases to amuse" thanks to its "quirky atmosphere" and "funny staff", whilst self-taught Irish chef Jonathan Hayes continues to win many admirers with his "delicious, rich" New French food; there's a patio garden as well.

Chiswick, The 🅂   20 | 14 | 16 | £30
131 Chiswick High Rd., W4 (Turnham Green), 0181-994 6887
☑ There's "posh nosh for reasonable dosh" at this "lively, loud" Chiswick eaterie that admirers call "good for all ages and budgets" thanks to "beautifully cooked" Modern British food; a few think it's "not worth the trek" and even some fans knock the "cramped" setting and service that can be "a little shaky", but the "great food" wins most over.

Chor Bizarre ⏺🅂   19 | 21 | 17 | £29
16 Albemarle St., W1 (Green Park), 0171-629 9802
☑ The "decor is very Indian, but the dishes are not" is how some see this "out-of-the-ordinary" Mayfair Indian, but others are more convinced by the "authentic" regional cooking: "reminded me of a great place in Delhi"; the atmosphere is "relaxing" and there's free cab service to nearby Theatreland plus delivery within a half mile.

Choys ⏺🅂   16 | 12 | 15 | £23
172 King's Rd., SW3 (Sloane Sq.), 0171-352 0505
☑ An "old-fashioned Chinese" on King's Road offering "dependable food" and a "friendly" reception from staff with "zero turnover"; a few doubters shrug "ok, not great."

Christopher's ⏺🅂   18 | 18 | 16 | £35
18 Wellington St., WC2 (Covent Garden), 0171-240 4222
☑ "One of Covent Garden's better choices" thanks to a "convivial atmosphere", "prompt service" and "consistently good", "American-style" cooking highlighted by "great lobsters" and steaks; a few find the menu "limited" and "expensive for what it is", but it's a popular media haunt and "excellent for champagne brunch" or "after the theatre."

Chuen Cheng Ku ◐S   17 | 8 | 11 | £17
17 Wardour St., W1 (Leicester Sq.), 0171-437 1398

■ "Fantastic dim sum" served from trolleys is the main "claim to fame" of this "sprawling" Chinatown eaterie that draws "lots of Chinese" as well as "tourists"; "if you ignore" the "offhand service" and "ordinary decor", most say you'll enjoy the dumplings and other "good, honest food."

Churchill Arms S   21 | 13 | 13 | £13
119 Kensington Church St., W8 (High St. Kensington/Notting Hill Gate), 0171-727 4242

■ The "funky back room" of a "cluttered" pub near Notting Hill Gate might seem "an unlikely place" to find "terrific" Thai food, but this "unexpected surprise" receives many plaudits for just that, with some rating it the "best value in London for Thai"; "book at least one week in advance."

Chutney Mary ◐S   19 | 19 | 17 | £32
535 King's Rd., SW10 (Fulham Broadway), 0171-351 3113

☑ Recently refurbished (with a new upstairs dining room), this "colonial-style" Chelsea Indian still strikes fans as "good all-round", offering an "inventive menu" that "blends Indian and British" influences; although critics call it "overrated" and even some fans find it "slightly overpriced" with "oh so slow" service, most enjoy its "different" approach.

Chutney's ◐S   18 | 12 | 15 | £17
124 Drummond St., NW1 (Euston/Euston Sq.), 0171-388 0604

■ It doesn't look like much, but this vegetarian Indian in Euston has an "eat-all-you-want" lunch buffet for "under £5", making it a "bargain" and "good for a large family outing."

Cibo S   19 | 14 | 15 | £35
3 Russell Gardens, W14 (Olympia/Shepherd's Bush), 0171-371 2085

☑ A "fun" Italian near Olympia that wins applause for "wonderful fresh pasta", "great fish" and "professional" service; critics (a minority) say it "started well years ago" but has declined and suggest it's "time for a face-lift."

Cicada   18 | 16 | 17 | £27
132 St. John St., EC1 (Farringdon), 0171-608 1550

■ "Doesn't get the plaudits it deserves" say fans of this "stylish" restaurant/bar in Clerkenwell with "innovative" Pan-Asian fare that's "good value" and "worth fighting the throng in the bar for"; a few cite "unreliable food", but the appealing "mix of clients" and "attractive" staff help keep it "busy."

Cicoria S   13 | 11 | 13 | £19
(fka Billboard Cafe)
280 West End Ln., NW6 (West Hampstead), 0171-431 4188

☑ This "slightly pretentious but cute" West Hampstead "local" with "loud music" and "bland decor" has a "yuppie Californian and Italian" menu, which some label "unexciting" but which fans sum up as "good food, good price."

Circus ◐ 19 | 18 | 18 | £35

1 Upper James St., W1 (Piccadilly Circus), 0171-534 4000

◪ The decor of this "painfully trendy" Soho "media" hangout is "smart and stylish" to some, "chilly and minimalist" to others ("like an ad agency reception" area), and the Modern British cooking also polarises diners: "excellent" vs. "needs more consistency", "pricey"; the most unanimous praise goes to the "fantastic" downstairs bar that attracts "those who want to be seen, but not eat."

City Miyama ▽ 21 | 11 | 19 | £33

17 Godliman St., EC4 (St. Paul's), 0171-489 1937

■ This "great City restaurant" near St. Paul's Cathedral offers little in the way of decor but redeems itself with "the best sushi", teppanyaki and other Japanese fare; "friendly" service also helps make it a popular business option.

City Rhodes 24 | 19 | 21 | £45

1 New Street Sq., EC4 (Blackfriars/Chancery Ln.), 0171-583 1313

◪ Celebrity chef Gary Rhodes wins many admirers at this first-floor Holborn venue thanks to "thrilling" Modern British dishes featuring "unusual combinations that work"; to a minority, however, the food is "not as special as the price suggests" and there are also complaints about a "dull" setting that "lacks soul", but "unobtrusive service" is appreciated and overall most judge it "excellent."

Claridge's Bar [S] 19 | 22 | 22 | £27

Claridge's Hotel, Brook St., W1 (Bond St.), 0171-629 8860

◪ The former Causerie restaurant at this Mayfair hotel has been converted into a "smart, sleek" bar catering to a largely "business" crowd; whilst most appreciate the "good" Modern British menu of sophisticated snacks, some feel the room has "lost its lustre" and find the ambience "uptight."

Claridge's Restaurant [S] 23 | 22 | 24 | £52

Claridge's Hotel, Brook St., W1 (Bond St.), 0171-629 8860

■ Now past the century mark, Mayfair's "grand" "jewel" of a hotel dining room still has many admirers who "could not fault it in any way", from the "trusty" French fare to the "professional" staff; if a few feel it could use an "innovative touch given such high prices", more are charmed by the "old-fashioned panache" of this "privileged" "step back in time."

CLARKE'S 25 | 19 | 23 | £43

124 Kensington Church St., W8 (Notting Hill Gate), 0171-221 9225

■ "Perfect for the indecisive", Sally Clarke's "lovely little place" in Kensington offers a "no choice" set dinner menu but most "don't mind being told what to eat" since the Modern British–Med cooking is "bursting with flavour" and "beautifully presented"; although some complain of "stiff atmosphere" and "terrible acoustics", to the majority it's a "consistently top class" experience that's going "from strength to strength"; P.S. lunch offers some choice.

CLUB GASCON 25 | 19 | 19 | £35
57 West Smithfield, EC1 (Barbican/Farringdon), 0171-796 0600
■ "Don't tell anyone – it's hard enough to get a table" at this "exciting", stylish Smithfield debutant, which some consider the year's "best newcomer" thanks to an "innovative" menu with "a tempting array of Southwestern French specialties in small helpings" ("a French answer to tapas"); some point to "suspect service" and a "strangely restricting wine list", but most say you'll "want to go again, again, again."

Coast ●S 19 | 17 | 17 | £38
26B Albemarle St., W1 (Green Park), 0171-495 5999
☑ This "modern" Mayfair "goldfish bowl" (a former car showroom) "could do with more atmosphere", but still attracts "hip" "beautiful people" who don't seem to mind if there's debate over the Modern British menu: "really interesting" vs. "ordinary"; "slow", "gruff service" also comes in for some stick.

Coffee Republic ⌖ 13 | 12 | 14 | £7
French Connection, 99-103 Long Acre, WC2 (Covent Garden), 0171-240 9725 S
80 The Strand, WC2 (Charing Cross), 0171-836 6660 S
8 Pembridge Rd., W11 (Notting Hill Gate), 0171-229 6698 S
58 Queensway, W2 (Bayswater), 0171-792 3600 S
39 Great Marlborough St., W1 (Oxford Circus), 0171-734 5529 S
2 S. Molton St., W1 (Bond St.), 0171-629 4567 S
157 King's Rd., SW3 (Sloane Sq.), 0171-351 3178 S
30-32 Ludgate Hill, EC4 (St. Paul's), 0171-329 2522
147 Fleet St., EC4 (Blackfriars), 0171-353 0900
47 London Wall, EC2 (Moorgate), 0171-588 2220
Additional locations throughout London.
☑ To fans, these "cool coffee hangouts" are "excellent" for an "early morning wake-up" cup or a sandwich or cake "on the run", but to critics, the brews are "bland" and the snacks "average"; on balance, most give it a thumbs-up and like the "frequent buyer cards – a plus" for caffeine junkies.

Collection, The ● 16 | 19 | 14 | £36
264 Brompton Rd., SW3 (South Kensington), 0171-225 1212
☑ "Lost its edge" but "become friendlier" is one view on this "party" spot in Brompton Cross where diners "check in at the drawbridge" and move through to a "noisy", bi-level space (restaurant upstairs, bar/brasserie down) that's "excellent for people-watching" ("go in Prada or else"); the Pacific Rim fare is "interesting" to some, "average" to others, but the "hip-hop" bar is a "cool place to hang out."

Como Lario ● 18 | 15 | 18 | £30
22 Holbein Pl., SW1 (Sloane Sq.), 0171-730 2954
☑ "They always find you a table" at this "noisy" Italian "locals' hangout" behind Sloane Square; dissenters think the cooking is "variable" and "not as good as it was", but the "sunny" service helps make it "an old favourite."

Condotti ◐ 19 | 16 | 18 | £18
4 Mill St., W1 (Oxford Circus), 0171-499 1308
■ An "upmarket pizzeria" for "the Mayfair set" that's "fast, furious" and "reliable", offering "good pizzas" at "good value" in a "friendly atmosphere" with art on the walls; as one fan says: "you'd think we'd get bored of this, but no."

CONNAUGHT HOTEL, RESTAURANT [S] 25 | 23 | 26 | £59
Connaught Hotel, Carlos Pl., W1 (Bond St./Green Park), 0171-499 7070
■ "All-round excellence" is the trademark of this "elegant", "discreet" (some say "staid") Mayfair hotel dining room, where Michel Bourdin's "outstandingly good" Traditional British–French cooking is smartly served in a setting of "stylish" "luxury"; blending "old-fashioned charm with old-fashioned food", it's "fit for a king" and a fine place "to take the parents – or let them take you, at these prices"; the hotel's intimate (11 tables) Grill Room offers similar fare plus "great" Georgian-style decor.

Cookhouse, The ▽ 21 | 15 | 23 | £28
56 Lower Richmond Rd., SW15 (Putney Bridge), 0181-785 2300
■ This tiny, dinner-only Putney eaterie offers "wonderful", "inventive" Modern British food from an "excellent value" menu, but the "simple" room can get crowded, straining the usually "friendly service"; the BYO policy is "welcome."

Coq d'Argent [S] 18 | 19 | 17 | £40
No. 1 Poultry, EC2 (Bank), 0171-395 5000
◪ There's a "bird's eye view of the Square Mile" from Terence Conran's "sophisticated" City newcomer with a stunning rooftop garden (though, as one diner observes, it "failed to impress on a cold, wet night and can only work in summer"); the regional French cooking is generally considered "good" ("Conran can still do it"), and if some complain that it's "not very imaginative" and "overpriced", others simply advise "bring your expense account."

Cork & Bottle ◐ [S] 16 | 13 | 15 | £19
44-46 Cranbourn St., WC2 (Leicester Sq.), 0171-734 7807
◪ Something of an "institution", this "reliable" basement wine bar near Leicester Square offers "honest", "reasonably priced" French-Mediterranean cooking, and whilst most agree that the place could do with "some tarting up", the "sizzling atmosphere" and "strong wine list" make it a "great place to unwind after work", even if it's always a "tight fit."

Corney & Barrow 12 | 13 | 13 | £21
116 St. Martin's Ln., WC2 (Charing Cross/Leicester Sq.), 0171-655 9800 ◐ [S]
44 Cannon St., EC4 (Mansion House), 0171-248 1700
37A Jewry St., EC3 (Aldgate), 0171-680 8550
16 Royal Exchange, EC3 (Bank), 0171-929 3131

Corney & Barrow (Cont.)
1 Leadenhall Pl., EC3 (Bank/Monument), 0171-621 9201
109 Old Broad St., EC2 (Bank/Liverpool St.), 0171-638 9308
12-14 Mason's Ave., EC2 (Bank/Moorgate), 0171-726 6030
5 Exchange Sq., EC2 (Liverpool St.), 0171-628 4367
19 Broadgate Circle, EC2 (Liverpool St.), 0171-628 1251
9 Cabot Sq., E14 (Canary Wharf), 0171-512 0397
Additional locations throughout London.
◪ With its City locations (plus one Theatreland branch) and simple but "tasty" Eclectic snacks such as "nice smoked salmon on bagels", this "slick" wine bar chain is considered a "good place to go with work colleagues" for a "casual chat and quick bite"; those who find the food "bland and expensive for what you get" content themselves with the "good selection of wines."

Costa's Grill ⊄   15 | 11 | 17 | £15
12-14 Hillgate St., W8 (Notting Hill Gate), 0171-229 3794
■ "A local jewel in Notting Hill" that's been "family-run since the '50s", offering a "friendly welcome" and "tasty", "basic Greek food" at "an amazing price" in a "caff-style" setting with a "beautiful garden"; next door is a "very good" fish restaurant owned by the same family.

Côte à Côte 🆂   12 | 12 | 11 | £14
74-76 Battersea Bridge Rd., SW11 (Sloane Sq.), 0171-228 9096
■ It's "not the Titanic", but this unusual Battersea spot does have two "cool boats" to sit in, making it ideal for "an office party once a year" or a change of pace anytime; the French-Italian fare is "basic" but "good" and "cheap" (£5 for lunch) and there's a small garden area, but the "grumpy waiters" leave something to be desired.

Cottons Rhum Shop, Bar &   ▽ 18 | 17 | 16 | £23
Restaurant 🆂
55 Chalk Farm Rd., NW1 (Chalk Farm), 0171-482 1096
■ Bar-goers are "very happy" with the "great cocktails" at this "very hip" Camden eaterie, whilst those seeking solid sustenance will find "hot, spicy" Caribbean fare with a West Indian bias served by pleasantly "mad waiters"; most consider it a "good all-round" effort, and those unimpressed by the cooking say "after a few rum punches, who cares?"

County Hall Restaurant 🆂   17 | 20 | 16 | £34
London Marriott County Hall, Queens Walk, SE1
(Waterloo/Westminster), 0171-902 8000
◪ All agree the Thameside location is "a gift" with its "great view" of the Houses of Parliament, but beyond that, opinion diverges on this yearling; fans praise the "imaginative" Modern European cooking of David Ali (ex The Canteen), as well as the "warm welcome" and "romantic" setting, whilst others report "nondescript" food, "unpolished service" and "soulless" ambience; perhaps it still needs time to settle in.

Cow Dining Room S 19 | 16 | 16 | £25
89 Westbourne Park Rd., W2 (Westbourne Park), 0171-221 0021
■ Though this "quiet, simple" first-floor dining room "lacks the atmosphere of the pub downstairs", it rustles up "tantalising food" from a "small but well thought-out" menu of Modern British–Pacific Rim dishes; it's a "friendly", "warm" Notting Hill option that's only open for dinner or "a truly great Sunday lunch."

Cranks 16 | 11 | 12 | £11
8 Adelaide St., WC2 (Charing Cross/Embankment), 0171-836 0660 🏳
17-19 Great Newport St., WC2 (Leicester Sq.), 0171-836 5226 S
9-11 Tottenham St., W1 (Goodge St.), 0171-631 3912 S
23 Barrett St., W1 (Bond St.), 0171-495 1340 S 🏳
8 Marshall St., W1 (Oxford Circus/Piccadilly Circus), 0171-437 9431
☑ Some think "the new-style Cranks" with "updated decor" has finally "shed its weirdo veggie image", whilst others say the name still "says it all", but either way this chain dishes up "solid", "wholesome" Vegetarian grub with "no surprises"; detractors point to "chaotic" service and sometimes "dull" fare, but it's "fine for lunch" or "when you need to do penance after too many no-nos."

Crescent, The ◑S 18 | 15 | 19 | £22
99 Fulham Rd., SW3 (South Kensington), 0171-225 2244
■ A "cramped but convenient" split-level wine bar in Brompton Cross with a "superb wine list" (nearly 20 by the glass) and a "varied" Eclectic menu including a "terrific value" £6.95 set lunch; if some say the "nibbles are good but the real food needs work", most find it "pleasant" anyway.

CRITERION BRASSERIE ◑S 20 | 25 | 15 | £38
224 Piccadilly, W1 (Piccadilly Circus), 0171-930 0488
☑ Marco Pierre White's "grand dame" of Piccadilly dining boasts "technically well-prepared" and even "awesome" French-Med cooking that most agree "is almost up to the level of the spectacular" neo-Byzantine setting; critics say meals can be "marred" by "perfunctory" service and food that can "vary from visit to visit", but the "divine atmosphere" and "golden mosaic decor" help make it a true "experience."

Cuba ◑S 11 | 13 | 12 | £20
11-13 Kensington High St., W8 (High St. Kensington), 0171-938 4137
☑ "If you like fried bananas, this is the spot" and the "drinks are good" too at this "very lively", recently refurbed restaurant/bar in Kensington with "ok" Cuban food (plus some British dishes) that's not helped by "poor service"; still, most enjoy the "good atmosphere" at this place that claims to have the longest happy hour in town (noon to 8.30 PM); there are also salsa dancing lessons downstairs.

Cuba Libre & Havana Bar ◐S   12 | 15 | 12 | £19
72 Upper St., N1 (Angel), 0171-354 9998

☒ Though the "small portions" of "average" Cuban cooking are "disappointing" to many, this "brash" Islingtonian makes for a "fun night out" thanks to "great atmosphere", "good cocktails", "loud" music and reasonable prices (£10 set menu at dinner); "up the food quality, and it'd be worth returning."

Cucina S   20 | 16 | 19 | £30
45A South End Rd., NW3 (Belsize Park), 0171-435 7814

■ An "adventurous", "imaginative" Pacific Rim menu is served in a "leafy Hampstead setting" at this popular local; though a few suggest it's "losing its edge" and is "overpriced for the quality of the cooking", more report "excellent", "consistent" fare and "friendly" service ("very tolerant of our two-year-old"), calling it "ideal for Sunday lunch."

Dakota S   19 | 18 | 16 | £33
127 Ledbury Rd., W11 (Notting Hill Gate/Westbourne Park), 0171-792 9191

■ This "lively" American Southwestern "star" still excites most, attracting "fashionable people" with its "classy combo of flavours, colours and atmosphere" ("beats Mt. Rushmore by 4,000 miles"); however, critics find it "overhyped and underwhelming", citing "amateur service" and "miserly portions" ("do people from Dakota eat so little?"); pluses include a "nice bar downstairs" and "brilliant" brunch.

Dan's   16 | 16 | 18 | £34
119 Sydney St., SW3 (Sloane Sq./South Kensington), 0171-352 2718

☒ An "elegant", "friendly" Chelsea eaterie that fills a need as a "good neighbourhood restaurant", offering British fare that's "not great, but good" – "the sort of food you had as a treat at boarding school in the '60s"; it's "better in summer" thanks to the "beautiful garden", but do "book in time."

Daphne ◐   19 | 16 | 20 | £25
83 Bayham St., NW1 (Camden Town), 0171-267 7322

■ "No pretensions, just good Greek food without the broken plates" is what most find at this "relaxing" Camden Town eaterie that's "pleasant enough, without being exciting"; there are "enough interesting things on offer" to make it an "enjoyable experience", complete with "chatty" service.

Daphne's ◐S   19 | 21 | 17 | £41
112 Draycott Ave., SW3 (South Kensington), 0171-589 4257

☒ "Rub shoulders with stars" at Brompton Cross' "buzzy" "socialite" scene that some say "keeps getting better" but others claim is "not as impressive as its reputation"; fans cite "glorious" Italian food and "much improved" service, whilst foes find an "overpriced", "disappointing" menu and urge the staff to "lighten up – it's a restaurant, not the Vatican"; either way, the "chic, smart" set "still goes" here.

Daquise 🟥　　　　　　　13 | 8 | 13 | £15
20 Thurloe St., SW7 (South Kensington), 0171-589 6117
◪ This "rather quaint piece of Polish history" is "like being in
another time and world" and should be "preserved as a
branch of the V&A museum nearby"; whilst it could do with
a "face-lift", fans say the "plain and nourishing" Polish-
Continental cooking hits the mark as "great value" "comfort
food", making it "one of South Ken's best nooks."

Deals 🟥　　　　　　　　11 | 12 | 12 | £21
Bradmore House, Queen Caroline St., W6 (Hammersmith),
0181-563 1001
14-16 Foubert's Pl., W1 (Oxford Circus), 0171-287 1001
Harbour Yard, Chelsea Harbour, SW10 (Earl's Court),
0171-795 1001
■ They may be "chainy and ordinary", but this trio of
"dressed-up burger bars" is appreciated as a "cheap
and cheerful" option for "huge portions" of "standard"
American-style diner fare (with a few Thai dishes for
variety); they're especially "good with kids on weekends."

De Cecco 🟥　　　　　　　20 | 14 | 17 | £29
189 New King's Rd., SW6 (Parsons Green), 0171-736 1145
■ "Still good after all these years" is the consensus on
this "popular, busy" Parsons Green Italian that gets "oh
so noisy" in the evenings; the "excellent", "good value"
menu includes "killer" lobster spaghetti that's "a real
favourite" amongst regulars.

Deco 🟥　　　　　　　　– | – | – | M
294 Fulham Rd., SW10 (Fulham Broadway/South Kensington),
0171-351 0044
This small, art deco–style newcomer near Stamford Bridge
is establishing itself as a casual neighbourhood spot with
reasonably priced Modern European fare and cheery service;
the downstairs cocktail bar also serves food.

Defune　　　　　　　▽ 21 | 10 | 16 | £34
61 Blandford St., W1 (Baker St.), 0171-935 8311
◪ The few who reported on this Marylebone traditional
Japanese say it's worth overlooking the "humble" decor
to enjoy the "best sushi and sashimi" – but as you might
expect, the price reflects the quality: "stone me!"; the fact
that it's over 20 years old is testimony to its appeal.

Del Buongustaio 🌓🟥　　　22 | 14 | 17 | £31
283 Putney Bridge Rd., SW15 (East Putney), 0181-780 9361
■ It looks "like a down-market cafe from the outside",
but fans say this "unpretentious", "rustic" Putney eaterie
"transports you to Italy" with its "atmosphere, smells and
tastes", offering a "gutsy, authentic" regional menu with
"unusual concoctions" that yield "more hits than misses";
some even call it the "most underrated just-around-the-
corner Italian" in town.

Delfina Studio Cafe ▽ 19 18 17 £25
Delfina Gallery, 50 Bermondsey St., SE1 (London Bridge),
0171-357 0244
■ "Hidden away" in Bermondsey ("went there once and
can't remember how to get there") is this "stylish", lunch-
only studio cafe in a converted chocolate factory with an
"imaginative", "well-priced" Modern British menu and lots
of space; it's "a great place" to those who know it.

dell'Ugo ◐ 16 15 14 £30
(nka 6 Degrees)
56 Frith St., W1 (Leicester Sq./Tottenham Court Rd.),
0171-734 8300
◨ "Pick your floor" from the three options (cafe/bar, bistro,
restaurant) at this "popular" Soho eaterie which draws its
share of "corporate lunching" and "hen parties"; however, a
post-*Survey* redo, as well as a switch to a Pacific Rim menu
may outdate the above food and decor scores.

Denim ◐ S ▽ 15 20 13 £31
4A Upper St. Martin's Ln., WC2 (Leicester Sq.), 0171-497 0376
■ This "trendy", tri-level Theatreland hot spot with "cool
decor and a friendly bouncer" is a "great place to start a
fun night", though it can be "difficult to get a drink" in the
two "crowded" bars; those who've tried the ground-floor
restaurant report "good food" from a Pacific Rim–Modern
British menu, though "service is perhaps a little too relaxed."

Depot Waterfront Brasserie S 18 18 16 £25
Tideway Rd., Mortlake High St., SW14 (Barnes Bridge B.R.),
0181-878 9462
■ An "excellent setting overlooking the Thames" and "good
atmosphere" ("so relaxing at lunch, watching the world go
by") are strong points at this "refreshingly unpretentious"
brasserie at Barnes; it also wins fans with "consistently
good" Modern British fare that some say has "improved
dramatically" of late, but a few doubters cite "dull,
predictable" dishes and service that "tries, but is trying."

Dibbens – – – E
2-3 Cowcross St., EC1 (Farringdon), 0171-250 0035
After Mange-2 closed, new owners re-opened its Smithfield
premises as a cool eaterie with generous space between
tables and an unashamedly populist Modern British menu
from Mark Ovid (ex Harvey Nichols' Fifth Floor); whilst the
food may be down-to-earth, prices suit expense-accounters.

Diverso ◐ S 18 18 18 £34
85 Piccadilly, W1 (Green Park), 0171-491 2222
■ "Should be more popular" say fans of this Italian in a
"good location" overlooking Green Park, praising its
"excellent" cooking, "lovely decor" and "a 'welcome home'"
reception for regulars; the few who find anything to knock
("inept service", "feels naff") are outvoted.

DKNY Bar　　　　　　　　14 | 16 | 13 | £15

DKNY, 24 Old Bond St., W1 (Bond St./Green Park), 0171-499 8089
■ When "cruising down Bond Street", this in-store cafe
is "just right for a quick bite", with "surprisingly good food"
from a "good value" menu of American snacks: "wonderful
salads", bagels, etc.; there's also fun "people-watching."

Dôme S　　　　　　　　　12 | 13 | 12 | £16

8-10 Charing Cross Rd., WC2 (Leicester Sq.), 0171-240 5556
32 Long Acre, WC2 (Covent Garden), 0171-379 8650
35A-B Kensington High St., W8 (High St. Kensington),
0171-937 6655
57-59 Old Compton St., W1 (Leicester Sq./Piccadilly Circus),
0171-287 0770 ●
194-196 Earl's Court Rd., SW5 (Earl's Court), 0171-835 2200
354 King's Rd., SW3 (Sloane Sq.), 0171-352 2828
Unit 2, Kingswell Ctr., 58-62 Heath St., NW3 (Hampstead),
0171-431 0399
341 Upper St., N1 (Angel), 0171-226 3414
57-59 Charterhouse St., EC1 (Farringdon), 0171-336 6484
Additional locations throughout London.
☑ To most, this chain of "Franglais" cafes functions as a
"reliable fallback" for "robust", "decent value" bistro fare
served in "spacious" settings with a "friendly atmosphere";
others say it leaves "no lasting impression" and ask "does
service exist here?", but the fact that "you can usually get
a table" makes it an "easy" option.

Don Pepe ●　　　　　　▽ 18 | 14 | 19 | £26

99 Frampton St., NW8 (Edgware Rd.), 0171-262 3834
■ There's "real Spanish atmosphere" at this "small", "old-
style venue" off Edgware Road, where "steady", "reliable"
Spanish fare is served with the accompaniment of live
guitar music; "very friendly" service is another reason
why it's considered a "great local."

Dorchester, Bar S　　　　20 | 21 | 22 | £30

The Dorchester, Park Ln., W1 (Hyde Park Corner), 0171-629 8888
■ "One expects Fred Astaire to saunter in any moment" at
the "lovely" bar of this glossy Mayfair hotel that's "terrific
for celeb-spotting" and quite "enjoyable" for eating, too,
thanks to "excellent" Italian food plus the likes of a "world-
class club sandwich"; it's "good for a weekend" lunch or
a "relaxing" evening complete with piano music.

Dorchester, Grill Room S　　23 | 23 | 24 | £49

The Dorchester, Park Ln., W1 (Hyde Park Corner), 0171-317 6336
■ "Still wonderful" say devotees of this "grand dining
experience" in "one of the nicest hotels in London", where
Willy Elsener's "high-class" Traditional British fare is
"impeccably" served in a "very elegant" Mayfair dining
room; a few find it "a bit stuffy" and "unspectacular", but
to most it's "classy and reliable", just "as you would expect
the Dorchester to be."

Dorchester, Oriental   23 | 21 | 23 | £54
The Dorchester, Park Ln., W1 (Hyde Park Corner), 0171-317 6328
■ "If you can afford it", this "refined" Chinese in a Mayfair hotel is considered "as good (and expensive) as anything in Hong Kong", with "delicately flavoured, beautifully presented" food and "graceful service" with a favourable "waiters-to-customers ratio"; those who say it's "overrated, overpriced" and "almost too polished" are overruled by those who sigh "oh, to be able to dine here every day."

Dover Street Restaurant & Bar ●   13 | 14 | 12 | £28
8-10 Dover St., W1 (Green Park), 0171-629 9813
☑ Many "come for the music, not the food" to this "good late-night venue" (3 AM license) in Mayfair that's now bigger and "better after a refurbishment"; critics take aim at "forgettable" Mediterranean cooking and "disorganised staff", but the "buzzy environment" and live jazz in the evenings make it "popular."

Down Mexico Way ●S   12 | 15 | 13 | £21
25 Swallow St., W1 (Piccadilly Circus), 0171-437 9895
■ "A great party restaurant down Piccadilly way" describes this "lively" Mexican with a "good club atmosphere" and "lovely tiled" decor; there's little enthusiasm for the food ("nothing authentic") or service ("uninterested"), but that doesn't matter since the "great live music" and "excellent salsa show" are the real attractions – "arriba!"

Drones   16 | 18 | 16 | £35
1 Pont St., SW1 (Knightsbridge), 0171-259 6166
☑ Post-*Survey*, this colourful Belgravia eaterie with an adjoining grocery shop introduced a new Eclectic menu (having transferred the chef from sister Zoe), which may change the minds of critics who feel this former star has "never got back to its best" since its '80s heyday; in any case, fans enjoy its "good" ambience and "pleasant" service.

Duke of Cambridge S   – | – | – | M
30 St. Peter's St., N1 (Angel), 0171-359 3066
It looks a little down-at-heel, but this minimalist Islington gastropub serves unpretentious Modern European cooking that boasts of being 100% organic 'where humanly possible', a claim that extends to the wines and beers; alfresco dining is possible on the front patio and there's a competitively priced £6 weekday lunch menu.

Duke of Cambridge S   20 | 17 | 16 | £17
228 Battersea Bridge Rd., SW11 (Clapham Junction B.R.), 0171-223 5662
☑ This "relaxed" Battersea spot (sibling to The Queens) serving good "quality" Modern British cooking in "great surroundings" is considered "perfect for a casual dinner with friends", although a few find it "expensive for a pub"; the large outdoor terrace gets crowded in warm weather.

Eagle, The [S] ⌀ 22 | 14 | 14 | £18

159 Farringdon Rd., EC1 (Farringdon), 0171-837 1353

◪ Most feel this "fun", "crowded" Farringdon "foodie pub" "gets it right" by offering "superior" fare at "reasonable prices" from a "consistently excellent" Mediterranean menu, but to a minority, it's "not really worth" having to "arrive very early" to get a seat and then finding it "too noisy to listen or talk"; still, it "remains a much-visited favourite despite its faults."

East One ◐ [S] 16 | 12 | 13 | £20

175-179 St. John St., EC1 (Farringdon), 0171-566 0088

◪ A "novel" Chinese stir-fry concept near Smithfield Market where patrons choose "raw ingredients and watch the chef cook them"; fans say it's "always fun" whilst cynics suggest it "all tastes the same" and think the idea "has had its day", but being able to "eat as much as you like" (with lunch "for a tenner") makes it a "bargain."

Ebury Wine Bar [S] 17 | 14 | 15 | £25

139 Ebury St., SW1 (Victoria), 0171-730 5447

◪ Lovers of this "cosy" haunt on the Belgravia-Pimlico border find it "charming for a casual meal" with "consistent" Modern British fare "at reasonable prices" and a "good wine list"; others think it's "past its sell-by date", citing "cramped", "stuffy" quarters ("get the air con sorted!") and "red-nosed businessmen", but this "institution" is not known as the "great survivor" for nothing.

Eco 21 | 16 | 14 | £17

4 Market Row, SW9 (Brixton), 0171-738 3021
162 Clapham High St., SW4 (Clapham Common), 0171-978 1108 [S]

■ "Fab pizzas" with "interesting toppings" and "good people-watching" are the hallmarks of this "vibrant" Clapham pizzeria, and whilst some object to the "noise" and say you "sometimes feel as if you are rushed to finish", that doesn't deter those who rate it "one of the best" of its kind in London; no dinner at the Brixton sibling.

Ed's Easy Diner [S] 13 | 14 | 15 | £13

Pepsi Trocadero Ctr., 38 Shaftesbury Ave., W1 (Piccadilly Circus), 0171-287 1951 ◐
12 Moor St., W1 (Leicester Sq./Tottenham Court Rd.), 0171-439 1955 ◐
362 King's Rd., SW3 (Sloane Sq.), 0171-352 1956 ◐
Brent Cross Shopping Ctr., NW4 (Brent Cross), 0181-202 0999
O_2 Ctr., 255 Finchley Rd., NW3 (Finchley Rd.), 0171-431 1958

◪ This "brash, loud" chain of "American-style diners" with "'50s decor" and "slightly affected staff (resting actors!)" is a "great hangout for under-16s", and even many adults enjoy its "tasty burgers" and other "artery-clogging" fare; doubters claim it's "past its prime as a theme restaurant" and say "they do what they do well, but is what they do good?"

Efes Kebab House ◐ 19 | 13 | 17 | £21
175-177 Great Portland St., W1 (Great Portland St.), 0171-436 0600 [S]
80 Great Titchfield St., W1 (Oxford Circus), 0171-636 1953
■ "London's top Turk" rave fans of these "authentic Turkish" canteens serving "the tenderest marinated meat" ("ideal for carnivores") and other "straightforward, no-nonsense" fare at "bargain" prices in a "happy atmosphere"; the "belly dancer" (at the Great Portland Street venue) and "good takeaway service" earn brownie points.

El Blason 19 | 15 | 19 | £31
8-9 Blacklands Terrace, SW3 (Sloane Sq.), 0171-823 7383
■ Expect a "warm welcome" at this "friendly", "tucked-away" Spaniard in Chelsea that's "a bit pricey" but serves "the real thing": "great paella and tapas" that are "made with love" and "fresh ingredients"; some favour the ground-floor tapas bar over the first-floor restaurant.

Elena's L'Etoile 21 | 18 | 21 | £33
30 Charlotte St., W1 (Goodge St.), 0171-636 1496
■ Elena Salvoni is "a real trooper who knows how to run a restaurant", making everyone feel "welcome" at this "old-fashioned but still fashionable" Fitzrovia brasserie with "superb atmosphere", "charming" service and Classic French cooking that's "very good", if "a bit rich"; although a few find it "disappointing" ("what went wrong?"), most think it's "just how a French restaurant should be."

El Gaucho ◐ [S] ≠ 20 | 14 | 16 | £25
Chelsea Farmers Mkt., 125 Sydney St., SW3 (South Kensington), 0171-376 8514
■ This "excellent, down-to-basics Argentinean steakhouse" in Chelsea Farmers Market serves "steak as it should be" – "simple", "without sauces" – though some report "impolite" service; the terrace is "nice on a summer night."

Elistano 19 | 15 | 18 | £27
25-27 Elystan St., SW3 (Sloane Sq./South Kensington), 0171-584 5248
■ A popular "neighbourhood Italian joint" in Chelsea that gets "really busy" and "impossibly noisy", serving "inexpensive", "dependable" food in a "fun atmosphere" with a "welcoming" staff; it's a "smartish place to fill up at" – the "only problem is getting a booking at short notice"; N.B. new owners took over post-*Survey.*

El Metro ◐ [S] 15 | 12 | 14 | £19
10-12 Effie Rd., SW6 (Fulham Broadway), 0171-384 1264
■ "Is all of Spain really like this?"; there's usually an "incredible party atmosphere" at this "crowded, cramped" Fulham Spaniard, where the likes of "decent tapas" and "paella to die for" are washed down with "cheap wine"; live music and a terrace in front add to its appeal.

El Prado ◐ [S] ▽ 19 | 9 | 18 | £27
766 Fulham Rd., SW6 (Putney Bridge), 0171-731 7179
■ Although some feel it's "become too expensive", this Spaniard near Putney Bridge has a following thanks to "consistently good", "authentic" cooking plus "friendly service" and a warm welcome from owner Felix Velarde.

Emile's 21 | 14 | 20 | £26
96-98 Felsham Rd., SW15 (Putney Bridge), 0181-789 3323
144 Wandsworth Bridge Rd., SW6 (Fulham Broadway/ Parsons Green), 0171-736 2418
■ They're "not very innovative", but this pair of "intimate", "homey" neighbourhood eateries in the Putney vicinity serve "well-made, reasonably priced" fare from a "regularly changing" Modern British–Eclectic menu; expect "no fuss, no muss", just "good food" and "friendly, attentive" service.

Emporio Armani Express 17 | 17 | 15 | £23
191 Brompton Rd., SW3 (Knightsbridge), 0171-823 8818
■ "Surprisingly good food for a fashion place" is what most find at this "stylish" in-store cafe in Knightsbridge with a short Italian menu; though a few call it "overpriced" and "exclusively for lunching ladies" (which might explain the "extremely hunky waiters"), there's no doubt it's "good for what it is" – "a welcome break from a shopping expedition."

Engineer, The [S] 18 | 15 | 15 | £22
65 Gloucester Ave., NW1 (Camden Town/Chalk Farm), 0171-722 0950
■ There's "great summer eating" in the "very pleasant" garden of this "relaxed" Primrose Hill "gastro"-pub, but it's also "worth the trip in the winter" for Eclectic fare that's "more adventurous than most pub food"; a few call it "disappointing of late" and knock the "two sittings" policy, but most would happily "beg for a space on a sunny Sunday."

English Garden ◐ [S] 19 | 20 | 20 | £41
10 Lincoln St., SW3 (Sloane Sq.), 0171-584 7272
◪ "Foreign visitors" "love the Englishness" of this "cute" townhouse off King's Road, but whilst fans consider it "underrated" with "excellent" British cooking and staff with "charm and wit", foes find it "a bit precious" with "average" food; still, the "cosy" conservatory is popular; N.B. Richard Corrigan has taken over and plans a refurb.

English House ◐ [S] 18 | 19 | 18 | £39
3 Milner St., SW3 (Sloane Sq.), 0171-584 3002
◪ Another magnet for "tourists", this "courteous" Chelsea sibling of the English Garden has decor worthy of a "glossy magazine" and "reliable" British dishes that satisfy most, even if prices are rather "high" and some find the menu "slightly fussy"; fans think it "really should be more popular."

Enoteca Turi   22 | 15 | 19 | £32
28 Putney High St., SW15 (Putney Bridge), 0181-785 4449
☑ "Pasta as in Italy" is "worth the drive across the river" to Putney say admirers of this "understated" neighbourhood eaterie with "well-prepared" Modern Italian food that some say is "much improved" of late; critics find it "authentic but somehow bland", though the "extensive, interesting wine list" (over 10 choices by the glass) is a winner.

Enterprise, The 🅂   17 | 17 | 15 | £26
35 Walton St., SW3 (South Kensington), 0171-584 3148
■ There's a "great local scene" along with "interesting" International fare at this "upscale pub" in Chelsea, but it can get "too crowded to really enjoy" (no evening reservations) and they "need to 'beam up' more attentive waiters"; still, it's "a good choice for lunch when shopping in Knightsbridge."

Esarn Kheaw 🅂   20 | 8 | 14 | £21
314 Uxbridge Rd., W12 (Shepherd's Bush), 0181-743 8930
■ This "low-key" Shepherd's Bush canteen is "extremely cramped" and looks like a "living room", but the "excellent", "inexpensive" Thai food "makes up for it" (at least one fan is "seriously stuck on the sticky rice"); an outvoted few find it "overrated" and even some fans lament "very slow" service – "take a book, it can be worth it."

est 🅂   16 | 14 | 15 | £21
54 Frith St., W1 (Leicester Sq./Tottenham Court Rd.), 0171-437 0666
■ Ratings may be on the modest side, but most have warm praise for this "well-run" Soho bar/restaurant; the Mediterranean menu is "interesting and well prepared", and the "great atmosphere" and "friendly staff" at the bar help make it a popular meeting place.

Euphorium 🅂   18 | 15 | 16 | £31
203 Upper St., N1 (Highbury & Islington), 0171-704 6909
☑ "Islington's finest" say fans of this "trendy, cool" eaterie, praising its "very tasty", "inventive" Modern British fare, "fun" bar and "laid-back but surprisingly efficient" staff; others think it's "overpriced" and "let down" by "offhand service" and "uncomfortable chairs", but all agree the next-door bakery is "great", selling "fab cakes, etc."

Fairuz 🅂   – | – | – | M
3 Blandford St., W1 (Baker St./Marble Arch), 0171-486 8108
A "very pleasant Lebanese" newcomer to Marylebone that's "nothing fancy" in terms of looks, but which rustles up "good, healthy food"; the cost can be "a bit steep" if you order an array of dishes, but service is "always friendly" and odds are "you'll walk out happy."

Fakhreldine ◑S   20 | 15 | 18 | £32
85 Piccadilly, W1 (Green Park), 0171-493 3424
Fakhreldine Express ◑S
92 Queensway, W2 (Bayswater/Queensway), 0171-243 3177
■ "Middle East at its best" say fans of these "warm"
Lebanese eateries in Mayfair and Queensway; there's a
"high standard of cooking" with an emphasis on "tasty"
ingredients, and if some find it "a bit expensive", you get
your money's worth: "was not hungry for a week" after.

Fatboy's Cafe S⊅   17 | 12 | 16 | £16
10A-10B Edensor Rd., W4 (Turnham Green), 0181-994 8089
■ Serving "good" burger bar fare by day, this Chiswick cafe
offers "exemplary Thai" food at night; it's reasonably priced
and "great with children" thanks to "friendly" staff.

Feng Shang Floating Restaurant S   17 | 18 | 16 | £26
*Cumberland Basin, Prince Albert Rd., NW1 (Camden Town),
0171-485 8137*
◪ A "wonderful setting" on a barge moored beside Regent's
Park plus "excellent" Chinese food add up to "a delightful
dining experience" according to most; though some find it
"overpriced" with occasionally "rushed" service ("hold on
to your plate"), it's "good for parties" and enjoyable for kids.

ffiona's ◑S   20 | 18 | 22 | £25
*51 Kensington Church St., W8 (High St. Kensington/
Notting Hill Gate), 0171-937 4152*
■ This "intimate" Kensington eaterie is "run by a real
character", Ffiona Reid-Owen, who often "takes over" when
it comes to ordering from the menu of "rustic" British fare; if
the food reminds some of "boarding school days", most
enjoy this "step back in time" and have real affection for
the "amusing" Ffiona, "London's greatest hostess."

Fifth Floor ◑S   21 | 19 | 18 | £38
*Harvey Nichols, Knightsbridge, SW1 (Knightsbridge),
0171-235 5250*
◪ "Pose and be seen" at this "buzzy" Knightsbridge in-store
dining room that attracts a "formidable clientele" thanks to
Henry Harris' "superb", "consistently high standard" Modern
British cooking and a "chic" ambience; some object to
"noise from the adjacent bar" ("the best pick-up place")
and "slack", "aloof" service, but this "cool" venue remains a
flag-bearer: "if only all department stores had food like this."

Fifth Floor Cafe S   18 | 16 | 14 | £23
*Harvey Nichols, Knightsbridge, SW1 (Knightsbridge),
0171-823 1839*
■ This in-store cafe is "perfect for people-watching" or "a
breather while shopping" in Knightsbridge, and though many
are put off by the queue and "absurdly small tables", the
reward is "interesting" Modern British–Eclectic fare; service
that's "usually helpful" can be "offhand" when busy.

Film Café S   11 | 13 | 10 | £11

National Film Theatre, South Bank, SE1 (Waterloo),
0171-928 3535

■ The "film element is taken more seriously than the cafe element", but this "useful", all-day self-service venue inside the National Film Theatre is "fine for a snack" from a simple English menu of soups, salads and the like; "good views" from terrace seats by the Thames may be its "biggest asset."

Fina Estampa   ▽ 18 | 12 | 17 | £27

150 Tooley St., SE1 (London Bridge), 0171-403 1342

■ "Perfect for that Peruvian moment"; this "interesting find" near Tower Bridge has a "homely" feel, "friendly staff" and an "authentic", "unusual" Peruvian menu ("100 ways with potatoes") that's "good value" and "nice for a change."

First Floor ◑S   13 | 18 | 14 | £30

186 Portobello Rd., W11 (Ladbroke Grove/Notting Hill Gate),
0171-243 0072

☑ "Lots of candles" and a great view along Portobello Road make for a "nice atmosphere" at this rustic Portobello haunt, but many find the Modern British–Eclectic cooking "disappointing" ("tries to be too clever", perhaps); N.B. new owners took over recently, tarting up the decor and introducing a new chef to improve matters – the jury awaits.

Fish!   – | – | – | E

Cathedral St., Borough Mkt., SE1 (London Bridge), 0171-836 3236

Opposite Southwark Cathedral is this boisterous newcomer (resembling a fishbowl thanks to a huge window facia) from the team behind Bank; offering a fairly priced Eclectic menu of simply cooked fish plus easygoing, child-friendly service, it's made an auspicious debut; there's a fishmonger next door and three siblings are planned before the millennium.

Floriana   21 | 23 | 19 | £50

15 Beauchamp Pl., SW3 (Knightsbridge), 0171-838 1500

☑ "Like its owner – rich, Italian and a magnet for ladies who lunch" is one way to describe Riccardo Mazzucchelli's "elegant" Knightsbridge newcomer; fans rave about the "super ambience" (with piano music), "attentive servers" and Fabio Trabocchi's "delicate" cooking, but others think it's "vastly overrated" and "pricey", with food that's "over the top"; either way, it's made an impact on London's top-end dining scene; a chic, horseshoe-shaped bar opened at press time.

Florians S   20 | 15 | 18 | £28

4 Topsfield Parade, Middle Ln., N8 (Highgate), 0181-348 8348

☑ "Something of a gastronomic oasis" in Crouch End ("which can't be a bad thing"), with an "authentic Italian" menu of "good, hearty food" and an "excellent wine list"; some find the bar "noisy and smoky" and the restaurant "lacking in ambience", but "happy, helpful" service and the outside patio help make amends.

Food for Thought [S] ⊄ 19 | 8 | 13 | £11
31 Neal St., WC2 (Covent Garden), 0171-836 9072
■ There's "zero decor" and it's "not for the claustrophobic", but this "informal", "crowded" Covent Garden basement Vegetarian serves "delicious wholesome food" that's "nutritious, filling" and "good for a quick meal"; it's "cheap" too – "if only it were bigger or there were more of them!"

Footstool Restaurant ▽ 15 | 15 | 10 | £15
St. John's, Smith Sq., SW1 (Westminster), 0171-222 2779
■ If some call the Modern British–European fare "ordinary", the same can't be said of the setting in a 1700s church crypt in Westminster; serving weekday lunch plus light suppers on church concert evenings, it's a "versatile venue for a quick snack or something more special" and the £13.50 set lunch has takers from nearby political offices.

Formula Veneta ◐ 17 | 14 | 16 | £31
14 Hollywood Rd., SW10 (Earl's Court), 0171-352 7612
■ "All the taste without any arrogance" is what fans find at this "friendly Italian" in Chelsea where owner Gianni "always tries his best" to look after a "noisy" local crowd; faultfinders call it "a little expensive" and report "ups and downs", but the "good food" and "great garden" convince most.

Fortnum's Fountain 16 | 16 | 16 | £23
Fortnum & Mason, 181 Piccadilly, W1 (Green Park/ Piccadilly Circus), 0171-973 4140
◪ "A great institution", this all-day, in-store eaterie on the lower ground floor of the St. James's gourmet store is "wonderful when your mother or grandmother is visiting"; the "traditional" British fare strikes some as "dull", but most call it "fine for what it is" (especially the "great sundaes"), though "stiff-upper-lip service" raises a few eyebrows.

Foundation Restaurant & Bar [S] 14 | 14 | 11 | £26
Harvey Nichols, Knightsbridge, SW1 (Knightsbridge), 0171-201 8000
◪ This basement eaterie with "trendy" decor never gets "too crowded as it's difficult to find" in this Knightsbridge store, but fans say its Eclectic menu can be "excellent"; foes cite "clinical" ambience and staff "too busy looking gorgeous" to provide much service, but the "noisy bar" has appeal.

Four Regions [S] ▽ 16 | 17 | 18 | £26
County Hall, Riverside Bldg., SE1 (Waterloo/Westminster), 0171-928 0988
■ There are "wonderful views" over the Thames to Big Ben and the Houses of Parliament from this "wonderfully quiet" recent arrival within the County Hall complex, and most feel the multiregional Chinese menu measures up fairly well to the surroundings; "really friendly staff" and a waterside terrace are pluses.

Four Seasons Chinese ◑ S   21 | 11 | 13 | £23
84 Queensway, W2 (Bayswater), 0171-229 4320
■ Fans laud this "brilliant" Bayswater Chinese for offering "tasty", "authentic" fare (including "great roast duck") at modest prices; given the "quality", most don't mind the simple decor and service that can be "kind" or "acid-tongued."

Four Seasons Hotel, Lanes Restaurant S   23 | 21 | 23 | £45
Four Seasons Hotel, Hamilton Pl., W1 (Hyde Park Corner), 0171-499 0888
■ Reopened after a "jolly nice" revamp, this airy dining room in a luxury hotel overlooking Park Lane hits the mark with those who say it offers "wonderful", "top-drawer" Eclectic food from Shaun Whatling plus an "excellent wine linst" in a "beautiful" setting; still, a few find it a "bit boring" and note the odd "chairman entertaining his 'niece'."

Fox & Anchor   18 | 14 | 16 | £17
115 Charterhouse St., EC1 (Farringdon), 0171-253 4838
■ This "unchanging" (est. 1898) all-day pub on the edge of Smithfield Market has a "wonderful atmosphere" and serves "surprisingly good", "classic" pub grub at moderate prices; but it's probably most renowned for serving full English breakfasts all day, with the "7 AM breakfast and pint" (or "great Bloody Mary") having entered London folklore.

Foxtrot Oscar   16 | 12 | 15 | £25
79 Royal Hospital Rd., SW3 (Sloane Sq.), 0171-352 7179 S
16 Byward St., EC3 (Tower Hill), 0171-481 2700
◪ It may be "past its heyday" and in need of "a face-lift", but the Chelsea original remains a "fun" haunt for "a relaxed evening" according to regulars who don't mind if the American-British fare is "nothing special"; the City sibling has a similar menu but serves lunch only.

Francofill S   13 | 10 | 13 | £16
1 Old Brompton Rd., SW7 (South Kensington), 0171-584 0087
■ "Just what was needed" in the area say fans of this French bistro in a "handy location near South Ken tube", offering "good, robust" fare (some call it "classy fast food") at moderate prices, albeit with service that can be "a bit unpredictable"; the opening of a connecting bar may help mollify complaints about "cheerless" decor.

Frederick's ◑   20 | 20 | 19 | £35
106 Camden Passage, N1 (Angel), 0171-359 2888
■ "Traditional and contemporary at the same time", this "stylish" Islingtonian is a "favourite" thanks to a "superb" conservatory that "looks out to a lovely garden" and a Modern British menu that most find "reliably good" (though there's debate as to whether it's "never exciting" or "more innovative than its reputation suggests"); "unobtrusive" service and "fairly priced wines" add to the pleasure.

Freedom Brewing Company S　12 | 16 | 12 | £20
(fka Soho Brewing Company)
41 Earlham St., WC2 (Covent Garden), 0171-240 0606
■ Though some find the Modern British fare "surprisingly good for such a warehouse", all agree that "beers are the attraction" at this Covent Garden microbrewery with "interesting" beers in an industrial setting; there's "friendly" service and a "nicely laid-out bar", but the place can get so "lively" you may not "be able to hear yourself speak."

French House Dining Room ●　18 | 14 | 16 | £27
49 Dean St., W1 (Piccadilly Circus), 0171-437 2477
■ "A great institution" "hidden" above a Soho pub, this tiny room is "as far from modern British surroundings as you can get"; it's "a haven of intelligent food and conversation" with a "well-executed" if "eccentric" ("festival of offal") Modern British menu, and though a few report "patchy cooking" and "slow service", that doesn't bother the "same old luvvies" enjoying a "long lunch" or dinner.

Friends ●S　▽ 22 | 18 | 18 | £24
6 Hollywood Rd., SW10 (Earl's Court/South Kensington), 0171-376 3890
■ "Great appetisers" and pizzas "like in Italy" hit the mark at this "excellent value", cramped Chelsea Italian (part-owned by footballer Roberto Di Matteo), but it's noisy, crowded and not for the claustrophobic: "the smoke can be so thick you need a knife to cut it."

Frith Street Restaurant　23 | 20 | 22 | £38
63-64 Frith St., W1 (Tottenham Court Rd.), 0171-734 4545
■ This "outstanding new Soho restaurant" has made a "fabulous" start, receiving high praise for "fine" Modern European cooking featuring "daring flavour combinations"; however, this "cosy" spot may be in for changes now that chef Stephen Terry has resigned (post-*Survey*) and been replaced by sous chef Jason Atherton – stay tuned.

Fung Shing ●S　21 | 12 | 14 | £25
15 Lisle St., WC2 (Leicester Sq.), 0171-437 1539
■ The "great variety" of "authentic" Chinese dishes served at this "lively" Chinatown haunt "makes a change from the usual", and whilst a few suggest it's "not as good as it was 10 years ago", others say it's "still probably the best cooking in Chinatown" – "not a bad dish in 20 years!"

Futures!!　15 | 10 | 13 | £16
8 Botolph Alley, EC3 (Monument), 0171-623 4529
2 Exchange Sq., EC2 (Liverpool St.), 0171-638 6341
◪ These "convenient" City Vegetarians have fans ("great breakfast", "my regular lunch spot"), but they also have foes who find them "uncomfortable" and "boring" (some admit they "miss meat", which might be telling); Botolph Alley is takeaway only and Exchange Square is drinks-only at night.

Galicia [S] ▽ 20 | 14 | 15 | £22

323 Portobello Rd., W10 (Ladbroke Grove), 0181-969 3539

■ The "decor's not special" and the staff may seem a bit "too serious", but this unprepossessing tapas specialist in Notting Hill serves "proper Spanish food", attracting a clientele spanning everyone from "trendy" neighbourhood regulars to "old men with berets."

Garbo's [S] ▽ 18 | 12 | 19 | £23

42 Crawford St., W1 (Baker St./Marylebone), 0171-262 6582

■ It "helps to be Scandinavian", but even those who aren't appreciate the "unusual dishes" from a "good, basic" Swedish menu at this "cosy, friendly" Marylebone eaterie; the £8.95 smorgasbord lunch (£9.95 for Sunday brunch) has a following amongst workers from nearby offices.

Garlic & Shots ◐ [S] 11 | 9 | 12 | £20

14 Frith St., W1 (Leicester Sq.), 0171-734 9505

■ Prepare to "reek for a week" because this "noisy" Soho Eclectic with "funky staff and freaky decor" is "great if you're in the mood" for its garlic-laced menu; those averse to the pungent bulb say it's "not my cup of tea", but even they admire the "wonderful hidden garden."

Gate, The 23 | 16 | 19 | £20

51 Queen Caroline St., W6 (Hammersmith), 0181-748 6932

■ A "fine example of what veggie food should be like" is the consensus on the "imaginative" Vegetarian fare served by "enthusiastic staff" at this converted artist's studio in Hammersmith; the decor is rather "spartan" but there's a "lovely" summer courtyard, and whilst a few feel it's "not as good as its reputation", the fact that it can be "impossible to get a table" proves they're outvoted.

Gaucho Grill ◐ [S] 20 | 18 | 18 | £30

19 Swallow St., W1 (Piccadilly Circus), 0171-734 4040
64 Heath St., NW3 (Hampstead), 0171-431 8222

■ "No better steaks in London" proclaim partisans of these "reasonably priced" chophouses in Piccadilly ("best use of a basement space") and Hampstead ("funky decor"); the "top-quality", "melt-in-the-mouth" meat is imported vacuum-packed from Argentina, and if there's "not much else" on the menu for "squeamish vegetarians", it's a "favourite" for a "beef fix."

Gaudi Restaurante 20 | 18 | 17 | £32

63 Clerkenwell Rd., EC1 (Farringdon), 0171-608 3220

■ "You either love or hate" the "surreal" Gaudí-esque decor at this Clerkenwell Spaniard, but most appreciate its "surprisingly good", "modern" cooking that provides a welcome "alternative to the usual"; even if a few find the food "uneven", "friendly" service and a "great Spanish wine list" help make it a "terrific find."

Gay Hussar   18 | 17 | 19 | £31
2 Greek St., W1 (Tottenham Court Rd.), 0171-437 0973
■ "One leaves feeling well equipped to face an Hungarian winter" from this "earthy" Soho stalwart that "provides solid, appetising Eastern European food" in "plush" surroundings with "real old-world charm" ("a slap in the face of minimalist decor"); though some say it's "not what it used to be", this "institution" remains a reassuring "old favourite" for many.

Geale's 🅂   17 | 9 | 14 | £17
2 Farmer St., W8 (Notting Hill Gate), 0171-727 7528
☑ "Great fish 'n' chips like they used to make" plus grilled fish and "mushy peas" draw regulars to this Notting Hill eaterie, though some "subtract points" for the "boring menu" and "cramped" room; new owners are "sprucing up" decor that some found "depressing" ("reminds me of wet seaside holidays"), but loyalists "hope it stays exactly as it is forever."

Giraffe 🅂   – | – | – | M
6-8 Blandford St., W1 (Bond St.), 0171-935 2333
46 Rosslyn Hill, NW3 (Hampstead), 0171-435 0343 ◗
It's a squeeze to get in, but locals have taken to this "funky, nonsmoking" Hampstead yearling that's "great for kids", with a "low-cost" International menu (including a good choice of vegetarian dishes) and "fun" ambience; a revamp is planned and a sibling opened in Marylebone post-*Survey.*

Gladwins   ▽ 21 | 16 | 18 | £33
Minster Ct., Mark Ln., EC3 (Bank/Monument), 0171-444 0004
■ Given that it's the "the cost-cutting '90s", some find Peter Gladwin's lunch-only City basement venue "pricey" (£28 for two courses), but the International menu is "very good" and there's "goodwill gained" from the "free mineral water policy"; N.B. it's available for private use weekday evenings.

Glaister's Garden Bistro ◗🅂   15 | 15 | 16 | £25
8-10 Northcote Rd., SW11 (Clapham South), 0171-924 6699
4 Hollywood Rd., SW10 (Earl's Court/South Kensington), 0171-352 0352
☑ "Relatively cheap and very cheerful", these bistros please most with their "good", "reliable" Anglo-French cooking, even if a few contrarians call the menu "limited" and "dull"; the Chelsea site boasts a "lovely" "walled garden" and its Northcote Road sibling has a pavement terrace, which help make them favoured "Sunday lunch spots."

Glasshouse, The 🅂   – | – | – | E
14 Station Parade, Kew (Kew Gardens), 0181-940 6777
Two celebrated restaurateurs – Nigel Platts-Martin (The Square) and Bruce Poole (Chez Bruce) – are behind this "much-awaited", glass-fronted Kew entry; small and classy, it's winning fans thanks to "great flavours" on a Modern British menu with French accents, a quality wine list and "superlative service" overseen by Maurice Bernard.

Globe [S] 18 | 17 | 19 | £24
100 Avenue Rd., NW3 (Swiss Cottage), 0171-722 7200
◪ "A real find for NW3" say admirers of this "buzzy" Swiss Cottage eaterie, where "large portions" of "imaginative", "refreshingly different" Modern British fare are served by a well-trained staff in "pleasant surroundings"; some find the food simply "ok", but to most it's "decent enough", thus it can be "difficult to get into", especially at weekends.

Golden Dragon ◐ [S] 21 | 12 | 13 | £21
28-29 Gerrard St., W1 (Leicester Sq.), 0171-734 2763
■ This big, "authentic" Chinese rates as one of Soho's "best", offering "plenty" of "extremely good, no-nonsense food" in an atmosphere that's like "being in Hong Kong"; whilst the staff's "attitude" has foes breathing fire, fans have "never been disappointed" by the cooking and recommend it for a "quick pre-theatre meal."

Good Earth [S] 20 | 14 | 17 | £29
233 Brompton Rd., SW3 (Knightsbridge), 0171-584 3658
143-145 The Broadway, NW7 (Mill Hill), 0181-959 7011
■ "Good as always" is the word on this "down-to-earth" (if "pricey") Chinese duo in Knightsbridge and Mill Hill; "face-lifts are definitely needed", but the "relaxing atmosphere" and "nice service" make amends, and there's "fast delivery."

Goolies Bar & Restaurant [S] 18 | 16 | 17 | £29
21 Abingdon Rd., W8 (High St. Kensington), 0171-938 1122
■ It's just "ging gang great" at Kensington's "buzzy" "little secret" where a "glamorous" local crew is content with "simple, tasty" Modern British cooking delivered at "consistently good value" in a narrow room; some feel the experience would be enhanced if there were "more space between tables."

Gopal's of Soho ◐ [S] 19 | 11 | 15 | £22
12 Bateman St., W1 (Piccadilly Circus/Tottenham Court Rd.), 0171-434 0840
◪ "Stuck in a groove – but a nice one", this Soho "Indian institution" offers an "old-school" menu that devotees rate "rock solid" ("fantastic vindaloo"), complemented by "civilised" if "slow" service; nonetheless, a fussy few are "less than impressed" by "bland" flavours.

GORDON RAMSAY 27 | 21 | 25 | £64
68 Royal Hospital Rd., SW3 (Sloane Sq.), 0171-352 4441
■ "An eating experience not to be missed": this showcase for "celeb chef" Gordon Ramsay's "breathtaking" New French cuisine "did not miss a beat" after his '98 move from Aubergine to the former home of La Tante Claire in Chelsea; whilst some "don't understand the fuss", citing "overelaborate" food at "second-mortgage" prices in a "plain room", most detect "no weakness" and insist it's "well worth saving up for."

Goring Dining Room [S] 19 20 23 £35
The Goring Hotel, Beeston Pl., SW1 (Victoria), 0171-396 9000
■ This stately Victoria "haven" in a "family-run hotel" maintains its "old English charm and style" with "high-quality", "very traditional" British cooking accompanied by "steady, gracious" service; allies say it "tries harder" than many a restaurant, and its "discreet" ambience helps it attract its share of politicians for "power breakfasts."

Granita [S] 21 16 18 £32
127 Upper St., N1 (Angel/Highbury & Islington), 0171-226 3222
◪ "Cool, elegant and light" ("austere" to some), this Islingtonian wins support for its "stimulating", "cutting-edge" Eclectic mix of "wonderful tastes and textures" matched with "excellent service"; a few feel it's "overrated" ("fussy" food, "noisy"), but to its followers (including members of "the Labour party") it's "well done" all-round.

Grano ▽ 23 15 21 £36
162 Thames Rd., W4 (Gunnersbury), 0181-995 0120
■ It's "worth the journey" to Chiswick for "fabulous Italian cuisine" and "friendly" service at this "very promising" Tentazioni offshoot split over two floors; it aims for a fresh, simple look (exposed brick walls, wooden floors), but some find the setting a bit "sterile" and prices a bit high.

Great Eastern Dining Room ▽ 19 18 18 £28
54 Great Eastern St., EC2 (Liverpool St./Old St.), 0171-613 4545
◪ There's a "good buzz" at this "stylish" Shoreditch newcomer that attracts "relaxed" City folk ("hope the suit quota doesn't up") and "trendy" locals as much with its bar action as with its "excellent" Modern Italian menu; a few cite "overrated" cooking and noise, but the latter is testimony to its appeal.

Great Nepalese ◐ [S] 20 9 17 £18
48 Eversholt St., NW1 (Euston), 0171-388 6737
■ Perhaps some people "don't expect great dishes from Nepal", but this "winner" brings the "specialised taste" of that "interesting" cuisine to an insalubrious "fringes-of-Euston" locale; though "overcrowded" and plain, it offers a "laid-back" ambience, "friendly" service and "value."

Greek Valley ◐ 18 12 20 £20
130 Boundary Rd., NW8 (Maida Vale/Swiss Cottage), 0171-624 3217
■ Known for its "genuine, friendly" atmosphere, this taverna in St. John's Wood is appreciated for its "homestyle" Greek-Cypriot fare as well as its very "helpful" service; the decor is in a ratings valley, but it's been the same for years and loyalists take comfort in the "cheap" prices.

Green Cottage S
18 | 9 | 15 | £18

9 New College Parade, Finchley Rd., NW3 (Finchley Rd./ Swiss Cottage), 0171-722 5305

◪ It may "need a spring clean" and the "location is a bit of a turnoff", but this Finchley Road Chinese is "popular" for its "wonderful", "consistent" Cantonese cooking and "honest value"; although a few rate it "run-of-the-mill", "fast service" makes it "an ideal pre-movie" choice.

Greenhouse, The S
21 | 19 | 19 | £41

27A Hay's Mews, W1 (Green Park), 0171-499 3331

◪ A "suity" crowd frequents this "straightforward", "comforting" Mayfair stalwart, drawn by new chef Jeff Galvin's "superb" (if not "cutting-edge") Modern British fare; critics charge it "lives on its reputation", but they're outvoted by partisans who pronounce it "good all-round" and worth the expense-account prices.

Green Olive S
21 | 18 | 20 | £32

5 Warwick Pl., W9 (Warwick Ave.), 0171-289 2469

■ "What a gem" gush fans of this "cosy", "charming" trattoria serving "outstanding" Italian fare in an "out-of-the-way" Little Venice locale; as with "its sisters" (Red Pepper, White Onion, Purple Sage), a "warm atmosphere" sets the tone for "refined cuisine" that most consider "a treat" – "I'll wait in line for this one any day."

Green's Restaurant
20 | 18 | 20 | £39

36 Duke St., SW1 (Green Park/Piccadilly Circus), 0171-930 4566

■ "When out-of-towners ask for an 'English' restaurant", they're often directed to this "clubby", "civil" St. James's haunt where fish (including "excellent Dover sole") "is the strength" on the "good", if "expensive", Traditional British menu; whilst a bit "basic", it's a "lunchtime pleasure" for ichthyophiles from local galleries and businesses.

Grenadier S
16 | 21 | 15 | £24

18 Wilton Row, SW1 (Hyde Park Corner), 0171-235 3074

■ This "first-rate pub" in a Belgravia mews has a "fantastic ambience" (complete with "a resident ghost and fireplace") that makes it a "quaint" option for "tourists" or "business lunches"; the Traditional British "pub grub" is "not brilliant" but it's "good" and arrives in "seriously hearty portions."

Gresslin's S
21 | 14 | 18 | £29

13 Heath St., NW3 (Hampstead), 0171-794 8386

◪ "What a find!"; fans of this Hampstead eaterie's "inspired" Modern European fare (with Asian touches) call it an "oasis in a culinary desert"; whilst foes "don't understand the hype", boosters point to "friendly service" and "solid" food, saying "this is what one wants in the neighbourhood"; N.B. a refurb was to be completed shortly after press time.

Grissini ◗ S
21 | 19 | 18 | £38

*Hyatt Carlton Tower, 2 Cadogan Pl., SW1 (Knightsbridge/
Sloane Sq.), 0171-858 7171*

☒ "Get a window table and enjoy the view" of local gardens
at this "comfortable" Knightsbridge hotel dining room
serving "dainty", "thoroughly enjoyable" Modern Italian
cuisine; though it's "a bit lacking in atmosphere" (and
sometimes "empty"), it's "surprisingly good for a hotel"
and suitable for "expense-account dinners."

Groucho Club, The
16 | 16 | 17 | £31

Private club; inquiries: 0171-439 4685

☒ The decor's a "bit tatty, but it adds to the charm" of this
"very relaxed" (if "noisy") Soho private club, and it's always
"great to see who's there" as it draws an "extraordinary
cross section" of "wanna-bes" and "artsy types"; opinions
on the Modern British cooking range from "good" to
"disappointing", but it's always a "hub of colourful activity"
and a fine place to drink or "talk deals."

Grumbles ◗ S
– | – | – | M

35 Churton St., SW1 (Pimlico/Victoria), 0171-834 0149

A "cosy", "rustic wine bar" in Pimlico serving "great"
British-French bistro cooking from an "extensive menu with
blackboard specials"; a few find the atmosphere "dingy",
but "friendly" service and moderate prices compensate.

Guinea, The
22 | 14 | 18 | £36

30 Bruton Pl., W1 (Bond St./Green Park), 0171-409 1728

■ "Pity about all the tourists" say regulars at this rather
"stuffy" room behind a Mayfair pub, but there are few gripes
about the "very traditional" British fare including "the best
steaks this side of Texas" and a prize-winning steak-and-
kidney pie; even those who note the decor is "past its
sell-by date" can't deny the "meats are ambrosia."

Gung-Ho ◗ S
21 | 17 | 18 | £28

328-332 West End Ln., NW6 (West Hampstead), 0171-794 1444

☒ A "best-kept secret", this "stylish" Hampstead Chinese
has gung-ho admirers for its "excellent" Szechuan cooking;
spoilers snipe "not cheap enough" and say "service needs
some attention", but most enjoy its "pleasant", "unhurried"
ambience with an appealing "air of exclusivity."

Halepi ◗ S
20 | 13 | 17 | £27

*18 Leinster Terrace, W2 (Lancaster Gate/Queensway),
0171-262 1070*
48-50 Belsize Ln., NW3 (Belsize Park), 0171-431 5855

■ "Crowded", "cramped" and "a bit pricey" it may be,
but this "lively", "friendly" Greek-Cypriot on the north side
of Hyde Park "just goes on and on", scoring points for its
"authentic", "consistently good" cooking; its new, busy
Belsize Lane sibling is off to a "roaring" start with an
"above-average menu" and a "fun" feel.

HALKIN HOTEL, STEFANO CAVALLINI RESTAURANT S
25 | 22 | 23 | £52

Halkin Hotel, 5 Halkin St., SW1 (Hyde Park Corner), 0171-333 1234

■ The "minimalist" decor of this dining room in a Belgravia hotel is not to everyone's taste ("cool elegance" vs. "clinical" "starkness"), but Stefano Cavallini's "sophisticated" Modern Italian fare draws lavish praise: "divine food that defies description" and "justifies the expense"; "efficient" service is another reason why diners "feel like a million dollars" at what some call "the best Italian this side of Milan."

Harbour City ◖S
18 | 9 | 13 | £19

46 Gerrard St., W1 (Leicester Sq./Piccadilly Circus), 0171-439 7859

■ If you're looking for "some of the best dim sum" in town, this "bankable" Chinatown eaterie is "exactly what you need"; there's also a "good quality" menu with "excellent pricing", and regulars say "service improves" with familiarity.

Hard Rock Cafe ◖S
15 | 18 | 16 | £20

150 Old Park Ln., W1 (Green Park/Hyde Park Corner), 0171-629 0382

☑ "Been there, done that and boy, do I have the T-shirt"; this "colourful" outpost of the rock 'n' roll–themed chain has a "buzzing ambience" and "never fails with kids"; fans say the memorabilia and "enormous" portions of "classic" American fare are "worth becoming a tourist for", but others object to queues and noise, shrugging "seen one, seen them all."

Harrods
18 | 16 | 16 | £24

Harrods, 87-135 Brompton Rd., SW1 (Knightsbridge), 0171-730 1234

☑ Knightsbridge's shopping mecca offers 20-plus sites for "spur-of-the-moment eating"; most "can't complain" about them, but they're "not inspiring" and may be "overpriced"; the sushi bar and Georgian Restaurant are popular.

HARRY'S BAR
24 | 23 | 25 | £55

Private club; inquiries: 0171-408 0844

■ "Everybody's favourite club" is this "simply superb" private venue in Mayfair serving the "most amazing" Italian food in "glamorous", "opulent" surroundings with a "chic crowd" that's "great for people-spotting"; prices may be "ridiculous", but it's in a "league of its own" and many consider it the "ultimate" "special occasion" treat.

Havana ◖S
13 | 17 | 12 | £21

17 Hanover Sq., W1 (Bond St./Oxford Circus), 0171-629 2552
490 Fulham Rd., SW6 (Fulham Broadway), 0171-381 5005

■ "Wear your dancing shoes" and prepare to cha-cha at this Cuban-themed "disco" duo; they're "ideal for a lively night out", and though most "don't come for the food", the "mediocre" fare may well taste "better after the drinks."

Havelock Tavern S⊘   19 | 15 | 15 | £18
57 Masbro Rd., W14 (Olympia/Shepherd's Bush), 0171-603 5374
■ "Pucker pub tucker" awaits at this "low-key" Brook
Green gastropub that's "always crowded" thanks to "hearty"
Modern British fare at "reasonable prices"; no reserving is
the major gripe: "arrive early or there's no hope of a table."

Helter Skelter   – | – | – | M
50 Atlantic Rd., SW9 (Brixton), 0171-274 8600
"Brixton passersby keep patrons amused" at this revamped,
glass-fronted Modern British–Eclectic where the few diners
reporting are "impressed with the food" and service.

Henry J. Bean's S   12 | 12 | 11 | £17
195-197 King's Rd., SW3 (Sloane Sq.), 0171-352 9255
◪ "Good-value lowbrow eating" is what some find at this
"smoky, crowded" American-style diner in King's Road
where teens like to "hang out", "especially in summer"
thanks to the beer garden at the rear; but few would rate
the food higher than "average"; N.B. it was just renovated.

Hilaire ◑   21 | 16 | 20 | £40
68 Old Brompton Rd., SW7 (South Kensington), 0171-584 8993
■ Though the decor's "a tad tired", this "cosy bistro" in
South Kensington ("convenient for Christie's") is a "reliable"
stop for "excellent" Modern British fare; some find it
"expensive" for a local spot, but admirers appreciate its good
quality, "charming" ambience and staff with "personality."

Hi Sushi S   17 | 15 | 16 | £20
40 Frith St., W1 (Leicester Sq.), 0171-734 9688
■ "A deserved success" say admirers of this Soho
Japanese with an "interesting" setting on two floors
(downstairs with its sunken tables is "one of the funkiest
spaces around") and "wonderful" fare, both raw and
cooked, complemented by "friendly service"; add moderate
prices and you have a "gem of a restaurant."

Ho Ho   17 | 11 | 14 | £23
29 Maddox St., W1 (Oxford Circus), 0171-493 1228
■ This "well-placed" Chinese near Regent Street is "useful"
during "West End shopping", offering "excellent Peking
duck" and other fare at "relatively modest" prices; some
find the ambience "sterile", but there's always takeaway.

Home Bar Lounge & Kitchen   ▽ 20 | 19 | 17 | £21
100-106 Leonard St., EC2 (Old St.), 0171-684 8618
■ "Too trendy for your shoes", this bohemian restaurant/bar
may have "questionable surroundings" in a crowded City
basement, but that helps give it "great atmosphere"; whilst
very popular as a drinking venue, it can also claim fans
for its "inventive" Modern British menu; N.B. a renovation
should bring the dining above ground by autumn '99.

Home House [S] ▽ 16 22 16 £41

Private club; inquiries: 0171-670 2100

■ "Like being in *Sense and Sensibility* directed by Ken Russell" is how some feel at London's latest private club, a lavishly restored historical townhouse north of Oxford Street; it features bars, bedrooms, a gym and an upstairs dining room serving "fairly good" Modern European fare that's "more modern than the decor"; some say both the kitchen and service could use more "vigilance", however.

Honest Cabbage [S] 17 13 18 £18

99 Bermondsey St., SE1 (London Bridge), 0171-234 0080

■ "Welcome to good food at fair prices in Bermondsey – hooray!"; it's "not chic, not pretentious" and not easy to find, but this "basic" pub "does exactly" what it's supposed to, i.e. offer a "hearty" (if "limited") Traditional British menu that's "very good for what it is" and "excellent value" too.

Hothouse, The [S] ▽ 15 15 13 £21

78-80 Wapping Ln., E1 (Tower Hill), 0171-488 4797

◪ It's "pleasantly situated" in a converted Wapping spice warehouse and the Modern British–Med food is "good" enough, but service can be "offhand" and some say take the setting away and "there wouldn't be much to talk about."

House on Rosslyn Hill ◐ [S] 15 14 12 £21

34 Rosslyn Hill, NW3 (Belsize Park/Hampstead), 0171-435 8037

◪ "Always packed" ("mysteriously popular" is how critics put it), this "lively" Hampstead brasserie is "more scene than restaurant", supplying a "posey crowd" with International fare that's "passable" if not terribly exciting; some prefer it for lunch or an "easygoing breakfast", since it can be "too noisy and frantic" at night; N.B. a takeaway cafe is now open next door.

Hunan ◐ 20 11 17 £30

51 Pimlico Rd., SW1 (Sloane Sq.), 0171-730 5712

■ The "leave-it-to-them feast is a great way to discover what's not on the menu" at this "family-style Chinese" in Pimlico; with a "great range" of "excellent" Hunan-style fare (notably "spicy specials") served by "swift", "friendly" staff, it's "always crowded, and with good reason."

Ibla 20 13 17 £31

89 Marylebone High St., W1 (Baker St./Bond St.), 0171-224 3799

◪ There's "little ambience" to speak of at this Marylebone Italian with "sparse" "modern" decor, but that allows patrons to focus on the "delightful", "simple" Sicilian cuisine ("peasant food with class") served by a "conscientious staff"; if a few find it "overpriced", more feel it "easily lives up to expectations."

Icon, The 🅂 18 | 15 | 16 | £39
21 Elystan St., SW3 (South Kensington), 0171-589 3718
☑ This "intimate" (some say "cramped") Chelsea yearling
boasts a "small" but "excellent" French-Med menu from
Thierry Laborde (ex Le Gavroche); however, critics feel
the place is "lacking its own identity" and let down by
"service with a peculiar attitude", with one calling it an
"overambitious" version of "what should be a solid local."

Idaho Restaurant & Bar 🅂 – | – | – | E
13 North Hill, N6 (Highgate), 0181-341 6633
This welcome Highgate arrival (sibling to Canyon, Dakota
and Montana) has a vibrant bar area downstairs serving
light snacks, a tree-lined terrace for outside dining and
an attractive, high-ceilinged restaurant upstairs offering
adventurous, colourful American Southwestern cooking at a
fair price; the wine list has an intriguing organic selection.

Ikeda ▽ 19 | 13 | 19 | £31
30 Brook St., W1 (Bond St.), 0171-629 2730
■ It may be ordinary-looking, but the "authentic" cooking
(including a "perfect" sushi and tempura combo) at this
long-established Japanese near Bond Street provides
insight into "how the Japanese enjoy their food – and the
price they pay"; the £19 set lunch menu is appreciated, as
is the takeaway service.

Ikkyu 🅂 17 | 10 | 13 | £21
7 Newport Pl., WC1 (Leicester Sq.), 0171-439 3554
67A Tottenham Court Rd., W1 (Goodge St.), 0171-636 9280
☑ "Cheap", "quick" and "crowded", these Japanese
siblings in Chinatown and Tottenham Court Road offer
"excellent sushi" and the like in an "authentic" setting
("right down to the smoky atmosphere"), but a few claim
the food is "not as good as it was"; the "fantastic all-you-
can-eat" evening menu is a big draw at the Chinatown site.

Il Falconiere ◑ 15 | 11 | 15 | £29
84 Old Brompton Rd., SW7 (South Kensington), 0171-589 2401
■ It's "nothing extraordinary", but this "very obliging" South
Kensington "neighbourhood Italian" serves a purpose with a
simple menu that provides "the closest thing to mama's
pasta" its fans can find; "good value" doesn't hurt either.

Imperial City 18 | 17 | 15 | £29
Royal Exchange, Cornhill, EC3 (Bank), 0171-626 3437
☑ In the vaulted cellars under the Royal Exchange, this
"cavernous", "buzzy" venue wins votes as the "best modern
Chinese in the City" (though advocates admit "competition is
low in the area"); fans prize its "delicious", "consistent"
food and "brisk service", and if cynics claim it "could try
harder" and "needs a sense of humour", it remains a
"fantastic setting" for a "business lunch."

Inaho   ▽ 18 | 12 | 16 | £23
4 Hereford Rd., W2 (Notting Hill Gate), 0171-221 8495
■ This "great local sushi spot" in Bayswater is "smaller than your kitchen" ("reservations are a must") but it makes a big impression with its "superior", wallet-friendly Japanese menu; even those who feel it's "not as good" as in the past concede that it's "still going strong" with regulars.

Indigo ●S   19 | 19 | 18 | £33
One Aldwych, 1 Aldwych, WC2 (Covent Garden/Holborn), 0171-300 0400
☑ On the mezzanine overlooking the lobby of an impressive new Strand hotel, this all-day dining room strikes some as a "very pleasant place to hide" whilst others say "it feels a bit like an afterthought"; but the word on the Modern British menu is "so good so far", even if it is a bit "pricey."

Istanbul Iskembecisi ●S   ▽ 22 | 13 | 19 | £20
9 Stoke Newington Rd., N16 (Highbury & Islington/ Liverpool St.), 0171-254 7291
■ "A small piece of Turkey in London", this "wonderful" Stoke Newington venue serves "authentic Turkish fare" at a "reasonable price"; there's "not much atmosphere" by day, so go "late if you want it lively" (there's a 5 AM license).

I-Thai S   21 | 24 | 19 | £56
Hempel Hotel, 31-35 Craven Hill Gardens, W2 (Lancaster Gate), 0171-298 9001
☑ "Amazing decor" and a refreshingly "silent atmosphere" set this "minimalist" Bayswater hotel dining room apart, as does its unusual Italian-Thai menu; whilst critics find it "pretentious" with portions as pared-down as the decor, champions say "pricey, yes, but always memorable."

itsu S   18 | 17 | 16 | £26
(fka t'su)
118 Draycott Ave., SW3 (South Kensington), 0171-584 5522
☑ "Imaginative" sushi on a conveyor belt pleases patrons of this Chelsea venue, and even those who find it "not 100 percent authentic" enjoy the "lively" ambience; however, the new Pan-Asian menu has drawn mixed response and seems to have inspired some confusion amongst critics: "too expensive for what it is – and what is it?"

IVY, THE ●S   25 | 23 | 23 | £41
1 West St., WC2 (Leicester Sq.), 0171-836 4751
■ So sought-after (No. 1 for Popularity) that the "tables are traded on the futures market", this Theatreland "class act" is called the "one place you can't go wrong"; despite "media hype", it's a "down-to-earth" place with a "supremely consistent" Modern British–European menu, an airy setting and "great stargazing"; some ask "why the fuss?" and look for flaws following last year's Belgo takeover, but to the vast majority it's "pretty damn close to perfection."

Iznik [S] ▽ 21 | 22 | 20 | £19

19 Highbury Park, N5 (Highbury & Islington), 0171-354 5697

■ Though not well known outside Highbury and Islington, this "crowded" Turk has a large local following thanks to "authentic", "home-cooked" "Ottoman food" served in a "cheerful", "cosy" room with "enchanting decor"; in sum, a trusty "fuel stop" offering "fantastic value."

Jade Garden ◐ [S] 18 | 13 | 13 | £21

15 Wardour St., W1 (Leicester Sq.), 0171-437 5065

■ "Excellent dim sum" is the main draw at this "authentic" Chinatown Chinese, but there's also a "good variety" of other "innovative" fare; however, a jaded few feel it's "pricing itself out of the market" and cite "offhand" service.

Japanese Canteen 16 | 13 | 12 | £16

305 Portobello Rd., W10 (Ladbroke Grove), 0181-968 9988 [S]

5 Thayer St., W1 (Bond St.), 0171-487 5505 ⊄

21 Exmouth Market, EC1 (Farringdon), 0171-833 3521 [S]

394 St. John St., EC1 (Angel), 0171-833 3222 [S]

◪ "Spartan" but "convenient" chain of sushi bars (spread from East to West London) that are good for an "easy" meal at "amazing value", though perhaps "not worth going out of your way for"; a few purists rate the food "below average" and those who report "slow" service advise "take a book."

Jason's [S] 22 | 18 | 18 | £36

Jason's Wharf, opposite 60 Blomfield Rd., W9 (Warwick Ave.), 0171-286 6752

■ A "lovely setting right on the canal" is the perfect backdrop for the "terrific" "fresh" fish served at this "intimate" Little Venice seafooder with an "imaginative" Mauritian-influenced menu; a few find it "pricey" and "not the same since the chef left" (to go to Offshore), but more feel it "lives up to its reputation, and then some"; N.B. there are boats available for private dining.

Jen ◐ [S] ▽ 21 | 9 | 15 | £21

7 Gerrard St., W1 (Leicester Sq.), 0171-287 8193

■ There's "no atmosphere" to speak of, but this "cordial" Chinatown newcomer offers "something different from the usual Chinese restaurant" – namely an "inventive" menu of 125-plus Hong Kong–style dishes.

Jenny Lo's Tea House ⊄ 18 | 10 | 14 | £14

14 Eccleston St., SW1 (Victoria), 0171-259 0399

◪ This "hideaway" near Victoria is a "cheap", "crowded" outlet for a "host of quick Chinese dishes" ("love those noodles!") chased with "energising green teas"; regulars report it "still does the business every time" and the "reliable takeaway/delivery service" is a popular option.

Jim Thompson's Flaming Wok S   17 | 20 | 15 | £24
408 Upper Richmond Rd., SW15 (Putney East), 0181-788 3737
617 King's Rd., SW6 (Fulham Broadway/Parsons Green),
0171-731 0999
141 The Broadway, SW19 (Wimbledon), 0181-540 5540
◪ To fans, this Southeast Asian chain is an "interesting" concept, with decor that recalls "an Eastern market" and a "lively" ambience that's enjoyable "for large groups"; the food "can be good", but quality may "vary by location" and critics snub them as an "uneasy mix of pub and restaurant."

Jin Kichi ◑S   20 | 11 | 17 | £24
73 Heath St., NW3 (Hampstead), 0171-794 6158
■ "The shabbier, the better" say admirers of this "different" Japanese in Hampstead that "looks like a hole-in-the-wall" but is "always crowded" thanks to "superb quality" fare including "fantastic grilled fish" and "great sushi"; the less impressed call it "nothing to write home about", but perhaps the "high Japanese client base tells all."

Joe Allen ◑S   17 | 17 | 17 | £27
13 Exeter St., WC2 (Covent Garden), 0171-836 0651
◪ Even if "nobody famous goes anymore" (except "C-grade celebs"), supporters "never tire of this great old standby" in a "drab-looking" Covent Garden basement; it serves "dependable Anglo-American bistro" fare from a "good value", "no-frills" menu, and if some sigh "the thrill is gone", it's still a "lively" place and "brilliant for a large group."

Joe's S   18 | 17 | 16 | £28
126 Draycott Ave., SW3 (South Kensington), 0171-225 2217
■ "Beautiful people" like "to be seen" at this "fashionable", "small", "very '80s" Brompton Cross daytime eaterie offering "interesting", "surprisingly good" Modern British food; it's handy for a "heart-to-heart" or "coffee and Sunday breakfast", but nostalgists "wish they still did dinner."

Joe's Brasserie S   15 | 15 | 14 | £23
130 Wandsworth Bridge Rd., SW6 (Fulham Broadway),
0171-731 7835
◪ "It's Sunday morning, I'm hungover – only Joe's can cure me" declares one believer in this "relaxed", "reliable" Fulham local liked for its hearty (and apparently restorative) Modern British–Pacific Rim fare as well as its "busy bar" ("great" for "meeting friends" and scoping the "posey clientele"); a few penny-pinchers pronounce it "pricey."

Joe's Restaurant Bar   18 | 18 | 16 | £26
16 Sloane St., SW1 (Knightsbridge), 0171-235 9869
■ With a "good location" in the basement of a smart Knightsbridge fashion store, this Modern British cafe is a favourite for a "great light lunch"; N.B. reservations (made before 1 PM) are advised; last orders at 5.30 PM.

Joy King Lau ●S   21 | 11 | 14 | £20
3 Leicester St., WC2 (Leicester Sq./Piccadilly Circus),
0171-437 1133
■ This "relaxed" Chinatown eaterie has "lovely dim sum"
and other "very good, authentic" food at "reasonable
prices", but some say it helps "if you know what you are
doing" or better yet, "if you can read the Chinese menu";
service gets mixed reports ("with a smile" vs. "poor") but
it's taken as a good sign that "so many Chinese eat here."

J. Sheekey ●S   22 | 19 | 20 | £40
28-32 St. Martin's Ct., WC2 (Leicester Sq.), 0171-240 2565
■ The "revival of this old restaurant" (by The Ivy/Le Caprice
team) is receiving raves in Theatreland as diners discover
a seafood "triumph" behind an exterior that "looks like a
pub"; enthusiasts are hooked by its "faultless fish" and
"slick service", and if some find it "pricey" and "rushed",
it may simply need to "settle down" after a "good start."

Julie's S   17 | 21 | 17 | £34
133-137 Portland Rd., W11 (Holland Park), 0171-229 8331
◪ This "golden oldie" in Notting Hill "never fails to please"
fans who laud its "simple, tasty" Traditional British fare
and "quaint", "cosy" interior that's "perfect" for "romance"
or a "relaxing" Sunday lunch; others concede that the
ambience is "unique" ("so '70s!") but find prices "a bit
steep" for "unimaginative" fare; still, the "amazing
alcoves" provide a "nice place to escape."

Just Around the Corner S   15 | 11 | 19 | £22
446 Finchley Rd., NW2 (Golders Green), 0171-431 3300
◪ There's "always a warm welcome" and a "home from
home" feel at this Finchley French, but what really intrigues
diners is the "novel" price plan that allows them to "pay
what they think is appropriate" for the "satisfactory" bistro
fare; jokesters say it's "incredible value, if you're mean"
whilst others "always pay OTT", but the system "must
work" since they've been around a while.

Justin's Italian Fresh Pasta   16 | 14 | 15 | £23
(fka Justin de Blank)
120 Marylebone Ln., W1 (Bond St.), 0171-486 5250
◪ Now reincarnated as a specialist in Italian pastas and
salads, Justin de Blank's "minimalist" Marylebone venue
still has a "light" look to complement its newly lightened
menu; N.B. the food rating does not reflect the revamp.

Kai S   24 | 22 | 21 | £38
65 S. Audley St., W1 (Bond St./Marble Arch), 0171-493 8988
■ "Worth the Mayfair prices" say those who like this
"proper, grown-up Chinese" with a "beautiful interior" and
"first-class" Szechuan-biased cooking that's prepared
"with flair"; to cognoscenti, the "menu is an interesting
read", though it's all a "bit too serious" for a few.

Kaifeng S
20 | 15 | 15 | £30 |

51 Church Rd., NW4 (Hendon Central), 0181-203 7888

■ "For those strictly kosher with a Chinese penchant", this curious Hendon hybrid serves "good, authentic" fare that some rate "the best kosher Chinese in the UK" ("you don't even miss the prawns"); but it's a "shame it isn't cheaper" and some think "service drops" when they're busy.

Kalamaras Micro S
17 | 7 | 16 | £23 |

66 Inverness Mews, W2 (Bayswater/Queensway), 0171-727 9122

◪ "Home cooking at a reasonable price" continues to draw regulars to this "noisy", "crowded" Greek stalwart in Queensway where the "excellent meze" and BYO policy are draws; although some former fans think it's "sadly not the same anymore", at least it's "a reminder of the real thing."

Kastoori S
▽ 24 | 12 | 19 | £17 |

188 Upper Tooting Rd., SW17 (Tooting Bec/Tooting Broadway), 0181-767 7027

■ "A vegetarian Indian to travel a long way for", this low-key, family-run Tooting venue produces "unique", "first-rate" Gujarati- and Kathiwadi-style dishes that get the thumbs-up as "some of the most imaginative veggie food to be found" – and "what a bargain."

Kavanagh's S
▽ 19 | 16 | 19 | £30 |

26 Penton St., N1 (Angel/King's Cross), 0171-833 1380

■ The "lovely atmosphere" at this "unpretentious", recently expanded Islington "local" makes for a "great Sunday lunch" or "a fun evening out", and it's enhanced by "friendly service" and "yummy" Modern British fare; the "small, well-chosen set menu" is a deal for £10 (lunch and pre-theatre).

Kensington Place ◑S
20 | 16 | 17 | £34 |

201-207 Kensington Church St., W8 (Notting Hill Gate), 0171-727 3184

◪ "Love the food, hate the noise" is a common refrain over this Notting Hill eaterie that's "still exciting" and a "firm favourite" for fans (a majority) who say its "reliable" Modern British cooking "overcomes the decibels"; but it's "lost its sparkle" for others who are "tired" of the menu and "rather impersonal" atmosphere: "just like a busy railway station"; N.B. it was sold to the Avenue/Circus team post-*Survey*.

Kettners ◑S
14 | 16 | 14 | £21 |

29 Romilly St., W1 (Leicester Sq.), 0171-734 6112

◪ A "glorified" "pizza joint with bar, pianist and white starched tablecloths" in a "civilised", if rather "tired-looking", Soho townhouse that's "full of luvvies" and a "jolly" media crowd; most are content with the International menu dominated by "great pizzas" and burgers, but some say the "champagne bar's the only asset" of this "old favourite" that's "fading fast"; "quick" service is "good for pre-theatre."

Khan's ◑ 🅂 17 | 11 | 11 | £16 |
13-15 Westbourne Grove, W2 (Bayswater/Queensway),
0171-727 5420
■ "It's as busy as a beehive" at Bayswater's "noisy" Indian
"institution", a "student favourite" that's something of a
"madhouse" with "annoying" waiters who are "a bit too
fast for comfort", persuading people to "wait and share
tables"; the environmental downsides are "compensated"
for by "decent" dining that's "excellent value" – it's "the
epitome of good 'fast food'!"

Khan's of Kensington ◑ 🅂 17 | 12 | 14 | £22 |
3 Harrington Rd., SW7 (South Kensington), 0171-581 2900
■ "Not the best Indian, but if you're near it – go"; this small,
subdued South Kensington Indian (unrelated to its more
famous Bayswater namesake) has a "nice ambience" and
"speedy" service, and whilst the "tasty" cooking is "good",
"not great", it has its followers: "I suppose it's a ritual."

Khun Akorn ▽ 18 | 17 | 17 | £26 |
136 Brompton Rd., SW3 (Knightsbridge), 0171-225 2688
■ "If you're in Harrods and want Thai", there's "particularly
well-presented, subtly spiced food" to be had nearby at
this Knightsbridge specialist; service may strike some
as "a bit glum", but the "good food" and "good location"
override any drawbacks.

King's Road Cafe 🅂 ▽ 16 | 16 | 15 | £16 |
Habitat, 208 King's Rd., SW3 (Sloane Sq.), 0171-351 6645
■ A "good view" over King's Road is part of the "pleasant"
ambience at this "airy" in-store, all-day cafe, a "shopping
standby" for a "light" breakfast or lunch from an Italian
menu of simple snacks and "fresh juices" as well as a few
more "creative dishes"; "polite" service is appreciated.

Koi 🅂 ▽ 18 | 14 | 15 | £35 |
1E Palace Gate, W8 (Gloucester Rd./High St. Kensington),
0171-581 8778
■ Few surveyors have commented on this Kensington
newcomer (owned by the Ikkyu team), but those who have
praise the "high standard" of "excellent", if "expensive",
Japanese food, including "fresh sushi", that's also available
for takeaway; the place is spread over three floors, with
koi fish in a display aquarium.

Kulu Kulu Sushi 20 | 10 | 11 | £16 |
76 Brewer St., W1 (Piccadilly Circus), 0171-734 7316
■ It's "low on charm", but this "quick", "unpretentious"
Piccadilly Japanese has fans who say it offers the "best
quality/price ratio" for a "conveyor belt" sushi bar; whilst
it may "not be suitable for a big eater" and some pine for
"more choices", most diners "can fill up for a little money"
on "excellent sashimi" and "prime sushi."

Lab ◑ — | — | — | M
12 Old Compton St., W1 (Leicester Sq./Piccadilly Circus), 0171-437 7820
This sophisticated Soho bar concocts a comprehensive selection of cocktails and fruit juices and also whips up inexpensive bar food from an all-day Eclectic menu (available 9 AM–midnight); the relaxed downstairs lounge offers some respite from the hip bar above.

La Belle Epoque: La Brasserie ◑S 13 | 17 | 10 | £30
151 Draycott Ave., SW3 (South Kensington), 0171-460 5015
◪ "You feel like you're on a cruise with too few passengers" at this "always empty" all-day dining area in the huge Brompton Cross eating complex; though the British-French brasserie cooking does have a few admirers, many find it "disappointing", "overpriced" and not helped by "rude service"; one plus: outside tables to "watch people walk by."

La Belle Epoque: La Salle ◑S 16 | 18 | 13 | £43
151 Draycott Ave., SW3 (South Kensington), 0171-460 5005
◪ The main dining area of this Brompton Cross restaurant complex (same ownership as Le Palais du Jardin) polarises opinions: some applaud the "wonderful space", "friendly service" and "quality food" from a New French menu, whilst others blast "'70s disco" decor, cooking with "no depth" and staff "running around like headless chickens"; a chef change in the past year may improve matters.

La Bersagliera ◑ 15 | 9 | 14 | £20
372 King's Rd., SW3 (Sloane Sq.), 0171-352 5993
■ This World's End Italian with "squeezed" tables serves "superb" pastas and pizzas, though some say "you may as well go alone because you can't hear anything over the music"; still, the "patient" servers cope well when it's crowded; N.B. open weekday evenings and all day Saturday.

La Bouchée S 17 | 14 | 14 | £24
56 Old Brompton Rd., SW7 (South Kensington), 0171-589 1929
■ A "warm, cosy" bistro in South Kensington that gets "busy and noisy" in the evenings, but is "nice for a small group on a cold night" with "good, home-cooked" French fare that includes some "original, exciting" combinations; the £5.95 set "lunches are good value."

La Brasserie ◑S 18 | 16 | 15 | £25
272 Brompton Rd., SW3 (South Kensington), 0171-581 3089
◪ Like "a touch of Paris – bustling, yet laid-back", this all-day Brompton Cross eaterie is "looking good after a face-lift" and drawing praise for its "great atmosphere" and Classic French food; even doubters who insist it "doesn't quite make it" as a Gallic bistro and find "nothing earth-shattering" on the menu like the fact that it "serves till late."

La Brasserie du Marché aux Puces S   ▽ 15 14 17 £25
349 Portobello Rd., W10 (Ladbroke Grove), 0181-968 5828
▣ To some, this down-to-earth Portobello brasserie looks "a bit seedy", but it strikes a chord with admirers as a "relaxed" neighbourhood spot with an "ultra French" atmosphere, handy outside tables and a menu that ranges from bistro fare to Contemporary and Classic dishes.

La Cage Imaginaire S   ▽ 16 16 16 £27
16 Flask Walk, NW3 (Hampstead), 0171-794 6674
▪ A "romantic" eaterie that's just "like one would find in a French town", with "discreet" service and "good" New French fare; in sum, a "charming" Hampstead choice.

La Candela   – – – E
135 Kensington Church St., W8 (Notting Hill Gate), 0171-727 5452
Making a low-key debut, this Notting Hill newcomer (on the former Boyd's site) offers simple, fairly priced Modern Italian food in a narrow setting helped by modern art exhibits.

L'Accento Italiano ◐S   18 12 18 £28
16 Garway Rd., W2 (Bayswater/Queensway), 0171-243 2201
▪ Regulars say there's "a warm welcome" and "authentic Italian" ambience at this Bayswater "find" with "imaginative" cooking and an £11.50 set menu that "changes so often you can go a lot and not be bored"; but it's "noisy at times."

La Delizia ◑S   16 10 12 £18
246 Old Brompton Rd., SW5 (Earl's Court), 0171-373 6085
63-65 Chelsea Manor St., SW3 (Sloane Sq.), 0171-376 4111
▣ There's "authentic Italian – the waiters' chat up lines, that is!" – at this pair (a third site at Chelsea Farmers Market closed) of "pleasant" Chelsea pizzerias; the pies are mostly lauded as "consistently superior" and "good value", and the "reasonably priced wine" also goes down well.

La Dordogne S   21 17 17 £32
5 Devonshire Rd., W4 (Turnham Green), 0181-747 1836
▣ This "lovely little place" in Chiswick creates a "very good impression" amongst fans who praise the "very French" atmosphere and "excellent" French menu that's especially "good for fish" ("delicious lobster dishes"); a few suggest diners allow "plenty of time", particularly when it's busy.

La Famiglia ◑S   20 16 18 £34
7 Langton St., SW10 (Fulham Broadway/Sloane Sq.), 0171-351 0761
▣ It's got "real staying power" (25 years worth), but this "jolly" World's End Italian with a "lovely garden" has critics who claim the cooking is "variable" and "not up to the price"; still, loyalists swear this "very pleasing" spot "beats its new, trendier competition" and is "great on a summer's night" or "for Sunday lunch with children and celebrities."

La Finca ◐ S
13 | 13 | 14 | £20

185 Kennington Ln., SE11 (Kennington), 0171-735 1061
96-98 Pentonville Rd., N1 (Angel/King's Cross), 0171-837 5387

☑ For most, the "dancing is better than eating" at these "fun", "smoky" Spaniards in north and south London serving "cheap" if "not particularly memorable" food; but fans do reserve applause for the "excellent", "consistent" tapas; salsa lessons are available at Pentonville Road.

La Fontana ◐ S
▽ 21 | 13 | 21 | £34

101 Pimlico Rd., SW1 (Sloane Sq.), 0171-730 6630

■ "Walked in off the street and was pleasantly surprised" says one new admirer of this unimpressive-looking Pimlico Italian that cognoscenti consider "a must during truffle season" (October–January), when the prized and pricey wild edibles are highlights on the otherwise standard menu; the family-run charm of the place is a plus in any season.

Lahore Kebab House ◐ S ⌿
21 | 6 | 11 | £13

2 Umberston St., E1 (Aldgate East/Whitechapel), 0171-481 9737

■ Some think it's "lost its charm since it expanded" and was "spruced up", but this "casual", "unfancy" East End eaterie still prepares "heavenly kebabs" and "deliciously fresh", "authentic" Pakistani fare from a "cheap", if "limited", menu; it's "not a place to linger", but the food's "the real thing."

L'Altro ◐ S
16 | 15 | 14 | £23

210 Kensington Park Rd., W11 (Ladbroke Grove), 0171-792 1066

☑ "Reminiscent of Italy" say fans of this "friendly" Notting Hill Italian with an "earthy feel" and "great atmosphere", serving "huge portions" of "great-value" fare with an emphasis on seafood; but it's not quite unanimous, with dissenters reporting "disappointing" food and service.

La Mancha S
16 | 15 | 15 | £24

32 Putney High St., SW15 (Putney Bridge), 0181-780 1022

☑ "Authentic decor", "Spanish waiters" and a "brilliant atmosphere" characterise this "very lively" Putney Spaniard, and whilst some also praise "great food" and "varied tapas" at "reasonable prices" (£7.50 set lunch), others find it all rather "average" ("more Benidorm than Barcelona"); still, it's "good if you're going to the movies across the road."

Landmark London, Dining Room S
20 | 22 | 21 | £41

The Landmark London, 222 Marylebone Rd., NW1 (Marylebone), 0171-631 8230

☑ There's a "high level of luxury" in the "lovely" dining room of this impressively restored Marylebone hotel with "very sound" Euro–Classic French cooking that delights some ("hotel food at its best") but lets down others ("hugely expensive", "boring"); most enjoy the live jazz band at Sunday brunch, as well as the hotel's "awesome atrium" which serves all-day snacks.

Lanesborough Conservatory ◐⬛ | 21 | 24 | 21 | £42 |
The Lanesborough, 1 Lanesborough Pl., SW1
(Hyde Park Corner), 0171-259 5599
☑ The "stunning gothic-meets-Brighton Pavilion decor"
makes eating in the "chichi" all-day conservatory dining
room of this "posh" Hyde Park Corner hotel a "unique" affair,
but opinions are split on the International menu: "fantastic"
vs. "ordinary for the price"; still, service is "accommodating"
and it's "perfect for a classy breakfast" or "splendid" tea.

Langan's Bistro | 19 | 19 | 19 | £34 |
26 Devonshire St., W1 (Baker St.), 0171-935 4531
☑ Marylebone's Langan sibling strikes fans as "more
grown-up than the brasserie", with "very nice decor" (fine
art on the walls) and Traditional British–French bistro food
that most rate "pleasant enough"; though some say it's
"getting a little tired" now, this stalwart stays "lively" and
"bustling" as it's "good for business" or a "late-night meal."

Langan's Brasserie ◐ | 19 | 20 | 19 | £37 |
Stratton St., W1 (Green Park), 0171-491 8822
☑ "It seems fashionable to knock" this famous Piccadilly
institution as "vaguely naff" and "living on reputation alone",
but for many, it's "still a strong favourite", with "superb
atmosphere" ("better in a group than a couple") and
"generous portions" of "consistent" British-French bistro
fare; at its best, it can feel "magical", with plenty of stars
("if you're lucky") and a "fun" "sense of decadence."

Langan's Coq d'Or ⬛ | 15 | 16 | 15 | £34 |
254-260 Old Brompton Rd., SW5 (Earl's Court), 0171-259 2599
☑ "Needs to mature a little" but "fun to be in" is the word
on this "big, brash" Earl's Court all-day newcomer from
Richard Shepherd (owner of Langan's), offering a "basic"
French bistro menu that "could be more imaginative";
opinions on the service range from "very friendly" to
"often arrogant", but the "terrace in summer" has fans.

Lansdowne, The ⬛ | 18 | 15 | 14 | £21 |
90 Gloucester Ave., NW1 (Chalk Farm), 0171-483 0409
☑ "Arrive early for a fireside seat" at this "cramped"
Primrose Hill "gastropub", where the "hearty" Modern
British fare in "generous portions" satisfies many ("terrific",
"brilliant value") but not all ("very ordinary"); in autumn, a
new first-floor restaurant with a roof terrace is set to open.

La Perla Bar & Grill ⬛   ▽ | 18 | 19 | 20 | £19 |
28 Maiden Ln., WC2 (Charing Cross/Covent Garden),
0171-240 7400 ◐
803 Fulham Rd., SW6 (Parsons Green), 0171-471 4895
☑ "Mexican fabness" and "mind-blowing margaritas" are
the real pull at this duo in Covent Garden and Fulham, which
is just as well since the "basic" Mexican food is "good" at
best – just "don't drink on an empty stomach!"

La Piragua ◗⬛≠　　　　　▽ | 15 | 9 | 17 | £21
176 Upper St., N1 (Angel/Highbury & Islington), 0171-354 2843
⬛ "Still one of Islington's hidden secrets" say those who
know this "fun", characterful South American outpost
with a "simple" menu of "unsophisticated filler food" that
"pleases" most ("great tastes, great prices"), even if a few
report "some odd juxtapositions"; it's a quirky but "reliable
old standard" for locals.

La Porchetta Pizzeria ⬛　　　　– | – | – | M
147 Stroud Green Rd., N4 (Finsbury Park), 0171-281 2892
"A queue down the street every night" speaks volumes
about the appeal of this "lively", "noisy" Finsbury Italian
that produces "cheap", "magnificent pizzas"; as one fan
puts it: "London's best – I don't care what anyone says."

La Porte des Indes ◗⬛　　　　21 | 24 | 20 | £34
32 Bryanston St., W1 (Marble Arch), 0171-224 0055
⬛ Owned by The Blue Elephant team, this "flamboyant"
Indian near Marble Arch has similarly "stunning decor"
("see a waterfall, walk on nutshells") as backdrop to an
"interesting, subtle menu" featuring regional recipes
from former French colonies; despite a few naysayers (a
"letdown"), most find the fare "inventive" and "beautiful",
and whilst also "expensive", the buffet lunch and "superb"
Sunday brunch are a "bargain."

La Poule au Pot ◗⬛　　　　21 | 21 | 19 | £33
231 Ebury St., SW1 (Sloane Sq.), 0171-730 7763
⬛ "An unchanging romantic gem" "with character" on
Pimlico Green that's "nice for a wintry weekend" thanks
to "great candlelit decor" and also appealing in summer
at outside tables; the French "country cooking" is "fine
but not too exciting" and service is generally "friendly"
and "unobstrusive" if "uneven" – overall, it's "charming"
and the set lunch is an "amazingly good value."

L'Artiste Musclé ◗⬛　　　　17 | 16 | 16 | £20
1 Shepherd Mkt., W1 (Green Park), 0171-493 6150
⬛ "Rather than a 'muscle', one feels like a sardine here"
quips one diner about this "cramped", "classic Parisian"
Shepherd Market bistro that "can get very busy" but is
"always fun"; the "good, simple" menu is perhaps "never
high quality" but is a "glorious bargain."

La Rueda ◗⬛　　　　14 | 13 | 15 | £22
102 Wigmore St., W1 (Bond St.), 0171-486 1718
642 King's Rd., SW6 (Fulham Broadway), 0171-384 2684
66-68 Clapham High St., SW4 (Clapham North), 0171-627 2173
⬛ "No complaints can really be made" about these "busy",
"lively" tapas bars serving "fairly cheap" Spanish food
that's "ok", though most agree it "could be better"; their
real appeal is the "great atmosphere and dancing at the end
of the evening" when they transform into "fun nightclubs."

LA TANTE CLAIRE 26 21 24 £61

Berkeley Hotel, Wilton Pl., SW1 (Knightsbridge), 0171-823 2003

◪ Reactions to the move of Pierre Koffmann's "extremely civilised" Classic French restaurant from Chelsea to a wing of the Berkeley Hotel are mixed: critics find it "more impersonal", "less magical" and say "service has suffered", whilst admirers insist it "remains one of the best" thanks to "exquisite", "imaginative" cooking that's still "the gold standard" (although it may be "cheaper to take the Eurostar to Paris"); despite a two-point drop in food and service ratings, scores remain commendably high.

latitude [S] – – – E

163 Draycott Ave., SW3 (South Kensington), 0171-589 8464

The adjacent spaces near Brompton Cross that formerly housed Cafe O and Nippon Tuk have been combined to create this modern wine bar/Japanese restaurant, with a muted, sparsely decorated interior that contrasts with the noisy, colourful drinking crowd; the menu is surprisingly accessible but plays second fiddle to the bar action.

Launceston Place ◐ [S] 21 20 20 £39

1A Launceston Pl., W8 (Gloucester Rd./High St. Kensington), 0171-937 6912

◪ It's "like being invited to somebody's house" at this "discreet", "comfortable" Kensington "class act" serving "quality" Modern British "home cooking" in a setting with "tables arranged" for "private" conversations; nonfans find it "a bit too quiet" compared "with its sister" (Kensington Place) and complain that it's "tired, dated" and "too expensive", but it remains a "solid performer" "for people who want to eat well, without fuss"; N.B. it was taken over post-*Survey* by the Avenue/Circus crew.

Laurent ▽ 22 9 19 £19

428 Finchley Rd., NW2 (Golders Green), 0171-794 3603

■ "Go for the couscous, the couscous, the couscous" is the simple refrain for this "honest" North African in Golders Green that's "a pleasure to visit" thanks to "unaffected" service and "delicious" cooking "for a fraction of the price" of central London – "lucky North Londoners."

Lavender, The 17 14 14 £21

171 Lavender Hill, SW11 (Clapham Common), 0171-978 5242 [S]

24 Clapham Rd., SW9 (Oval), 0171-793 0770 [S]

112 Vauxhall Walk, SE11 (Vauxhall), 0171-735 4440

61 The Cut, SE1 (Waterloo), 0171-928 8645

■ "Great for an informal bite", this expanding chain of bistro/wine bars attracts a "lively" crowd with "tasty" Eclectic food and "good value"; a few argue that there's "too little choice" on the weekly changing blackboard menu and complain of "cramped seating", but those are quibbles.

L'Aventure   23 | 19 | 18 | £36
3 Blenheim Terrace, NW8 (St. John's Wood), 0171-624 6232
■ An "archetypal French restaurant" in St. John's Wood
that's "excellent in all respects", with "a charming owner",
"delightful" terrace and "authentic", "great value" regional
fare; a handful claim it's "overrated", but most are fans who
plead "don't tell too many about this tucked-away oasis."

Lawn Restaurant 🅂   20 | 20 | 16 | £35
(fka One Lawn Terrace)
1 Lawn Terrace, SE3 (Blackheath B.R.), 0171-379 0724
☑ Now owned by the team behind Bank, this spacious,
"minimalist" venue has been reincarnated with a British
menu; thus far it leaves some fawning ("a revelation", "a
feather in Blackheath's cap") and others yawning ("average
for the price"), but it's a popular family fixture at the
weekend, when it can resemble a "playground outing."

Le Bouchon Bordelais 🅂   ▽ 13 | 12 | 12 | £25
*5-9 Battersea Rise, SW11 (Clapham Junction B.R.),
0171-738 0307*
Le Bouchon Lyonnais 🅂   ▽ 19 | 15 | 15 | £26
38-40 Queenstown Rd., SW8 (Clapham Common), 0171-622 2618
☑ This "buzzy" Battersea bistro (with a similar sibling in
Clapham) serves what most call "good honest French food",
though some suspect that the servers "orbit in a different
galaxy"; it's "too cramped" for some, but "sit outside on a
summer day and be a fan forever."

Le Boudin Blanc 🅂   19 | 17 | 17 | £27
51 Trebeck St., W1 (Green Park), 0171-499 3292
■ "The secret is out" sigh boosters of this "too crowded"
but "romantic" Gallic bistro that serves "excellent French
food" ("c'est magnifique"); a few report occasionally
"snotty" staff, but concede it's "good value for Mayfair" –
especially the pre-theatre menu.

Le Cafe du Jardin ◖🅂   18 | 17 | 16 | £30
28 Wellington St., WC2 (Covent Garden), 0171-836 8769
☑ The "pleasant surroundings" of this "French-style" Covent
Garden bistro make it "feel more upmarket than the bill
suggests", which enhances the appeal of the "pretty good"
Med-Eclectic fare; though a few call it a "disappointing
attempt to replicate" a Parisian bistro, it's "an old favourite
with many" and the "fast service" is appreciated pre-theatre.

Le Café du Marché   21 | 19 | 19 | £34
22 Charterhouse Sq., EC1 (Barbican), 0171-608 1609
■ "Deserves wider recognition" say those who know this
"hidden" French gem "tucked away" in a "difficult to find"
location near Smithfield Market; it's "just what you hope a
restaurant will be", offering a "friendly welcome", an
"informal" setting and "great French country food" from
an "authentic" menu – "one for long, long lunches."

LE CAPRICE ◗⧈　　　24 ┃ 21 ┃ 23 ┃ £42 ┃
Arlington House, Arlington St., SW1 (Green Park), 0171-629 2239
■ "It's a boost to the ego just to get a table" at this "slick, chic" Piccadilly "institution" that's like a "mini Hollywood" "fizzing with atmosphere" (and "plenty of rubbernecking"), but where mere mortals are also "made to feel like a celebrity"; most extol its "customary culinary excellence" displayed in "robust, tempting" Modern British–European fare, and whilst a few question whether it's "losing its edge", "there's just something about this place that attracts."

Le Colombier ⧈　　　18 ┃ 17 ┃ 20 ┃ £34 ┃
145 Dovehouse St., SW3 (South Kensington), 0171-351 1155
☑ "A great French newcomer on a previously jinxed site" in Chelsea with an "authentic", if "unambitious", brasserie menu, a big terrace and a "cozy upstairs" (some say "drab"); whilst a few feel it's "nothing special", there's loyal support for this "lively" place: "trying hard and should make it."

Lee Fook ◗⧈　　　22 ┃ 13 ┃ 16 ┃ £20 ┃
98 Westbourne Grove, W2 (Bayswater/Notting Hill Gate), 0171-727 0099
■ The "dubious decor" is "uninspiring", but this Queensway Chinese prepares "first-class", "exquisite" dishes that are relatively "expensive" but "authentic"; regulars "ask for the specials" and warn service can be "slow."

Lee Ho Fook ◗⧈　　　16 ┃ 10 ┃ 12 ┃ £19 ┃
15-16 Gerrard St., W1 (Leicester Sq./Piccadilly Circus), 0171-494 1200
☑ "Not as good as it used to be" claim some, but this "medium-level" Chinatown Chinese offers "well-cooked", "good-value" dishes and "reliable" dim sum that satisfy most patrons – which is not always the case with "abrupt" staff members who expect diners to "turn up on time."

LE GAVROCHE　　　27 ┃ 22 ┃ 26 ┃ £63 ┃
43 Upper Brook St., W1 (Marble Arch), 0171-408 0881
■ For "old-fashioned French spoiling" that's "heavy on the wallet" but "worth every pampered moment", this "never-let-you-down venue" in a Mayfair basement ("don't go for the ambience") is a "client pleaser", with "marvellous" Classic French food from Michel Roux backed up by "superb" wines, a "fabulous cheese board" and service that leaves "no stone unturned"; all in all, a "remarkable experience."

Le Gothique　　　▽ 15 ┃ 19 ┃ 15 ┃ £24 ┃
Royal Victoria Patriotic Bldg., Fitzhugh Grove, Trinity Rd., SW18 (Clapham Junction B.R.), 0181-870 6567
■ An "intriguing, hidden restaurant with hidden qualities" in an "amazing" historic building in Wandsworth; despite mixed reviews for its Country French menu ("can't be faulted" vs. "ordinary"), it's "full of Gallic charm" and "good value", and can be "magical for alfresco dining."

Leith's ◐ — 24 [illegible]

92 Kensington Park Rd., W11 (Notting Hill Gate), 0171-229 44[illegible]

■ This "perpetual star" in Notting Hill has many admirers (including "chattering media/publisher" types) of its "comfortable" yet "classy" atmosphere ("much less stuffy than you might expect") and Alastair Ross' "fantastic, sophisticated" Modern British cooking; critics say it's "sometimes let down" by "slow" service, but it's highly recommended for "all those special occasions."

Leith's Soho ◐ — 20 | 17 | 19 | £37

41 Beak St., W1 (Piccadilly Circus), 0171-287 2057

◪ It's a bit "small and bare", but this "discreet", "minimalist" Soho sibling to the Notting Hill original has a "pleasant staff" and an "exciting" Modern British menu prepared by Alex Floyd (who opened here after 10 years at Leith's); "Soho luvvies" say it's "great for lunches", whilst the £16.50 prix fixe menu attracts some pre-theatre business.

Le Mercury ◐ [S] — 11 | 11 | 13 | £16

140A Upper St., N1 (Angel/Highbury & Islington), 0171-354 4088

◪ Although many suggest that this "understaffed" bohemian French bistro in Islington has "gone downhill" (an opinion borne out by the ratings), it still offers "amazing value" (particularly the £5.50 prix fixe lunch), hence it's "always packed" with bargain hunters.

Le Metro [S] — 16 | 14 | 14 | £26

L'Hotel, 28 Basil St., SW3 (Knightsbridge), 0171-591 1213

■ Few know about this low-key wine bar in a discreet hotel basement near Harrods, but those who do say it's a "favourite haunt" for Knightsbridge shoppers with simple Modern British food and "one of the best by-the-glass wine selections anywhere" (in excess of 50 bottles).

Lemonia ◐ [S] — 19 | 18 | 19 | £24

89 Regent's Park Rd., NW1 (Chalk Farm), 0171-586 7454

◪ "Real Greek and great" proclaim lovers of this "warmly welcoming", family-run taverna in Primrose Hill with a "fab atmosphere" and "solidly good food" that's "tangy" and "very tasty"; a few think it "got too successful for its own good" and is "a touch complacent", but the fact that it's "mad on a Saturday night" suggests locals are happy with "probably the closest thing to a perfect neighbourhood" spot.

Le Muscadet — 19 | 13 | 16 | £34

25 Paddington St., W1 (Baker St.), 0171-935 2883

◪ "When you can get through the door" (it often remains shut by the owner) of this dated-looking Marylebone bistro, respondents report there's "good" Gallic fare to be had; some object to occasionally "moody" service, particularly when trying to book dinner before the 7.30 PM opening time.

LE PALAIS DU JARDIN ◐ [S] 20 | 19 | 17 | £33

136 Long Acre, WC2 (Covent Garden/Leicester Sq.), 0171-379 5353

◪ "Excellent for its type" is how most see this "airy", "buzzy" Covent Garden brasserie with a "reliable" New French menu strong on "very good seafood" that's "not too pricey"; many are aggravated by "patchy" service and some think the tables are "far too close together", but it's a "perfect pre-theatre" option and the "bar provides a valuable meeting place."

Le Piaf [S] 13 | 11 | 13 | £19

75 Southampton Row, WC1 (Holborn), 0171-580 7800 ◐
156A Chiswick High Rd., W4 (Turnham Green), 0181-995 1398
16 Percy St., W1 (Tottenham Court Rd.), 0171-636 5289
40 Wimbledon Hill Rd., SW19 (Wimbledon), 0181-946 3823 ◐
146 Upper Richmond Rd., SW15 (East Putney), 0181-780 3833 ◐
75-77 Dulwich Village, SE21 (North or West Dulwich B.R.), 0181-693 9331

◪ There's "nothing spectacular" about these "safe", "relaxed" French bistros, but for many they're "a local staple" for "basic", "casual" eating in a "typical check tablecloth" setting; though critics of the "unmemorable" cooking and "poor service" rail "Edith would turn in her grave!", moderate prices convince most.

LE PONT DE LA TOUR ◐ [S] 22 | 22 | 19 | £45

Butlers Wharf Bldg., 36D Shad Thames, SE1 (London Bridge/ Tower Hill), 0171-403 8403

◪ "Fabulous outdoor seating" with a "view that can't be beaten" are magnets at Terence Conran's "grown-up", "ideal all-rounder" next to Tower Bridge that also wins "brownie points" for "consistently good", if "pricey", Modern European cooking and a "fantastic wine list"; dissenters claim the "food varies" and is "not as inventive as it was", but the fact that "it's good enough for the PM" (and Bill Clinton) seems to make it "good enough" for most.

L'Escargot ◐ 22 | 20 | 20 | £39

48 Greek St., W1 (Leicester Sq./Tottenham Court Rd.), 0171-437 6828

◪ If "its specialness was lost in the past", this famous Soho stalwart (since 1927) is still a "place to be taken to", with a "civilised, classy" atmosphere and a "slightly old-fashioned but intriguing" Classic French menu, served in an "elegant" ground-floor restaurant and a "rather formal" (some say "stuffy") first-floor dining room; boosters say the £14.95 pre-theatre menu is "one of London's best."

Le Soufflé [S]
24 | 18 | 24 | £52

Hotel Inter-Continental, 1 Hamilton Pl., W1 (Hyde Park Corner), 0171-409 3131

■ "Discover it – it's perfection" rave admirers of this "comfortable", if rather dated, dining room in the Hotel Inter-Continental, where the respected Peter Kromberg prepares "amazing" New French fare that "deserves more recognition" (though it's a "little rich" for some); "attentive service" and live piano music are appreciated and there are a number of set menus spanning two to five courses.

L'Estaminet
18 | 18 | 20 | £35

14 Garrick St., WC2 (Covent Garden/Leicester Sq.), 0171-379 1432

■ "Close your ears and you could be in France" at this "top of the range" Covent Garden bistro that's "more typically French than most" thanks to "subtle", rustic decor and "hearty French fare"; it's "good for a date", whilst its "quick service" and three-course menu for less than £11 also make it "first-rate for a pre-theatre meal."

Le Suquet ◐[S]
21 | 16 | 17 | £41

104 Draycott Ave., SW3 (South Kensington), 0171-581 1785

◪ "Left over from a bygone age" say some about this "tired-looking", "pricey" Brompton Cross seafooder, but loyalists praise the "upbeat feel" and "great seafood", including the "best plate of fruits de mer"; "swift service" also draws kudos for being "charming – contrary to its reputation."

Lexington, The
16 | 15 | 17 | £29

45 Lexington St., W1 (Oxford Circus/Piccadilly Circus), 0171-434 3401

◪ "Love it, love its piano" – this "quirky" Soho "old favourite" draws an "arty farty" crowd that "loves the piano player" (Wednesday–Friday evenings) and "odd decor" in a narrow, somewhat funky room more than they love the "uninventive" Modern European menu; still, it "holds its own versus stiff competition" and the £11.95 prix fixe menu has takers.

L'Incontro ◐[S]
21 | 17 | 19 | £42

87 Pimlico Rd., SW1 (Sloane Sq.), 0171-730 3663

◪ Admirers of this "wonderfully smooth" Pimlico Italian call it a "great place for dinner" with contemporary cooking that's "definitely good", if "a bit expensive"; but critics ask "what's all the fuss?", citing "small portions."

Little Bay ◐[S]🚫💳
14 | 11 | 14 | £13

228 Belsize Rd., NW6 (Kilburn Park), 0171-372 4699

■ "Don't know how they do it for the price" marvel fans who say that "pound for pound", this "cheap" bistro in Kilburn offers "unbeatable value" (though it's a "good job the lights are dim"); the "basic, but very reasonable" French menu invites little criticism since "you get what you pay for."

Little Havana ◐[S] 13 | 18 | 14 | £23

Queens House, 1 Leicester Pl., WC2 (Leicester Sq.), 0171-287 0101

■ Cuban-Caribbean "madness" to the tune of "fun dancing [and] drinking" enlivens this large, "nicely decorated" Leicester Square venue (not to be confused with the Havana chain) with three bars, a dance floor and cigar shop, but "sadly, food is at the bottom of their list of priorities" – not a problem if the only reasons for going are "Cuban cigars and dancers!"

Little Italy ◐[S] 18 | 13 | 15 | £24

21 Frith St., W1 (Leicester Sq./Tottenham Court Rd.), 0171-734 4737

■ "Little by name, large by nature" says one surveyor about the "good portions" of "nice, traditional" Italian fare dished up at this "atmospheric" Soho venue; although the "cute waiters" can be "painfully slow", it matters little when making use of the 4 AM license: "always the last stop for one more beer."

Livebait ◐ 20 | 15 | 17 | £32

21 Wellington St., WC2 (Charing Cross/Covent Garden), 0171-836 7161

41-45 The Cut, SE1 (Waterloo), 0171-928 7211

◪ "Very good fish belies the casual atmosphere" of these Waterloo and Theatreland seafooders with decor that's likened to a "stylish pie-and-mash shop"; comments on the cooking range from "first-class", "innovative" to "weird combinations" at "fancy prices", but regulars defend the "wonderful concept", claiming it's "maintained standards during expansion" from its humble Waterloo origins.

Lobster Pot 21 | 17 | 19 | £34

3 Kennington Ln., SE11 (Kennington), 0171-582 5556

◪ "Ideal if you enjoy being serenaded by seagulls", this "erratically lovely" Kennington seafooder is the "ultimate in marine kitsch" (seagull noises greet your entry) with "kooky" decor and "robust French cooking" that's "pricey but excellent"; fans say it's "worth a short detour as it will take you straight to Brittany", whilst others find it a "strange place" that's "a bit like being extras in *'Ello 'Ello*!"

L'Odeon ◐ 18 | 17 | 16 | £36

65 Regent St., W1 (Piccadilly Circus), 0171-287 1400

◪ "Seems to be slipping from very good to just good" is a not uncommon view of the "overpriced" New French menu and "iffy" service at this first-floor Piccadilly eaterie that's "comfortable" and "stylish" to some, but "a weird room" to others ("great view of the top deck as buses go by"); but defenders praise the "chic", "bustling" scene and "reliable" dishes "with substance", insisting it's "becoming a classic."

Lola's S
20 | 18 | 20 | £33

The Mall Bldg., 359 Upper St., N1 (Angel), 0171-359 1932

☑ This "spacious" dining room in a converted tram shed in Islington has many admirers for its ambience ("West End meets N1"), "imaginative" Eclectic fare and "wonderful staff", but others "can't understand the hype", claiming "everything is good but nothing is memorable"; on balance, the ayes have it, voting this "professional" venture "great for couples" and a "place to hang out for Sunday lunch."

L'Oranger S
23 | 21 | 21 | £45

5 St. James's St., SW1 (Green Park), 0171-839 3774

☑ Last year's temporary, but high-profile, closure following the departure of Marcus Wareing to Petrus led to Kamel Benamar's appointment as chef at this "quite formal" St. James's New French with "top-quality" cooking and "immaculate surroundings" that are "perfect for a discreet business lunch"; if a few find it "a bit too fussy" and "missing the spark to be exceptional", the fact that many feel "it's like it never closed" speaks volumes.

Lou Pescadou ◐ S
18 | 15 | 17 | £34

241 Old Brompton Rd., SW5 (Earl's Court), 0171-370 1057

☑ "A Provençal breeze in The Boltons" – there's a "cheeky", "fun" attitude from the "very French service" ("especially if France has just won at rugby") at this "usually reliable" Earl's Court bistro that's strong on fish; whilst critics point to "some unappealing concoctions" on the menu, the £9.50 prix fixe lunch is an "extraordinary value."

Luc's
19 | 18 | 19 | £30

22 Leadenhall Market, EC3 (Bank/Monument), 0171-621 0666

☑ "As good as the City gets" say fans of this "watering hole" in Leadenhall Market that offers "good value" for lunch (no dinner) with a sensibly priced Classic French menu; some warn about noise: "don't go for a quiet chat."

Luigi's Delicatessen
22 | 10 | 15 | £17

359 Fulham Rd., SW10 (Gloucester Rd./South Kensington), 0171-351 7825

■ The "best language lessons in London" can be found at this "small slice of Italy" in Chelsea, a "busy, low-key deli" that's "crowded" with Italians enjoying the "excellent", if simple, cooking; it's a "friendly" option "when you don't want to do it yourself."

Luigi's of Covent Garden ◐
18 | 15 | 18 | £28

15 Tavistock St., WC2 (Covent Garden), 0171-240 1789

■ The "waiters look like extras from *Goodfellas*" at this "old-fashioned, upmarket" Covent Garden veteran with "straightforward", "affordable" Italian food; it may be "run-of-the-mill", but it's "nicely done" and perfect "when you've worked up a hunger after a day of shopping."

Luna Nuova [S] 16 | 13 | 15 | £20

22 Shorts Gardens, WC2 (Covent Garden), 0171-836 4110

◪ Most "can't complain" about this "reliable pit stop" in Covent Garden which is "never too busy" for comfort, offering the standard Italian meal: "couple of starters, couple of pizzas, couple of bottles of vino"; critics say it "can be inconsistent", but few dispute it's "good for the price."

Lundum's [S] ▽ 19 | 19 | 21 | £35

119 Old Brompton Rd., SW7 (Gloucester Rd./South Kensington), 0171-373 7774

■ "The Danes are back!"; this "lovely" South Kensington newcomer (on the former Shaw's site) attracts "homesick Scandinavians, all enjoying an excellent smorgasbord" and other "homemade" fare; as for its wider appeal, "Danish food is an acquired taste, but this is a good way to acquire it" as the place is "trying hard and deserves recognition."

Mackintosh's Brasserie ◐ [S] 13 | 12 | 15 | £19

142 Chiswick High Rd., W4 (Turnham Green), 0181-994 2628

■ This "nice, buzzy" Chiswick local has followers who "use it frequently" for casual dining from an affordably priced American grill menu (with Cajun-Creole accents); it's "good for Saturday lunch with the kids" ("you can write on the tables") and live jazz on Sundays draws adults; no reserving.

Made in Italy ◐ [S] 15 | 13 | 14 | £21

249 King's Rd., SW3 (Sloane Sq.), 0171-352 1880

◪ "Perfect for a quick bite before a movie" or a "weeknight out" is how some see this family-run King's Road Italian that's "showing its age" but "has character"; critics hint there's "room for improvement": "cheap – but that's about it."

Maggie Jones's [S] 19 | 20 | 17 | £28

6 Old Court Pl., W8 (High St. Kensington), 0171-937 6462

◪ "So dark, you can't see your date" (which "may be useful!"), this "cosy" (some say "cramped") Kensington hideaway sets the mood with "country clutter" and "hearty" Traditional British fare; sceptics are "still not convinced" and feel it's "getting tired", but given "quaint" decor and service that verges on "camp", it's "always an experience."

Maggiore's ◐ [S] ▽ 20 | 15 | 16 | £24

17-21 Tavistock St., WC2 (Covent Garden), 0171-379 9696

■ Covent Garden's "Italian starlet in an area of much mediocrity" is "as comfortable as well-worn Gucci loafers" and much admired for its "consistently good" food and "attentive" service; in sum, a "reliable local 'trat'."

Magno's Brasserie ◐ 18 | 15 | 18 | £28

65A Long Acre, WC2 (Covent Garden), 0171-240 0662

◪ "Ideal pre- or post-theatre", this Covent Garden brasserie sets a "lively" stage for "tasty" French fare; those who call it "average" with "variable" service say the main draw is "location", but fans call the act "good enough for the price."

Ma Goa
20 | 11 | 16 | £23

*244 Upper Richmond Rd., SW15 (East Putney),
0181-780 1767*

■ It's "a bit out of the way", but this "homey" Putney eaterie beckons with its "unusual take on Indian cuisine", offering "authentic", "always excellent" Goan "family" fare that's "lovingly prepared" and served by "friendly", "careful" staff; the decor may be simple, but it's an "exciting" alternative and "not for lager louts."

Maison Bertaux S⊘
21 | 14 | 15 | £11

*28 Greek St., W1 (Piccadilly Circus/Tottenham Court Rd.),
0171-437 6007*

■ Established in 1871, this "splendid cafe/pâtisserie in a quiet corner of Soho" is celebrated for its "wonderful" tea and cakes, the "best croissants" around and other "yummy snacks"; fans insist the "quirky" service "adds to its charm", but the same might not be true of the "uncomfortable" seats.

Maison Novelli ◐
22 | 16 | 17 | £38

29 Clerkenwell Green, EC1 (Farringdon), 0171-251 6606

◪ Believers vow it's "worth a trek to Clerkenwell" to sample "super-chef" Jean-Christophe Novelli's "creative", "beautifully art-directed" New French cooking with "substance", even if a few feel the setting (more casual than smart) "lacks atmosphere" and service "can let it down"; on balance, most report "really enjoyable dining" at this "pleasant" "original."

Malabar ◐S
20 | 14 | 18 | £22

27 Uxbridge St., W8 (Notting Hill Gate), 0171-727 8800

■ A good place to "introduce the uninitiated" to Indian fare, this "Notting Hill gem" offers a "somewhat different" menu of "delicious" dishes; "quiet" and discreet, it's appreciated for its "consistent quality" and "fast service" – no mean feat as it's "always full"; there's takeaway too.

Malabar Junction ◐S
▽ 22 | 17 | 18 | £26

*107 Great Russell St., WC1 (Tottenham Court Rd.),
0171-580 5230*

■ Bloomsbury's "upmarket Indian" with a "delightful" "conservatory setting" is considered "a real find" and "sadly underrated" by those who tout its "tasty South Indian food", including some "superior vegetarian" options; "good service" is also appreciated, even if it's sometimes "slow."

Mandalay
▽ 19 | 12 | 21 | £15

444 Edgware Rd., W2 (Edgware Rd.), 0171-258 3696

■ "Bring the kids" to this "friendly", family-run Burmese "pit stop" on Edgware Road; it's rather "cluttered and cramped" but delivers "excellent value" on "good food – period!"; even those who claim to have "waited aeons for service" bear no grudges as the plates are presented with "lordly charm."

Mandarin Kitchen ◐Ⓢ   22 | 10 | 14 | £29
14-16 Queensway, W2 (Bayswater/Queensway), 0171-727 9012
■ "Booking a table is irrelevant" as evidenced by the "huge queues" at this Queensway Chinese, but connoisseurs consider the "amazing" food "worth every bit of the wait", with particular praise for the "best seafood" ("lobster noodles reign supreme"); once seated, service is "efficient" and the cost-conscious happily note that the bill is "not expensive."

Mandeer   19 | 11 | 14 | £16
8 Bloomsbury Way, WC1 (Tottenham Court Rd.), 0171-242 6202
■ "Veggie food at its best" is the verdict from the meat-free mob on the "well-prepared" fare at this Bloomsbury Indian, which also pleases those with "slimmer wallets"; the "new location" (it moved from Tottenham Court Road) is "rather sleepy", but it's "a haven" for the faithful, even if a few carnivores scoff at "self-righteous", "bland" fare.

Mandola Café Ⓢ⇗   ▽ 19 | 10 | 14 | £19
139-143 Westbourne Grove, W11 (Notting Hill Gate), 0171-229 4734
■ A small band of cheerleaders calls this simply appointed Sudanese in Bayswater one of the "best cheap eats in London" thanks to "interesting" fare and "excellent value", with a £15 prix fixe and an economical BYO policy (£1 corkage); it clearly has a following, judging by last year's expansion which nearly doubled its capacity.

Manzi's ◐Ⓢ   18 | 13 | 17 | £29
1-2 Leicester St., WC2 (Leicester Sq./Piccadilly Circus), 0171-734 0224
◪ It's "beginning to seem very old-fashioned" (after all, it has been around since 1928), but longtime loyalists "just can't kick the habit" given the "simple, unfussy" cooking and "warm", "friendly service" at this "traditional" Piccadilly seafooder; even if foes insist it's "dull" and "living on past glories", it's a pillar of "nostalgia" and "dependable" dining.

Mao Tai ◐Ⓢ   23 | 20 | 18 | £33
58 New King's Rd., SW6 (Parsons Green), 0171-731 2520
◪ An "unusual", "designer Chinese" experience can be had at this "intimate" Parsons Green venue with "dim lighting", "trendy decor" and "occasionally fabulous" Szechuan dishes; service varies ("expert, friendly" vs. "indifferent") and spoilers decry "minuscule portions", but they are outvoted by fans who rank it "among London's best Chinese."

Marine Ices Ⓢ   18 | 8 | 14 | £15
8 Haverstock Hill, NW3 (Chalk Farm), 0171-482 9003
■ "Häagen-Dazs, eat your heart out"; this "old stalwart" in Chalk Farm is famed for serving "the best gelato outside Italy", even if the rest of the Italian menu is deemed "nothing special" (though offered at "low-end" prices); it's "welcoming for families", who are urged to "stick to the ice cream."

MARK'S CLUB
24 | 26 | 27 | £62

Private club; inquiries: 0171-499 2936

■ "The air is thick with exclusivity" at Mark Birley's "outstanding" private dining club in Mayfair where the "old money" set comes for "sublime", "expensive" Traditional British–French fare served by "divinely accommodating" staff in a "swish" setting that "feels like a private house"; if some deem it "self-consciously smug", most consider it a "wonderful" treat, with "good celeb-watching" thrown in.

Maroush ◐ⓢ
21 | 13 | 15 | £25

68 Edgware Rd., W2 (Marble Arch), 0171-224 9339
21 Edgware Rd., W2 (Marble Arch), 0171-723 0773
62 Seymour St., W1 (Marble Arch), 0171-724 5024
38 Beauchamp Pl., SW3 (Knightsbridge), 0171-581 5434

◪ "At 2 AM, nothing hits the spot like" the "really authentic" Lebanese dishes at these eateries around Marble Arch and Knightsbridge with "fast" service; critics say the food "can be inconsistent", but fans insist the value "cannot be beaten", especially the "first-class" takeaways.

Marquis
▽ 19 | 16 | 19 | £38

121A Mount St., W1 (Bond St./Green Park), 0171-499 1256

◪ Regulars consider this family-run Mayfair veteran "perfect for lunch", citing "interesting" Mediterranean cuisine and a "good wine list"; others find the menu "limited", but it's hard to complain too loudly about the £14.50 prix fixe option at lunch and dinner.

Mas Café ◐ⓢ
16 | 15 | 13 | £22

6-8 All Saints Rd., W11 (Ladbroke Grove), 0171-243 0969

■ This "ultratrendy" Notting Hill haunt attracts stylish young things ("at 40, we felt the oldest") with its "great atmosphere" and "reliable", "cheap" Cal-Med food; it's "relaxing" for brunch and "brilliant for an office lunch" or "buzzy" Saturday night; N.B. the membership system has been discontinued.

Mash ◐
15 | 17 | 13 | £29

19-21 Great Portland St., W1 (Oxford Circus), 0171-637 5555

◪ "Weird", "Trek-y" decor sets the scene at Oliver Peyton's "noisy", "gimmicky" all-day complex (restaurant, deli, bar and microbrewery) behind Oxford Street, where a "cool crowd" digs into Eclectic fare that draws mixed reviews: "surprisingly good" vs. "canteen-quality"; service doesn't always impress either ("staff was hungover"), but what counts for many is the "marvellous buzz."

Matsuri
21 | 17 | 21 | £43

15 Bury St., SW1 (Green Park), 0171-839 1101

■ It "could do with a face-lift", but this traditional Japanese in a St. James's basement is lauded for "wonderful" food, "especially the teppanyaki" ("you have your own chef") and "very, very good sushi"; there's a prix fixe menu, but otherwise it can make for "an expensive night out."

Maxwell's ◐ [S] — 12 | 11 | 13 | £19
8-9 James St., WC2 (Covent Garden), 0171-836 0303
76 Heath St., NW3 (Hampstead), 0171-794 5450
◪ These "Americana"-style burger joints are "acceptable" "standbys for good, hearty" "retro" eating, not least because "you get plenty" of food; the Hampstead branch is particularly "kid-friendly" and both are "quick, easy" and "reliable" – but "that's about all."

Mediterraneo ◐ [S] — 21 | 16 | 18 | £28
37 Kensington Park Rd., W11 (Ladbroke Grove), 0171-792 3131
■ A "cute" "corner cafe" in Notting Hill, this "delightful" Italian yearling (sibling of nearby Osteria Basilico) has proved to be something of a "success story" (thus it's "difficult to get a table"), drawing a "fun" local crowd with its "genuine", "excellent value" food; "decent, friendly service" also gets a thumbs-up.

Melati ◐ [S] — 19 | 9 | 12 | £19
21 Great Windmill St., W1 (Piccadilly Circus), 0171-437 2745
◪ Opinions on the Malaysian-Indonesian cooking vary from "promising" to "hit-and-miss", but supporters say this "long-running" Soho entry is "always worth" a try, particularly as prices are "cheap"; whilst some find it "cramped" and "a bit too hurried", others say it's "often busy, so it must be good."

Memories of China [S] — 21 | 17 | 18 | £36
353 Kensington High St., W8 (High St. Kensington), 0171-603 6951 ◐
67-69 Ebury St., SW1 (Victoria), 0171-730 7734
◪ They still remember "old-fashioned Chinese" at this duo in Belgravia (the 20-year-old original) and Kensington, praised for "peerless" dishes and "outstanding flavours" from a "Westernised" menu that's "reassuringly expensive"; doubters find them "a bit stuffy" and "corporate", claiming they've "lost the touch of the late founder" (Ken Lo), but fans think he would be "very proud."

Memories of India [S] — ▽ 18 | 12 | 19 | £25
18 Gloucester Rd., SW7 (Gloucester Rd.), 0171-581 3734
◪ "Reliably good food" is what admirers focus on at this low-key South Kensington Indian, even if the decor is hardly memorable and some feel the place relies "on its reputation"; complaints that it's "a bit expensive" do not apply to the prix fixe lunch and dinner menus.

Mesclun [S] — ▽ 21 | 12 | 20 | £25
24 Stoke Newington Church St., N16 (Manor House), 0171-249 5029
■ "Every neighbourhood should have one" according to advocates of this casual, dinner-only Mediterranean, "one of the finer Stoke Newington" establishments; whilst it's "pricey for the area, the food is worth it" – "too bad you have to book so far ahead."

Meson Don Felipe 17 | 15 | 15 | £21

53 The Cut, SE1 (Waterloo), 0171-928 3237

◩ "Iberia in Waterloo" describes this Spaniard, where "reliable" tapas and a "fun" ambience enlivened by flamenco guitar ensure it's "good for a group"; though some bewail the "cramped" setting and "pre-theatre chaos" (the Old & Young Vics are nearby), most hail it as a "unique experience."

Met Bar ◐[S] 13 | 15 | 11 | £27

Private club; inquiries: 0171-447 5757

◩ This "happening" private bar in the Metropolitan Hotel by Hyde Park strikes fans as a "funky", "zippy" place to "see and be seen" and "celeb-spot", but to sceptics it's an "achingly hip enclave" that's "not all it's cracked up to be"; there is a snack menu, but the room can get "too crowded for food at night", hence some "only use it as a bar."

Mezzo ◐[S] 17 | 18 | 15 | £34

100 Wardour St., W1 (Leicester Sq./Piccadilly Circus), 0171-314 4000

◩ Those who no longer buy the "bigger is better" concept feel that Terence Conran's "daunting" Soho "gastrodome" seems "a little tired", with "all the charm of a crowded station" and "sometimes stressed service"; but it still has fans who call it "a great place to meet friends" for "good-quality" Modern European fare in a "buzzing" ambience with live music; in sum, "fun if you like that sort of thing."

Mezzonine ◐ 16 | 15 | 14 | £24

100 Wardour St., W1 (Leicester Sq./Piccadilly Circus), 0171-314 4000

◩ Mezzo's "busy", "loud" ground-floor space serves "interesting" Med-Asian cooking that's "good value for the quality", but the "canteen-style layout leaves a lot to be desired" and shared tables may mean being seated with "people you don't want to eat with"; still, it's "good for a quick bite in Soho" and worthwhile "for the experience."

Mildreds [S]🚫 19 | 9 | 16 | £14

58 Greek St., W1 (Tottenham Court Rd.), 0171-494 1634

◩ "Should be a chain" say fervent fans of this "funky, laid-back" Soho Vegetarian serving "large plates" of "cheap", "very healthy" fare, albeit from a "limited menu"; but a few mock it as a "studenty" place for "eccentrics and cheapskates" where "everything tastes the same."

Mimmo d'Ischia ◐ 21 | 17 | 18 | £39

61 Elizabeth St., SW1 (Sloane Sq./Victoria), 0171-730 5406

◩ "Mimmo's still a fine host" who "panders to regulars" at this Belgravia Italian, a "lovable" local trattoria "even if the menu and decor are dated to the '70s"; to fans it's an "ideal all-rounder" with "huge portions" that inspire "pasta mania", and though critics claim it's "costly" for "run-of-the-mill" fare, it's been a popular "haunt" for nearly 30 years.

Ming ◐   ▽ 17 14 14 £28
*35-36 Greek St., W1 (Leicester Sq./Piccadilly Circus),
0171-734 2721*

◪ This Soho eaterie scores some points with its Northern
Chinese cuisine (one booster even calls it "best in London"),
but others rate it a "medium-level" performer and wish it
were "more interesting" (that goes for the "insipid decor"
as well); still, the £10 lunch/pre-theatre menu has takers.

Min's 🅂   ▽ 16 20 18 £26
*31 Beauchamp Pl., SW3 (Knightsbridge/South Kensington),
0171-589 5080*

◼ The "gorgeous setting" of this "warm, cosy" split-level
townhouse newcomer in Chelsea wins high praise ("like a
sumptuous old home"), and the changing Eclectic menu also
wins mostly approval; most consider it "a great find",
especially as a "secret retreat after a heavy day's shopping."

MIRABELLE ◐🅂   23 22 20 £47
56 Curzon St., W1 (Green Park), 0171-499 4636

◼ "A big-city restaurant for grown-ups", this "glamorous"
Mayfair basement (with a patio) presents "Marco Pierre
White at his most accessible", thanks to "well-executed"
Modern British–Classic French fare, an "unbeatable" (if
"expensive") wine list and "great staff"; some snipe at
"fussy" food and an "irritating" two-sittings policy at night,
but to most it's a winner offering real "value for money."

Mitsukoshi   ▽ 21 15 19 £34
*Dorland House, 14-20 Regent St., SW1 (Piccadilly Circus),
0171-930 0317*

◪ "They need some improvement in decor", but this rather
sparsely decorated Japanese in the basement dining area of
a St. James's Asian department store supplies "excellent,
fresh" sushi and grilled items; however, it's pricey and
service can come across as "rushed."

Miyama 🅂   23 13 18 £40
38 Clarges St., W1 (Green Park), 0171-499 2443

◼ This Mayfair Japanese may not look like much but it wins
hearts with its "great food" ("number one for noodles") and
"sweet" service; some feel the menu "needs explanation
for non-Japanese", whilst others say "the guys at the
Japanese embassy eat here – that's all you need to know."

Momo ◐   17 24 16 £36
25 Heddon St., W1 (Piccadilly Circus), 0171-434 4040

◪ "Getting a table is murder, but worth it" claim champions
of this "bustling" Moroccan off Regent Street that's "sexy
and fun" even if the food (dominated by couscous) is
"nothing special"; cynics sniff "the novelty wears thin" and
dismiss "theme-park" decor and "rude" service, but the
room's "electricity" makes for a "really different evening."

Mona Lisa [S] 🚭 ▽ 17 | 11 | 14 | £15

417 King's Rd., SW10 (Earl's Court/Sloane Sq.), 0171-376 5447

■ "This cafe is remarkable value" enthuse advocates of this "cheap and cheerful" World's End "local" where casual customers come for a "good English breakfast" and basic Eclectic fare; nonpuffers warn of a "smoky atmosphere."

Monkeys 20 | 16 | 19 | £38

1 Cale St., SW3 (Sloane Sq./South Kensington), 0171-352 4711

■ To some it seems "a bit cramped and down-at-heel", but this "cosy" Chelsea eaterie is like "a friend's home", serving "reliable" "comfort food" from a "very good" French-British menu (insiders advise "go for [seasonal] game"); "nice wines" and a proprietor who "loves the sound of his own voice" keep the mood relaxed.

Mon Plaisir 🌙 21 | 19 | 19 | £33

21 Monmouth St., WC2 (Covent Garden), 0171-836 7243

■ There are "great nooks and crannies" at this "romantic" "little bit of Paris in Covent Garden" that has "everything one would expect" from an "authentic French restaurant": "very reliable food", "great chips", a "good wine list" – and "what a cheese board!"; it's a "perennial" pleasure, especially for its pre-theatre prix fixe.

MONSIEUR MAX [S] 25 | 18 | 22 | £34

133 High St., Hampton Hill (Fulwell B.R.), 0181-979 5546

■ "Wish it weren't so far" sigh devotees of Max Renzland's "*magnifique*" Hampton Hill destination for "very French" dining "on the rich side"; it's pronounced "excellent on all counts", from its "consistently good" classic fare ("best in Southwest London") to its "professional" service and "top value" – helped along by the BYO option (£5 corkage).

Montana [S] 20 | 17 | 17 | £32

125-129 Dawes Rd., SW6 (Fulham Broadway), 0171-385 9500

◪ "Not your usual American joint", this Fulham "oasis" offers "innovative" American Southwestern food accompanied by "excellent jazz" (Wednesdays–Sundays); whilst some are less impressed, knocking a "pricey" "pseudo Tex-Mex" menu, most maintain it offers "a nice change", not to mention an "amazing brunch."

Monte's 🌙 21 | 19 | 21 | £50

Private club; inquiries: 0171-245 0892

◪ This "luxurious", "intimate" Knightsbridge private club comprises a restaurant, bar, cigar shop (featuring its namesake Montecristos) and nightclub for "smoochy dancing"; its new "bargain" menus coax a "swelling number of diners" in to enjoy "excellent" French-Med fare and "great" service, though foes still find the scene "pretentious"; N.B. changes to the dinner menu are planned.

Montpeliano ●Ⓢ   17 | 16 | 18 | £36
13 Montpelier St., SW7 (Knightsbridge), 0171-589 0032
▣ As far as fans are concerned, this Knightsbridge veteran is "reliable" for "generous portions" of "proper Italian food" served in "pleasant surroundings" by "friendly" staff; detractors dismiss it as "expensive" and "boring", but it remains "popular with locals", "businessmen" and a "somewhat older" set.

Monza ●Ⓢ   20 | 14 | 20 | £31
6 Yeoman's Row, SW3 (Knightsbridge), 0171-591 0210
■ Bedecked with the "enthusiastic owner's" motor-racing mementoes, this "no-frills" Knightsbridge trattoria stays "full of regulars" enjoying "innovative", "top-level" Modern Italian cooking; "welcoming" and "unpretentious", it's a very useful "neighbourhood" pit stop.

Moro   22 | 17 | 19 | £30
34-36 Exmouth Mkt., EC1 (Angel/Farringdon), 0171-833 8336
■ "Make a beeline for it" urge fans of this Clerkenwell "find", which "shows inspiration" by way of "adventurous" (albeit "quirky") Southern Mediterranean cuisine enlivened by "Moorish magic"; a few claim the "food's not quite as good as it looks", but it remains "relentlessly popular" with a "wonderful mix" of patrons who come to "thrill the taste buds" in a "trendy" yet "casual" setting.

Mortimer, The   – | – | – | M
40 Berners St., W1 (Goodge St.), 0171-436 0451
An open plan, minimalist gastropub (from The Chapel team) on the site of a former estate agent off Oxford Street, offering a regularly changing, midpriced Mediterranean (with Asian influences) menu; it attracts after-work gatherings thanks to a good bar selection and large outside terrace.

Morton's The Restaurant ●   20 | 21 | 19 | £45
28 Berkeley Sq., W1 (Bond St./Green Park), 0171-493 7171
■ Now open to nonmembers, the "stunning" dining room on the first floor of this Berkeley Square private club offers an "expensive", "well-presented" British–Classic French menu, now prepared by Philip Reynolds (who took over after Garry Hollihead's post-*Survey* departure); most consider the cooking "memorable" enough to "match the setting" ("at last!") and award credit for the "extra space between tables."

Moshi Moshi Sushi   17 | 12 | 12 | £18
7-8 Limeburner Ln., EC4 (St. Paul's/Thames City), 0171-248 1808
Unit 24, Liverpool St. Station, EC2 (Liverpool St.), 0171-247 3227
Cabot Pl. East, level 2, E14 (Canary Wharf), 0171-512 9911
▣ Perhaps they're "frowned on by real sushi aficionados", but these "quick", "convenient" conveyor-belt sushi spots in the City (with a new Canary Wharf sibling) have schools of loyal followers who find them "addictive" for a "good, fresh" fish fix at moderate prices; tip: "come early to avoid queues."

MOSIMANN'S ◐   25 | 26 | 25 | £55
Private club; inquiries: 0171-235 9625
◧ "Anton [Mosimann's] club is still the business" declare fans of this "magical" private venue in the "fascinating surroundings" of a former Belgravia church, offering "exquisite" International fare (including a "best value ladies' lunch") and "excellent service"; whilst a few think it's "not up to old standards", most deem it "superb – as usual."

Motcomb's S   20 | 18 | 19 | £33
26 Motcomb St., SW1 (Knightsbridge/Sloane Sq.), 0171-235 6382
■ "Consistently good for many years" (over 30, in fact), this cosy Belgravia basement haunt offers "enormous portions of delicious" International fare; a few feel the act is growing "too old", but "friendly staff" who are "always pleased to see you" and an interesting art collection work in its favour.

Movenpick Marché S   14 | 12 | 10 | £16
Portland House, Stag Pl., SW1 (Victoria), 0171-630 1733
◧ "Self-service" market stalls at this Victoria Swiss-International allow patrons to select "fresh" ingredients and hand them over to be cooked as they watch; some "enjoy the freedom of choice" and "good value", others find the setup "confusing" and the food just "passable", but it's fine if "tired of the same old sandwich" or in search of a place "for kids."

Moxon's S   ▽ 23 | 17 | 23 | £28
14 Clapham Park Rd., SW4 (Clapham Common), 0171-627 2468
■ It's not in the smartest part of Clapham, but this newcomer is a "good standby" for "spot-on", reasonably priced fish; "great" service and a few "trendy" patrons help make this "one of the nicer places" in an area where options are limited.

Mr. Chow ◐S   19 | 16 | 17 | £39
151 Knightsbridge, SW1 (Knightsbridge), 0171-589 7347
◧ A Knightsbridge stalwart for 30 years, this "stylish" Chinese has backers who boast they can "eat and eat" the "lovely food", and if some say it dispenses "disappointing" "Western"-style fare, it's hard to knock the £9.50 lunch.

Mr. Kong ◐S   20 | 7 | 12 | £23
21 Lisle St., WC2 (Leicester Sq.), 0171-437 7341
■ This "practical", "old-fashioned" Chinatown Chinese has an "interesting", "varied" menu (emphasising Cantonese fare) that offers both "excellent quality" and "value"; the decor is bare-bones and service can be "rushed", but last orders at 2.45 AM makes it a winner for a "late-night dinner."

Mr. Wing ◐S   20 | 21 | 18 | £33
242 Old Brompton Rd., SW5 (Earl's Court), 0171-370 4450
■ "Amid a jungle of greenery" diners discover "excellent" Chinese fare (plus a few Thai dishes) at this "lush" Earl's Court eaterie; the "high quality" comes at high prices, but a new 30-foot aquarium and the introduction of live jazz (Thursdays–Saturdays) are lending it "upmarket" appeal.

Museum Street Cafe   18 | 14 | 16 | £24
47 Museum St., WC1 (Holborn/Tottenham Court Rd.),
0171-405 3211
☑ "Absolutely delicious vegetarian" dishes dominate the
"creative but small" Modern British menu at this "charming"
daytime (no dinner) Bloomsbury cafe near the British
Museum; light lunchers hail "great salads", but a few wish
there were more for carnivores: "shame it has gone cranky."

Mustards Smithfield Brasserie   15 | 13 | 15 | £23
60 Long Ln., EC1 (Barbican), 0171-796 4920
☑ Next to Smithfield Market, this multilevel restaurant/wine
bar has a "nice atmosphere" and "consistently reliable"
Eclectic fare that works well as "comfort" food "on a cold
day"; it's on the "unimaginative" side, but supporters say
"cheap prices" make it a "meat-market must."

Nachos 🆂   11 | 11 | 12 | £19
29 Chiswick High Rd., W4 (Stamford Brook), 0181-995 0945
147-149 Notting Hill Gate, W11 (Notting Hill Gate),
0171-221 5250 ◑
36 High St., SW19 (Wimbledon), 0181-944 8875 ◑
212 Fulham Rd., SW10 (Fulham Broadway/South Kensington),
0171-351 7531
57 Upper St., N1 (Angel), 0171-354 3340 ◑
☑ Defenders of this "pretty tacky" Tex-Mex chain call it a
"fun" place to "kick back a few Coronas and fajitas" and dig
into "a good version of its namesake", but contras consider
it a "tired" "Mexi-McDonald's" with "ersatz food and service
to match"; all agree the "loud", "smoky" environment is
better "for a big group" than "a romantic meal."

Naked Turtle 🆂   14 | 15 | 14 | £27
505-507 Upper Richmond Rd. West, SW14 (Richmond),
0181-878 1995
☑ A "lively crowd" can be found at this East Sheen "gem"
enjoying "lots of fun" plus a "well-executed" Modern British
menu featuring a few "Antipodean delights" (e.g. kangaroo,
emu); doubters "don't get the big deal", citing a "pricey"
menu and service that "could be better", but outside tables
and a "loud pianist" are diversion enough for most.

Nam Long Le Shaker ◑   17 | 15 | 12 | £31
159 Old Brompton Rd., SW5 (Gloucester Rd./South Kensington),
0171-373 1926
☑ The legendary "crazy cocktails" ("if you have a Flaming
Ferrari, make sure you have nothing to do the next day")
will "blow your mind" at this "loose, loud" South Ken
bar/restaurant with "expensive" Vietnamese food that
some rate "average" and others find "delicious enough"
to offset the "smoke and din"; either way, it's "a place to
be seen" that "survives on buzz."

Nancy Lam's Enak Enak ▽ 20 | 8 | 18 | £26

56 Lavender Hill, SW11 (Clapham Junction B.R.), 0171-924 3148

■ "Bless her – probably the only TV chef who cooks every dish on the menu personally" say fans of Nancy Lam, who attracts many admirers to this no-frills Lavender Hill Indonesian-Malaysian to "experience her cooking and her unique style" (which some say is "not for the fainthearted"); N.B. when she takes her act to the airwaves the restaurant is closed, so reservations are required.

Nautilus Fish 🚫 23 | 9 | 17 | £16

27-29 Fortune Green Rd., NW6 (West Hampstead), 0171-435 2532

◪ There's little doubt that this "unpretentious" West Hampstead stalwart is "hard to beat" for "huge portions" of "delicious, fresh" fish and chips at "prices paupers can afford", so it doesn't matter if they're served in "old-style" surroundings with "no atmosphere"; it's "one of the best" in the eyes of the faithful.

Navajo Joe 🌙 16 | 16 | 15 | £22

34 King St., WC2 (Covent Garden), 0171-240 4008

◪ A "well-stocked bar" makes this Covent Garden spot "fun" for a drink, and some say the American Southwestern–Mexican fare is "a change from the mundane", offering a "good choice and prices" plus some "very intense flavours"; sceptics who are "not overimpressed" say "don't expect too much" and you'll do fine.

Neal Street Restaurant 22 | 18 | 20 | £44

26 Neal St., WC2 (Covent Garden), 0171-836 8368

◪ "Magic" mushrooms prepared "every which way" are the main attraction at celeb chef Antonio Carluccio's "narrow", "cramped" Covent Garden Italian; whilst it's looking "a bit tired and worn" and "high prices" rankle, it remains a "business lunch" standout for "power people" – not to mention "mushroom lovers."

New Culture Revolution [S] 17 | 11 | 14 | £16

442 Edgware Rd., W2 (Edgware Rd.), 0171-402 4841
157-159 Notting Hill Gate, W1 (Notting Hill Gate), 0171-313 9688
305 King's Rd., SW3 (Sloane Sq.), 0171-352 9281
43 Parkway, NW1 (Camden Town), 0171-267 2700
42 Duncan St., N1 (Angel), 0171-833 9083 🌙

◪ Fans ignore the "bare-bones" surroundings at these Chinese noodle shops and focus on the "hearty pick-me-up food" that's "cheap and filling" ("one bowl usually does the job"); cynics suggest it "needs a revolution", dismissing "bland" flavours and "slow service", but they're in the minority; "easy takeaway" is a plus.

New World ◐ [S] — 16 10 10 £17

1 Gerrard Pl., W1 (Leicester Sq.), 0171-434 2508

■ All the "hustle and bustle of Hong Kong" animates this "very crowded, chaotic", no-frills Chinatown Chinese, home to a "great variety" of multiregional dishes plus "plenty" of "excellent dim sum" served from the "best travelling cart" around; insiders advise "come early to avoid" queues.

Nico Central — 20 16 19 £35

35 Great Portland St., W1 (Oxford Circus), 0171-436 8846

■ Some wish they'd "change the menu more often", but this civilised Classic French off Oxford Street (no longer owned by Nico Ladenis) pleases most with "no-nonsense", "flavoursome" cooking that's "pricey" but delivers "value"; a few judge it "somewhat ordinary" and there's debate over service ("attentive" vs. "snooty"), but "satisfying" meals appear to be the norm here.

Nicole's — 18 18 17 £32

Nicole Farhi, 158 New Bond St., W1 (Green Park), 0171-499 8408

■ The "perfect venue for ladies who shop": this "trendy" eaterie in the basement of Nicole Farhi's Bond Street store is popular as a "great lunch place" (but quiet in the evenings) with "delicious", "well-presented" Modern European fare; it's certainly a pleasant place "to rest" your shopping bags.

Nikita's — 14 16 17 £32

65 Ifield Rd., SW10 (Earl's Court), 0171-352 6326

■ "Vodka with everything" is the rule at this rowdy Earl's Court Russian, pouring 26 "flavoured vodkas" to make up for rather unconvincing Slavic fare (few "remember the food" the next day anyway); it's "great fun" for "large, uninhibited parties" and "at least you fall upstairs leaving."

NOBU [S] — 26 22 21 £51

The Metropolitan Hotel, 19 Old Park Ln., W1 (Hyde Park Corner), 0171-447 4747

◪ "Wear black" to this "frighteningly à la mode" Japanese overlooking Hyde Park, which most deem "unbeatable" thanks to "artistic" sushi and other "exquisite", "new-wave" dishes with a South American touch; the few who snipe at "snooty" attitude and "sterile" "canteen decor" are outvoted by fans of this "glamorous" showstopper, "a gastronomical event at astronomical prices" that's "worth every penny" (but better "on expenses").

Nontas ◐ — ▽ 14 9 17 £21

14-16 Camden High St., NW1 (Camden Town), 0171-387 4579

■ According to regulars, "the unvarying quality of the food" accounts for the longevity of this Camden Greek stalwart (25 years and rising); though ratings are modest and some hint the "'70s time-warp" interior "needs a face-lift", it benefits from sensible prices and a "wonderful summer garden."

Noor Jahan ●⧗   21 | 13 | 18 | £26
2A Bina Gardens, SW5 (South Kensington), 0171-373 6522
■ Aficionados of "good, honest curry" applaud this long-standing South Kensington Indian as an "underrated" "favourite" with a "terrific" "traditional" menu; even those who complain of "inauthentic, Western" cooking "keep going back – call it habit."

North Pole ⧗   ▽ 16 | 16 | 19 | £24
131 Greenwich High Rd., SE10 (Greenwich B.R.), 0181-853 3020
■ "Never suspected such a gem" (and a "much-needed" one) could be found in Greenwich declare fans of this pub conversion with an upstairs restaurant offering "mouthwatering" Modern British fare and "very good" service at a "reasonable" cost; a few nitpickers knock "meagre portions" and "not very appealing" decor (the "goldfish in the light fittings" attract much comment).

Noto   ▽ 20 | 10 | 15 | £14
7 Bread St., EC4 (Bank/Mansion House), 0171-329 8056 ⊅
2-3 Bassishaw Highwalk, EC2 (Moorgate), 0171-256 9433
■ "Huge, comforting bowls of noodles" and "very fresh fish" distinguish these "pleasant", low-cost Japanese noodle bars near Moorgate and Mansion House; "quick service" and "good takeaway" appeal to those on the run, whilst others appreciate a "decent spot for people-watching."

Novelli EC1   19 | 16 | 16 | £35
29 Clerkenwell Green, EC1 (Farringdon), 0171-251 6606
▨ The "younger, funkier neighbour" of Maison Novelli, this "high-class" Clerkenwell bistro "never fails to please" admirers who applaud "creative" Northern French fare with "inventive flavours"; however, others cite "variable" quality and "lack of atmosphere", with some suggesting it "suffers" because Jean-Christophe Novelli (with ventures from here to South Africa) has "too many interests" these days.

Novelli W8   19 | 14 | 15 | £33
122 Palace Gardens Terrace, W8 (Notting Hill Gate),
0171-229 4024
▨ "Too cramped for pleasure" is a common charge against this "narrow" Notting Hill bistro ("tables so close, could only talk to my neighbour and lost my date to hers"); still, fans find it "cosy" and report "unusual, great Novelli nosh", though some feel it's "not always up to scratch" and say service can be "charming" or expert at "benign neglect."

Nusa Dua ●⧗   ▽ 18 | 12 | 16 | £21
11-12 Dean St., W1 (Oxford Circus), 0171-437 3559
▨ Regulars rave about "superb", "mind-blowing cuisine" from the "really authentic", budget-priced Indonesian menu at this small, bi-level eatery on a Soho corner; but others are a bit less impressed, suggesting it's let down by "poor service" and a lack of atmosphere.

OAK ROOM MARCO PIERRE WHITE ◐ 26 | 23 | 23 | £70
Le Meridien Piccadilly, 21 Piccadilly, W1 (Piccadilly Circus), 0171-437 0202
◪ It's "OTT" and "ludicrously expensive", but this "classy" Piccadilly hotel dining room sustains "extremely high standards", led by chef Marco Pierre White's "memorable", "truly faultless" Classic French cooking; whilst some find the cost and "corporate" ambience "intimidating" ("so whispery and snooty, I get the giggles"), most would agree it's a "perfect place to spend other people's money."

Oceana ◐ 17 | 16 | 16 | £33
Jason Ct., 76 Wigmore St., W1 (Bond St.), 0171-224 2992
■ Submerged in a Marylebone basement, this "well-hidden" Modern British–Eclectic is a "find" thanks to "interesting", "consistently good" fare and "well-spaced tables"; though a few say the "menu could change more often" and service could be speedier, most consider it a "very nice surprise."

Odette's [S] 22 | 22 | 21 | £34
130 Regent's Park Rd., NW1 (Chalk Farm), 0171-586 5486
■ "Primrose Hill's great neighbourhood staple" is this "really romantic" Modern British eaterie that "goes from strength to strength" with "excellent", "satisfying" food and a "beautifully decorated" setting; if some say "nice but not exciting", more consider it a "great little oasis" for bypassing the "bustle of the West End."

Odin's 20 | 22 | 21 | £40
27 Devonshire St., W1 (Baker St.), 0171-935 7296
◪ "Step back in time" at this "elegant" Marylebone "gem", where "splendidly discreet" service and "stylish", "classy", art-filled surroudings enhance the "dependable", if rather "old-fashioned", Franco-British menu; the food is "appealing" enough, but it's the uniquely "formal but friendly" ambience that makes it a business diners' "favourite."

Offshore [S] – | – | – | E
148 Holland Park Ave., W11 (Holland Park), 0171-221 6090
Sylvain Ho Wing Cheong, who made his name with a successful three-year stint at Jason's, is off to a "fine" start as chef-owner of this seafood newcomer in Holland Park, creating "exciting, innovative" dishes blending Mauritian and Creole influences; if service can be "a bit off", it may simply need more time to find its sea legs.

Old Delhi [S] ▽ 24 | 16 | 20 | £31
48 Kendal St., W2 (Marble Arch), 0171-723 3335
■ The decor is rather "uninspiring" but the welcome is "gracious" and it's followed by "excellent" Indian and Persian fare at this "reliable" Marble Arch venue; though "pricey for what it is", a live harpist on Wednesdays and Saturdays (£2 cover charge) helps soothe the sting.

Oliveto S
20 | 14 | 16 | £25

49 Elizabeth St., SW1 (Sloane Sq./Victoria), 0171-730 0074

■ Fans proclaim this "cheerful" Olivo spin-off in Belgravia the "best high-class pizza parlour in town" on the merits of its "decent" thin pizzas with unusual toppings and other "simple" Italian standards; some find it "pricey" for a "casual" local place, but there's always a "good buzz" and even occasional "star-spotting"; N.B. reservations required.

Olivo S
21 | 16 | 19 | £31

21 Eccleston St., SW1 (Victoria), 0171-730 2505

■ Supplying "Italian for foodies" in Victoria, this "cosy", "bright" Sardinian "never fails to please" its followers with "simple", "well-prepared" dishes that are "always top drawer"; "friendly" and "unpretentious", it's "very good for the neighbourhood" and "perfect for a low-key date."

1 Lombard Street
21 | 21 | 18 | £40

1 Lombard St., EC3 (Bank), 0171-929 6611

◪ Chef Herbert Berger concocts "varied and interesting" New French fare at this "stylish", "airy", high-ceilinged restaurant-cum-brasserie in a converted banking hall; its "exciting" ambience makes it "a welcome addition to City" dining, though critics object to the "too-loud" brasserie acoustics and "expense-account" pricing.

190
18 | 17 | 16 | £35

190 Queen's Gate, SW7 (Gloucester Rd./High St. Kensington), 0171-581 5666

◪ There's an "innovative" Mediterranean menu featuring some "great fish" dishes at this South Kensington basement with a "relaxed atmosphere", but some say it's "overpriced" and marred by "mediocre" service; all agree the location is "fabulous" for those headed to or from the Royal Albert Hall.

192 ◐S
18 | 16 | 14 | £31

192 Kensington Park Rd., W11 (Ladbroke Grove/Notting Hill Gate), 0171-229 0482

◪ This "long-standing standby" in Notting Hill is a "fun", "buzzing" venue with a "great bar", an "interesting crowd" and a bi-level dining section; boosters of the Modern British menu declare it "excellent" and "reliable", and though a fussy few are "disappointed", it's a "hardy perennial" for locals and a fine "Sunday lunch alternative."

One-O-One S
21 | 17 | 19 | £41

Sheraton Park Tower, William St., SW1 (Knightsbridge), 0171-290 7101

■ This spacious hotel dining room on the Knightsbridge-Belgravia border offers "excellent" French fare highlighted by some of "the best fish" around and complemented by "attentive, anticipatory service"; however, some say it's "too dear for its own good": "at first I thought the name was part of the address – now I know it's the price per person."

Oriel S
14 | 15 | 13 | £26
50-51 Sloane Sq., SW1 (Sloane Sq.), 0171-730 2804

▣ "Good at what it's trying to do", this "trendy, buzzing" Sloane Square bar/brasserie is a "great location" for "meeting" or "people-watching" over "laid-back" Modern European "comfort food"; however, since some say the menu delivers "good hits and bad misses", it may work best "for a quick meal" rather than anything more ambitious.

Orrery Restaurant S
23 | 21 | 21 | £46
55 Marylebone High St., W1 (Baker St./Regent's Park), 0171-616 8000

▣ The "most subtle Conran" say fans of this "intimate" Terence Conran venture in Marylebone with a "cool", "relaxing" feel and Modern French fare that's "pricey" but "high quality"; some find "nothing 'wow' on the menu" and service treads a line between "superb" and "a little oppressive", but most rate it "quietly excellent" and "wine snobs" rejoice in the fine list; there's a new terrace.

Orsino ●S
19 | 18 | 17 | £33
119 Portland Rd., W11 (Holland Park), 0171-221 3299

■ "Tucked away" in Holland Park, "Orso's kid brother" is "a bright, modern" eatery that "combines comfort and style" with "no loss of sophistication"; the "tasty" Modern Italian menu is "efficiently cooked", and though some snipe at service that "can be sloppy", it's a "good neighbourhood spot" and sometimes attracts a few "famous faces."

Orso ●S
19 | 15 | 17 | £33
27 Wellington St., WC2 (Covent Garden), 0171-240 5269

▣ This "reliable" Modern Italian in a Covent Garden basement has a "great" "urban ambience" and gets "very noisy in full flow" as fans feast on "fantastic" food presented "on big plates" by servers who are "pleasant" if "often rushed"; to a minority it "feels tired" and "ordinary", but for many it's still the "only place to go after the theatre."

Oslo Court
23 | 15 | 23 | £35
Prince Albert Rd., NW8 (St. John's Wood), 0171-722 8795

■ "It's in a time warp" and oddly located in a block of flats, but this French veteran near Regent's Park has "character" and is a "firm favourite for family celebrations" – the servers are "superb" with "the over-80s" and "many renditions of 'Happy Birthday'" accompany the big "helpings of traditional" food; the "small space" fills up, so "book in advance."

Osteria Antica Bologna S
18 | 13 | 15 | £25
23 Northcote Rd., SW11 (Clapham Junction B.R.), 0171-978 4771

■ "How lucky for Battersea"; this "rustic" trattoria may get "noisy" and "crowded", but the "robust", "authentic", "very filling" Modern Italian menu "always gives pleasure" with its "myriad flavours"; thoughtfully selected wines and an £8.50 prix fixe lunch menu keep things "interesting."

Osteria Basilico S

20 | 16 | 17 | £25

29 Kensington Park Rd., W11 (Ladbroke Grove), 0171-727 9957

■ A "regular for regulars", hence it can be "hard to get a table" at this "buzzy", "packed" Notting Hill trattoria with an "excellent" Modern Italian menu ("pasta as in Italy", "nice pizza") and a "warm, rustic feel"; "large" portions add to the "value" and the "friendly waiters" are "great with kids."

OXO TOWER ● S

20 | 24 | 17 | £42

Oxo Tower Wharf, Barge House St., SE1 (Blackfriars/Waterloo), 0171-803 3888

◪ "Smashing", "unrivalled views" ("if you get the right table") distinguish this "very swish" top-floor room in a South Bank landmark, but the rest of the package gets mixed marks: fans praise "superb" Modern British cooking and "attentive" staff, whilst foes find it "erratic" and "expensive"; on balance, the ayes have it and it's the "best place in town to watch the sun go down."

Oxo Tower Brasserie ● S

19 | 23 | 17 | £34

Oxo Tower Wharf, Barge House St., SE1 (Blackfriars/Waterloo), 0171-803 3888

◪ Oxo Tower's "noisy" neighbour boasts the "same view" as its floormate but is "more chummy" and "slightly cheaper"; the Med-Asian menu is "delicious" to some, "a letdown" to others, but either way the "superb" vista "upstages" everything else at this "lively" South Bank option.

Pacific Oriental

– | – | – | E

1 Bishopsgate, EC2 (Bank), 0171-621 9988

"A great surprise" say those who know this impressive-looking, weekday-only City newcomer with a brasserie/bar serving sushi, tempura and the like and a more refined Pacific Rim restaurant upstairs; slightly incongruous features include a microbrewery and wide-screen TVs in the bar; other siblings are planned.

Pacific Spice

▽ 15 | 16 | 15 | £21

42 Northampton Rd., EC1 (Farringdon), 0171-278 9983

◪ "Bring your compass" when navigating a course to this "out-of-the-way" Clerkenwell pub conversion where "reasonably good" Thai-Malaysian fare is served in a bi-level setting with "delightful", airy dining areas and a noodle bar; mutineers maintain it's "a little overpriced" and advise "place a homing device on your waiter."

Palio ● S

16 | 14 | 13 | £25

175 Westbourne Grove, W11 (Notting Hill Gate), 0171-221 6624

◪ This bright, colourful bistro near Portobello Road offers "good variety" on a "serviceable" Mediterranean menu, though detractors deem the results "hit-and-miss"; still, it can be agreeable for "lightweight brunches" and provides "excellent atmosphere" for live jazz (Thursday nights); N.B. a recent refurb may not be reflected in the decor score.

Palm Court S   ▽ 19 21 19 £30
Le Meridien Waldorf, Aldwych, WC2 (Covent Garden), 0171-836 2400
☒ According to fans, there's "a real buzz" surrounding this "romantic", "serene" dining area in a famous Aldwych hotel, serving "lovely" Modern British fare and high tea that's "a wonderful treat"; foes find its cachet "difficult to understand", but it's "an experience to be here" and "quick service" makes it a good business dining option.

Paparazzi Cafe ◐S   11 13 12 £21
58 Fulham Rd., SW3 (South Kensington), 0171-589 0876
Paparazzi Lounge ◐
9 Hanover St., W1 (Oxford Circus), 0171-355 3337
☒ "Dancing on the tables" might cap off a meal at this "fun" South Ken Italian (recently joined by a Regent Street sibling), which "serves its purpose" as a "noisy", "hot" nightspot with live soul/Latin music; "no one goes here for the food", but one patron puts in a word for "penne from heaven."

Park, The ◐S   – – – E
105 Salisbury Rd., NW6 (Queen's Park), 0171-372 8882
In Queen's Park premises formerly owned by the Royal National Institute for the Blind, this big, split-level Italian newcomer has hit the ground running, drawing a trendy, upbeat crowd with Modern Italian fare ranging from wood-oven pizzas to more adventurous dishes, all served by youthful staff; there are plans to open an adjacent deli.

Park Restaurant S   ▽ 24 23 20 £37
Mandarin Oriental Hyde Park Hotel, 66 Knightsbridge, SW1 (Knightsbridge), 0171-201 3635
☒ There's a "magnificent view of Hyde Park" from this dining room in a grandly renovated Knightsbridge hotel, and whilst you "pay for the location", the deal includes efficient service ("always had good treatment") and David Nicholls' well-regarded French-Med cooking; hedgers rate it "just ok", but ratings side with those who say "worth a visit."

Pasha ◐S   17 23 16 £37
1 Gloucester Rd., SW7 (Gloucester Rd.), 0171-589 7969
☒ "Lovely decor" invokes "a different world" at this "romantic" South Kensington Moroccan, and the kitchen follows through with "interesting" food; doubters deem it "faddish" ("all show, no go") and "not really authentic", but to most it's a refreshing "change from the norm" (just watch out for "low chairs" that some find "uncomfortable").

Pasha ◐S   17 18 20 £27
301 Upper St., N1 (Angel/Highbury & Islington), 0171-226 1454
■ A "cute place" with "a warm feeling", this Islington Turk is "good at what it aims to do", i.e. deliver "decent" fare and "friendly" service; if "nothing stands out", it offers "good value", with set-price menus at lunch (£5) and dinner (£9.95).

Passione　　　　　　　　　- | - | - | E |
10 Charlotte St., W1 (Goodge St.), 0171-636 2833
A trio of staffers from Antonio Carluccio's Neal Street
Restaurant have branched out with their own venture in a
narrow, bustling Fitzrovia space, offering a Modern Italian
menu that mixes and matches regional dishes, keeping the
accent on wild mushrooms and herbs.

Patara ▣　　　　　　　21 | 14 | 18 | £28 |
(fka S&P)
*9 Beauchamp Pl., SW3 (Knightsbridge/South Kensington),
0171-581 8820*
181 Fulham Rd., SW3 (South Kensington), 0171-351 5692
■ The name may have changed but the cooking is "still
reliable" ("make sure you like it hot!") according to boosters
of this Thai twosome; if a few claim it's "not as good as a
few years ago", more are won over by the "great-tasting"
food, "friendly service" and "good value."

Patisserie Valerie　　　　20 | 15 | 15 | £14 |
8 Russell St., WC2 (Covent Garden), 0171-240 0064 ▣
44 Old Compton St., W1 (Leicester Sq.), 0171-437 3466 ▣
*Royal Institute British Architects, 66 Portland Pl., W1
(Oxford Circus), 0171-631 0467*
*105 Marylebone High St., W1 (Baker St./Bond St.),
0171-935 6240* ▣
215 Brompton Rd., SW3 (Knightsbridge), 0171-823 9971 ▣
■ "If you don't have a ticket on Eurostar, the next best thing"
is a trip to these "casual", "bustling" all-day French-style
cafes with "great pastries", "unbelievable cakes" and
"good" Franco-Italian snacks at "amazing value"; if service
is sometimes "confused", it's understandable given this
chain's popularity, particularly that of the "atmospheric",
septuagenarian Soho original.

Peasant, The　　　　　　19 | 17 | 16 | £25 |
(aka Room 240)
240 St. John St., EC1 (Angel/Farringdon), 0171-336 7726
◪ Though some suggest that this "informal" dining room
above an Islington pub is "an acquired taste" ("almost too
peasanty to be exciting"), it pleases most with its "fine (if
smallish) menu" of "nouveau" British-Mediterranean fare
served in a "relaxed" ambience; the terrace is "lovely" and
it's "convenient for Saddler's Wells."

Pelham Street ▣　　　　　17 | 11 | 17 | £32 |
93 Pelham St., SW7 (South Kensington), 0171-584 4788
■ This low-key Brompton Cross eaterie, which fans credit
with "good potential", has made some post-*Survey* changes:
chef Trevor Blythe has left and the Modern European menu
has been lightened with Eclectic–Pacific Rim touches (thus
putting the food rating into question), whilst the basement
has been turned into a separate eaterie, Pizza Chelsea;
there's live jazz at weekends.

People's Palace [S] 18 | 19 | 19 | £32

Royal Festival Hall, South Bank Ctr., SE1 (Embankment/ Waterloo), 0171-928 9999

◪ Despite "mega" river views, this "spacious" Modern British eaterie in the South Bank's Royal Festival Hall takes knocks for "institutional" decor and "no atmosphere" ("like an airport foyer"), but many are "pleasantly surprised" by the "quite tasty" food and "motivated" service; outvoted dissenters find the cooking "hit-and-miss", but it's certainly a "convenient" "pre-concert" option.

Pepe Nero ◐ – | – | – | M

133 Lavender Hill, SW11 (Clapham Junction B.R.), 0171-978 4863

Alberto Chiappa and Antonio Raillo (ex Toto's and Criterion Brasserie respectively) are behind this casual, split-level Lavender Hill newcomer that serves reasonably priced Mediterranean fare to a mostly local crowd; the large windowed front opens on warm days for pavement dining.

Pepper Tree [S] 20 | 13 | 17 | £16

19 Clapham Common Southside, SW4 (Clapham Common), 0171-622 1758

■ It's "cramped" and "noisy" with "refectory tables", but this Clapham canteen serves "tasty" (some say "faultless") Thai food that's "phenomenal value"; it's a "favourite" of locals who hope it doesn't get any more popular.

Pescatori 22 | 17 | 18 | £29

57 Charlotte St., W1 (Goodge St.), 0171-580 3289 ◐

11 Dover St., W1 (Green Park), 0171-493 2652

◪ The long-running (since 1961) Charlotte Street original of this Italian seafooder group is known for "seriously well-presented" "fresh fish" and "super service", but some find it "overpriced for what it is"; "newish decor" distinguishes the Dover Street venue.

Pétrus ▽ 23 | 25 | 25 | £54

33 St. James's St., SW1 (Green Park), 0171-930 4272

■ After his exit from L'Oranger last year, Marcus Wareing has resurfaced in St. James's to rejuvenate the former '33', turning it into an intimate, discreet room with a distinctly opulent air; "marvellous" New French fare and a 300-label wine list enhance the prospects of this power-eating upstart.

Pharmacy Restaurant [S] 17 | 19 | 15 | £37

150 Notting Hill Gate, W11 (Notting Hill Gate), 0171-221 2442

◪ Though the "hype" has subsided, opinions on this "eye-catching" Notting Hill hot spot remain polarised: some say it's "surprisingly good", praising Michael McEnearay's "first-class" Modern European fare and the "fantastic" arty decor, but critics call it "a concept in search of a restaurant" with an "annoying chemist theme" and "slow" service; few deny it's "way cool", so "go to say you've been."

Phoenicia ◐Ⓢ   21 | 14 | 19 | £28

11-13 Abingdon Rd., W8 (High St. Kensington), 0171-937 0120
◪ This "civilised", family-run Kensington Lebanese has
won many hearts with its "excellent", "authentic" cooking
and "helpful" staff, even if a few contrarians complain of
"ordinary food" in a "dull room" with service that "could
not be slower"; there's a "great value buffet" with a "wide
choice" that's ideal for the very "hungry."

Phoenix Bar & Grill Ⓢ   20 | 17 | 17 | £32

162 Lower Richmond Rd., SW15 (Putney Bridge), 0181-780 3131
■ Similar to its elder sib Sonny's ("but a bit more youthful"),
this "light", "relaxed", "neighbourhood" eatery in Barnes
rises to the occasion with "reliably good", "sometimes
excellent" Modern British food and "friendly" service; some
report "decibel problems" at busy times, but "summer
evenings on the terrace" get the thumbs-up.

Picasso ◐Ⓢ   12 | 9 | 14 | £14

127 King's Rd., SW3 (Sloane Sq.), 0171-352 4921
■ It's been a "true King's Road hangout for more than 30
years", and this "smoky" Italian still offers "'70s authenticity"
in an environment free of "creature comforts"; there are
no masterpieces on the menu of "traditional" fare, but it's
cheap and the pavement tables are a "posers' paradise."

PIED-À-TERRE   25 | 18 | 22 | £51

34 Charlotte St., W1 (Goodge St.), 0171-636 1178
■ Diners may debate whether it's a "lovely, simple setting"
or a "cramped", "small" space, but most agree that this
"congenial" Fitzrovian is home to "outstanding", "creative"
New French cooking by an "exciting chef", Tom Aikens;
you're "really well looked after" at this "secret treasure"
that's "pricey, but worth it."

Pierre Victoire ◐Ⓢ   13 | 11 | 13 | £16

5 Dean St., W1 (Tottenham Court Rd.), 0171-287 4582
◪ "Are there any left?"; yes, but this "mock French" chain
is now down to one location: the successful Soho branch,
offering "basic" Gallic fare that's "a bit hit-and-miss" but "a
bargain"; die-hard devotees "hope it rises from the ashes."

Pitcher & Piano   13 | 13 | 12 | £16

40-42 William IV St., WC2 (Charing Cross), 0171-240 6180 Ⓢ
18-20 Chiswick High Rd., W4 (Stamford Brook), 0181-742 7731 Ⓢ
10 Pollen St., W1 (Oxford Circus), 0171-629 9581
*69-70 Dean St., W1 (Leicester Sq./Tottenham Court Rd.),
0171-434 3585*
871-873 Fulham Rd., SW6 (Parsons Green), 0171-736 3910 Ⓢ
4-5 High St., SW19 (Wimbledon), 0181-879 7020 Ⓢ
8 Balham Hill, SW12 (Clapham South), 0181-673 1107 Ⓢ
*214 Fulham Rd., SW10 (Earl's Court/South Kensington),
0171-352 9234* Ⓢ
(Continues)

Pitcher & Piano (Cont.)
316 King's Rd., SW3 (Sloane Sq.), 0171-352 0025 S
68 Upper St., N1 (Angel), 0171-704 9974 S
200 Bishopsgate, EC2 (Liverpool St.), 0171-929 5914
Additional locations throughout London.
☑ An "alternative to the English pub", these "noisy, vibrant", "dip in and out" wine bars with "big comfy sofas" are popular "for a drink" or "after-hours" gatherings with "office mates", drawing a young crowd that doesn't mind if the Eclectic menu of "basic burgers and pub grub" is "consistent, but a little boring."

Pizza Chelsea S   – – – M
93 Pelham St., SW7 (South Kensington), 0171-584 4788
Chelsea locals who appreciated this pizzeria during its previous run at this site (it closed a few years ago to make way for Pelham Street) will be happy to see it reincarnated in a cosy basement space beneath Pelham Street (with a separate entrance); the good value Modern Italian menu has been dusted off and makes a welcome reappearance.

PIZZA EXPRESS ◗S   18 16 16 £15
9-12 Bow St., WC2 (Covent Garden), 0171-240 3443
137 Notting Hill Gate, W11 (Notting Hill Gate), 0171-229 6000
35 Earl's Court Rd., W8 (High St. Kensington), 0171-937 0761
29 Wardour St., W1 (Leicester Sq.), 0171-437 7215
198 Trinity Rd., SW17 (Wandsworth Town B.R.), 0181-672 0200
46-54 Battersea Bridge Rd., SW11 (Earl's Court/Sloane Sq.), 0171-924 2774
363 Fulham Rd., SW10 (Fulham Broadway), 0171-352 5300
895 Fulham Rd., SW6 (Parsons Green), 0171-731 3117
The Pheasantry, 152-154 King's Rd., SW3 (Sloane Sq.), 0171-351 5031
7 Beauchamp Pl., SW3 (Knightsbridge), 0171-589 2355
125 Alban Gate, London Wall, EC2 (Moorgate/St. Paul's), 0171-600 8880
Additional locations throughout London.
■ "Often imitated, occasionally equalled but never surpassed" say fans of this "justifiably popular" chain, a "mainstay of London living" thanks to "consistently above-average pizzas" (but "can't they be bigger?") and other "inoffensive" Italian dishes that are "a safe bet for a quick meal or with kids"; even if service can be "variable", this "well-priced" institution is the "pizza yardstick" for many.

PIZZA METRO S   24 14 19 £22
64 Battersea Rise, SW11 (Clapham Junction B.R.), 0171-228 3812
■ "Book early – the place is tiny", "packed" and "becoming too trendy"; this "chaotic" Battersea pizzeria is "loved by Italians", and many others, for its "wonderful Naples-style cuisine", including "outstanding pizzas" and the "best antipasto"; the decor is no-frills, but it's a "friendly" favourite that makes for a "fun night out."

Pizza on the Park ● S
18 | 17 | 16 | £20

11 Knightsbridge, SW1 (Hyde Park Corner),
0171-235 5273

■ This "posher, jazzed-up version" of the "unfailingly good" Pizza Express chain has a "great location" on Hyde Park Corner and is considered "worth the bit extra" for the "great" live jazz and cabaret acts; supporters recommend it for "a quick tummy fill" or before a concert.

Pizza Pomodoro ●
16 | 13 | 14 | £19

51 Beauchamp Pl., SW3 (Knightsbridge),
0171-589 1278 S
7 Steward St., E1 (Liverpool St.), 0171-377 6186

■ You're "guaranteed to exercise your vocal chords" at these "noisy", "cramped" pizzerias in the City and Knightsbridge, where the fairly "run-of-the-mill" Italian menu offers a respectable "price/quality ratio" and "great bands" (jazz/Latin/soul) inspire "music madness"; it's a "fun" choice for "parties" and "hen nights."

Pizza The Action ● S
16 | 12 | 15 | £16

678 Fulham Rd., SW6 (Parsons Green), 0171-736 2716

◪ Though some critics feel this Fulham pizzeria puts in a "varied performance" and has "been the same for too long", others laud its "good", cheap Italian fare, including what some call the "best pizzas in town"; since it can be "crowded and noisy", it must fulfil a need in the area.

Pizzeria Castello
21 | 12 | 19 | £16

20 Walworth Rd., SE1 (Elephant & Castle), 0171-703 2556

■ Still a "real local discovery" for some even after almost two decades, this "rustic", simply decorated Elephant & Castle pizzeria is "deservedly popular" thanks to Italian food that's "amazingly cheap" and "amazingly good"; those charmed by the "friendly" service ask "where do they find such polite waiters?"

PJ's Bar & Grill ● S
15 | 16 | 14 | £25

52 Fulham Rd., SW3 (South Kensington), 0171-581 0025

◪ "Once you've navigated the pickup bar, the food is good" say fans of this "casual" Chelsea eatery with "nice vibes" and a conventional International menu; if pickier types find the food "uninspiring" and wish they'd "turn down the music", most agree it's "handy" for "hanging out" and "ideal for brunch" lubricated by the "world's best Bloody Marys."

PJ's Grill ● S
15 | 15 | 14 | £27

30 Wellington St., WC2 (Covent Garden), 0171-240 7529

◪ Supporters say Brian Stein's original P.J.'s in a wood-panelled Covent Garden setting is "like being in the USA", with a "good" Eclectic menu supplemented by Pacific Rim dishes; the less impressed cite "average" food and deficient service, but the affordable pre-theatre menu packs them in.

Place Below 20 | 15 | 13 | £14

St. Mary-le-Bow Church, EC2 (St. Paul's), 0171-329 0789

■ In the Norman crypt of a church near St. Paul's, this "atmospheric" breakfast-and-lunch eaterie strikes fans as "the best place to eat healthy veggie food in the City" thanks to "filling, plentiful" fare; still, some find it "rather pricey" for a self-service "caff."

Planet Hollywood ◐ [S] 12 | 17 | 14 | £21

13 Coventry St., W1 (Leicester Sq./Piccadilly Circus), 0171-437 7827

◪ "Let's face it, the chef is unlikely to win an Oscar", but this "chaotic" Piccadilly branch of the cinema-themed chain can be "fun if you're in the mood" and is a "great place to take noisy kids" for "standard" Californian fare served in "portions as big as Arnie's pecs"; critics say the "cachet has gone" and it "should be a museum, not a restaurant."

Plummers ◐ [S] 18 | 16 | 16 | £23

33 King St., WC2 (Covent Garden), 0171-240 2534

◪ For a "romantic dinner" or a "pre-theatre" bite, fans laud this "cosy" Covent Garden stalwart with a "good value" Traditional British menu; foes find it rather "nondescript" and "boring", but they may be appeased by a recent refurb.

Poissonnerie de l'Avenue ◐ 20 | 17 | 19 | £41

82 Sloane Ave., SW3 (South Kensington), 0171-589 2457

◪ "Reliable quality year-in, year-out" has built the reputation of this "lovely, old-fashioned" Brompton Cross seafooder with a "quiet", "unhurried" ambience that attracts a "stylish, older customer base" and "business" crowd; some find it a bit "pompous" and warn bring a "fat wallet", but fans "love" its "traditional" takes on "beautifully fresh fish."

Pollo Bar ◐ [S] 🚫 15 | 9 | 13 | £11

20 Old Compton St., W1 (Leicester Sq.), 0171-734 5917

◪ "The queues can't be wrong" argue advocates of this "no-nonsense", "no-frills" Italian cafe in the "heart of Soho", home to "huge portions" of "very cheap" fare that's judged "one stage above average"; whilst snobs say "no thanks" to this "pauper's" paradise, most commend it as a "fast, friendly" and even "hip" fill-up – "when you can get in."

Polygon Bar & Grill [S] 19 | 18 | 18 | £30

4 The Polygon, Clapham Old Town, SW4 (Clapham Common), 0171-622 1199

◪ A "bit Conranesque" in feel (but not a Conran spot), this Clapham venue with attractive modern decor offers "flavoursome" grill/rotisserie fare from an Eclectic menu; the food benefits from "more consistency now", and if some find it "overpriced" and say "service could be improved", most enjoy the "good" ambience and "stylish bar."

Pomegranates ◐   20 | 17 | 21 | £34
94 Grosvenor Rd., SW1 (Pimlico), 0171-828 6560
☑ Maybe it's an "anomaly in today's London", but this "romantic", "quirky" Pimlico "find" offers a "pleasant change" with its "consistent" Eclectic fare and "excellent service" courtesy of "merry" (if "eccentric") owner Patrick Gwynne Jones; the "1975 time warp" style is "not everyone's cup of tea", though, and critics say it's "living on memories."

Poons ☒   18 | 12 | 14 | £21
4 Leicester St., WC2 (Leicester Sq.), 0171-437 1528 ◐
27 Lisle St., WC2 (Leicester Sq.), 0171-437 4549 ◐
Royal National Hotel, 50 Woburn Pl., WC1 (Euston/Russell Sq.), 0171-580 1188 ◐
Unit 205, Whiteleys Shopping Ctr., 151 Queensway, W2 (Bayswater/Queensway), 0171-792 2884
☑ "High-quality", "authentic" Chinese cooking ("crispy duck as it should be") is the main attraction at these "fast", basic-looking eateries in "convenient locations" around town, with service that some sense is "getting politer"; detractors deem them "uninspiring" but concede the two Chinatown sites are a "port in a storm" "before theatre or after."

Poons in the City   15 | 11 | 12 | £27
1 Minster Pavement, Minster Ct., Mincing Ln., EC3 (Monument/Tower Hill), 0171-626 0126
☑ It's "looking a little tired now", but defenders say the ornate, stylised basement setting of this Chinese in Minster Court (under different ownership from Poons) is still home to "good" multiregional food and dim sum; foes are less forgiving, citing "small portions" of "overpriced" fare with "no particular character."

Porters ◐☒   14 | 14 | 15 | £21
17 Henrietta St., WC2 (Covent Garden), 0171-836 6466
☑ There's a "warm atmosphere" at Lord Bradford's pub-style Covent Garden veteran, the better to complement "wholesome portions" of "good value" "trad British" food ("great bangers and mash"); nonfans find it "very ordinary", but it's a "useful" place to "take kids" or "your aunt who's up in town for the afternoon."

porters bar ☒   – | – | – | M
16 Henrietta St., WC2 (Covent Garden/Leicester Sq.), 0171-836 6466
porters bar at poland st. ☒
21-22 Poland St., W1 (Oxford Circus/Tottenham Court Rd.), 0171-460 7475
Next to Porters, his Covent Garden stalwart, Lord Bradford has installed this "good bar", a colourful, bi-level space serving affordable bar snacks that draw a lively, after-work crowd; a Poland street sibling is due to open at press time.

Prince Bonaparte [S] 18 | 13 | 12 | £15

80 Chepstow Rd., W2 (Bayswater/Notting Hill Gate), 0171-313 9491

■ "Rough and ready" (and arguably "getting rougher and readier"), this "good gastropub" in Westbourne Park wins "high praise for atmosphere" and its Eclectic menu of "bar snacks with style" offers "extreme value for money"; it's an "ideal" "Sunday lunch/evening drink" kind of place.

Princess Garden ◐[S] 22 | 18 | 19 | £41

8-10 N. Audley St., W1 (Bond St.), 0171-493 3223

◪ "Good quality food" and a grand setting complete with piano bar make this formal Mayfair Chinese (part of the Zen group) "lovely for family gatherings"; however, critics say "Chinese was never intended to be so stuffy" or "expensive."

Prism – | – | – | VE

147 Leadenhall St., EC3 (Bank/Monument), 0171-256 3888

The latest addition to the Harvey Nichols portfolio is this stylised venue in the heart of the City, a former banking hall that now houses an airy restaurant with handsome columns, towering windows and high ceilings, plus a downstairs bar and private rooms; the accomplished Modern British cooking with International accents doesn't come cheap, though the simpler bar menu is more affordable.

Pucci Pizza ◐[S]🚫 16 | 9 | 12 | £17

205 King's Rd., SW3 (Sloane Sq.), 0171-352 2134

■ Even those who give it "no points for decor or service" admit they "can't resist" the "hard-to-beat" pizzas and "fun Eurotrash atmosphere" at this cramped, "laid-back" Chelsea pizzeria; it's also "great value" – "especially for Chelsea."

Purple Sage 20 | 17 | 14 | £25

92 Wigmore St., W1 (Bond St.), 0171-486 1912

■ A "great addition to the family" that includes Red Pepper, White Onion and Green Olive, this newcomer near Oxford Street offers "impressive", "fresh" "nouveau Italian fare without lira inflation", including "excellent" wood-oven pizzas; some say service "needs to improve" and beg for "bigger portions", but the "buzzing", "casual" ambience helps make it a "welcome arrival to an area in need."

Putney Bridge Restaurant & Bar [S] 17 | 21 | 14 | £36

1 Embankment, Lower Richmond Rd., SW15 (Putney Bridge), 0181-780 1811

◪ The "amazing view over the Thames" adds to the "beautiful atmosphere" at this New French in Putney, and the arrival of respected chef Anthony Demetre is now paying dividends as patrons praise his "imaginative" fare; spoilers still hark on about "snooty" service and an "impudently overpriced" menu, but backers call it "deservedly popular" and feel that with a bit of effort it could be "outstanding."

QUAGLINO'S ◐ⓈＳ　　　19 │ 20 │ 16 │ £37 │
16 Bury St., SW1 (Green Park), 0171-930 6767
▰ Be "famous for five seconds" descending the "impressive" staircase at Terence Conran's "stylish", "cavernous" Piccadilly basement eatery offering Modern British fare that most find "reliable" (if "slightly overpriced"), highlighted by "heavenly seafood"; if some say this "frantic" place with "overzealous" service and "dangerously high decibels" has "had its day", advocates argue it "may get a lot of stick" but it "still does the biz" and remains a "great place to entertain."

Quality Chop House ◐Ｓ　　　21 │ 15 │ 18 │ £29 │
94 Farringdon Rd., EC1 (Farringdon), 0171-837 5093
▰ Even those who "hate sharing tables" and balk at "hard benches" ("bring a cushion") admit they "keep going back" to this "interesting" Farringdon "original" for "good, old-fashioned" British "staples" like "the best pie and chips"; critics find it "mundane", but they're soundly outvoted; P.S. there's now a next-door seafood bar without bench seating.

Queens, The Ｓ　　　▽ 19 │ 13 │ 17 │ £21 │
49 Regent's Park Rd., NW1 (Chalk Farm), 0171-586 0408
▰ "Views of leafy Primrose Hill" appeal to the "nice younger crowd" that heads to this sibling of the Duke of Cambridge to down "consistent" Modern British "pub food"; it's likable enough for some to "swear by it."

Quincy's Ｓ　　　20 │ 17 │ 22 │ £28 │
675 Finchley Rd., NW2 (Golders Green), 0171-794 8499
▰ Boosters of this "hidden gem" in Finchley brand it a "wonderful local" with "first-class" Modern British food and service that treats patrons "like royalty"; a few feel it's "time for a fresh coat of paint" and protest the "rather squashed seating" ("no privacy"), but the fact that it's "hard to get a table" suggests something's being done right.

Quo Vadis ◐Ｓ　　　20 │ 18 │ 18 │ £41 │
26-29 Dean St., W1 (Leicester Sq./Tottenham Court Rd.), 0171-437 9585
▰ Marco Pierre White's "sleek" Soho "media hangout" wins mostly applause for its "imaginative" Modern European menu complemented by a wine list "thicker than the Yellow Pages" ("scary"); sceptics may call it a "snore", but it's still a "fashionable" "see-and-be-seen" spot that "hits all the right places – and the credit cards"; N.B. a post-*Survey* revamp followed the departure of Damien Hirst's artwork.

Rain Ｓ　　　19 │ 19 │ 18 │ £33 │
303 Portobello Rd., W10 (Ladbroke Grove), 0181-968 2001
▰ "Great New York atmosphere" and "creative Pan-Asian cuisine" (from a former Vong chef) distinguish this "offbeat and original" Portobello newcomer; "friendly, personal" service is a plus and the "cosy" (some say "tacky") setting showcases quirky modern art.

Rainforest Cafe S   11 | 22 | 16 | £20 |

20 Shaftesbury Ave., W1 (Piccadilly Circus),
0171-434 3111

☑ This "touristy", tropical-themed Piccadilly eaterie has a "Disney-ride feel" complete with animatronics, thunder and "annoying animal noises" to accompany "large portions" of "mediocre" American fare (which cynics say explains the "Tarzan screams"); it's "fun for family meals" (thus "overrun with kids"), but critics dub it "an endangered species that's not worth protecting"; N.B. it now takes reservations.

Randall & Aubin S   19 | 18 | 15 | £22 |

14-16 Brewer St., W1 (Piccadilly Circus), 0171-287 4447

■ Ed Baines' "buzzing, bar-style" venue in a converted Soho butcher shop has a "funky, laid-back" ambience plus "superb seafood", "pleasing rotisserie fare" and some charcuterie; the main gripe seems to be "uncomfortable seats", but it's a "unique" spot for a "quick" bite that's "not madly expensive."

Rani S   19 | 13 | 17 | £21 |

7 Long Ln., N3 (Finchley Central), 0181-349 4386

☑ "Even a non-veggie can enjoy it" say fans of this modestly priced Finchley Vegetarian Indian, where "tasty", "home-from-home cooking" (now including pizzas) attracts "discriminating" curry-heads in pursuit of "a real treat for the taste buds"; though a few feel it's "hugely overrated" and cite "detached" service, most give a thumbs-up to this "popular" spot.

Ransome's Dock S   21 | 19 | 21 | £32 |

35-37 Park Gate Rd., SW11 (Sloane Sq.), 0171-924 2462

■ There's a "real feeling the staff enjoy their work" at this "relaxed", "well-run" Modern British in a "strange" (yet somehow "charming") setting on the edge of a Battersea dock; featuring "interesting" if "simple" food matched with "fair-priced fine wines" and "always pleasant service", it's "great for parties" or an "outdoor brunch" at weekends.

Rasa S   24 | 18 | 21 | £23 |

6 Dering St., W1 (Bond St./Oxford St.), 0171-629 1346
55 Stoke Newington Church St., N16 (Angel),
0171-249 0344

Rasa Samudra

5 Charlotte St., W1 (Tottenham Court Rd.),
0171-637 0222

☑ A "fab Keralan veggie banquet" is how fans describe a meal at this Indian trio (Rasa Samudra also serves seafood), offering "unusual", "authentic" fare ("simply the best"), a "warm welcome" and "helpful" service; even those who don't normally like nonmeat cooking say "this is something special", though some prefer the original Stoke Newington "delight" to its West End spin-offs.

Ravi Shankar 🅂
19 ｜ 11 ｜ 14 ｜ £15

133-135 Drummond St., NW1 (Euston), 0171-388 6458
422 St. John St., EC1 (Angel), 0171-833 5849

■ "How can they produce such excellent food at such low prices?" wonder fans of these "dependable" Vegetarian Indians on the City fringes; sure, they skimp a bit on the "fast-foodish" ambience, but few mind given "amazingly cheap" "good eats"; N.B. the St. John Street branch is lunch-only and BYO.

Real Greek, The
– ｜ – ｜ – ｜ M

15 Hoxton Mkt., N1 (Old St.), 0171-739 8212

Due to open shortly after press time is this brainchild of Theodore Kyriakou, the originator of Livebait (who sold that venture to Groupe Chez Gerard); family-run and occupying a small, fresh-looking space in Hoxton Market, it hopes to take Greek food to a new level of authenticity, aided by an exclusively Greek wine list.

Rebato's
▽ 20 ｜ 16 ｜ 18 ｜ £27

169 S. Lambeth Rd., SW8 (Stockwell), 0171-735 6388

☑ "Off the beaten track" south of Vauxhall Bridge, this little-known Spaniard offers "tasty" tapas, though some feel the rest of the fare is "more your Spanish international hotel" variety; a singer helps distract from the "dated" decor.

Red Fort 🅂
19 ｜ 15 ｜ 16 ｜ £30

77 Dean St., W1 (Leicester Sq./Tottenham Court Rd.),
0171-437 2115

☑ Supporters swear by the "consistent" Indian cooking with a "creative twist" at this Soho stalwart, reporting it's "easy to eat too much" at the "wonderful", "good value" buffet (lunch and pre-theatre); however, a few doubters find the regular menu "overpriced" and the surroundings "scruffy" (though plans are in hand for a refurb).

Redmonds 🅂
22 ｜ 14 ｜ 19 ｜ £36

170 Upper Richmond Rd. West, SW14 (Hammersmith),
0181-878 1922

■ "If it were in Belgravia it would be booked solid – alas, it's in Sheen", but even so Redmond Hayward's "interesting", "well-presented" Modern British fare has many followers, hence this "modern" ("a little cold") space with "anodyne" decor can get "noisy when crowded"; there's also an appealing wine list with "plenty of half bottles."

Red Pepper 🅂
19 ｜ 13 ｜ 15 ｜ £23

8 Formosa St., W9 (Warwick Ave.), 0171-266 2708

☑ "Pizza with pizazz" is the big draw at this Italian "hidden treasure in Maida Vale", also serving "imaginative pastas" and "excellent grilled fish" in a "cramped party" setting; a few find the fare "a bit disappointing" and object to "rushed" service and "too many tables", but all agree it's "hard to beat the takeouts."

Reubens S
| | | | | 14 | 11 | 14 | £21 |

79 Baker St., W1 (Baker St.), 0171-486 0035

☑ Back "with a vengeance" say loyalists who find this classic kosher deli "as good" as ever in its new Marylebone premises, lauding its "salt beef sandwich to rival New York" and other "good, traditional food"; though not to everyone's liking ("dreary"), most would agree it's "not bad for a snack."

Reynier Wine Library
| 15 | 15 | 16 | £20 |

43 Trinity Sq., EC3 (Tower Hill), 0171-481 0415

■ "Food is not the point", it's the "excellent" wines (400-plus labels) that enthuse oenophiles at this lunch-only City venue in a former skittles alley, where the liquid offerings are augmented by a buffet of "interesting cheeses and pâtés"; the bottles are priced at retail plus £2 corkage, making it a "best-kept secret" for a "boozy lunch."

Rhodes in the Square S
| 23 | 18 | 20 | £46 |

Dolphin Sq. Hotel, Dolphin Sq., Chichester St., SW1 (Pimlico), 0171-798 6767

☑ Celeb chef Gary Rhodes shows off "precision cooking" at this Modern British yearling with "trendy decor" in a Pimlico luxury flats/hotel complex, and disciples liken the results to a "gastronomic dream" with "informed" service and a good wine list; a few critics balk at "heavy" food and matching prices, but the consensus is "very good indeed."

Rib Room & Oyster Bar ● S
| 20 | – | 20 | £47 |

Hyatt Carlton Tower, 2 Cadogan Pl., SW1 (Knightsbridge/Sloane Sq.), 0171-235 1234

■ "Fine beef served in fine style" is the forte of this Knightsbridge hotel dining room where the traditional British fare is "done well", including "quality" prime rib and "steaks for the Americans"; those who knock "staid" surroundings can look to a major revamp to be completed at press time that includes the addition of an oyster bar.

Riccardo's ● S
| 17 | 12 | 14 | £26 |

126 Fulham Rd., SW3 (South Kensington), 0171-370 6656

■ A "crowded" Chelsea Italian "hangout" notable for its "all-starter-portion" menu that offers "plenty of choice" and "value"; there's not much decor and some say service needs to "sharpen up", but it's a "great concept" and outside tables make for a "nice Sunday brunch"; it also serves breakfast.

Richard Corrigan at Lindsay House
| 24 | 20 | 21 | £46 |

21 Romilly St., W1 (Leicester Sq./Piccadilly Circus), 0171-439 0450

■ This "unusual little" Soho townhouse is home to Richard Corrigan's "inventive" Modern British fare that devotees rate "near perfection"; if a few feel it "lacks atmosphere" and claim prices "have escalated alarmingly", most have no complaints about this "quiet" place where "obliging" service adds to the sense that "everything is done with love."

Richoux [S] 14 | 14 | 13 | £19

172 Piccadilly, W1 (Green Park/Piccadilly Circus), 0171-493 2204
41A South Audley St., W1 (Bond St.), 0171-629 5228
86 Brompton Rd., SW3 (Knightsbridge), 0171-584 8300
3 Circus Rd., NW8 (St. John's Wood), 0171-483 4001

◪ For a "casual afternoon tea" or "coffee break", this "solid" if "rather dated" chain of tearooms can satisfy with "fabulous cakes" and "fresh" snacks; critics consider them "pedestrian" but even they admit they're "convenient."

RITZ RESTAURANT ◐ [S] 23 | 27 | 24 | £50

Ritz Hotel, 150 Piccadilly, W1 (Green Park), 0171-493 8181

■ "Dress up – they deserve it!"; with its "sumptuous", "aristocratic surroundings" and view over Green Park, this recently spruced-up Piccadilly hotel dining room is hailed as London's "prettiest" (No. 1 for Decor), and if some say the Classic French–British fare is not quite as spectacular, most find it "fabulous" enough and "impeccably" served, making this "perfect" for special occasions.

Riva [S] 23 | 15 | 19 | £35

169 Church Rd., SW13 (Hammersmith), 0181-748 0434

◪ Despite an "uninspired setting", there's "interesting", "proper" Northern Italian "food for foodies" at this "buzzy" Barnes eaterie owned by a "real character", Andreas Riva; though a few dissenters feel it's "slipped a notch" with cooking that's become "too fussy", it's still "very much a local favourite" and "crowded" most evenings.

RIVER CAFE [S] 25 | 20 | 20 | £45

Thames Wharf, Rainville Rd., W6 (Hammersmith), 0171-381 8824

◪ Devotees dub this "hard-to-find" Hammersmith Italian a "foodies' paradise" thanks to "robust", "creative" Modern Italian cooking that's "stunningly simple" but "unbelievably yummy"; foes feel it's "hyped beyond belief" ("the emperor's new foods") and "wildly overpriced", but since it's "still a hard booking to secure" they're outvoted; P.S. local regulations that "force you out" by 11 PM are lamented.

RK Stanley's ◐ 17 | 16 | 17 | £21

6 Little Portland St., W1 (Oxford Circus), 0171-462 0099

■ "Sausages meet upmarket diner" at this "busy", "down-to-earth" Oxford Circus sausage specialist with an "American-style setting" and "unpretentious", "good value" British "comfort food" "with a twist", served by "friendly" staff and accompanied by a huge selection of beers.

Rock Garden ◐ [S] 13 | 13 | 11 | £19

4 The Piazza, WC2 (Covent Garden), 0171-836 4052

◪ Whilst defenders say this Covent Garden haunt provides "fabulous burgers" and other American fare, critics dub it a "tourist trap" that's "too expensive"; its location and late hours make it handy pre- or post-theatre, but with live music and a "noisy" crowd, it's "not for a quiet tête-à-tête."

Rodizio Rico ◖Ⓢ   16 | 9 | 14 | £21
111 Westbourne Grove, W2 (Bayswater/Notting Hill Gate),
0171-792 4035
■ "Meat lovers" stampede to this Bayswater Brazilian
where they can "eat as much barbecued meat" and
"delicious salads" as they like for a moderate set price;
whilst foes say it doesn't "compare with real churrascarias"
in South America, live music (Thursdays) and a "friendly",
"mainly Brazilian staff" help make it "enjoyable."

Room, The   – | – | – | M
103-107 Waterloo Rd., SE1 (Waterloo), 0171-928 5707
Opposite Waterloo Station is this spacious, informal Modern
British newcomer with a contemporary-gothic interior and
chef Peter Lloyd's gently ambitious menu that has echoes
of his old haunt, RSJ; the wine list has a global selection.

Room at the Halcyon Ⓢ   23 | 20 | 23 | £45
Halcyon Hotel, 129 Holland Park Ave., W11 (Holland Park),
0171-221 5411
■ "Quiet sophistication" characterises this "smart" Holland
Park hotel dining room offering "lovely" New French food,
"good wines" and "attentive service"; critics feel it has "no
soul" and is "expensive", but to most it's a "hidden jewel"
with a dash of star appeal: "marvellous meal, then slept in
Madonna's bed whilst Mick Jagger was in the bar below."

Rotisserie Jules ◖Ⓢ   17 | 8 | 15 | £15
133A Notting Hill Gate, W11 (Notting Hill Gate), 0171-221 3331
6 Bute St., SW7 (South Kensington), 0171-584 0600
338 King's Rd., SW3 (Sloane Sq.), 0171-351 0041
■ These spit roast specialists in Chelsea and Notting Hill are
"very French" and "just right when you want" some "great-
value", "finger-lickin' chicken"; whilst they're not very good-
looking, that matters little given "efficient" takeaway/delivery.

Roussillon   ▽ 24 | 20 | 22 | £44
16 St. Barnabas St., SW1 (Sloane Sq.), 0171-730 5550
■ "Shame it's tucked away" in a "quiet" Pimlico street
say those who know this "lovely surprise" where Alexis
Gauthier "shows great promise" with an "unorthodox",
"remarkably good" French menu, served in a "sedate"
setting with "attentive service"; "would be a top favourite
if I could afford it on a regular basis" sighs one fan.

Rowley's Ⓢ   17 | 17 | 17 | £29
136 Brompton Rd., SW3 (Knightsbridge), 0171-823 8019
113 Jermyn St., SW1 (Piccadilly Circus), 0171-930 2707 ◖
◪ According to fans, this "traditional" St. James's venue
(with a new Brompton Road sibling) is a "dependable" if "not
cheap" source of "simple" British fare (including "always
good" steak and chips) served by "charming staff", but others
find the cooking "uninspired" and feel it could do with "more
imagination"; either way it's a good "pre-theatre" option.

ROYAL CHINA [S] 25 | 14 | 15 | £26
13 Queensway, W2 (Queensway), 0171-221 2535
40 Baker St., W1 (Baker St./Bond St.), 0171-487 3123
68 Queen's Grove, NW8 (St. John's Wood), 0171-586 4280
■ At this popular Chinese group, "reservations are like traffic lights in Naples – just indicative of an intention", but "you never know who you'll meet" in the queue and once seated there's "unbeatable dim sum" and other "delicious" fare served by "harried" staff amidst "camp disco decor"; fans say "you won't get closer to Hong Kong in London."

RSJ 21 | 16 | 18 | £33
13A Coin St., SE1 (Waterloo), 0171-928 4554
■ "Why can't there be more of these?" ask admirers of this "surprisingly good" South Bank "jewel" offering "solid" Modern British fare "at good prices" plus "professional service" and an "excellent" wine list; though sometimes "forgotten" ("ideal for illicit meetings"), it's "handy" if bound for a nearby show and worth it "with or without a visit to the theatre"; N.B. there's a new cafe offshoot a few doors away.

Rudland & Stubbs 20 | 15 | 18 | £27
35-37 Greenhill Rents, Cowcross St., EC1 (Farringdon), 0171-253 0148
◪ "The genuine article" when it comes to "great fish, simply cooked" to order say advocates of this tiled, traditional Smithfield seafooder; a few find the ambience "a bit middle-aged" and prices "too high", but it's good "for a City lunch", though some say "go with a regular" for the best service.

RULES ◐ [S] 20 | 22 | 19 | £36
35 Maiden Ln., WC2 (Covent Garden), 0171-836 5314
■ "It's not a happening place" and looking a bit "worn", but this "unique", "crowded" Covent Garden "bastion of British cuisine" (circa 1798) has "lots of atmosphere" plus "quintessential" "comfort food extraordinaire" including "fantastic game"; critics claim it's "a shadow of its former self" and "needs a shake-up", but more agree "if you want to wallow in old English" tastes and ambience, Rules "rules!"

Saffron ◐ [S] – | – | – | E
306B Fulham Rd., SW10 (Fulham Broadway), 0171-565 8183
Admirers say "brilliant Indian food" can be found at this neat, promising yearling midway down Fulham Road, offering accessible multiregional dishes plus several unusual, modern creations that are all reasonably priced given the quality; "great service" enhances the experience.

Saga [S] – | – | – | E
43 South Molton St., W1 (Bond St.), 0171-408 2236
The decor isn't noteworthy, but the creative sushi is at this Japanese near Bond Street with a ground-floor sushi bar and downstairs restaurant; though not widely known, it draws a Japanese clientele with its good quality and service.

Saigon ◗ ▽ 20 | 14 | 16 | £26
45 Frith St., W1 (Leicester Sq./Piccadilly Circus), 0171-437 7109
■ "Not flash, but a winner", this Soho Vietnamese offers "authentic" (some even call it "fantastic") fare in a simple but "cute" setting; budget-minded diners find it "expensive for what it is", but fans don't mind paying a bit more for "genuinely Vietnamese" cooking of a high calibre.

Saigon Thuy 🅂 – | – | – | M
189 Garratt Ln., SW18 (Earlsfield B.R./East Putney), 0181-871 9464
Not many surveyors know this dinner-only Wandsworth Vietnamese yearling, but those who have visited send back reports of "good food" served in a "basic" setting; moderate prices and a garden boost its appeal.

Saigon Times ▽ 17 | 13 | 16 | £22
17-20 Leadenhall Market, EC3 (Bank/Monument), 0171-621 0022
■ An "interesting mix of French and Oriental" flavours characterises the cooking at this weekday-only Franco-Vietnamese brasserie in the centre of Leadenhall Market; "bustling at lunchtime", it can be "empty in the evenings", which may be due to its early closing time (last orders 9 PM).

Saint Bar & Restaurant 15 | 17 | 12 | £29
8 Great Newport St., WC2 (Leicester Sq.), 0171-240 1551
◪ Most agree that the appeal of this "sleek" Soho bar/restaurant is due more to its "atmosphere" and "nightlife" than to its Modern British–Pacific Rim fare, though some report "surprisingly" good food for such a "trendy" venue; however, critics who complain of a less-than-saintly door policy ask "who could be bothered to fight their way in?"

Sale e Pepe 19 | 16 | 18 | £34
9-15 Pavilion Rd., SW1 (Knightsbridge), 0171-235 0098
◪ "As long as you don't mind the noise" and "crowded" tables, fans say "you'll come away feeling a lot better" after a visit to this Knightsbridge Italian where the "lively", "shouting staff" will "keep you laughing" whilst serving "excellent" food; those put off by the "frantic atmosphere" call it a "madhouse" and suggest "someone should tell them it's no longer the '70s."

Salloos ◗ 23 | 14 | 19 | £38
62 Kinnerton St., SW1 (Hyde Park Corner/Knightsbridge), 0171-235 4444
■ "Genuine Pakistani" cooking featuring "top-quality" ingredients earns "loyal customers" for this family-run spot in a quiet Knightsbridge mews; "authoritarian but caring" servers will "guide you through your order", and though it's "pricey", that doesn't dampen the ardour of enthusiasts: "when I'm abroad I miss two things: my dogs, and Salloos' food."

Salsa! 11 | 14 | 13 | £19
96 Charing Cross Rd., WC2 (Leicester Sq./
Tottenham Court Rd.), 0171-379 3277
■ It's a "party place – who remembers the food?" typifies
reaction to this "very passionate" Leicester Square salsa
restaurant, where the "vibes, music", "interesting cocktails"
and dancing create more sparks than the Latin cooking; not
surprisingly, it gets "very noisy", but that's part of the "fun."

Salt House S – | – | – | M
63 Abbey Rd., NW8 (St. John's Wood), 0171-328 6626
An offshoot of The Chiswick, this ebullient, spacious pub
conversion offers a reasonably priced, daily-changing
Modern British menu in an airy, pleasant space; it's a
welcome addition to St. John's Wood that's popular as a
drop-in bar as well as a local eatery.

Sambuca 19 | 17 | 21 | £33
62 Lower Sloane St., SW3 (Sloane Sq.), 0171-730 6571
■ Those who've visited this Italian since it moved to Lower
Sloane Street say the "new location is lovely, light and airy"
and the cooking is "nothing pretentious" but "consistently
good"; add a "warm welcome" and "accommodating"
service and you have a fine "neighbourhood restaurant"
that's "perfect for business" too.

Sandrini ● S 16 | 15 | 16 | £35
260 Brompton Rd., SW3 (South Kensington), 0171-584 1724
◪ To admirers, this Brompton Cross Italian is a "graciously
hosted" place that "seems to improve each visit", offering
"consistently good food" and "very accommodating"
service; critics sing a different tune ("outrun its course",
"not good value"), but perhaps they haven't visited often
enough: "once you're a regular, it's great."

San Lorenzo ● ⌿ 19 | 19 | 18 | £42
22 Beauchamp Pl., SW3 (Knightsbridge/South Kensington),
0171-584 1074
◪ It can be "very good in all respects", but "unless you're
a star" or part of "the in-crowd" you may encounter "serious
attitude" at this "see and be seen" Italian near Harrods; it's
"still a favourite after 33 years" for regulars who say it's
fun "watching the famous go by", but that doesn't sway
those who knock "ordinary food at ridiculous prices."

San Lorenzo Fuoriporta S ▽ 17 | 18 | 19 | £38
3A Worple Mews, SW19 (Wimbledon), 0181-946 8463
◪ The Italian fare served at this San Lorenzo offshoot in
Wimbledon Village may not generate much excitement
("dated menu", "expensive for what it is"), but it's "reliable"
and some consider this "the only decent restaurant in
SW19", with courtyard dining that's "a pleasure in summer."

San Martino ◐[S] 14 | 11 | 14 | £34
101-105 Walton St., SW3 (Knightsbridge/South Kensington), 0171-589 1356
◪ "Pretty good but not excellent" seems to be the verdict on this bright Chelsea Italian stalwart of 29 years; if some feel it "doesn't compare" with top-tier Italians, you certainly "won't stay hungy", though prices that are on the high side prompt some to call it "lacking value."

Santa Fe [S] – | – | – | E
75 Upper St., N1 (Angel), 0171-288 2288
This stylish Islington newcomer serves quality American Southwestern food prepared by Rocky Durham, who hails from the eponymous capital of New Mexico; expect a wait in the large bar area before being seated.

Santini ◐[S] 20 | 18 | 18 | £47
29 Ebury St., SW1 (Victoria), 0171-730 4094
◪ Supporters call this "classy" Italian near Victoria Station "expensive but excellent", whilst detractors balk at paying "an extraordinary price" for "ordinary" fare; waiters who "hover too close too often" also take a few knocks, but solid ratings across the board suggest that most are satisfied, though given the cost, it may be best for a "business" meal.

SARASTRO ◐[S] 13 | 25 | 17 | £26
126 Drury Ln., WC2 (Covent Garden/Holborn), 0171-836 0101
■ "A theatrical experience, but you wouldn't ask for a curtain call for the food" sums up reaction to this Theatreland Mediterranean where "first-time guests are always knocked out" by the "surreal", "theatrical bordello" decor, if not by the "rather bland" cooking; still, service is "attentive" and "the ambience alone is worth it" – "great for a crazy 'group evening' with low food expectations."

Sarkhel's Indian Cuisine [S] – | – | – | M
199 Replingham Rd., SW1 (Southfields), 0181-870 1483
Whilst the "decor is nothing to write home about" at this unpretentious Southfields Indian, chef-owner Udit Sarkhel (ex Bombay Brasserie) is impressing observers with "exquisite" regional food ("best I've ever had" raves one convert) and "charming" service; an expansion is planned.

Sartoria ◐[S] 19 | 20 | 18 | £42
20 Savile Row, W1 (Piccadilly Circus), 0171-534 7000
■ "Finally, a Conran you can converse in", and by most accounts you can also eat quite well in Terence Conran's "very grown-up", "smart and intimate" Modern Italian just off Regent Street, where "excellent food" is served in a "clean-lined" space with "clever" "sartorial touches"; faultfinders cite "mediocre service" and "overpriced wines", but fans have the vote sewn up.

Satsuma 🅂   19 | 17 | 16 | £17
56 Wardour St., W1 (Leicester Sq./Piccadilly Circus),
0171-437 8338
■ "Convivial bench seating" plus "light, simple, enjoyable Japanese food" (including "good sushi" and bento boxes) is a formula that's winning fans for this Soho newcomer; it's "not gourmet", but it is "a pleasant experience" and "hot competition" in the sushi/noodle bar field, with the benefit of "less queuing" ("not all the tourists have heard about it").

Sauce BarOrganicDiner 🅂   _ | _ | _ | M
214 Camden High St., NW1 (Camden Town),
0171-482 0777
It's a "great idea" – a colourful, all-day Camden diner serving an "appetising" menu of organic fare ranging from burgers, salads and sandwiches to the likes of seared oak-smoked salmon – but preliminary reports suggest that the results can be uneven; however, it's early days so the jury is still out.

Savoy Grill ◑   23 | 22 | 23 | £49
Savoy Hotel, The Strand, WC2 (Covent Garden/Embankment),
0171-836 4343
■ The "canteen of editors and tycoons", this "classic" hotel dining room on the Strand offers "much better cooking than many realise" (Traditional British plus Classic French) in an "unhurried" ambience with "sterling service"; it's "a bit of an old gentleman's club" and hardly cheap, but the pre-theatre menu is "a bargain" and it's hard to top for a taste of "old-world London."

Savoy River Restaurant ◑🅂   22 | 23 | 23 | £49
Savoy Hotel, The Strand, WC2 (Covent Garden/Embankment),
0171-836 4343
◪ "If you want to impress, get a window seat" and watch the Thames whilst basking in the "real glamour and sense of occasion" at this "classy" Strand hotel dining room; if some find the International fare "unmemorable" and claim service is "slipping", most feel the "superb food" is on a par with the "sumptuous" decor and "courteous" staff, making it "perfect for special occasions"; there's also a "decadent" breakfast and evening dancing.

Scalini ◑🅂   21 | 16 | 19 | £39
1-3 Walton St., SW3 (Knightsbridge/South Kensington),
0171-225 2301
■ It's "as noisy as ever" – "annoyingly so" for some, but regulars feel the "buzzy", "fun" atmosphere "always makes for a good feeling" and adds to the enjoyment of the "excellent" cooking at this "welcoming" Chelsea Italian; a few see "nothing special about the food", but given that it's "hard to get a table" they're clearly in the minority.

Scotts [S] 20 | 20 | 18 | £41

18-20 Mount St., W1 (Bond St./Green Park), 0171-629 5248

■ Established in 1851 and still considered "one of the best fish restaurants in London", this Mayfair veteran offers "fresh" fare ("must have swum here this morning") in a "luxurious" setting with the occasional famous face in the crowd (allowing for "a bit of celebrity-ignoring"); the "excellent, underused bar" downstairs has affordable set price menus plus live music.

Seafresh Fish Restaurant ▽ 14 | 11 | 15 | £19

80-81 Wilton Rd., SW1 (Victoria), 0171-828 0747

■ "Good fish" and "no pretensions" are the hallmarks of this fish and chips shop behind Victoria Station; it's not much to look at and quibblers call it "overrated", but most consider it "excellent" for what it is, with speedy service.

Searcy's at the Barbican [S] 18 | 14 | 17 | £30

Barbican Ctr., Silk St., EC2 (Barbican/Moorgate), 0171-588 3008

■ The atmosphere "could be more interesting", but the Modern British fare "continues to surprise by being so good" say admirers of this eaterie in the Barbican Centre; it's "handy" for "culture vultures" bound for a concert and has "good views" and service; in sum, a "nice" City place.

Seashell [S] 17 | 9 | 13 | £18

49-51 Lisson Grove, NW1 (Marylebone), 0171-724 1063

■ Decor is not a strong point, but that doesn't bother fans who flock to this Marylebone venue for "superior fish and chips" served by "friendly", "gossipy" waitresses who "add to the ambience"; a few critics claim it's "resting on its laurels" and "rather pricey", but "foreign visitors love it", as do the locals, particularly as it's "reliable" for takeaways.

755 ◐ [S] 24 | 16 | 23 | £35

755 Fulham Rd., SW6 (Parsons Green), 0171-371 0755

■ This "tiny" eaterie is "worth the trip down Fulham Road" for New French cooking that's "fabulous" if a bit "too rich" for certain palates; the ambience is "a little sedate" but service is "friendly" and the set price menus are "excellent value" – "now everyone is going to know" laments one regular who would have preferred to keep this "out-of-the-way gem" a secret.

Shepherd's 21 | 19 | 20 | £37

Marsham Ct., Marsham St., SW1 (Pimlico/St. James's Park), 0171-834 9552

■ An "upper-class", "business-oriented" Westminster venue offering "excellent" Traditional British fare to a crowd including "MPs and government employees"; it's a "relaxing" place with "well laid-out" tables and "energetic" service that "makes everyone feel like a regular."

Shimla Pinks
– – – **E**

7-8 Bishopsgate Church Yard, EC2 (Liverpool St.), 0171-628 7888
Intriguingly housed in former Turkish baths near Liverpool
Street, this sibling to Pacific Oriental serves ambitious
Northern Indian fare including some novel dishes, and if the
cooking doesn't always hit the bull's-eye, it makes amends
with attractive, classy-looking decor and polished service.

Shoeless Joe's
11 **12** **12** **£24**

Temple Pl., The Embankment, W1 (Temple), 0171-240 7865 **S**
555 King's Rd., SW6 (Fulham Broadway), 0171-534 0250
■ "For a sports bar, it's good" is the call on this Fulham
eaterie with a new Temple Place sibling; both offer games
on the telly and an Eclectic menu (overseen by consulting
chef John Burton-Race) that some find "surprisingly" tasty,
but which others mostly look to "for a snack."

Shogun **S**
22 **17** **17** **£41**

Britannia Hotel, Adam's Row, W1 (Bond St.), 0171-493 1255
■ "Wonderful sushi" and other "excellent" Japanese fare
served in a "cool setting" in the basement of a Mayfair hotel
makes this restaurant a "lovely" if rather pricey experience;
special praise goes to the "superb" sushi master: "to watch
him is like watching an artist", so "sit at the bar" and enjoy.

Shoreditch Electricity Showrooms **S**
▽ **14** **18** **16** **£18**

39A Hoxton Sq., N1 (Old St.), 0171-739 6934
☑ "Too trendy to be comfy", this newcomer in Hoxton
Square nevertheless attracts modish young locals with its
very '90s, minimalist open plan setting in a former electricity
showroom and its moderately priced Eclectic menu with
Mediterranean leanings; if you're looking for "hip" after-
work gatherings, it can definitely fit the bill.

Signor Sassi ❶
20 **16** **19** **£33**

14 Knightsbridge Green, SW1 (Knightsbridge), 0171-584 2277
■ It can seem like the "loudest restaurant in town" and the
waiters strike some as "quite mad", but this lively, "ever-
dependable" Knightsbridge Italian pleases most with its
"great ambience", "delicious" (if rather "old-fashioned")
food and "excellent hospitality"; it's a bit "expensive" though.

Signor Zilli Restaurant
19 **15** **17** **£30**

41 Dean St., W1 (Leicester Sq./Tottenham Court Rd.),
0171-734 3924
☑ Regulars, including many media-world types, "keep going
back" to this "small", "old-fashioned" Soho Italian for its
"good food, good value and nice reception", as well as for
the "very entertaining" presence of chef/owner/TV star
Aldo Zilli – he "makes this place a hit"; still, a few critics
find the cooking and service "wanting" and suggest that
"the TV appearances may have gone to his head."

Silks & Spice S
19 | 15 | 15 | £21

95 Chiswick High Rd., W4 (Turnham Green), 0181-995 7991
23 Foley St., W1 (Oxford Circus), 0171-636 2718
28 Chalk Farm Rd., NW1 (Chalk Farm), 0171-267 5751

◪ A "good range of Thai dishes" (Malaysian too), "friendly" staff and "better decor than at your usual Thai restaurant" add up to "a pleasurable experience" according to most who've visited this growing chain; dissenters find the food "very average" and cite "cramped" conditions, but they're outvoted by those who consider it a "superb cheapie."

Simply Nico S
20 | 15 | 17 | £37

48A Rochester Row, SW1 (St. James's Park/Victoria),
0171-630 8061
Simply Nico Barbican S
7 Goswell Rd., EC1 (Barbican), 0171-336 7677
Simply Nico London Bridge S
10 London Bridge St., SE1 (London Bridge), 0171-407 4536

◪ "Simply delicious" say admirers of this "smart" bistro group that can produce "excellent" French food; whilst the praise isn't unanimous ("could have been better", "starting to get quite expensive"), ratings side with those who "always have a good meal here."

Simpson's in The Strand S
17 | 19 | 19 | £36

100 The Strand, WC2 (Charing Cross), 0171-836 9112

◪ "Old England preserved" describes this vintage 1828 Strand veteran where the British food, decor and service can all be summed up in one word: "traditional"; critics would replace that word with "tired", but the post-*Survey* completion of a £2 million revamp (and the introduction of a more contemporary menu in the upstairs dining room) may change their minds; in any case, "tourists" love it and breakfast is "unbeatable."

Simpsons Tavern
▽ 17 | 14 | 17 | £21

Ball Ct., 38 Cornhill, EC3 (Bank), 0171-626 9985

■ An "excellent chophouse for City boys", this lunch-only weekday spot serves "delicious" "stockbroker's fare" (i.e. a Traditional British menu featuring charcoal-grilled dishes) in an ambience that's "wonderful in its own way"; since it's been around in some guise since 1759, it must fill a need.

Singapore Garden S
21 | 12 | 16 | £25

83 Fairfax Rd., NW6 (Swiss Cottage), 0171-328 5314
154-156 Gloucester Pl., NW1 (Baker St.), 0171-723 8233

■ "Excellent as a local restaurant" say habitués of this Southeast Asian duo (in Swiss Cottage and in a Marylebone basement) serving "above-average" Chinese, Malaysian and Singaporean fare that's "authentic, well prepared and well presented", not to mention "good value"; they can be "a bit crowded and noisy", but the cooking's "very reliable."

Singapura 18 15 17 £27

1-2 Limeburner Ln., EC4 (Blackfriars/St. Paul's), 0171-329 1133
78-79 Leadenhall St., EC3 (Aldgate/Tower Hill), 0171-929 0089

◪ "Reasonably authentic renditions" of Southeast Asian fare and "lovely" service earn mostly approval for these City Southeast Asians, and though a few find them "average" and say the "minimalist decor detracts" from the experience, most would agree they're "fine" options "in a location where one is not spoilt for choice"; Leadenhall is lunch only.

Smokey Joe's Diner [S]🚭 ▽ 14 10 14 £16

131 Wandsworth High St., SW18 (East Putney), 0181-871 1785

◪ If you're in the mood for something different, check out this tiny, 15-seat Wandsworth Caribbean cafe; it doesn't generate much comment ("some improvement needed" suggests one), but modest prices make it a low-risk pick.

Smollensky's on the Strand ◐[S] 14 14 15 £25

105 The Strand, WC2 (Charing Cross/Covent Garden), 0171-497 2101

◪ This all-day American eaterie on the Strand may be "nothing special" and "a bit dated", but it's a "reasonable postwork burger and steak joint" and "ideal for kids on Sunday", offering "good food", "good value" and a "fun" atmosphere, with music and dancing.

Snows on the Green [S] 20 15 17 £28

166 Shepherd's Bush Rd., W6 (Hammersmith), 0171-603 2142

■ "Very original" Modern British–Med cooking makes "every meal a surprise", and usually a pleasant one, according to admirers of this "reliable" Shepherd's Bush venue; "excellent value and staff" heighten its appeal, and regulars find the ambience particularly "cheerful" for lunch.

Sofra ◐[S] 18 12 15 £19

36 Tavistock St., WC2 (Covent Garden), 0171-240 3773
17 Charing Cross Rd., WC2 (Leicester Sq.), 0171-930 6090
18 Shepherd St., W1 (Green Park), 0171-493 3320
1 St. Christopher's Pl., W1 (Bond St.), 0171-224 4080

◪ "Yummy food, reasonable too, therefore too busy sometimes" pretty much sums up these Turkish cafes; the settings are "uninspired" and reports on service vary, but they're fine for a "cheap, fast, healthy" meal and the set menus are "bargains."

Soho House ◐[S] 20 19 17 £34

Private club; inquiries: 0171-734 5188

■ "Like being in a grand country house", this bohemian Soho private club has a "cosy, warm" atmosphere and a well-received Modern British menu enhanced by a "good wine list"; it's "great if you enjoy catching celebrities", but some say "beware the often very loud luvvies."

Soho Soho ☻   15 | 15 | 15 | £28
11-13 Frith St., W1 (Leicester Sq./Tottenham Court Rd.), 0171-494 3491
■ An "easygoing restaurant with easygoing food" is one way to describe this bi-level (restaurant upstairs, rotisserie/bar downstairs) Soho Mediterranean; whilst a few judge the food "average", most feel the "simple cooking works well" and the crowd provides a "great view of Soho life."

Soho Spice S   18 | 16 | 15 | £22
124-126 Wardour St., W1 (Leicester Sq./Tottenham Court Rd.), 0171-434 0808
◪ "Bold colours" set the scene for "modern Indian" food at this "hip" Soho eaterie with "funky" decor; fans call it a refreshing "break from the normal curry" house and appreciate its "excellent" set menus, but a few feel it emphasises "trendiness at the expense of taste."

Solly's S   19 | 14 | 14 | £22
148A Golders Green Rd., NW11 (Golders Green), 0181-455 2121
■ "Huge portions" of "good quality" kosher Middle Eastern fare (including "fabulous pita") explain why this Golders Green spot can be "madly busy", especially the downstairs takeaway; "value for money" is another draw, though some suggest you "order one portion for two to avoid waste."

Sonata S   – | – | – | M
36 Wigmore St., W1 (Bond St.), 0171-486 1111
Attached to Wigmore Hall is this low-key basement eaterie (owned by the Oceana team) that draws locals at lunch and concertgoers in the evenings with a straightforward Modern British menu, speedy service and moderate prices.

Sonny's S   22 | 18 | 18 | £33
94 Church Rd., SW13 (Hammersmith), 0181-748 0393
■ "Great decor, still great food" report surveyors who've visited this Barnes favourite since a major refurb gave it a lighter, more modern look; the Eclectic cooking is "consistently good" and service is "helpful", making it an "all-round winner" and "worth a trip to SW13."

Souk   – | – | – | M
27 Litchfield St., WC2 (Leicester Sq.), 0171-240 1796
This casual basement eaterie in Theatreland with Moroccan decor appeals to students and suits alike, serving midpriced North African cooking including dishes from Morocco, Tunisia and Algeria; service is laid-back but charming.

Sound Republic ☻S   15 | 17 | 16 | £21
Swiss Ctr., W1 (Leicester Sq./Piccadilly Circus), 0171-287 1010
■ "Music and eating" go hand in hand at this new Leicester Square theme eaterie comprising a Modern British–Thai restaurant and live music venue; whilst some find the food "lacking", it's drawing "twentysomethings" and the high decibels make it "great if you don't want to talk all night."

Soup Opera ⊭   20 | 15 | 18 | £7
2 Hanover St., W1 (Oxford Circus), 0171-629 0174
Cabot Pl., concourse level, E14 (Canary Wharf DLR),
0171-513 0880
■ "It sings to me" say supporters of this new chain of
gourmet soup bars, crediting it with a "lunchtime revolution"
thanks to its "wonderful creations and combinations of
flavours"; if some find the settings "stark" and the soups
"overpriced", others say "complimentary bread and fruit
make it a bargain" – "more please."

Soup Works   ∇ 19 | 10 | 16 | £7
29 Monmouth St., W2 (Leicester Sq.), 0171-240 7687 S
9 D'Arblay St., W1 (Oxford Circus/Tottenham Court Rd.),
0171-439 7687
56 Goodge St., W1 (Goodge St.), 0171-636 7438
■ A "souper idea", this chain offers "delicious soups in a
wide variety of innovative flavours"; some complain that it's
"rather expensive" ("this is soup, after all"), whilst others
call it a "good deal" for a "tasty, quick" meal.

Southeast W9 S   ∇ 21 | 12 | 17 | £22
239 Elgin Ave., W9 (Maida Vale), 0171-328 8883
■ The "best pad Thai this side of Bangkok" and other
"big servings" of "hot and spicy" Southeast Asian "fusion
cuisine" make this Maida Vale spot a "favourite"; for those
unimpressed by the minimalist decor, there's takeaway.

Spaghetti House   14 | 11 | 14 | £18
30 St. Martin's Ln., WC2 (Charing Cross), 0171-836 1626
24 Cranbourn St., WC2 (Covent Garden/Leicester Sq.),
0171-836 8168 S
Vernon Pl., 20 Sicilian Ave., WC1 (Holborn), 0171-405 5215
74-76 Duke St., W1 (Bond St.), 0171-629 6097 S
15 Goodge St., W1 (Goodge St.), 0171-636 6582 S
3 Bressenden Pl., SW1 (Victoria), 0171-834 5650
77 Knightsbridge, SW1 (Knightsbridge), 0171-235 8141 S
69-71 Haymarket, SW1 (Piccadilly Circus), 0171-839 3939 S
16 Jermyn St., SW1 (Piccadilly Circus), 0171-734 7334 S
☑ "Good, basic Italian food", "sensible prices" and a
"family atmosphere" make this chain a decent "pasta
standby" and "useful" for "a quick bite in a hurry"; though
critics dismiss it as a mere "hole-filler", more kindly folks
say it's "better than you'd think", if "at the right branch."

Spago ◑ S ⊭   18 | 12 | 14 | £20
6 Glendower Pl., SW7 (South Kensington), 0171-225 2407
Spago 2 ◑ S
45 Kensington High St., W8 (High St. Kensington), 0171-937 6471
■ "Great pizza", "super spaghetti" and other "authentic"
Italian food can be had at this dinner-only South Kensington
eaterie and its all-day Kensington High Street sibling;
but as ratings attest, the decor doesn't make much of an
impression and some complain of "slow", "sporadic service."

Spiga ◗🄢   18 | 15 | 14 | £26
84-86 Wardour St., W1 (Leicester Sq./Piccadilly Circus), 0171-734 3444

■ "Uncomplicated, delicious Italian food", highlighted by some of the "best pizza in town", is prepared with a "focus on good ingredients" at this Soho sister to Giorgio Locatelli's Spighetta; add "excellent value" and it's no surprise that this "modern" space can get "hectic" with "slow" service.

Spighetta 🄢   18 | 14 | 15 | £23
43 Blandford St., W1 (Baker St.), 0171-486 7340

■ "Serious food at lighthearted prices" is a winning formula for this bi-level Marylebone Italian from Giorgio Locatelli (Zafferano); though a few claim it's "not as good lately" and say it's a "shame about the acoustics", most have no complaints about the wood-oven pizzas and "first-rate pastas", recommending it for "really good casual" eating.

Sporting Page 🄢   16 | 16 | 13 | £17
6 Camera Pl., SW10 (Earl's Court), 0171-349 0455

■ "Simple, cheap pub grub", "good atmosphere" and the chance to watch sports on a big TV screen account for the popularity of this hangout off the King's Road; the "staff are mad but ace" and the place has the kind of comfortable feel that makes some wish it were their "local."

Sports Cafe 🄢   10 | 16 | 12 | £20
80 Haymarket, SW1 (Piccadilly Circus), 0171-839 8300

◪ "Let's face it, you go for the game, not the food", at this big Piccadilly sports-themed cafe, so beyond a nod to "good burgers", the American fare inspires little comment (one surveyor likens it to "eating cheap food in home stand at Leicester City"); the key factors appear to be "the TV", drinks and a "central" locale that draws "young office workers."

SQUARE, THE 🄢   26 | 22 | 24 | £55
6-10 Bruton St., W1 (Bond St./Green Park), 0171-495 7100

■ "A '90s restaurant that will soar into the millennium", this Mayfair New French this year breaks into the top 10 on the *Survey*'s Favourites and Food Ratings lists; diners praise Philip Howard for offering "superb" food in a "sophisticated setting that has buzz but is not deafening", with "well-selected" wines and service "that cares" as assets; if some find it a bit too "formal", more salute a "superbly professional" venue that's "worth the money – for a change."

Sri Siam ◗🄢   20 | 16 | 17 | £27
16 Old Compton St., W1 (Leicester Sq./Tottenham Court Rd.), 0171-434 3544

■ "Always lively, always tasty" say fans of this Soho Thai with "authentic", "dependable" food, "attentive service" and decor that's more "vibrant" than the norm; it's "very busy at lunch" and a "good pre-theatre place", though some find it "a bit pricey for what it is."

Sri Siam City
20 | 15 | 17 | £30

85 London Wall, EC2 (Liverpool St.), 0171-628 5772

■ "Smashing food" and a handy location for City workers keep this London Wall Thai "lively" (and sometimes "a bit noisy"); staff that some find "courteous" others term "bossy", but they get the job done: "fastest service" around.

Sri Thai
19 | 16 | 17 | £27

3 Queen Victoria St., EC4 (Bank), 0171-827 0202

■ Though not cheap, this City Thai is considered "good value" given the "high quality" of its cooking; "classic dishes" served in a setting that's "more subtle" than might be expected explain why fans "can never eat there enough."

Standard Tandoori ●S
17 | 7 | 15 | £17

21-23 Westbourne Grove, W2 (Bayswater/Queensway), 0171-727 4818

■ "You wouldn't go there for the decor", but even so this Queensway tandoori veteran is "always full" thanks to "well-executed" Punjabi dishes served by "courteous staff"; "better than the nearby competition" insist advocates.

Starbucks/Seattle Coffee Company
17 | 15 | 16 | £8

51-54 Long Acre, WC2 (Covent Garden), 0171-836 2100 S
25A Kensington High St., W8 (High St. Kensington), 0171-937 5446 S
34 Great Marlborough St., W1 (Oxford Circus), 0171-434 0778 S
111 Marylebone High St., W1 (Baker St.), 0171-486 9668 S
809 Fulham Rd., SW6 (Parsons Green), 0171-371 9491 S
39 Abbeville Rd., SW4 (Clapham South), 0181-673 4004 S
123A King's Rd., SW3 (Sloane Sq.), 0171-376 4678 S
Jerry's Home Store, 163 Fulham Rd., SW3 (South Kensington), 0171-823 7188 S
79 St. John's Wood High St., NW8 (St. John's Wood), 0171-586 4365 S
10-15 Queen St., EC4 (Mansion House), 0171-489 1229
365 Cabot Pl. East, E14 (Canary Wharf DLR), 0171-363 0040
Additional locations throughout London.

☑ Partisans hope the takeover by Starbucks "won't spoil" what they see as the "benchmark for that caffeine buzz"; "jolly good coffee" plus "good sandwiches" and pastries please most, but some turn bitter over "disorganised service", "annoying" queues and lack of seats, whilst others wonder "should coffee and a cake cost this much?"

Star of India ●S
21 | 17 | 16 | £31

154 Old Brompton Rd., SW5 (Gloucester Rd./South Kensington), 0171-373 2901

■ "A real star" say admirers of this South Ken Indian that's "different" – from its "innovative" food to its flamboyant owner (Reza Mahammad) and almost "Florentine" decor; there are grumbles about "slow service" and "expensive" prices, with some hinting it could do with "more care, less camp."

Stephen Bull 22 17 20 £36

12 Upper St. Martin's Ln., WC2 (Leicester Sq.), 0171-379 7811 ◐
5-7 Blandford St., W1 (Baker St./Bond St.), 0171-486 9696

■ "This man can do no wrong" enthuse acolytes of Stephen Bull, and if not everyone would go that far, most agree that his Marylebone and Theatreland duo provides "interesting", "consistently good" Modern British cooking featuring "novel, tasty combinations"; the decor strikes some as "a bit clinical" and prices are a bit high, but service is refreshingly "unstuffy" and most would gladly "go again."

Stephen Bull Smithfield 20 15 17 £31

71 St. John St., EC1 (Farringdon), 0171-490 1750

■ The atmosphere can be "rather cold", but the Modern British cooking "does not disappoint" according to fans of this Bull sibling in Smithfield; however, a few less impressed diners see it as "dependable, not spectacular."

Stepping Stone [S] 22 17 20 £32

123 Queenstown Rd., SW8 (Clapham Common), 0171-622 0555

■ According to enthusiasts, "some of the most inventive menus in London" can be found at this Battersea eaterie serving "very good" Modern British fare; it's a "casual", attractive place with "friendly owners" and "great value" – "if only there were more local restaurants of this quality."

Sticky Fingers ◐ [S] 15 14 15 £21

1 Phillimore Gardens, W8 (High St. Kensington), 0171-937 3657

◪ Aging Rolling Stones fans "feel young again" at Bill Wyman's American-style Kensington diner, and their kids "love" its "good burgers", "loud, lively" atmosphere and "really fun decor" featuring Stones memorabilia; however, those who get no satisfaction here rate it "average" and feel Bill should "stick to music."

St. John ◐ 20 17 19 £31

26 St. John St., EC1 (Farringdon), 0171-251 0848

■ "Great if you don't think about what you're eating", this "carnivore paradise" in an old Smithfield smokehouse has an "innovative" Modern British menu featuring "fabulous offal" – they do "wonderful things" with "strange bits of animals" ("pig intestines!"); the "white-walled" setting strikes some as "bleak", others as "groovy", but most simply focus on the "compelling, tasty" food; P.S. there's "wonderful bread" from the on-site bakery.

Stratford's [S] 20 16 17 £34

7 Stratford Rd., W8 (High St. Kensington), 0171-937 6388

■ "Deserves more patrons" is the word on this "excellent neighbourhood" place in a narrow Kensington townhouse, serving "delicious" Classic French seafood in a "quiet, quaint" ambience; it's "almost as good" as some of the high-profile fish houses and "far cheaper" – in sum, "a little gem."

Suan Neo
– | – | – | E

31 Broadgate Circle, EC2 (Liverpool St.), 0171-256 5045
This Southeast Asian in Broadgate Circle doesn't generate much surveyor response – perhaps a feeling that it's "overpriced" is to blame; still, the food is "interesting" and well presented in a glossy setting with staff in native dress.

SUGAR CLUB S
23 | 18 | 19 | £38

21 Warwick St., W1 (Piccadilly Circus), 0171-437 7776
■ Some say it's "even better" in its "slick" new bi-level home behind Regent Street whilst others claim it "lost the informal feel" it had, but this Eclectic still thrills most taste buds with its "innovative textures and flavours"; if some note that the dishes "don't always work" and feel it's "serving up a little too much attitude", more say it's "done London a big favour in introducing this interesting fusion-style cuisine."

Suntory S
23 | 18 | 22 | £53

72-73 St. James's St., SW1 (Green Park), 0171-409 0201
■ "Is this Japan?" – it's "expensive enough" to be, but in fact it's a "formal" Japanese veteran in St. James's serving "superb" food; though some feel it "needs redecoration", it's "nirvana" to devotees: "no other Japanese can beat it."

Sushi Wong S
▽ 16 | 13 | 16 | £26

38C-D Kensington Church St., W8 (High St. Kensington), 0171-937 5007
■ A "nice menu" including "good sushi" is available at this "quiet", bi-level Kensington spot; those who find the ground-floor sushi bar "too bright" prefer the less-modern-looking downstairs restaurant, and of course there's takeaway.

Sweetings ⊅
21 | 14 | 16 | £31

39 Queen Victoria St., EC4 (Mansion House), 0171-248 3062
■ This "blast from the past" (1889, to be precise) is a "traditional City lunch spot" offering "fish as it was meant to be – briskly served and eaten" in an "old-worldly" setting; expect "excellent food" and a "fun" ambience; no dinner.

Tajine
– | – | – | E

7A Dorset St., W1 (Baker St.), 0171-935 1545
Off to a promising start, this family-run newcomer near Baker Street strikes those who know it as a "North African delight", offering an interesting Moroccan menu that concentrates on tajines and couscous in a cosy, earthy environment; it's a tiny venue, so reservations are advisable.

Tamarind ●S
23 | 20 | 19 | £37

20 Queen St., W1 (Green Park), 0171-629 3561
■ At this chic Mayfair Indian, the "ambience and food are spectacular and the prices match" ("cheaper to fly to Delhi" grumble some), but admirers don't mind paying more for "superior" food from the northwest frontier; it's a "favourite for business dinners" and regulars say "let the waiters choose – you won't be disappointed."

Tandoori Lane ◑Ⓢ ▽ 19 13 17 £21
131A Minster Rd., SW6 (Fulham Broadway/Parsons Green), 0171-371 0440
■ The decor may be "aging" but the ambience is "cosy" and there's "lovely grub" at this Fulham Indian "old favourite"; "no gloppy curries" here, just "delicious", "good quality" fare in a "casual environment."

Tandoori of Chelsea ◑Ⓢ ▽ 19 15 21 £27
153 Fulham Rd., SW3 (South Kensington), 0171-589 7617
■ They "always remember patrons" at this "very pleasant" Chelsea Indian where "excellent service" enhances the food (special kudos for the "delicious rice"); a few feel the menu could use some "added pizazz", but most have no complaints about this "underrated" old reliable that's been around since 1964.

Tate Gallery Restaurant Ⓢ 17 19 16 £26
Tate Gallery, Millbank, SW1 (Pimlico), 0171-887 8825
■ "A great way to spend the day": visit the Tate, "then have lunch" in its "beautiful" basement dining room, where patrons can feast their eyes on a "lovely" Rex Whistler mural while enjoying "surprisingly good" Modern British fare and what some call the "best value wine list in town" in a "very chic, art world" ambience; no dinner.

Tatsuso 23 16 21 £48
32 Broadgate Circle, EC2 (Liverpool St.), 0171-638 5863
■ "If money is no object or the boss is paying" (conditions which seem to apply to "the majority of the clientele"), this bi-level Broadgate Japanese can provide a "mind-blowing" meal, whether downstairs for some of the "best sushi in town" or upstairs in the teppanyaki room; so bring your "corporate card" and enjoy an "outstanding" meal.

Tea Rooms des Artistes ◑Ⓢ 13 18 13 £20
697 Wandsworth Rd., SW8 (Clapham Common), 0171-652 6526
☑ Though some say it's "good for vegetarians" (there's seafood as well), this offbeat Clapham Eclectic set in a converted 16th-century barn is more bar than restaurant and popular as a "cool, laid-back" hangout with DJ music, outdoor seating and late hours.

Teatro ◑ 18 17 17 £38
93-107 Shaftesbury Ave., W1 (Leicester Sq.), 0171-494 3040
☑ Comprising a big, bright restaurant and an adjoining members bar, this Soho venture from Lee Chapman and Lesley Ash strikes supporters as "a great-looking addition", offering "surprisingly fine" New French fare in a setting whose "odd shape doesn't detract from a good experience"; however, it's "expensive" and some find it "dull."

TECA   20 | 14 | 16 | £38
54 Brooks Mews, W1 (Bond St.), 0171-495 4774
◼ Though the "accomplished cooking" at this Modern Italian in a discreet Mayfair mews earns solid ratings, reaction to the overall package is mixed: whilst boosters call it "underappreciated" and "enjoyable", others label it "too expensive for small portions" served in a "stripped-down", "high-teca" setting; an extensive Italian wine list and alfresco seating are points in its favour.

10   ▽ 14 | 10 | 13 | £34
10 Cutlers Gardens Arcade, Devonshire Sq., EC2 (Liverpool St.), 0171-283 7888
◼ The ratings are modest, but those who know this big, muraled City basement eaterie created by financier Terry Pullen say it's "perfect for business", with "well-spaced tables" and a Modern British menu to "please any taste"; if looking for quiet, note that it can be "empty" at dinner.

Tentazioni   23 | 14 | 22 | £35
Lloyd's Wharf, 2 Mill St., SE1 (London Bridge/Tower Hill), 0171-237 1100
◼ "Inventive" Modern Italian cooking yielding "beautiful food" makes this Italian next to Butlers Wharf a "real star" in the eyes of admirers; it's somewhat pricey but delivers "quality" for the money, with a "very good wine list", "nice service" and "intimate surroundings" adding to the value.

Tenth, The   ▽ 18 | 23 | 20 | £40
Royal Garden Hotel, 2-24 Kensington High St., W8 (High St. Kensington), 0171-361 1910
◼ "Breathtaking views" of Kensington Gardens can be enjoyed from this Eclectic dining room atop a Kensington hotel, and if not everyone feels that it has the "food to match" the vista, most find it all-round "impressive"; one quibble: some say you "never lose that hotel restaurant feeling."

Terrace, The 🆂   21 | 20 | 20 | £35
33C Holland St., W8 (High St. Kensington), 0171-937 3224
◼ It may be "small" in size, but the Modern British food is "big" in flavour and appeal at this "cosy", "charming" hideaway in Kensington; "good wines", efficient service and, true to the name, a pleasant terrace magnify its appeal: "if they can squeeze you in, you'll have fun."

Terrace, The 🆂   – | – | – | E
Le Meridien Piccadilly, 21 Piccadilly, W1 (Piccadilly Circus), 0171-465 1642
This hotel conservatory overlooking Piccadilly has benefited from a major refurb and the arrival of a respected consultant chef, Parisian Michel Rostang, who oversees a Classic French menu plus more innovative dishes; despite some pricey wines, it's cheaper than Marco Pierre White's Oak Room downstairs – but not by much.

Terraza S ▽ 16 17 14 £23
33 High St., Wimbledon Village, SW19 (Wimbledon),
0181-946 1920
4-5 King St., Richmond (Richmond), 0181-940 4362
■ They may not set the world on fire, but these Richmond and Wimbledon Mediterraneans are "very pleasant" options "when you can't be bothered" to cook, offering "consistently good" food, "friendly" service and "great atmosphere", not to mention moderate prices; there's occasional jazz too.

Texas Embassy Cantina ● S 14 16 14 £21
1 Cockspur St., SW14 (Charing Cross/Piccadilly Circus),
0171-925 0077
☑ "Sometimes you just need a Tex-Mex fix", and in those moments this "huge", "loud" Trafalgar Square cantina can do the job, even if critics claim the meal peaks with the "tortilla chips"; service is "hit-and-miss", but the decor is "cute" and there's "good booze" to keep things "lively."

Texas Lone Star ● S 13 13 14 £18
50-54 Turnham Green Terrace, W4 (Turnham Green),
0181-747 0001
154 Gloucester Rd., SW7 (Gloucester Rd.), 0171-370 5625
☑ Though these Tex-Mexers can produce "good ribs", burgers and the like, critics say they're "inconsistent" and "beginning to look tired"; still, portions are "huge" and some tout them for a "Sunday lunch with children."

T.G.I. Friday's ● S 12 13 15 £20
6 Bedford St., WC2 (Charing Cross/Covent Garden),
0171-379 0585
96-98 Bishop's Bridge Rd., W2 (Bayswater), 0171-229 8600
25-29 Coventry St., W1 (Leicester Sq./Piccadilly Circus),
0171-839 6262
☑ "Loyal to its core constituencies", i.e. "families" and "twentysomethings", this chain offers "no-surprises" American fare, "generous cocktails" and "bubbly" if sometimes "inefficient" service; however, critics call it "nothing special", citing "noise and indigestion."

Thai Kitchen ▽ 19 12 16 £20
108 Chepstow Rd., W2 (Westbourne Park), 0171-221 9984
■ The service is "utilitarian", ditto the decor, but "you don't go" to this dinner-only Thai near Queensway looking for luxury, just "tasty", affordable food; if some suggest the fare has been "adjusted to Western tastes", most don't mind.

Thai on the River S 21 18 18 £32
Chelsea Wharf, 15 Lots Rd., SW10
(Fulham Broadway/Sloane Sq.), 0171-351 1151
■ Given the "genuinely good" fare at this Thai near Chelsea Harbour, the "lovely setting on the river" is just "a bonus"; it's "pricey" and some cite "small portions" and service lapses, but "get a table with a view" and faults are forgotten.

Thierry's 🅂   19 | 16 | 18 | £31
342 King's Rd., SW3 (Sloane Sq.), 0171-352 3365
■ This Chelsea bistro serves "reliable" French fare "without pretension" in a setting that's "a bit crowded" but "elegant" (or, if you're in the right mood, "romantic"); a "welcoming" attitude is another reason why it's "still a favourite local."

Tiger Lil's ◐🅂   14 | 12 | 13 | £18
500 King's Rd., SW10 (Fulham Broadway/Sloane Sq.), 0171-376 5003
16A Southside Clapham Common, SW4 (Clapham Common), 0171-720 5433
270 Upper St., N1 (Highbury & Islington), 0171-226 1118
☑ "Excellent for gluttons, less so for gourmets" is how some rate these "do-it-yourself" Asians where diners "help themselves" to ingredients (all you can eat for a set price) then watch chefs cook the food "in front of you"; whilst fans call it a "refreshing concept", critics say the "novelty wears off quickly" and ask "why go out to queue?"

Titanic ◐🅂   14 | 17 | 13 | £33
81 Brewer St., W1 (Piccadilly Circus), 0171-437 1912
☑ When Marco Pierre White and team named this gigantic Piccadilly newcomer, they were asking for trouble, and critics take the bait: "most appropriately named restaurant in London", "titanic waste of time and money"; defenders say the Eclectic food, "great atmosphere" and hopping central bar are "good enough" to keep it "afloat", but foes blast it as "big, loud and boring", "full of wanna-bes" "waiting for somebody famous" to turn up.

Toast 🅂   – | – | – | E
50 Hampstead High St., NW3 (Hampstead), 0171-431 2244
A glossy newcomer above Hampstead tube station featuring a long, members-only bar/dining area with a leather-clad wall and a clean-looking restaurant (open to all comers) with huge windows and a pricey, French-accented Modern European menu that changes fortnightly.

Toff's   ▽ 20 | 4 | 12 | £13
38 Muswell Hill Broadway, N10 (Highgate), 0181-883 8656
☑ "Muswell Hill's sole claim to gastronomic fame" is this purveyor of fish-based fare (fish and chips, soups, etc.) that fans deem "excellent"; doubters label it "good not great" but ratings prove most are content, at least with the cooking – hence the takeaway service has a following.

Tokyo Diner ◐🅂   16 | 12 | 15 | £17
2 Newport Pl., WC2 (Leicester Sq.), 0171-287 8777
■ "Good, simple, inexpensive and sincere" sums up this Chinatown Japanese; though not much to look at and "rather cramped", it's "always reliable" and can provide a "very good introduction to sushi" for first-timers.

Tom's Delicatessen S   21 | 13 | 14 | £14

226 Westbourne Grove, W11 (Notting Hill Gate), 0171-221 8818

■ "Excellent, healthy food" has made Tom Conran's Notting Hill deli/cafe "a refreshing addition to London's dining scene"; its "unusual sandwiches, salads" and other Eclectic offerings are perfect for "gourmet-style informal" eating, but it's "too small" and some find it "hard work eating somewhere so cool"; N.B. it's now open evenings.

Tootsies S   15 | 11 | 14 | £17

120 Holland Park Ave., W11 (Holland Park), 0171-229 8567
148 Chiswick High Rd., W4 (Turnham Green), 0181-747 1869 ◗
35 James St., W1 (Bond St.), 0171-486 1611
48 High St., SW19 (Wimbledon), 0181-946 4135
147 Church Rd., SW13 (Hammersmith), 0181-748 3630
107 Old Brompton Rd., SW7 (South Kensington), 0171-581 8942
177 New King's Rd., SW6 (Parsons Green), 0171-736 4023 ◗
196-198 Haverstock Hill, NW3 (Belsize Park), 0171-431 3812 ◗
110 Kew Rd., Richmond (Kew Gardens/Richmond), 0181-948 4343 ◗

■ There may be "nothing distinctive" about this "cheerful" American-style chain, but it satisfies most surveyors with its "good burgers" and other "simple fare", not to mention its "solid value" and "helpful", "incredibly child-friendly" service; it's a "comfortable place for a single" diner and "perfect for young families" with kids.

Toto's ◗S   22 | 20 | 20 | £40

Walton House, Walton St., SW3 (Knightsbridge/ South Kensington), 0171-589 2062

■ "Mysteriously neglected" say devotees of this "lovely-looking" Italian in a "fine old townhouse" in Chelsea, praising its "seriously excellent" cooking, "charming garden" and "friendly, very welcoming" atmosphere; "expensive" prices may partially explain the mystery, but they don't deter well-heeled admirers.

Townhouse Brasserie ◗S   ▽ 17 | 15 | 15 | £22

24 Coptic St., WC1 (Tottenham Court Rd.), 0171-636 2731

■ "Excellent food for the money" (especially via the set price menus) can be had at this all-day Eclectic in a Bloomsbury townhouse; despite grumblings about "small portions" and "expensive" wine, fans say "you'll have a beautiful meal" in "nice premises."

Trader Vic's ◗S   16 | 20 | 17 | £35

London Hilton, 22 Park Ln., W1 (Hyde Park Corner), 0171-208 4113

◪ "Austin Powers is here", or so he should be since this Hilton veteran is called the "best cocktail bar in town" – it "takes you back to the '70s" (or earlier) with its "deliciously tasteless" Polynesian-theme setting and "those drinks" – yeah, baby!; there's also an "aggressively kooky" island-style menu, but the word is "restaurant ok, bar excellent."

Tramp
12 | 12 | 14 | £44

Private club; inquiries: 0171-734 0565

☑ "Who goes for the food?" – not many, judging by the ratings, but that doesn't matter since this legendary Piccadilly private nightclub that recently celebrated 30 years as a nocturnal magnet for glamour and fame always makes for "a good night out" thanks to its packed bar, sexy ambience and dancing; those who do eat here report that "great burgers" are a highlight amongst the Traditional British offerings; N.B. the first revamp in decades has recently been completed.

Troubadour, The 🅂⊘
13 | 18 | 9 | £13

265 Old Brompton Rd., SW5 (Earl's Court), 0171-370 1434

■ Perhaps the Traditional British food is "not great" and service can vary from "nice" to less so, but the arty atmosphere makes up for any shortcomings at this "real coffeehouse" in Earl's Court where music, poetry readings and the like are part of the appeal; it's a good place to hang out, "read the papers" or linger over a "weekend brunch."

Tui 🅂
21 | 11 | 15 | £26

19 Exhibition Rd., SW7 (South Kensington), 0171-584 8359

■ Enthusiasts say some of "the best" and "most authentic" Thai food in London can be found at this South Kensington eaterie, which explains why they're happy to overlook decor that's "not so good" and service that can be "nonchalant."

Tuk Tuk Thai 🅂
16 | 10 | 14 | £20

330 Upper St., N1 (Angel), 0171-226 0837

■ A "very good cheap and cheerful Thai" is the consensus on this "down-to-earth restaurant" in Islington; though a few critics cite "volatile" quality and "offhand service", they're outvoted by those who find the food "spot-on" and say the simple setting has a "feeling of Bangkok."

Turner's 🅂
20 | 18 | 19 | £43

87-89 Walton St., SW3 (Knightsbridge/South Kensington), 0171-584 6711

☑ Surveyors fail to see eye to eye on TV chef Brian Turner's Chelsea New French: to admirers it's "expensive but worth it" for "lovely food" served in a "discreet, upmarket ambience", whilst detractors find it "stuffy", calling it an "average restaurant with higher-than-average prices"; still, supporters have the edge and your odds of siding with them may increase if you "go for the prix fixe lunch."

Tuttons Brasserie ⬤🅂
14 | 12 | 12 | £23

11-12 Russell St., WC2 (Covent Garden), 0171-836 4141

■ "Don't expect a gastronomic experience to beat all", but this brasserie's International fare is generally considered "good value" and the location is hard to top if you want a handy "meeting place" near Covent Garden; it's especially "nice in summer" for alfresco meals.

Two Brothers Fish 22 | 11 | 17 | £18

297-303 Regent's Park Rd., N3 (Finchley Central), 0181-346 0469

■ "Fabulous fresh fish" and "oh, the chips – ecstasy!" explain why this "buzzing" Finchley fish and chips specialist is "hugely popular" with locals and "well worth a journey" from elsewhere; many consider it "one of the best" of its kind, and though it can be "cramped and crowded" with no reserving in the evening, there's always "fantastic takeaway."

Union Cafe 18 | 14 | 16 | £27

96 Marylebone Ln., W1 (Bond St.), 0171-486 4860

■ Though the "minimal" decor "lacks appeal" for some, the "simple but elegant" Modern British–Med cooking wins approval from most at this Marylebone cafe that's part of John Brinkley's stable – hence the "good value wine list"; "excellent brunch" on Saturdays adds to its appeal.

Uno ◐ 15 | 14 | 15 | £19

1 Denbigh St., SW1 (Pimlico/Victoria), 0171-834 1001

◪ Views on this Victoria Southern Italian run the gamut from "great neighbourhood restaurant", "best secret in London" to "quite dull", but ratings support those who take a moderate stance and simply report "good food" and "quick, friendly" service; "fantastic pizzas" are a highlight and they "do takeaway too."

Upper Street Fish Shop ⊄ 19 | 10 | 16 | £16

324 Upper St., N1 (Angel), 0171-359 1401

■ This Islington eaterie "gives fish and chips the good name it deserves" and also serves other "great" fish dishes and praiseworthy puddings in a setting that's "rather primitive" but "homey"; budget-watchers insist it's "overpriced" for what it is, but the BYO policy helps.

Upstairs at The Savoy ◐ 21 | 18 | 23 | £33

Savoy Hotel, The Strand, WC2 (Covent Garden/Embankment), 0171-420 2392

■ A "perfect hideaway", the Savoy's upstairs bar/cafe is "less formal" than the hotel's other eateries but still an "elegant" spot in which to enjoy "delicious" seafood (including recently added sushi and sashimi) and other light fare from a "limited but excellent" British-International menu; it's especially appreciated as a "lovely stop for pre-/post-theatre dining."

Vale, The ◐ [S] – | – | – | M

99 Chippenham Rd., W9 (Maida Vale/Westbourne Grove), 0171-266 0990

Low-key but promising Maida Vale start-up from Francesca Melman (ex The Cow), whose gutsy Modern British cooking is attracting an increasingly bohemian crowd; there are three separate conservatory-style dining areas at this down-to-earth haunt, one of which can be used for private dining.

Vama - The Indian Room ◐ S　　23　20　20　£30
438 King's Rd., SW10 (Sloane Sq.), 0171-351 4118
■ "In an entirely different category from other Indians" proclaim admirers of this World's End standout, praising its "utterly delicious" cooking ("tries and often succeeds in breaking new ground"), "tasteful", "modern" setting and "very warm welcome"; it "deserves to be better known", though regulars admit they "hope it remains a local secret."

Vasco & Piero's Pavilion　　18　15　19　£31
15 Poland St., W1 (Oxford Circus), 0171-437 8774
☑ Opinion is mixed on this Modern Italian on the northern fringes of Soho: what some see as a "nice place" offering "simple", "beautifully cooked" food at "good value", others describe as "overpriced and indifferent"; ratings suggest that supporters are in the majority, as does the fact that it's "always full" at lunchtime.

Veeraswamy ◐ S　　19　18　17　£30
99 Regent St., W1 (Piccadilly Circus), 0171-734 1401
☑ Whilst fans salute the "fabulous reincarnation" of this "long-established" (since 1926) Regent Street Indian, which now boasts "sleek", "trendy" decor and a "different" regional menu, critics say it "lost its good old imperial" ambience and claim the cooking "does not live up to the hype"; still, to the majority it's a "classy" "Indian dining experience", "not a curry house."

Vegia Zena S　　18　14　17　£28
17 Princess Rd., NW1 (Camden Town/Chalk Farm), 0171-483 0192
■ A "favourite secret" for boosters, this "quiet", "homey" Primrose Hill Italian offers "authentic, unusual" dishes (including some regional specialties) in an "intimate" setting with outdoor seating in summer; perhaps not every meal is a smash hit ("pleasant, not great"), but it's "worth a visit" for cooking that "can surprise" by its quality.

Vendome　　16　19　16　£32
20 Dover St., W1 (Green Park), 0171-629 5417
☑ Opinions on the Modern British–Med fare vary ("vastly underrated" vs. "inconsistent"), but the lush, "eclectic decor" and "good atmosphere" at this Piccadilly bar/restaurant make it a "stylish drop-in" for some surveyors; others simply recall "one point: too noisy."

Verbanella ◐ S　　18　13　20　£27
30 Beauchamp Pl., SW3 (Knightsbridge), 0171-584 1107
■ "Nothing to worry about here" say appreciative patrons of this "neighbourhood" Italian in Knightsbridge; "after 30 years" it's still offering "Italian soul food" in a "nice, quiet" setting with "very friendly" service, at prices that are reasonable by Beauchamp Place standards.

Veronica's ◗   20 | 17 | 22 | £24

3 Hereford Rd., W2 (Bayswater/Queensway), 0171-229 5079

■ "Your only chance in London to test historical English food – and it's good"; this "small, friendly" eatery off Westbourne Grove specialises in "old English recipes", and though some say "reading the menu is more interesting than eating the food", most applaud the cooking as well as the "delightful" owner-hostess, Veronica Shaw; "take your foreign friends here" for a different experience.

Vic Naylor   16 | 15 | 15 | £23

38-40 St. John St., EC1 (Barbican/Farringdon), 0171-608 2181

■ There's usually a "thriving bustle" at this "brash" Smithfield brasserie, though it may be the "fun bar" and "fab atmosphere" that draw people more than the "nice" Eclectic fare ("better for a drink and a nibble" say some); it's a "good place for a party" and attracts its share of the "in-crowd."

Viet Hoa ◗S   21 | 8 | 18 | £15

70-72 Kingsland Rd., E2 (Old St.), 0171-729 8293

■ It earns votes as "the best" and "most authentic" Vietnamese in town, so it's "worth the effort of finding" this "friendly, family-run" eatery in Shoreditch; the decor is "spartan" at best but that doesn't take away from the "incredible value."

Villandry Foodstore Restaurant S   19 | 15 | 14 | £27

170 Great Portland St., W1 (Great Portland St.), 0171-631 3131

◪ "The formula should work", yet some feel that this Eclectic bistro/food shop, now relocated to "spacious" Portland Street quarters, sometimes "just misses"; at its best it's a "gourmet's delight", offering "original" food from breakfast through dinner, but critics feel it's "not so nice since it moved", citing an "austere", "noisy" room and service that's "well-intentioned" but "a little chaotic."

Vine, The S   ▽ 17 | 16 | 14 | £29

86 Highgate Rd., NW5 (Kentish Town B.R.), 0171-209 0038

■ "Easy and comfortable", this "fave pub" in Kentish Town offers "good quality" cooking from an "interesting" Eclectic menu that's "excellent value"; some say it's a "shame about the service", but to most it's an all-round "refreshing dining experience" that's sort of "like a lazy Sunday party at home."

Vineet Bhatia ◗S   – | – | – | M

291 King St., W6 (Ravenscourt Park), 0181-748 7345

The restaurant Indian Summer didn't last long before morphing into this newcomer whose trademark is adding new twists to traditional Indian favourites; it's become a popular neighbourhood spot, but things may change again with the departure of the namesake chef-owner in spring '99.

Vingt-Quatre ◐ S　　　　13 | 10 | 13 | £18
325 Fulham Rd., SW10 (South Kensington), 0171-376 7224

■ It's a "cool place" and open round-the-clock, which are reasons enough to keep this "noisy" Chelsea Eclectic busy; it's "handy for odd-hour" cravings and "great" after clubbing.

Vinopolis S　　　　　　　　– | – | – | E
1 Bank End, SE1 (London Bridge), 0171-645 3700

Oenophiles will want to visit this new leisure complex devoted to wine, opening at press time near London Bridge; besides buying wines, taking courses, etc., visitors will be able to eat at Cantina (Eclectic fare), Root & Branch (a stylish wine bar) or opt for fine dining in a space due to open in early 2000, all overseen by restaurateurs Claudio Pulze and Trevor Gulliver.

VONG ◐ S　　　　　　　23 | 21 | 20 | £44
Berkeley Hotel, Wilton Pl., SW1 (Hyde Park Corner), 0171-235 1010

☑ A "super place to reawaken the taste buds", Jean-Georges Vongerichten's "stylish" Thai-French in a Hyde Park Corner hotel is "still going strong", offering "inspired" dishes that look "as exquisite as they taste"; it's "not for the credit card–impaired" and some cite "offhand service" and portions as "minimal" as the "sleek" decor, but to the majority it's "always an exciting" and "unique" experience.

Voodoo Lounge ◐ S　　　14 | 19 | 15 | £24
7-9 Cranbourn St., WC2 (Leicester Sq.), 0171-434 0606

☑ "Is it worth queuing for?" is the question when it comes to this Leicester Square nightclub/restaurant; the answer may be yes if you're looking for "funky atmosphere", but the Eclectic food (emphasising Californian fare) doesn't make much of an impression and some report "surly attitude."

Vrisaki ◐　　　　　　　▽ 22 | 11 | 16 | £20
73 Myddelton Rd., N22 (Bounds Green/Wood Green), 0181-889 8760

■ To "relive" your Aegean holidays, head to Wood Green and enjoy "basic" Greek food "cooked to perfection" and served in a "simple", "friendly" ambience; "if you like Greek-Cypriot meze, this is the place" and it's "economical" to boot.

WAGAMAMA S　　　　　19 | 15 | 16 | £15
4A Streatham St., WC1 (Tottenham Court Rd.), 0171-323 9223
26-40 Kensington High St., W8 (High St. Kensington), 0171-376 1717
101 Wigmore St., W1 (Bond St.), 0171-409 0111
10A Lexington St., W1 (Piccadilly Circus), 0171-292 0990
9-11 Jamestown Rd., NW1 (Camden Town), 0171-428 0800

■ "Wagawow!" shout fans of these "tasty, cheap" Japanese noodle bars that epitomise "efficient minimalism", from the decor to the food; "be prepared to share tables" and endure "outrageous" waits, but once seated service is "speedy" and the food "plentiful"; now "if only it weren't so popular."

Wakaba ▽ 21 | 16 | 18 | £38
122A Finchley Rd., NW3 (Finchley Rd.), 0171-586 7960
■ There's some "amazing food" and "excellent service" to be enjoyed at this "formal" Finchley Japanese, and whilst the setting is "very austere" it can also be "relaxing"; such "quality" comes "at a price", but for certain (presumably well-heeled) sushi and sashimi fanciers, it's a "top favourite."

Waterloo Fire Station S 16 | 14 | 13 | £21
150 Waterloo Rd., SE1 (Waterloo), 0171-620 2226
☑ "So trendy, so after-work" describes the scene at this restaurant/bar in an old Waterloo fire station; though critics claim that "increasing popularity" has meant "deteriorating quality", most enjoy its "tasty" Eclectic fare, "good value" and "lively" ambience; it's "convenient for the Old Vic" too.

Waxy O'Connor's Pub S 11 | 20 | 13 | £15
14-16 Rupert St., W1 (Piccadilly Circus), 0171-287 0255
☑ "Don't get lost" in the labyrinth-like setting of this big, "fun" Piccadilly Irish pub/restaurant with different theme rooms; as for the Irish fare, some call it "authentic" whilst others ask "why serve food when it only delays drinking?"

Westbourne, The S 18 | 16 | 13 | £20
101 Westbourne Park Villas, W2 (Royal Oak/Westbourne Park), 0171-221 1332
■ "If you aren't wearing black, don't come" to this "trendy" pub in Westbourne Park where patrons sport a fashionably "scruffy" look; the Eclectic food is "surprisingly good" and reasonably priced and there's "nice outdoor" seating too.

White Onion S 22 | 16 | 19 | £33
297 Upper St., N1 (Angel), 0171-359 3533
■ "Miles better than you would expect for a 'local'", this "unpretentious" Islington New French offers "excellent", "stylish cooking" in a "sophisticated" bi-level setting with a "relaxed" ambience; "friendly" service and fair prices are more reasons why nonlocals say "shame it's in Islington."

Wilson's ▽ 20 | 13 | 23 | £26
236 Blythe Rd., W14 (Hammersmith), 0171-603 7267
■ Despite solid ratings, Bob Wilson's small, Scottish-themed Shepherd's Bush eatery (with clan maps and tartan decor) doesn't arouse much comment; fans report "good" Traditional British food but say "watch out for the bagpipes."

Wilton's S 23 | 21 | 24 | £53
55 Jermyn St., SW1 (Green Park/Piccadilly Circus), 0171-629 9955
■ "They never change, thank God" say devotees of this "clubby, male-dominated" St. James's eatery "from a past era", where diners enjoy "excellent" British seafood and "wonderful service" whilst perhaps eavesdropping on the "cabinet minister at the next table"; it's "extremely English" and pricey, thus some say "on an expense account only."

Windows on the World S
21 | 23 | 21 | £47

London Hilton, 22 Park Ln., W1 (Hyde Park Corner),
0171-208 4021

■ "Magnificent views" across the whole of London are
the big draw at this 28th-floor bar/restaurant in the Hilton,
but the "excellent" French food does a respectable job of
competing with it; it's "great for special occasions" and
"always a pleasure to take someone who's never been
before"; P.S. "don't forget your jacket" for dinner.

Wine Factory S
▽ 12 | 13 | 16 | £20

294 Westbourne Grove, W11 (Notting Hill Gate), 0171-229 1877

◪ The Med-Eclectic food (pastas, pizzas, salads) may be
"unexciting", but "amazing value on wines" (sold at retail
prices) gets pulses racing at this Westbourne Grove venue;
though the bi-level setting is simple, it has "a touch of old-
world charm" bolstered by "very friendly" service.

Wine Gallery ●S
– | – | – | M

49 Hollywood Rd., SW10 (Earl's Court), 0171-352 7572

"Large portions" of "excellent value" British food and wine
at retail prices explain the appeal of this neighbourhood
wine bar in Chelsea; a few complain the menu "never
changes", but the pretty garden more than compensates.

Wiz S
17 | 17 | 16 | £27

123A Clarendon Rd., W1 (Holland Park), 0171-229 1500

◪ "New and buzzy", this "refreshingly different" concept
from Antony Worrall Thompson offers "tapas of many
nations" in an upbeat, modern bi-level Notting Hill space;
reaction is largely positive ("great idea", "brilliant choice of
dishes"), but a few call it a "mishmash that does not work."

Wòdka ●S
18 | 14 | 17 | £28

12 St. Alban's Grove, W8 (High St. Kensington), 0171-937 6513

◪ There's an "excellent" range of vodkas at this Kensington
eaterie, but "don't have too many or you'll forget how
delicious" the Polish–Eastern European cuisine is; whilst
ardent fans say the updated cooking "takes Polish food to
new heights", others find the results "nothing special" (ditto
the decor), but it's nice as "a departure from standard fare."

Wok Wok S
16 | 14 | 15 | £18

7 Kensington High St., W8 (High St. Kensington), 0171-938 1221
10 Frith St., W1 (Leicester Sq.), 0171-437 7080
51-53 Northcote Rd., SW11 (Clapham Junction B.R.),
0171-978 7181
140 Fulham Rd., SW10 (Fulham Broadway), 0171-370 5355
67 Upper St., N1 (Angel/Highbury & Islington), 0171-288 0333

■ "High-quality, low-cost Asian treats" including some of
the "best quick noodles in town" account for the success
of this "fast, friendly" chain; "modern decor" and "vibrant"
atmosphere ("can be unruly at times") are more reasons
why enthusiasts would happily "eat there every night."

Wolfe's Bar & Grill ◐ 17 12 16 £23

30 Great Queen St., WC2 (Covent Garden/Holborn), 0171-831 4442

■ "Wicked burgers" are the highlight at this Covent Garden veteran that fans credit with "some of the best American food in London"; it's not much to look at, but long hours and moderate prices make it practical.

Wong Kei [S]⊭ 13 4 5 £12

41-43 Wardour St., W1 (Leicester Sq./Piccadilly Circus), 0171-437 8408

◪ "Marvellously hostile staff" ("rudest restaurant in the world", "been thrown out several times", "if shouted at, shout back") is so much part of "the charm" of this Chinatown "madhouse" that those who experience "pleasant" service ask "what am I doing wrong?"; besides "the abuse gimmick", people come for "cheap, no-fuss Chinese grub", but don't expect much in the way of decor.

World Food Café ⊭ ▽ 19 18 19 £14

14 Neal's Yard, WC2 (Covent Garden), 0171-379 0298

■ "Refreshingly different for lunch", this Eclectic-Vegetarian cafe overlooking Neal's Yard in Covent Garden offers a "good variety" of "imaginative" dishes, served by "friendly" staff in a cramped space that gets busy at lunch; no dinner.

Ye Olde Cheshire Cheese [S] 12 18 12 £20

145 Fleet St., EC4 (Blackfriars), 0171-353 6170

◪ "Want olde England? – here it is", at this vintage 1667 Fleet Street tavern; it's a "quaint place" to "take visitors" for "real London" decor, but the pub food is "standard" and critics claim the place is "reliant on tourist popularity."

Yoshino ▽ 22 15 18 £29

3 Piccadilly Pl., W1 (Piccadilly Circus), 0171-287 6622

◪ You might "feel left out if not Japanese" (especially since the lunch menu is only in Japanese), but "don't be deterred" because this modern, stylish but discreet Piccadilly eaterie serves some of the "best" fish-based Japanese cuisine (but no sushi) around; it's "not frequented by tourists" either.

Yo! Sushi [S] 18 16 15 £20

Selfridges, 400 Oxford St., W1 (Bond St.), 0171-318 3944
52 Poland St., W1 (Oxford Circus), 0171-287 0443
Harvey Nichols, Knightsbridge, 5th fl., SW1 (Knightsbridge), 0171-235 6114
O_2 Ctr., 255 Finchley Rd., NW3 (Finchley Rd.), 0171-431 4499

◪ "Keep that sushi rolling!" shout fans of this growing chain of "very cool" Japanese eateries where sushi is served via conveyor belts and drinks are served by robots; dissenters call it "yo big deal" and say "gizmos don't replace good fish", but they're outvoted by those who feel it's "on the right track"; P.S. the Poland Street venue has opened a beer hall and sake cellar.

Yum Yum Thai S
▽ | 18 | 15 | 17 | £19

30 Stoke Newington Church St., N16 (Seven Sisters),
0171-254 6751

■ Only a few diners commented on this Stoke Newington Thai, but their impressions are positive: "good food, good buzz, very nice hosts"; on the downside is service that can "make one feel rushed", but that's the price of popularity and there's always takeaway.

ZAFFERANO S
25 | 20 | 22 | £41

15 Lowndes St., SW1 (Knightsbridge), 0171-235 5800

■ "As good as it gets in London for Italian food" is the consensus on Giorgio Locatelli's superpopular eaterie on the Knightsbridge-Belgravia border, where "class and quality go hand in hand", from the "innovative", "upscale" cooking to the "professional service", "good-looking" (if small) space and "cosmopolitan", "sophisticated" ambience; the main problem: trying to book "in the foreseeable future" – "if only they charged more, one might be able to get a table."

Zaika S
– | – | – | E

257-259 Fulham Rd., SW3 (South Kensington), 0171-351 7823

Claudio Pulze re-emerges after his departure from Aubergine, Zafferano, etc. as owner of this sophisticated, comfortable Fulham Road Indian, where the refined, innovative cooking of Vineet Bhatia is fairly priced and enhanced by a carefully chosen wine list put together by well-regarded consultant sommelier Yves Sauboua.

Zamoyski S
18 | 13 | 18 | £21

85 Fleet Rd., NW3 (Belsize Park), 0171-794 4792

■ "Good for Polinophiles" declares one surveyor, who may have been inspired to come up with that word after sampling the "great vodkas" at this Belsize Park Eastern European; though a few say the menu is "better than the meal", most have no qualms about the "real Polish food", "enthusiastic" service and "reasonable prices"; there's live music too.

Zen Central ◐S
20 | 16 | 16 | £36

20 Queen St., W1 (Green Park), 0171-629 8089

■ By most accounts, this Mayfair outpost of the Zen group remains a "reliable" choice for "excellent" Chinese fare served in a "minimal" setting; however, some feel that setting is "looking a bit tatty" these days and a few dissenters find the food "disappointing for the price."

Zen Chelsea ◐S
21 | 16 | 18 | £36

Chelsea Cloisters, 85 Sloane Ave., SW3 (South Kensington),
0171-584 9219

■ The first of the Zen group is still among "the best" for Chinese food according to admirers of this spacious Chelsea veteran's "tasty" cooking (with special praise for "good seafood"); service can vary from "cocky" to "attentive", but a meal here is "generally entertaining."

Zen Garden [S] 22 | 19 | 20 | £32
15-16 Berkeley St., W1 (Green Park), 0171-493 1381
■ Another "high-quality" member of the Zen group of Chinese restaurants, this one earning special praise for its "civilised", "elegant" Mayfair setting that's an "excellent eating environment"; there's an extensive menu with Northern Chinese dishes plus interesting specials.

ZeNW3 ◐ [S] 19 | 16 | 16 | £29
83 Hampstead High St., NW3 (Hampstead), 0171-794 7863
■ "Always packed, because the food is excellent and service is also good" say boosters of this Hampstead Chinese with a "clever name" and an "unhurried" ambience; it's seen as "a bit expensive" by critics and whilst some love the "modern" decor, others feel it's beginning to look "tired", but the "good mixture of Western-style dishes" broadens its "selling" appeal.

Ziani ◐ [S] 21 | 17 | 20 | £31
45 Radnor Walk, SW3 (Sloane Sq.), 0171-351 5297
■ "Great fun if you don't mind sitting in your neighbour's lap", this Chelsea Italian is "a favourite" with locals who appreciate its "consistently good, straightforward food", "warm welcome" and "real Italian ambience"; still, given the tight quarters and sometimes "rushed" service, you may "need to be in the right frame of mind to enjoy it."

Zilli Fish 21 | 16 | 17 | £33
36-40 Brewer St., W1 (Piccadilly Circus), 0171-734 8649
■ Though some come to Aldo Zilli's "very Soho" "media haunt" to "be seen, overhear gossip" and "network", the "delicious" Italian seafood is a draw in its own right ("spaghetti lobster – that's all to be said"); it's "pricey" and "cramped" but "always lively and enjoyable", with "attentive, efficient" service and "good atmosphere."

Zinc Bar & Grill ◐ 14 | 14 | 14 | £29
21 Heddon St., W1 (Piccadilly Circus), 0171-255 8899
◪ Admirers of this "lighthearted" Terence Conran brasserie near Regent Street insist it's "underrated", lauding its "useful location" and "all-day menu" featuring a "wide choice" of "well-cooked" Franco-British fare; critics call it "just another noisy Conran place" with "uninspired food" and "cold decor", but "the bar is lively enough" and lunch is considered a "good value."

Zoe ◐ 15 | 16 | 14 | £25
St. Christopher's Pl., 3-5 Barrett St., W1 (Bond St.), 0171-224 1122
■ "Reasonable food" for a "reasonable price" in a "very useful central location" makes this Mediterranean in St. Christopher's Place a handy option; it's especially "fun for lunch", with "good decor" and pleasant outdoor seats.

Zucca 🅂   17 | 15 | 17 | £27
188 Westbourne Grove, W11 (Notting Hill Gate),
0171-727 0060

■ An "interesting, evolving" Modern Italian menu plus "great" wood-oven pizzas are earning a following for this "trendy", minimalist spot, "currently the best in Notting Hill"; "friendly service" and "good value" don't hurt either, and the downstairs bar is "good for a group" outing.

Zuccato ◐🅂   – | – | – | M
O₂ Ctr., 255 Finchley Rd., NW3 (Finchley Rd.), 0171-431 1799

In the O₂ leisure complex on Finchley Road, this airy, stylish newcomer serves midpriced, trattoria-style Modern Italian–Med cooking in a setting adorned with huge '60s photos of Milan; other draws include booth seating, a popular bar and live music (Wednesdays).

Outside London

AMBERLEY CASTLE, `22 | 26 | 21 | £43`
QUEENS ROOM S
Amberley Castle, Amberley, West Sussex, 01798 831992
■ "With these surroundings, it cannot fail" say admirers of this 11th-century castle in a "beautiful" spot on the South Downs near Arundel, but besides the setting it also offers "super" Eclectic fare, an "impressive" (if "expensive") wine list and "polite" service; if a few spoilers claim "nothing else" lives up to the location, most "feel like royalty" here, especially "for romantic weekends."

Angel Restaurant S `▽ 21 | 18 | 17 | £31`
Angel Inn, 47 Bicester Rd., Long Crendon, Buckinghamshire, 01844 208268
■ A cosy 16th-century Buckinghamshire pub/restaurant with a large conservatory dining room (which underwent a recent refurb) and an "innovative", reasonably priced Pacific Rim menu with "fantastic fish" dishes; if the food is "occasionally not up to standard", it's "usually very good."

Auberge du Lac S `▽ 26 | 23 | 24 | £50`
Brocket Hall, Welwyn, Hertfordshire, 01707 368888
■ This former hunting lodge overlooking Broadwater Lake on the 500-acre Brocket Hall Estate is a "decadent" indulgence, offering "exquisite" Classic French fare and "great wines" from a 4,000-bottle cellar; some find it "way over the top", from cost to decor that's "a bit overdone", but to fans it's "worth it" and "lovely" for a "Sunday lunch."

Bear Restaurant S `20 | 20 | 19 | £35`
Bear Hotel, Park St., Woodstock, Oxfordshire, 01993 811511
■ Suckers for "ye olde coaching inns" will fall for this "cosy", "relentlessly British" Oxfordshire stalwart that "luckily doesn't change" from year to year; it may be a little "frayed" but has "great atmosphere" plus "excellent" British-French fare; in sum, a "lovely country establishment" and a "must for lunch when visiting Blenheim Palace."

Beetle & Wedge S `23 | 22 | 20 | £38`
Beetle & Wedge Hotel, Ferry Ln., Moulsford-on-Thames, Oxfordshire, 01491 651381
■ "Arrive by boat if you can" to this "idyllic setting" on the Thames in Oxfordshire with a "comfortable" conservatory dining room and a less formal Boathouse where meats and fish are cooked on open grills; both are lauded for their "well-prepared" Modern British–French fare as well as their "attention to detail" and outside tables: "perfect in summer."

Bell Inn S   20 | 18 | 19 | £39
Bell Inn, London Rd., Aston Clinton, Aylesbury,
Buckinghamshire, 01296 630252
With its "enjoyable" setting, this 17th-century coaching inn has fans who say it's "worth a drive" to Buckinghamshire, but the Modern British fare (with French touches) doesn't arouse much excitement and some feel this family-run venue is "living on its reputation"; still, there's confidence it "could be great again" and it's "nice" for "family gatherings."

Bishopstrow House S   21 | 21 | 21 | £43
Bishopstrow House, Boreham Rd., Warminster, Wiltshire,
01985 212312
To some, this handsome Georgian country house hotel (with indoor tennis court and pool) is a "wonderful oasis" in the Wiltshire countryside that impresses with its pricey Modern British fare and "unobtrusive service", but others find the food "rather bland" and service sometimes lacking; solid ratings suggest disappointments are rare.

Buckland Manor S   23 | 23 | 24 | £49
Buckland Manor, Buckland, Broadway, Gloucestershire,
01386 852626
The "gracious surroundings" at this "lovely country" manor on the outskirts of a pretty Cotswold village are admired, and the "fine" British-French fare is a worthy match, served in a "comfortable" dining room steeped in "old-world charm"; in sum, "excellent for a weekend."

Chapter One S   – | – | – | E
Farnborough Common, Locksbottom, Kent, 01689 854848
A surprisingly sophisticated venue near Locks Bottom in Kent serving Modern European food in a spacious room with an adjoining bar/brasserie area; its better-known sibling, Chapter Two, opened last year in Blackheath.

Cherwell Boathouse S   ▽ 20 | 17 | 17 | £27
Bardwell Rd., Oxford, Oxfordshire, 01865 552746
This unpretentious Oxfordshire riverside boathouse looks "bleak" to some, but others like its "funky" ambience and "excellent", "well-thought-out" British-French menu that offers "value for money", with a "great wine list" (200 strong) and "interesting sherries" to enhance the meal; besides, there's "nowhere else to eat" for miles (bookings advised).

CHEWTON GLEN HOTEL S   27 | 25 | 26 | £55
Chewton Glen Hotel, Christchurch Rd., New Milton,
Hampshire, 01425 275341
"Best behaviour required" at this "luxurious" "special hideaway" in the New Forest, which "gets it exactly right" according to fans, offering "remarkable" British-French fare in a "beautiful", "peaceful" setting; not everyone agrees ("overpriced", "overhyped"), but to believers it's "the best in all departments" and "great for a weekend break."

CLIVEDEN, WALDO'S   24 | 26 | 25 | £55

Cliveden Hotel, Taplow, Berkshire, 01628 668561

🔲 "Worth every haricot bean" is how most see this "very elegant" dining room in the basement of a famous country home in Berkshire (40 minutes from London), where the "impressive" French-International menu is enhanced by "wonderful service"; if some find it "pompous", more consider it "a gem" and tops for "special occasions."

Compleat Angler, Riverside Restaurant 🅂   18 | 21 | 18 | £40

Compleat Angler Hotel, Marlow Bridge, Buckinghamshire, 01628 484444

🔲 The Thameside location of this Buckinghamshire hotel owned by Granada's Heritage Hotels is "beautiful", but some feel the "pricey" International food "doesn't quite match"; still, it's "good" enough for many, with special praise for "the best afternoon tea"; N.B. a more casual dining option, Mange 2, recently opened in the conservatory.

Dining Room, The   24 | 21 | 22 | £35

59A High St., Reigate, Surrey, 01737 226650

◼ "If you are lucky", TV chef "Tony Tobin will be circulating" at this "formal" first-floor dining room in Reigate that perhaps "lacks atmosphere" but redeems itself with "excellent, hearty" Modern British fare; "go midweek for a real bargain" in the form of a £13.50 prix fixe lunch menu.

Eastwell Manor 🅂   ▽ 22 | 24 | 23 | £42

Eastwell Manor, Eastwell Park, Ashford, Kent, 01233 213000

◼ One of those "lovely country" venues with "beautiful grounds", a long driveway and great ambience, this Kent hotel/restaurant strikes fans as "up-and-coming" thanks to "good English fare", "friendly" service and "elegant" decor; but there is a faint note of dissent ("overrated") and prices are of the "special occasion" variety.

Fat Duck, The 🅂   23 | 18 | 19 | £45

High St., Bray, Berkshire, 01628 580333

🔲 "If only it were closer" to London lament admirers of Heston Blumenthal's "lovely pub-style restaurant" in Berkshire (40 minutes along the M4), where the "inventive" New French cooking takes a "fresh approach" and service is "knowledgeable"; critics find the food and prices "too rich" and claim the place is "self-satisfied, like its name."

Fawsley Hall 🅂   ▽ 21 | 24 | 23 | £38

Fawsley Hall, Fawsley, Northamptonshire, 01327 892000

◼ After a "wonderful restoration", this "quiet" Northampton mansion (handy for Silverstone and Althorp Park) is a "real getaway" with "fabulous" bedrooms and an alcoved dining room serving "delicious" Classic French fare; if some feel it has "not quite got it right for a luxury hotel", it's still early days for this yearling, part of the Halcyon Hotel stable.

Feathers Hotel 🅢   22 | 20 | 21 | £38
Feathers Hotel, Market St., Woodstock, Oxfordshire,
01993 812291
⬛ A "delightful place in a delightful part of the world" say
fans of this hotel in a 17th-century building at the gates of
Oxfordshire's Blenheim Palace, serving "creative" Modern
British fare in a "calming" atmosphere; whilst a few find it
"too formal" and "overpriced" with "stuffy" service, it rates
as a "favourite stop for lunch" and the walled garden is
"stunning" in summer.

Flitwick Manor 🅢   ▽ 22 | 22 | 21 | £37
Flitwick Manor Hotel, Church Rd., Flitwick, Bedfordshire,
01525 712242
⬛ This Georgian mansion in Bedfordshire is "upmarket
but also relaxed" with "jolly" service, making it "excellent
for corporate entertaining"; whilst some feel the setting is
"smarter than the food", others salute an "imaginative chef",
Richard Salt, for preparing Anglo-French fare "with flair",
but as is often the case, it may be most enjoyable "when
someone else is paying."

French Horn 🅢   22 | 21 | 21 | £48
French Horn Hotel, Sonning-on-Thames, Berkshire,
01189 692204
⬛ "The swans gliding by this little Thames backwater" add
to the "great view" at this "lovely" 19th-century building
near Henley, where "excellent" Traditional British–French
fare is enhanced by an "extensive wine list" and "old-style
service" that's "slow, but who cares?"; fans say it's "very
good for Sunday lunch" and "worth travelling miles for."

Gravetye Manor 🅢   24 | 24 | 25 | £50
Gravetye Manor Hotel, East Grinstead, West Sussex,
01342 810567
⬛ "England at its best": the long drive through "lovely
grounds" to this "magnificent" Elizabethan manor in Sussex
whets many an appetite for Mark Raffan's "quality" British-
Eclectic cooking, served by "courteous" staff in a "beautiful
setting"; whilst it's "expensive" and some find the ambience
"starchy" with a liberal sprinkling of "company directors",
admirers "never had a dull meal" here and "long to go back."

HAMBLETON HALL 🅢   25 | 25 | 25 | £53
Hambleton Hall, Hambleton, Oakham, Rutland,
01572 756991
⬛ "A surprise to find in Rutland", this "oasis of excellence"
delights many as an "enjoyable" "weekend retreat" with
"very beautiful" gardens, a "quiet, romantic" atmosphere
and well-regarded Modern British fare from chef Aaron
Patterson; even those who say the food "lacks originality"
concede that he "does cook well", though such quality
comes at a price.

HARTWELL HOUSE [S] 23 | 25 | 24 | £44

Hartwell House, Oxford Rd., Aylesbury, Buckinghamshire, 01296 747444

■ The "grand setting" of this "beautiful" Buckinghamshire mansion (with a Jacobean and Georgian heritage) wins universal acclaim, and as ratings attest most find the "excellent" British food to be a good match; add "friendly" service and a "peaceful" atmosphere and it's "just marvellous", whether for a meal or an overnight stay.

Horsted Place Hotel, Pugin Restaurant [S] ▽ 21 | 22 | 22 | £38

Horsted Place Hotel, Little Horsted, East Sussex, 01825 750581

■ A Pugin-designed, "wonderful country house hotel" on the edge of Sussex's South Downs offering British-Eclectic fare showcasing "good local produce", with special praise for the "best British breakfast anywhere"; if some see it as a "seminar venue" and note that it gets its share of "wedding receptions", others swear by it "for impressing friends and winning mistresses."

Hotel du Vin & Bistro [S] 23 | 21 | 21 | £36

Hotel du Vin & Bistro, Crescent Rd., Tunbridge Wells, Kent, 01892 526455

Hotel du Vin & Bistro, 14 Southgate St., Winchester, Hampshire, 01962 841414

■ "Excellent in all respects" say fans of this hotel/bistro duo in Winchester and Tunbridge catering to a "clientele of food and wine lovers" with "simple" but "sublime" French fare, "young, keen service" and advice from an "outstanding sommelier" ("tough to enjoy if you have to drive home" lament some); those who would like to "see more of them" will be pleased that a Bristol sibling is due to open before the millennium.

King's Head, The [S] ▽ 23 | 20 | 23 | £40

Station Rd., Ivinghoe, Buckinghamshire, 01296 668264

◪ A "relaxed" 17th-century Buckinghamshire country inn that "continues to satisfy under the watchful eye of the smooth French maitre d'", Georges, who still "reigns supreme" after 36 years; with "excellent" British-French food and service, it makes for a "delightful meal", even if some feel the place has become "very touristy."

Leaping Hare [S] – | – | – | E

Wyken Vineyards, Stanton, Bury St. Edmunds, Suffolk, 01359 250287

American-born Carla Carlisle recreated a choice bit of California in Suffolk when she transformed a 400-year-old barn into a cafe/country store serving such Americana as crab cakes; set on 1,000 acres, it also boasts enchanting vineyards and gardens; open daytime Wednesday–Sunday, serving dinner Friday and Saturday only.

Leatherne Bottel [S] 21 | 21 | 20 | £41

The Bridleway, Goring-on-Thames, Berkshire, 01491 872667

◩ It's "lovely to eat on a summer's day a few feet from the Thames", and in winter, Keith Read's "truly different" Berkshire eaterie is a cosy spot for "innovative" Modern British fare; a few find the menu "strange" and "pricey" and the nude pin-ups don't charm everyone, but the "excellent" cooking and "idyllic setting" win most over.

LE MANOIR AUX QUAT'SAISONS [S] 28 | 26 | 26 | £65

Le Manoir aux Quat'Saisons, Church Rd., Great Milton, Oxfordshire, 01844 278881

■ "The ultimate ecstasy – foodwise, of course"; ardent fans say this 15th-century Cotswold manor house is "culinary heaven on earth" and the "best England has to offer" (with ratings to back up the claim) thanks to Raymond Blanc's "fabulous" New French fare served in a "restful" conservatory setting that's "even more beautiful" after a refurb (which upped bedrooms to 32); though it's costly and some point to "rather stiff service", the consensus is "perfect for special occasions" and "worth a detour."

Le Petit Blanc [S] 22 | 18 | 21 | £30

The Queens Hotel, The Promenade, Cheltenham, Gloucestershire, 01242 266800
71-72 Walton St., Oxford, Oxfordshire, 01865 510999

■ "Raymond Blanc on the high street"; expect "competent, confident" French cooking "without frills" at this "casual" duo in Oxford ("filling a big hole") and Cheltenham ("modern, funky" decor), which both offer "pleasant service" ("terrific with kids") and "fantastic value" set price menus; some are less impressed ("disappointingly average", tables "crammed together"), but to most they're a good concept and "particularly welcome" for tea.

Le Talbooth [S] 21 | 22 | 20 | £47

Maison Talbooth Hotel, Gun Hill, Dedham, Essex, 01206 323150

■ This "elegant", 16th-century Tudor-style building enjoys a "phenomenal location" along Essex's River Stour, making it "particularly nice" in summer and "even better if you stay overnight"; though "expensive", the Modern British food is "consistently good" and service is of a similar standard (if "a bit slow"), causing fans to ask "what more can you want?"

L'ORTOLAN [S] 26 | 21 | 23 | £58

The Old Vicarage, Church Ln., Shinfield, Berkshire, 01189 883783

◩ "Real class without the hype" purr fans of John Burton-Race's "excellent" Classic French fare at this "lovely" vicarage near Reading with two separate dining areas (including a "warm conservatory") and service that wows admirers ("unbelievable quality"); yet the raves aren't quite unanimous: a few find the cooking "overrated" and fume "how anyone can justify the prices is a mystery."

Lucknam Park S   23   23   24   £50
Lucknam Park Hotel, Colerne, Wiltshire, 01225 742777
☑ To some, this 18th-century Palladian mansion (with 42 bedrooms) set in 500 acres of Wiltshire parkland is the "best place to go for a weekend", offering "great" Modern British–Eclectic cooking, "elegant" decor and "faultless service", but others find it a bit "stuffy" with "outrageous prices"; in any event, it caters to active types with a gymnasium, pool and equestrian centre.

Lygon Arms, The S   18   22   20   £44
The Lygon Arms, Broadway, Worcestershire, 01386 852255
☑ The Savoy Group's "extremely picturesque" 16th-century Cotswold coaching inn features a "distinguished" baronial-style dining hall serving Modern British fare that divides diners ("special" vs. "substandard"); still, given the setting, supporters "fully recommend" it as a "honeymoon" venue or somewhere "cosy" to have a "nice cream tea."

Mallory Court S   ▽ 24   25   24   £46
Mallory Court Hotel, Harbury Ln., Leamington Spa, Warwickshire, 01926 330214
■ A "calming" country house hotel close to Leamington Spa in Warwickshire with an elegant oak-panelled dining room where chef-owner Allan Holland offers British-French fare with "flair"; a new wing has increased the bedrooms from 10 to 18, whilst pretty gardens, a swimming pool and croquet pitch add appeal for overnight guests.

Marsh Goose, The S   ▽ 20   18   19   £36
High St., Moreton-in-Marsh, Gloucestershire, 01608 653500
☑ This characterful former coaching stable with traditional Cotswold stone walls and several eating areas offers "pleasant surroundings" for a quiet country meal, but whilst some call the Modern British fare "good", others find the menu "slightly bizarre" and "expensive."

Old Bridge Hotel S   ▽ 22   18   21   £38
Old Bridge Hotel, 1 High St., Huntingdon, Cambridgeshire, 01480 452681
■ The "comfortable" surroundings and "efficient staff" of this ivy-clad Cambridgeshire hotel win applause, and its two dining areas (The Terrace and the more formal Restaurant) offer a "high standard" of Modern British fare; there's a competitively priced wine list with helpful tasting notes.

One Paston Place   ▽ 22   14   21   £37
1 Paston Pl., Brighton, West Sussex, 01273 606933
■ An "excellent husband/wife team" (the Emmersons) runs this "rather cramped" dining room in a Brighton townhouse that fans say is "the equal" of "top-quality London" eateries thanks to "terrific" New French food and "friendly service"; those who feel there's "more atmosphere in a funeral parlour" might want to indulge more in the "good wine list."

Orange Balloon 🅂　　20 | 18 | 18 | £30

83 Fore St., Hertford, Hertfordshire, 01992 535666
249 High St., Berkhamsted, Hertfordshire, 01442 878978
2 Bromley Rd., Beckenham, Kent, 0181-650 0999
150-152 High St., Tonbridge, Kent, 01732 368008
50 High St., Cranleigh, Surrey, 01483 271555
58-62 The Green, Twickenham, Middlesex, 0181-893 8998

☑ "West End prices" is a complaint some level at this expanding chain of bistros in provincial outposts around London, but most seem content with the "pleasant, tasty" Modern British fare (with an International bent) served in "light", "modern" surroundings with "good service"; whilst a few remain unconvinced ("bit too trendy", "neither bistro nor restaurant"), fans proclaim these neighbourhood options "excellent" – "for a chain."

Pennyhill Park, Latymer Restaurant 🅂　　21 | 21 | 21 | £43

Pennyhill Park Hotel, London Rd., Bagshot, Surrey, 01276 471774

■ This creeper-clad Victorian manor in Surrey offers a "romantic setting" in which "to propose" or recover "after a bad day at Ascot races", and it also draws a "corporate" contingent for "business lunches" in the "elegant" dining room; the British food (with French and Italian accents) is "good" if "a little predictable", though "expensive prices" may induce "sweating before the bill arrives"; there's lighter fare in the more casual brasserie.

Pink Geranium　　▽ 23 | 19 | 18 | £40

25 Station Rd., Melbourn, Cambridgeshire, 01763 260215

☑ Entering the dining room of this pretty, thatched cottage in Cambridgeshire feels "like walking into a beautiful dinner party"; both the Modern British cooking and service are "good" and if some find the experience "overpriced", the "special midweek set meal" is considered reasonable value; one surveyor can't resist asking, "why, oh why, is owner Steven Saunders on the telly all the time?"

Royal Oak 🅂　　▽ 18 | 20 | 18 | £42

Royal Oak Hotel, The Square, Yattendon, Berkshire, 01635 201325

■ "Not too over the top", this Berkshire restaurant/hotel (with five bedrooms) boasts a "perfect English cosy country" setting, and if some claim the "quite pricey" British-French cooking "varies", others find it "excellent" and praise "attentive" service that's "keen to please."

Sir Charles Napier 🅂　　22 | 20 | 19 | £38

Spriggs Alley, Chinnor, Oxfordshire, 01494 483011

■ A "casual, comfortable" Oxfordshire inn with "quirky", "eclectic decor", a "relaxed", "fun" attitude and Modern British cooking that most judge "first-rate", though a few suggest the kitchen "goes over the top trying to dream up unusual dishes" that don't always succeed; still, the entire package is "well worth the effort to drive from London."

Stapleford Park S 20 | 22 | 22 | £42

Stapleford Park Hotel, Melton Mowbray, Stapleford,
Leicestershire, 01572 787522

■ Deep in the Leicestershire countryside ("still trying to
find it...") is this impressive, isolated former stately home
with "beautiful" rooms individually designed by the likes
of Nina Campbell and David Hicks; the Modern British fare
strikes some as "average" compared with the "great"
setting, but solid scores suggest that most are content.

Stonor Arms S ▽ 19 | 16 | 17 | £35

Stonor Arms Hotel, Henley-on-Thames, Oxfordshire,
01491 638866

◪ Though the Modern British food doesn't set pulses racing
("good" is the highest praise it receives) and service can
be "a teeny bit slow", this 18th-century coaching inn near
Henley-on-Thames offers big portions and "pleasant" decor
with three eating areas (a "lovely bar", dining room and
conservatory), making it a "delight in delightful country."

Three Lions, The S – | – | – | E

Three Lions Hotel, Stuckton, near Fordingbridge,
Hampshire, 01425 652489

Run by Mike and Jayne Womersley, this "country pub
restaurant" in a remote Hampshire village near Fordingbridge
offers "excellent", if "quite rich", Modern British cooking
and "friendly service"; however, some find the rather
simple decor "disappointing."

WATERSIDE INN S 27 | 24 | 26 | £65

Waterside Inn, Ferry Rd., Bray-on-Thames, Berkshire,
01628 620691

■ "Superb from start to finish", Michel Roux's *magnifique*
riverside French in Berkshire is "the real deal", with
"heavenly", "technically brilliant" cooking, "seamless
service" and a "perfect", "romantic" setting; a few object
to its "formality" and claim only "bank robbers" can afford it,
but to most "it's everything it's supposed to be", especially if
you "complete the experience and stay the night" in one
of the pretty guestrooms.

Indexes to Restaurants

Special Features and Appeals

CUISINES

Argentinean
El Gaucho (SW3)
Gaucho Grill (multi. loc.)

Asian
Asia de Cuba (WC2)
Cicada (EC1)
itsu (SW3)
Jim Thompson's (multi. loc.)
Mezzonine (W1)
Rain (W10)
Singapura (multi. loc.)
Southeast W9 (W9)
Suan Neo (EC2)
Tiger Lil's (multi. loc.)
Wok Wok (multi. loc.)

Bar-B-Q
Arkansas Cafe (E1)

Belgian
Belgo Centraal (WC2)
Belgo Noord (NW1)
Belgo Zuid (W1)
Bierodrome (N1)

Brasserie
Balans (W1)
Bluebird (SW3)
Brasserie Rocque (EC2)
Brasserie St. Quentin (SW3)
Browns Rest. (multi. loc.)
Café Delancey (NW1)
Café des Amis du Vin (WC2)
Café Flo (multi. loc.)
Cafe Rouge (multi. loc.)
Camden Brasserie (NW1)
Chez Gérard (multi. loc.)
Dôme (multi. loc.)
House/Rosslyn Hill (NW3)
Joe's Brasserie (SW6)
La Brasserie (SW3)
La Brasserie du Marché (W10)
Langan's Brasserie (W1)
Le Metro (SW3)
Le Palais du Jardin (WC2)
Mackintosh's (W4)
Magno's (WC2)
Novelli EC1 (EC1)
Oriel (SW1)

Oxo Tower Brasserie (SE1)
Quaglino's (SW1)
Randall & Aubin (W1)
Saigon Times (EC3)
Salt House (NW8)
Townhouse (WC1)
Tuttons (WC2)
Vic Naylor (EC1)
Zinc B&G (W1)

Brazilian
Rodizio Rico (W2)

British (Modern)
Admiral Codrington (SW3)
Alastair Little (W1)
Alastair Little/Lanc. Rd. (W11)
Alfred (WC2)
All Bar One (multi. loc.)
Andrew Edmunds (W1)
Anglesea Arms (W6)
Apprentice (SE1)
Atlantic B&G (W1)
Avenue (SW1)
Axis (WC2)
Bear (Oxon)
Beetle & Wedge (Oxon)
Belair House (SE21)
Bell Inn (Bucks)
Belvedere (W8)
Bishopstrow Hse. (Wilts)
Bistrot 190 (SW7)
Bistrot 2 Riverside (SE1)
Bluebird (SW3)
Brackenbury (W6)
Bradley's (NW3)
Brinkley's (SW10)
Browns Rest. (multi. loc.)
Buckland Manor (Glos)
Byron's (NW3)
Cafe at Sotheby's (W1)
Cafe de Paris (W1)
Cantaloupe B&G (EC2)
Chapel (NW1)
Charco's (SW3)
Chelsea Ram (SW10)
Cherwell Boathse. (Oxon)
Chez Bruce (SW17)
Chiswick (W4)
Circus (W1)

City Rhodes (EC4)
Claridge's Bar (W1)
Clarke's (W8)
Coast (W1)
Cookhouse (SW15)
Corney & Barrow (multi. loc.)
Cow Dining Room (W2)
Dan's (SW3)
Delfina Studio Cafe (SE1)
dell'Ugo (W1)
Depot Waterfront (SW14)
Dibbens (EC1)
Dining Room (Surrey)
Duke of Cambridge (SW11)
Eastwell Manor (Kent)
Ebury Wine Bar (SW1)
Emile's (multi. loc.)
Engineer (NW1)
English Garden (SW3)
Euphorium (N1)
Feathers Hotel (Oxon)
ffiona's (W8)
Fifth Floor (SW1)
Fifth Floor Cafe (SW1)
First Floor (W11)
Flitwick Manor (Beds)
Footstool (SW1)
Frederick's (N1)
Freedom Brewing Co. (WC2)
French House (W1)
Glaister's Garden (SW10)
Glasshouse (Kew)
Globe (NW3)
Goolies (W8)
Gravetye Manor (W. Sus)
Greenhouse (W1)
Hambleton Hall (Rut)
Harrods (SW1)
Hartwell House (Bucks)
Havelock Tavern (W14)
Helter Skelter (SW9)
Hilaire (SW7)
Home Bar Lounge (EC2)
Horsted Place, Pugin (E. Sus)
Hothouse (E1)
Indigo (WC2)
Ivy (WC2)
Joe's (SW3)
Joe's Brasserie (SW6)
Joe's Rest. Bar (SW1)
Kavanagh's (N1)
Kensington Place (W8)

Lansdowne (NW1)
Launceston Place (W8)
Lawn (SE3)
Leaping Hare (Suffolk)
Leatherne Bottel (Berks)
Le Caprice (SW1)
Leith's (W11)
Leith's Soho (W1)
Le Metro (SW3)
Le Petit Blanc (multi. loc.)
Le Talbooth (Essex)
Lucknam Park (Wilts)
Lygon Arms (Wocs)
Mallory Court (Warwks)
Marsh Goose (Glos)
Mirabelle (W1)
Museum St. Cafe (WC1)
Naked Turtle (SW14)
North Pole (SE10)
Oceana (W1)
Odette's (NW1)
Old Bridge Hotel (Cambs)
192 (W11)
Orange Balloon (multi. loc.)
Oxo Tower (SE1)
Palm Court (WC2)
Peasant (EC1)
Pennyhill Park, Latymer (Surrey)
People's Palace (SE1)
Phoenix B&G (SW15)
Pink Geranium (Cambs)
Prism (EC3)
Quaglino's (SW1)
Queens (NW1)
Quincy's (NW2)
Ransome's Dock (SW11)
Redmonds (SW14)
Reynier Wine Library (EC3)
Rhodes in Square (SW1)
Richard Corrigan (W1)
RK Stanley's (W1)
Room (SE1)
Rowley's (multi. loc.)
Royal Oak (Berks)
RSJ (SE1)
Saint Bar & Rest. (WC2)
Salt House (NW8)
Searcy's/Barbican (EC2)
Sir Charles Napier (Oxon)
Snows on Green (W6)
Sonata (W1)
Sound Republic (W1)

Sporting Page (SW10)
Stapleford Park (Leics)
Stephen Bull (multi. loc.)
Stephen Bull Smithfield (EC1)
Stepping Stone (SW8)
St. John (EC1)
Stonor Arms (Oxon)
Tate Gallery (SW1)
10 (EC2)
Terrace (W8)
Three Lions (Hants)
Union Cafe (W1)
Upstairs/The Savoy (WC2)
Vale (W9)
Vendome (W1)
Waterloo Fire Station (SE1)
Wine Gallery (SW10)

British (Traditional)

alistair Greig's Grill (W1)
Atrium (SW1)
Bear (Oxon)
Bentley's (W1)
Boisdale (SW1)
Buckland Manor (Glos)
Butlers Wharf (SE1)
Chelsea Bun (multi. loc.)
Chelsea Kitchen (SW3)
Connaught Hotel (W1)
Dorchester, Grill Rm. (W1)
English Hse. (SW3)
Fatboy's Cafe (W4)
ffiona's (W8)
Flitwick Manor (Beds)
Fortnum's Fountain (W1)
Fox & Anchor (EC1)
Foxtrot Oscar (multi. loc.)
French Horn (Berks)
Goring Dining Rm. (SW1)
Gravetye Manor (W. Sus)
Greenhouse (W1)
Green's Rest. (SW1)
Grenadier (SW1)
Grumbles (SW1)
Guinea (W1)
Harrods (SW1)
Hartwell House (Bucks)
Honest Cabbage (SE1)
Horsted Place, Pugin (E. Sus)
Julie's (W11)
King's Head (Bucks)
La Belle Epoque/Brasserie (SW3)
Langan's Bistro (W1)

Langan's Brasserie (W1)
Lawn (SE3)
Maggie Jones's (W8)
Mallory Court (Warwks)
Monkeys (SW3)
Morton's (W1)
Odin's (W1)
Pennyhill Park, Latymer (Surrey)
Plummers (WC2)
Porters (WC2)
porters bar (WC2)
porters bar/poland st. (W1)
Prince Bonaparte (W2)
Quality Chop Hse. (EC1)
Rib Room (SW1)
Richoux (multi. loc.)
Ritz Rest. (W1)
RK Stanley's (W1)
Royal Oak (Berks)
Rules (WC2)
Savoy Grill (WC2)
Scotts (W1)
Shepherd's (SW1)
Simpsons Tavern (EC3)
Simpson's/The Strand (WC2)
Titanic (W1)
Troubadour (SW5)
Veronica's (W2)
Wilson's (W14)
Wilton's (SW1)
Wine Gallery (SW10)
Ye Olde Cheshire (EC4)
Zinc B&G (W1)

Burmese

Mandalay (W2)

Cajun/Creole

Boardwalk (W1).

Caribbean

Cottons Rhum Shop (NW1)
Little Havana (WC2)
Smokey Joe's Diner (SW18)

Chinese

Aroma Chinese (multi. loc.)
Bayee House (multi. loc.)
Cheng-Du (NW1)
China Blues (NW1)
China City (WC2)
China Jazz (W1)
Choys (SW3)
Chuen Cheng Ku (W1)

Dorchester, Oriental (W1)
East One (EC1)
Feng Shang (NW1)
Four Regions (SE1)
Four Seasons Chinese (W2)
Fung Shing (WC2)
Golden Dragon (W1)
Good Earth (multi. loc.)
Green Cottage (NW3)
Gung-Ho (NW6)
Harbour City (W1)
Ho Ho (W1)
Hunan (SW1)
Imperial City (EC3)
Jade Garden (W1)
Jen (W1)
Jenny Lo's (SW1)
Joy King Lau (WC2)
Kai (W1)
Kaifeng (NW4)
Lee Fook (W2)
Lee Ho Fook (W1)
Mandarin Kitchen (W2)
Mao Tai (SW6)
Memories of China (multi. loc.)
Ming (W1)
Mr. Chow (SW1)
Mr. Kong (WC2)
Mr. Wing (SW5)
New Culture Rev. (multi. loc.)
New World (W1)
Poons (multi. loc.)
Poons in the City (EC3)
Princess Garden (W1)
Royal China (multi. loc.)
Singapore Garden (multi. loc.)
Trader Vic's (W1)
Wong Kei (W1)
Zen Central (W1)
Zen Chelsea (SW3)
Zen Garden (W1)
ZeNW3 (NW3)

Chophouses

alistair Greig's Grill (W1)
Butlers Wharf (SE1)
Christopher's (WC2)
El Gaucho (SW3)
Gaucho Grill (multi. loc.)
Guinea (W1)
Quality Chop Hse. (EC1)
Simpsons Tavern (EC3)

Coffeehouses

Aroma (multi. loc.)
Caffè Nero (multi. loc.)
Coffee Republic (multi. loc.)
Maison Bertaux (W1)
Starbucks/Seattle Co. (multi. loc.)

Cuban

Asia de Cuba (WC2)
Cuba (W8)
Cuba Libre (N1)
Havana (multi. loc.)
Little Havana (WC2)

Danish

Lundum's (SW7)

Dim Sum

China City (WC2)
Chuen Cheng Ku (W1)
Dorchester, Oriental (W1)
Four Regions (SE1)
Golden Dragon (W1)
Harbour City (W1)
Jade Garden (W1)
Lee Ho Fook (W1)
New World (W1)
Pacific Oriental (EC2)
Poons (multi. loc.)
Poons in the City (EC3)
Royal China (multi. loc.)
Zen Chelsea (SW3)
Zen Garden (W1)

Eclectic/International

Amberley Castle, Queens (W. Sus)
Andrew Edmunds (W1)
Anglesea Arms (W6)
Arcadia (W8)
Archduke (SE1)
Axis (WC2)
Balans (W1)
Balans Knightsbridge (SW3)
Balans West (SW5)
bali sugar (W11)
Bibendum (SW3)
Bibendum Oyster (SW3)
Birdcage (W1)
Blakes (NW1)
Blakes Hotel (SW7)
Blue Legume (N16)
Blue Print Cafe (SE1)

Books for Cooks (W11)
Brackenbury (W6)
Brasserie Rocque (EC2)
Brinkley's (SW10)
Browns Rest. (multi. loc.)
Che (SW1)
Chez Moi (W11)
Cliveden, Waldo's (Berks)
Compleat Angler (Bucks)
Corney & Barrow (multi. loc.)
Crescent (SW3)
Drones (SW1)
Emile's (multi. loc.)
Engineer (NW1)
Enterprise (SW3)
Fifth Floor Cafe (SW1)
First Floor (W11)
Fish! (SE1)
Food for Thought (WC2)
Foundation (SW1)
Four Seasons, Lanes (W1)
Garlic & Shots (W1)
Giraffe (multi. loc.)
Gladwins (EC3)
Granita (N1)
Gravetye Manor (W. Sus)
Harrods (SW1)
Helter Skelter (SW9)
Horsted Place, Pugin (E. Sus)
House/Rosslyn Hill (NW3)
Lab (W1)
Lanesborough (SW1)
Lansdowne (NW1)
Lavender (multi. loc.)
Le Cafe du Jardin (WC2)
Lola's (N1)
Lucknam Park (Wilts)
Mash (W1)
Min's (SW3)
Mona Lisa (SW10)
Motcomb's (SW1)
Movenpick Marché (SW1)
Mustards Smithfield (EC1)
Oceana (W1)
Odette's (NW1)
Pelham St. (SW7)
Pitcher & Piano (multi. loc.)
PJ's Bar & Grill (SW3)
PJ's Grill (WC2)
Polygon B&G (SW4)
Pomegranates (SW1)
Prince Bonaparte (W2)

Sauce BarOrganicDiner (NW1)
Savoy River Rest. (WC2)
Shoeless Joe's (SW6)
Shoreditch Electricity (N1)
Sonny's (SW13)
Soup Opera (multi. loc.)
Soup Works (multi. loc.)
Sugar Club (W1)
Tea Rms. des Artistes (SW8)
Tenth (W8)
Titanic (W1)
Tom's Deli (W11)
Townhouse (WC1)
Tuttons (WC2)
Upstairs/The Savoy (WC2)
Vic Naylor (EC1)
Vine (NW5)
Vingt-Quatre (SW10)
Vinopolis (SE1)
Voodoo Lounge (WC2)
Waterloo Fire Station (SE1)
Westbourne (W2)
Wine Factory (W11)
Wiz (W1)
World Food Café (WC2)

Fish 'n' Chips
Brady's (SW18)
Geale's (W8)
Nautilus Fish (NW6)
Rudland & Stubbs (EC1)
Seafresh Fish (SW1)
Seashell (NW1)
Sweetings (EC4)
Toff's (N10)
Two Brothers (N3)
Upper St. Fish Shop (N1)

French Bistro
Abingdon (W8)
Bear (Oxon)
Bibendum Oyster (SW3)
Bistro Daniel (W2)
Bistrot 190 (SW7)
Café Boheme (W1)
Café Delancey (NW1)
Café Flo (multi. loc.)
Cafe Rouge (multi. loc.)
Chez Gérard (multi. loc.)
Chez Max (SW10)
Cork & Bottle (WC2)
Côte à Côte (SW11)
Dôme (multi. loc.)

Francofill (SW7)
Glaister's Garden (multi. loc.)
Grumbles (SW1)
Hotel du Vin (multi. loc.)
Just Around the Corner (NW2)
La Belle Epoque/Brasserie (SW3)
La Bouchée (SW7)
Langan's Bistro (W1)
Langan's Coq d'Or (SW5)
La Poule au Pot (SW1)
L'Artiste Musclé (W1)
Le Bouchon Bordelais (SW11)
Le Bouchon Lyonnais (SW8)
Le Café du Marché (EC1)
Le Gothique (SW18)
Le Mercury (N1)
Le Palais du Jardin (WC2)
Le Petit Blanc (multi. loc.)
Le Piaf (multi. loc.)
Little Bay (NW6)
Mon Plaisir (WC2)
Monsieur Max (Hampton Hill)
Novelli EC1 (EC1)
Patisserie Valerie (multi. loc.)
Pierre Victoire (W1)
Randall & Aubin (W1)
Rotisserie Jules (multi. loc.)
Thierry's (SW3)
Villandry Foodstore (W1)
Zinc B&G (W1)

French (Classic)

Auberge du Lac (Herts)
Beetle & Wedge (Oxon)
Beotys (WC2)
Black Truffle (NW1)
Brasserie St. Quentin (SW3)
Buckland Manor (Glos)
Caviar Kaspia (W1)
Chewton Glen Hotel (Hants)
Chez Gérard (multi. loc.)
Chez Max (SW10)
Chez Nico (W1)
Claridge's Rest. (W1)
Cliveden, Waldo's (Berks)
Connaught Hotel (W1)
Coq d'Argent (EC2)
Elena's L'Etoile (W1)
Fawsley Hall (N'hants)
Flitwick Manor (Beds)
French Horn (Berks)
Hotel du Vin (multi. loc.)
Icon (SW3)

La Bouchée (SW7)
La Brasserie (SW3)
La Brasserie du Marché (W10)
La Dordogne (W4)
Landmark, Dining Rm. (NW1)
Langan's Brasserie (W1)
La Poule au Pot (SW1)
La Tante Claire (SW1)
L'Aventure (NW8)
Le Boudin Blanc (W1)
Le Café du Marché (EC1)
Le Colombier (SW3)
Le Gavroche (W1)
Le Muscadet (W1)
L'Escargot (W1)
L'Estaminet (WC2)
Le Suquet (SW3)
Lobster Pot (SE11)
L'Ortolan (Berks)
Lou Pescadou (SW5)
Luc's (EC3)
Mirabelle (W1)
Monkeys (SW3)
Mon Plaisir (WC2)
Monsieur Max (Hampton Hill)
Morton's (W1)
Nico Central (W1)
Oak Room MPW (W1)
Odin's (W1)
Oslo Court (NW8)
Ritz Rest. (W1)
Roussillon (SW1)
Royal Oak (Berks)
Simply Nico (multi. loc.)
Stratford's (W8)
Terrace (W1) (W1)
Waterside Inn (Berks)
Windows on World (W1)

French (New)

Abingdon (W8)
Amandier (W2)
Aubergine (SW10)
Bam-Bou (W1)
Bank (WC2)
Beetle & Wedge (Oxon)
Belair House (SE21)
Bibendum (SW3)
Big Chef (E14)
Birdcage (W1)
Bleeding Heart (multi. loc.)
Brown's Hotel, 1837 (W1)
Buckland Manor (Glos)

Café des Amis du Vin (WC2)
Cafe des Arts (NW3)
Canteen (SW10)
Capital Rest. (SW3)
Cave (W1)
Chez Bruce (SW17)
Chez Max (SW10)
Chinon (W14)
Club Gascon (EC1)
Coq d'Argent (EC2)
Côte à Côte (SW11)
Criterion Brasserie (W1)
Fat Duck (Berks)
Flitwick Manor (Beds)
Gordon Ramsay (SW3)
Gravetye Manor (W. Sus)
La Belle Epoque/La Salle (SW3)
La Bouchée (SW7)
La Cage Imaginaire (NW3)
La Dordogne (W4)
Le Manoir/Quat'Saisons (Oxon)
Le Palais du Jardin (WC2)
Le Soufflé (W1)
L'Odeon (W1)
L'Oranger (SW1)
Maison Novelli (EC1)
Novelli EC1 (EC1)
Novelli W8 (W8)
Oak Room MPW (W1)
1 Lombard St. (EC3)
One-0-One (SW1)
One Paston Place (W. Sus)
Orrery (W1)
Park Rest. (SW1)
Pétrus (SW1)
Pied-à-Terre (W1)
Putney Bridge (SW15)
Room/Halcyon (W11)
755 (SW6)
Simply Nico (multi. loc.)
Square (W1)
Teatro (W1)
Turner's (SW3)
Vong (SW1)
Waterside Inn (Berks)
White Onion (N1)

Greek

Beotys (WC2)
Costa's Grill (W8)
Daphne (NW1)
Greek Valley (NW8)
Halepi (multi. loc.)
Kalamaras Micro (W2)
Lemonia (NW1)
Nontas (NW1)
Real Greek (N1)
Vrisaki (N22)

Hamburgers

Babe Ruth's (multi. loc.)
Big Easy (SW3)
Break for the Border (WC2)
Capital Radio Cafe (multi. loc.)
Chelsea Ram (SW10)
Chicago Rib Shack (SW7)
Deals (multi. loc.)
Ed's Easy Diner (multi. loc.)
Fatboy's Cafe (W4)
Foxtrot Oscar (multi. loc.)
Hard Rock Cafe (W1)
Henry J. Bean's (SW3)
Joe Allen (WC2)
Kettners (W1)
Mackintosh's (W4)
Maxwell's (multi. loc.)
PJ's Bar & Grill (SW3)
PJ's Grill (WC2)
Planet Hollywood (W1)
Rock Garden (WC2)
Shoeless Joe's (multi. loc.)
Smollensky's/Strand (WC2)
Sports Cafe (SW1)
Sticky Fingers (W8)
Texas Lone Star (multi. loc.)
T.G.I. Friday's (multi. loc.)
Tootsies (multi. loc.)
Vingt-Quatre (SW10)
Wolfe's B&G (WC2)

Hungarian

Gay Hussar (W1)

Ice Cream Parlours

Fortnum's Fountain (W1)
Harrods (SW1)
Marine Ices (NW3)

Indian

Bengal Clipper (SE1)
Bengal Trader (E1)

Bombay Bicycle (SW12)
Bombay Brasserie (SW7)
Cafe Lazeez (multi. loc.)
Cafe Spice Namaste (multi. loc.)
Chor Bizarre (W1)
Chutney Mary (SW10)
Chutney's (NW1)
Gopal's of Soho (W1)
Great Nepalese (NW1)
Kastoori (SW17)
Khan's (W2)
Khan's of Kensington (SW7)
Lahore Kebab Hse. (E1)
La Porte des Indes (W1)
Ma Goa (SW15)
Malabar (W8)
Malabar Junction (WC1)
Mandeer (WC1)
Memories of India (SW7)
Noor Jahan (SW5)
Old Delhi (W2)
Rani (N3)
Rasa (multi. loc.)
Ravi Shankar (multi. loc.)
Red Fort (W1)
Saffron (SW10)
Salloos (SW1)
Sarkhel's Indian (SW1)
Shimla Pinks (EC2)
Soho Spice (W1)
Standard Tandoori (W2)
Star of India (SW5)
Tamarind (W1)
Tandoori Lane (SW6)
Tandoori of Chelsea (SW3)
Vama (SW10)
Veeraswamy (W1)
Vineet Bhatia (W6)
Zaika (SW3)

Irish
ArdRí/O'Conor Don (W1)
Waxy O'Connor's (W1)

Italian (Contemporary)
Alba (EC1)
Al San Vincenzo (W2)
Arancia (multi. loc.)
Assaggi (W2)
Bertorelli's (WC2)
Bertorelli's Cafe Italian (W1)
Black Truffle (NW1)
Buona Sera (multi. loc.)

Buona Sera/Jam (SW3)
Café Milan (SW3)
Caraffini (SW1)
Caravaggio (EC3)
Cecconi's (W1)
Cibo (W14)
Cicoria (NW6)
Como Lario (SW1)
Daphne's (SW3)
Del Buongustaio (SW15)
Diverso (W1)
Dorchester, Bar (W1)
Elistano (SW3)
Emporio Armani (SW3)
Enoteca Turi (SW15)
Floriana (SW3)
Florians (N8)
Formula Veneta (SW10)
Grano (W4)
Great Eastern (EC2)
Green Olive (W9)
Grissini (SW1)
Halkin, Stefano Cavallini (SW1)
Ibla (W1)
I-Thai (W2)
Justin's (W1)
King's Rd. Cafe (SW3)
La Candela (W8)
L'Accento Italiano (W2)
La Delizia (multi. loc.)
L'Altro (W11)
L'Incontro (SW1)
Luigi's/Covent Garden (WC2)
Luna Nuova (WC2)
Mediterraneo (W11)
Monza (SW3)
Neal St. (WC2)
Oliveto (SW1)
Olivo (SW1)
Orsino (W11)
Orso (WC2)
Osteria Antica Bologna (SW11)
Osteria Basilico (W11)
Paparazzi Lounge (multi. loc.)
Park, The (NW6)
Passione (W1)
Pescatori (W1)
Pizza Chelsea (SW7)
Purple Sage (W1)
Red Pepper (W9)
Riva (SW13)
River Cafe (W6)

Sandrini (SW3)
San Lorenzo Fuoriporta (SW19)
San Martino (SW3)
Santini (SW1)
Sartoria (W1)
Spago (multi. loc.)
Spiga (W1)
Spighetta (W1)
Teca (W1)
Tentazioni (SE1)
Toto's (SW3)
Uno (SW1)
Vasco & Piero's (W1)
Verbanella (SW3)
Zafferano (SW1)
Ziani (SW3)
Zucca (W11)
Zuccato (NW3)

Italian (Traditional)

Ask Pizza (multi. loc.)
Bice (W1)
Black Truffle (NW1)
Buona Sera (multi. loc.)
Buona Sera/Jam (SW3)
Café Milan (SW3)
Caffè Nero (multi. loc.)
Cantinetta Venegazzu (SW11)
Caraffini (SW1)
Casale Franco (N1)
Cecconi's (W1)
Como Lario (SW1)
Condotti (W1)
Côte à Côte (SW11)
Daphne's (SW3)
De Cecco (SW6)
Dorchester, Bar (W1)
Elistano (SW3)
Emporio Armani (SW3)
Friends (SW10)
Il Falconiere (SW7)
La Bersagliera (SW3)
L'Accento Italiano (W2)
La Famiglia (SW10)
La Fontana (SW1)
Little Italy (W1)
Luigi's/Covent Garden (WC2)
Luigi's Deli (SW10)
Made in Italy (SW3)
Maggiore's (WC2)
Marine Ices (NW3)
Mimmo d'Ischia (SW1)
Montpeliano (SW7)

Picasso (SW3)
Pizza Metro (SW11)
Pollo Bar (W1)
Red Pepper (W9)
Riccardo's (SW3)
Sale e Pepe (SW1)
Sambuca (SW3)
Sandrini (SW3)
San Lorenzo (SW3)
San Lorenzo Fuoriporta (SW19)
San Martino (SW3)
Scalini (SW3)
Signor Sassi (SW1)
Signor Zilli (W1)
Spaghetti House (multi. loc.)
Spiga (W1)
Vegia Zena (NW1)
Verbanella (SW3)
Ziani (SW3)
Zilli Fish (W1)
Zuccato (NW3)

Japanese

Aykoku-Kaku (EC4)
Benihana (multi. loc.)
Cafe Japan (NW11)
City Miyama (EC4)
Defune (W1)
Harrods (SW1)
Hi Sushi (W1)
Ikeda (W1)
Ikkyu (multi. loc.)
Inaho (W2)
itsu (SW3)
Japanese Canteen (multi. loc.)
Jin Kichi (NW3)
Koi (W8)
Kulu Kulu Sushi (W1)
latitude (SW3)
Matsuri (SW1)
Mitsukoshi (SW1)
Miyama (W1)
Moshi Moshi Sushi (multi. loc.)
Nobu (W1)
Noto (multi. loc.)
Saga (W1)
Satsuma (W1)
Shogun (W1)
Suntory (SW1)
Sushi Wong (W8)
Tatsuso (EC2)
Tokyo Diner (WC2)
Wagamama (multi. loc.)

Wakaba (NW3)
Yoshino (W1)
Yo! Sushi (multi. loc.)

Jewish

Bloom's (NW11)
Kaifeng (NW4)
Reubens (W1)
Solly's (NW11)

Korean

Bu-San (N7)

Kosher

Bloom's (NW11)
Kaifeng (NW4)
Reubens (W1)
Solly's (NW11)

Malaysian/Indonesian

Melati (W1)
Nancy Lam's Enak Enak (SW11)
Nusa Dua (W1)
Pacific Spice (EC1)
Silks & Spice (multi. loc.)
Singapore Garden (multi. loc.)
Suan Neo (EC2)

Mediterranean

Atrium (SW1)
Back to Basics (W1)
Beach Blanket Babylon (W11)
Bistrorganic (W10)
Café dell'Ugo (SE1)
Cafe des Arts (NW3)
Cafe Med (multi. loc.)
Camden Brasserie (NW1)
Cantaloupe B&G (EC2)
Canteen (SW10)
Cantina del Ponte (SE1)
Chapel (NW1)
Clarke's (W8)
Cork & Bottle (WC2)
Criterion Brasserie (W1)
dell'Ugo (W1)
Dover Street (W1)
Eagle (EC1)
est (W1)
Halepi (W2)
Hothouse (E1)
Icon (SW3)
Le Cafe du Jardin (WC2)
Marquis (W1)
Mas Café (W11)

Mesclun (N16)
Mezzonine (W1)
Moro (EC1)
Mortimer (W1)
Olivo (SW1)
190 (SW7)
Oxo Tower Brasserie (SE1)
Palio (W11)
Peasant (EC1)
Pepe Nero (SW11)
Sarastro (WC2)
Snows on Green (W6)
Soho Soho (W1)
Terraza (multi. loc.)
Union Cafe (W1)
Vendome (W1)
Waterloo Fire Station (SE1)
Wine Factory (W11)
Zoe (W1)

Mexican/Tex-Mex

Break for the Border (multi. loc.)
Café Pacifico (WC2)
Down Mexico Way (W1)
La Perla B&G (multi. loc.)
Nachos (multi. loc.)
Navajo Joe (WC2)
Salsa! (WC2)
Texas Embassy (SW14)
Texas Lone Star (multi. loc.)

Middle Eastern

Al Bustan (SW1)
Al Hamra (W1)
Alounak (multi. loc.)
Al Sultan (W1)
Beiteddine (SW1)
Fairuz (W1)
Fakhreldine (multi. loc.)
Maroush (multi. loc.)
Phoenicia (W8)
Solly's (NW11)

Modern European

Admiral Codrington (SW3)
Bar Bourse (EC4)
Brompton Bay (SW3)
Builders Arms (SW3)
Chapter One (Kent)
Chapter Two (SE3)
County Hall (SE1)
Duke of Cambridge (N1)
Fifth Floor Cafe (SW1)

Footstool (SW1)
Frith Street (W1)
Gresslin's (NW3)
Ivy (WC2)
Landmark, Dining Rm. (NW1)
Le Caprice (SW1)
Le Pont de la Tour (SE1)
Lexington (W1)
Mezzo (W1)
Nicole's (W1)
Oriel (SW1)
Pharmacy (W11)
Quo Vadis (W1)
Teatro (W1)
Toast (NW3)
Vine (NW5)

Moroccan

Adams Cafe (W12)
Momo (W1)
Pasha (SW7) (SW7)
Tajine (W1)

Nepalese

Great Nepalese (NW1)

North African

Adams Cafe (W12)
Laurent (NW2)
Momo (W1)
Pasha (SW7)
Souk (WC2)
Tajine (W1)

North American

Arkansas Cafe (E1)
Babe Ruth's (multi. loc.)
Big Easy (SW3)
Blues Bistro (W1)
Boardwalk (W1)
Break for the Border (WC2)
Cactus Blue (SW3)
Canyon (Richmond)
Capital Radio Cafe (multi. loc.)
Cheers (W1)
Chelsea Bun (multi. loc.)
Chicago Rib Shack (SW7)
Christopher's (WC2)
Cicoria (NW6)
Dakota (W11)
Deals (multi. loc.)
DKNY Bar (W1)
Ed's Easy Diner (multi. loc.)
Foxtrot Oscar (multi. loc.)

Hard Rock Cafe (W1)
Henry J. Bean's (SW3)
Idaho (N6)
Joe Allen (WC2)
Leaping Hare (Suffolk)
Mackintosh's (W4)
Mas Café (W11)
Maxwell's (multi. loc.)
Montana (SW6)
Navajo Joe (WC2)
PJ's Bar & Grill (SW3)
PJ's Grill (WC2)
Planet Hollywood (W1)
Rainforest Cafe (W1)
Reubens (W1)
Rock Garden (WC2)
Santa Fe (N1)
Shoeless Joe's (multi. loc.)
Smokey Joe's Diner (SW18)
Smollensky's/Strand (WC2)
Sports Cafe (SW1)
Sticky Fingers (W8)
Texas Embassy (SW14)
Texas Lone Star (multi. loc.)
T.G.I. Friday's (multi. loc.)
Tootsies (multi. loc.)
Wolfe's B&G (WC2)

Pacific Rim

Angel (Bucks)
Birdcage (W1)
Collection (SW3)
Cow Dining Room (W2)
Cucina (NW3)
Denim (WC2)
Joe's Brasserie (SW6)
Pacific Oriental (EC2)
Saint Bar & Rest. (WC2)
Sugar Club (W1)
Vine (NW5)
Voodoo Lounge (WC2)

Persian

Alounak (multi. loc.)
Old Delhi (W2)

Peruvian

Fina Estampa (SE1)

Pizza

Ask Pizza (multi. loc.)
Buona Sera (SW11)
Café Milan (SW3)
Calzone (multi. loc.)

Cantina del Ponte (SE1)
Casale Franco (N1)
Condotti (W1)
Eco (multi. loc.)
Friends (SW10)
Harrods (SW1)
Kettners (W1)
La Delizia (multi. loc.)
La Porchetta Pizzeria (N4)
Luigi's Deli (SW10)
Luna Nuova (WC2)
Made in Italy (SW3)
Marine Ices (NW3)
Mash (W1)
Oliveto (SW1)
Orso (WC2)
Osteria Basilico (W11)
Paparazzi Lounge (SW3)
Pizza Chelsea (SW7)
Pizza Express (multi. loc.)
Pizza Metro (SW11)
Pizza on the Park (SW1)
Pizza Pomodoro (multi. loc.)
Pizza The Action (SW6)
Pizzeria Castello (SE1)
Pucci Pizza (SW3)
Purple Sage (W1)
Red Pepper (W9)
Spago (multi. loc.)
Spiga (W1)
Spighetta (W1)
Terraza (SW19)
Zucca (W11)

Polish

Daquise (SW7)
Wòdka (W8)
Zamoyski (NW3)

Russian

Caviar Kaspia (W1)
Nikita's (SW10)

Scottish

Boisdale (SW1)
Buchan's (SW11)
Wilson's (W14)

Seafood

Aquarium (E1)
Back to Basics (W1)
Belgo Centraal (WC2)
Belgo Noord (NW1)
Belgo Zuid (W1)

Bentley's (W1)
Bibendum Oyster (SW3)
Bluebird (SW3)
Brady's (SW18)
Café Fish (W1)
Cave (W1)
Chez Liline (N4)
Fish! (SE1)
Green's Rest. (SW1)
Harrods (SW1)
Jason's (W9)
J. Sheekey (WC2)
Le Palais du Jardin (WC2)
Le Suquet (SW3)
Livebait (multi. loc.)
Lobster Pot (SE11)
Lou Pescadou (SW5)
Manzi's (WC2)
Moxon's (SW4)
Offshore (W1)
190 (SW7)
One-O-One (SW1)
Pescatori (multi. loc.)
Poissonnerie/l'Avenue (SW3)
Quaglino's (SW1)
Quality Chop Hse. (EC1)
Randall & Aubin (W1)
Rudland & Stubbs (EC1)
Scotts (W1)
Stratford's (W8)
Sweetings (EC4)
Upper St. Fish Shop (N1)
Upstairs/The Savoy (WC2)
Wilton's (SW1)
Zilli Fish (W1)

South American

La Piragua (N1)

Spanish

Barcelona Tapas (multi. loc.)
Bar Madrid (W1)
Cambio de Tercio (SW5)
Don Pepe (NW8)
El Blason (SW3)
El Metro (SW6)
El Prado (SW6)
Galicia (W10)
Gaudi (EC1)
La Finca (multi. loc.)
La Mancha (SW15)
La Rueda (multi. loc.)
Meson Don Felipe (SE1)

Moro (EC1)
Rebato's (SW8)

Sudanese
Mandola Café (W11)

Swedish/Scandinavian
Anna's Place (N1)
Garbo's (W1)
Lundum's (SW7)

Swiss
Movenpick Marché (SW1)

Thai
Bangkok (SW7)
Bedlington Cafe (W4)
Ben's Thai (WC1)
Birdcage (W1)
Blue Elephant (SW6)
Blue Jade (SW1)
Busabong Too (SW10)
Busabong Tree (SW10)
Chiang Mai (W1)
Churchill Arms (W8)
Esarn Kheaw (W12)
Fatboy's Cafe (W4)
I-Thai (W2)
Khun Akorn (SW3)
Pacific Spice (EC1)
Patara (multi. loc.)
Pepper Tree (SW4)
Silks & Spice (multi. loc.)
Sound Republic (W1)
Sri Siam (W1)
Sri Siam City (EC2)
Sri Thai (EC4)
Thai Kitchen (W2)
Thai on River (SW10)
Tui (SW7)
Tuk Tuk Thai (N1)

Vong (SW1)
Yum Yum Thai (N16)

Turkish
Efes Kebab Hse. (multi. loc.)
Istanbul Iskembecisi (N16)
Iznik (N5)
Pasha (N1)
Sofra (multi. loc.)

Vegetarian
Blah! Blah! Blah! (W12)
Blue Legume (N16)
Chutney's (NW1)
Cranks (multi. loc.)
Food for Thought (WC2)
Futures!! (multi. loc.)
Gate (W6)
Kastoori (SW17)
Lanesborough (SW1)
Leith's (W11)
Mandeer (WC1)
Mildreds (W1)
Place Below (EC2)
Rani (N3)
Rasa (multi. loc.)
Ravi Shankar (multi. loc.)
Soup Opera (multi. loc.)
Soup Works (multi. loc.)
Tea Rms. des Artistes (SW8)
World Food Café (WC2)

Vietnamese
Bam-Bou (W1)
Bonjour Vietnam (SW6)
Nam Long Le Shaker (SW5)
Saigon (W1)
Saigon Thuy (SW18)
Saigon Times (EC3)
Viet Hoa (E2)

LOCATIONS

CENTRAL LONDON

Belgravia
Al Bustan
Beiteddine
Drones
Ebury Wine Bar
Grenadier
Grissini
Halkin, Stefano Cavallini
Lanesborough
La Tante Claire
Memories of China
Mimmo d'Ischia
Motcomb's
Oliveto
One-O-One
Pizza on the Park
Rib Room
Salloos
Santini
Vong
Zafferano

Bloomsbury
Alfred
Ask Pizza
Back to Basics
Bam-Bou
Bertorelli's Cafe Italian
Birdcage
Caffè Nero
Chez Gérard
Cranks
Efes Kebab Hse.
Elena's L'Etoile
Ikkyu
Le Piaf
Malabar Junction
Mandeer
Mash
Museum St. Cafe
Nico Central
Passione
Patisserie Valerie
Pescatori
Pied-à-Terre
Poons
Rasa
Silks & Spice

Soup Works
Spaghetti House
Townhouse
Vasco & Piero's
Villandry Foodstore
Wagamama

Chinatown
Aroma Chinese
China City
Chuen Cheng Ku
Fung Shing
Golden Dragon
Harbour City
Ikkyu
Jade Garden
Jen
Manzi's
Mr. Kong
New World
Poons
Tokyo Diner
Wong Kei

Covent Garden
All Bar One
Aroma
Asia de Cuba
Axis
Bank
Belgo Centraal
Beotys
Bertorelli's
Browns Rest.
Buona Sera
Café des Amis du Vin
Café Flo
Café Pacifico
Cafe Rouge
Caffè Nero
Capital Radio Cafe
Chez Gérard
Christopher's
Coffee Republic
Corney & Barrow
Cranks
Denim
Dôme
Food for Thought

Freedom Brewing Co.
Indigo
Ivy
Joe Allen
J. Sheekey
La Perla B&G
Le Cafe du Jardin
Le Palais du Jardin
L'Estaminet
Little Havana
Livebait
Luigi's/Covent Garden
Luna Nuova
Maggiore's
Magno's
Maxwell's
Mon Plaisir
Navajo Joe
Neal St.
Orso
Palm Court
Patisserie Valerie
Pitcher & Piano
Pizza Express
PJ's Grill
Plummers
Porters
porters bar
Rock Garden
Rules
Salsa!
Sarastro
Savoy Grill
Savoy River Rest.
Shoeless Joe's
Simpson's/The Strand
Smollensky's/Strand
Sofra
Sound Republic
Soup Works
Spaghetti House
Starbucks/Seattle Co.
Stephen Bull
T.G.I. Friday's
Tuttons
Upstairs/The Savoy
Wolfe's B&G
World Food Café

Knightsbridge

Aroma
Balans Knightsbridge
Brasserie St. Quentin

Cafe Rouge
Capital Rest.
Chez Gérard
Chicago Rib Shack
Emporio Armani
Fifth Floor
Fifth Floor Cafe
Floriana
Foundation
Good Earth
Harrods
Joe's Rest. Bar
Khun Akorn
Le Metro
Maroush
Min's
Montpeliano
Monza
Mosimann's
Mr. Chow
Park Rest. (SW1)
Patara
Patisserie Valerie
Pizza Express
Pizza Pomodoro
Richoux
Rowley's
Sale e Pepe
San Lorenzo
Signor Sassi
Spaghetti House
Verbanella
Yo! Sushi

Marylebone

All Bar One
ArdRí/O'Conor Don
Chapel
Chutney's
Defune
Fairuz
Garbo's
Giraffe
Great Nepalese
Ibla
Japanese Canteen
Justin's
Landmark, Dining Rm.
Langan's Bistro
La Porte des Indes
La Rueda
Le Muscadet
Mandalay

Maroush
New Culture Rev.
Oceana
Odin's
Orrery
Purple Sage
Ravi Shankar
Reubens
RK Stanley's
Royal China
Seashell
Singapore Garden
Sofra
Sonata
Spighetta
Starbucks/Seattle Co.
Stephen Bull
Tajine
Tootsies
Union Cafe
Wagamama
Yo! Sushi
Zoe

Mayfair
Al Hamra
alistair Greig's Grill
All Bar One
Al Sultan
Aroma
Ask Pizza
Bar Madrid
Benihana
Bice
Break for the Border
Brown's Hotel, 1837
Browns Rest.
Cafe at Sotheby's
Caffè Nero
Caviar Kaspia
Cecconi's
Chez Gérard
Chez Nico
China Jazz
Chor Bizarre
Claridge's Bar
Claridge's Rest.
Coast
Coffee Republic
Condotti
Connaught Hotel
Cranks

DKNY Bar
Dorchester, Bar
Dorchester, Grill Rm.
Dorchester, Oriental
Dover Street
Four Seasons, Lanes
Greenhouse
Guinea
Havana
Ho Ho
Ikeda
Kai
Langan's Brasserie
L'Artiste Musclé
Le Boudin Blanc
Le Gavroche
Le Soufflé
Marquis
Mirabelle
Miyama
Morton's
Nicole's
Nobu
Paparazzi Lounge
Pescatori
Princess Garden
Rasa
Richoux
Saga
Sartoria
Scotts
Shogun
Sofra
Soup Opera
Spaghetti House
Square
Starbucks/Seattle Co.
Tamarind
TECA
Trader Vic's
Veeraswamy
Vendome
Windows on World
Zen Central
Zen Garden

Piccadilly
Aroma
Atlantic B&G
Bentley's
Cafe de Paris
Café Flo
Cheers

Criterion Brasserie
Diverso
Down Mexico Way
Ed's Easy Diner
Fakhreldine
Gaucho Grill
Hard Rock Cafe
L'Odeon
Mitsukoshi
Momo
Oak Room MPW
Planet Hollywood
Rainforest Cafe
Richoux
Sports Cafe
Terrace (W1)
Titanic
Yoshino
Zinc B&G

Soho

Alastair Little
All Bar One
Andrew Edmunds
Aroma
Aroma Chinese
Balans
Blues Bistro
Boardwalk
Break for the Border
Café Boheme
Café Fish
Café Flo
Cafe Med
Cafe Rouge
Caffè Nero
Chiang Mai
Circus
Coffee Republic
Cork & Bottle
Deals
dell'Ugo
Dôme
Ed's Easy Diner
est
French House
Frith Street
Garlic & Shots
Gay Hussar
Gopal's of Soho
Hi Sushi
Ikkyu
Joy King Lau

Kettners
Kulu Kulu Sushi
Lab
Lee Ho Fook
Leith's Soho
Le Piaf
L'Escargot
Lexington
Little Italy
Maison Bertaux
Melati
Mezzo
Mezzonine
Mildreds
Ming
Mortimer
Nusa Dua
Patisserie Valerie
Pierre Victoire
Pitcher & Piano
Pizza Express
Pollo Bar
porters bar/poland st.
Quo Vadis
Randall & Aubin
Red Fort
Richard Corrigan
Saigon
Saint Bar & Rest.
Satsuma
Signor Zilli
Sofra
Soho Soho
Soho Spice
Souk
Soup Works
Spiga
Sri Siam
Sugar Club
Teatro
Voodoo Lounge
Wagamama
Waxy O'Connor's
Wok Wok
Yo! Sushi
Zilli Fish

St. James's

Avenue
Cave
Che
Fortnum's Fountain
Green's Rest.

Le Caprice
L'Oranger
Matsuri
Pétrus
Quaglino's
Ritz Rest.
Rowley's
Spaghetti House
Suntory
Texas Embassy
Wilton's

Victoria

Ask Pizza
Boisdale

Goring Dining Rm.
Jenny Lo's
Movenpick Marché
Olivo
Seafresh Fish
Simply Nico
Spaghetti House
Uno

Westminster

Atrium
Coffee Republic
Footstool
Shepherd's
Tate Gallery

EAST/SOUTH EAST LONDON

Blackfriars/City

Alba
All Bar One
Arkansas Cafe
Aroma
Aykoku-Kaku
Bar Bourse
Barcelona Tapas
Ben's Thai
Brasserie Rocque
Café Flo
Caffè Nero
Caravaggio
Chez Gérard
City Miyama
City Rhodes
Coffee Republic
Coq d'Argent
Corney & Barrow
Futures!!
Gladwins
Imperial City
Lahore Kebab Hse.
Luc's
Moshi Moshi Sushi
Noto
1 Lombard St.
Pacific Oriental
Pitcher & Piano
Pizza Pomodoro
Place Below
Poons in the City
Prism
Ravi Shankar
Saigon Times

Searcy's/Barbican
Shimla Pinks
Simply Nico
Simpsons Tavern
Singapura
Sri Siam City
Sri Thai
Starbucks/Seattle Co.
Suan Neo
Sweetings
Tatsuso
10
Ye Olde Cheshire

Canary Wharf/Docklands

Babe Ruth's
Big Chef
Cafe Rouge
Cafe Spice Namaste
Corney & Barrow
Hothouse
Moshi Moshi Sushi
Soup Opera
Starbucks/Seattle Co.

Clerkenwell/Smithfield

All Bar One
Bleeding Heart
Cafe Lazeez
Cicada
Club Gascon
Dibbens
Dôme
Eagle
East One
Fox & Anchor

Gaudi
Japanese Canteen
Le Café du Marché
Maison Novelli
Moro
Mustards Smithfield
Novelli EC1
Pacific Spice
Quality Chop Hse.
Rudland & Stubbs
Stephen Bull Smithfield
St. John
Vic Naylor

Greenwich/Blackheath

Chapter Two
Lawn
Le Piaf
North Pole

Shoreditch/Spitalfields

Bengal Trader
Cantaloupe B&G
Great Eastern
Real Greek
Shoreditch Electricity
Viet Hoa

South Bank

Archduke
Bistrot 2 Riverside
Café dell'Ugo
Delfina Studio Cafe
Film Café
Fina Estampa

Honest Cabbage
La Finca
Oxo Tower
Oxo Tower Brasserie
People's Palace
Simply Nico

Tower Bridge

Apprentice
Aquarium
Arancia
Bengal Clipper
Blue Print Cafe
Butlers Wharf
Cantina del Ponte
Fish!
Foxtrot Oscar
Le Pont de la Tour
Reynier Wine Library
Tentazioni
Vinopolis

Waterloo

Aroma
County Hall
Four Regions
Lavender
Livebait
Meson Don Felipe
Rebato's
Room
RSJ
Waterloo Fire Station

NORTH/NORTH WEST LONDON

Camden Town/Kentish Town/Chalk Farm

Ask Pizza
Belgo Noord
Blakes (NW1)
Café Delancey
Camden Brasserie
Cheng-Du
China Blues
Cottons Rhum Shop
Daphne
Engineer
Feng Shang
Lansdowne
Lemonia
Marine Ices

New Culture Rev.
Nontas
Odette's
Queens
Sauce BarOrganicDiner
Silks & Spice
Vegia Zena
Vine
Wagamama
Zamoyski

Golders Green/Finchley

Babe Ruth's
Bloom's
Bradley's
Cafe Japan
Capital Radio Cafe

Ed's Easy Diner
Globe
Just Around the Corner
Kaifeng
Laurent
Quincy's
Solly's
Two Brothers
Wakaba
Yo! Sushi
Zuccato

Hampstead/Kilburn

Black Truffle
Byron's
Cafe des Arts
Caffè Nero
Calzone
Cicoria
Cucina
Dôme
Gaucho Grill
Giraffe
Good Earth
Green Cottage
Gresslin's
Gung-Ho
Halepi
House/Rosslyn Hill
Jin Kichi
La Cage Imaginaire
Little Bay
Maxwell's
Nautilus Fish
Park, The (NW6)
Rani
Singapore Garden
Toast
Tootsies
ZeNW3

Highgate/Muswell Hill

Florians
Idaho
Toff's
Vrisaki

Islington

All Bar One
Anna's Place
Bierodrome
Bu-San
Café Flo
Cafe Med

Calzone
Casale Franco
Chez Gérard
Cuba Libre
Dôme
Duke of Cambridge (N1)
Euphorium
Frederick's
Granita
Home Bar Lounge
Istanbul Iskembecisi
Iznik
Japanese Canteen
Kavanagh's
La Piragua
Le Mercury
Lola's
Nachos
New Culture Rev.
Pasha (N1)
Peasant
Pitcher & Piano
Santa Fe
Tiger Lil's
Tuk Tuk Thai
Upper St. Fish Shop
White Onion
Wok Wok

St. John's Wood

Benihana
Cafe Med
Cafe Rouge
Don Pepe
Greek Valley
Green Olive
Jason's
L'Aventure
Oslo Court
Red Pepper
Richoux
Royal China
Salt House
Southeast W9
Starbucks/Seattle Co.
Vale

Stoke Newington

Blue Legume
Chez Liline
La Porchetta Pizzeria
Mesclun
Rasa
Yum Yum Thai

SOUTH/SOUTH WEST LONDON

Barnes
Browns Rest.
Depot Waterfront
Riva
Sonny's

Battersea
Buchan's
Cantinetta Venegazzu
Chelsea Bun
Côte à Côte
Duke of Cambridge (SW11)
Glaister's Garden
Le Bouchon Bordelais
Le Bouchon Lyonnais
Osteria Antica Bologna
Pizza Express
Pizza Metro
Ransome's Dock
Stepping Stone

Brixton/Clapham
Arancia
Bombay Bicycle
Buona Sera
Cafe Spice Namaste
Eco
Helter Skelter
La Rueda
Lavender
Lobster Pot
Moxon's
Nancy Lam's Enak Enak
Pepe Nero
Pepper Tree
Pitcher & Piano
Pizzeria Castello
Polygon B&G
Starbucks/Seattle Co.
Tiger Lil's
Wok Wok

Chelsea
Admiral Codrington
Ask Pizza
Aubergine
Benihana
Big Easy
Bluebird
Brinkley's
Brompton Bay
Browns Rest.

Builders Arms
Buona Sera/Jam
Busabong Too
Busabong Tree
Café Flo
Café Milan
Cafe Rouge
Calzone
Canteen
Caraffini
Charco's
Chelsea Bun
Chelsea Kitchen
Chelsea Ram
Choys
Chutney Mary
Coffee Republic
Dan's
Daphne's
Deals
Dôme
Ed's Easy Diner
El Blason
El Gaucho
Elistano
English Garden
English Hse.
Enterprise
Formula Veneta
Foxtrot Oscar
Friends
Glaister's Garden
Gordon Ramsay
Henry J. Bean's
Icon
itsu
King's Rd. Cafe
La Belle Epoque/Brasserie
La Belle Epoque/La Salle
La Bersagliera
La Delizia
La Famiglia
latitude
Le Colombier
Le Suquet
Made in Italy
Mona Lisa
Monkeys
New Culture Rev.
Oriel
Paparazzi Lounge

Picasso
Pitcher & Piano
Pizza Express
PJ's Bar & Grill
Poissonnerie/l'Avenue
Pucci Pizza
Riccardo's
Rotisserie Jules
Sambuca
San Martino
Scalini
Sporting Page
Starbucks/Seattle Co.
Tandoori of Chelsea
Thai on River
Thierry's
Tiger Lil's
Toto's
Turner's
Vama
Vingt-Quatre
Wine Gallery
Wok Wok
Zaika
Zen Chelsea
Ziani

Dulwich

Barcelona Tapas
Belair House

Earl's Court

Balans West
Cambio de Tercio
Chez Max
Dôme
La Delizia
Langan's Coq d'Or
Lou Pescadou
Mr. Wing
Nikita's
Troubadour

Fulham

All Bar One
Blue Elephant
Bonjour Vietnam
Café Flo
Cafe Med
De Cecco
Deco
El Metro
Emile's

Havana
Jim Thompson's
Joe's Brasserie
La Perla B&G
La Rueda
Mao Tai
Montana
Nachos
Pitcher & Piano
Pizza Express
Pizza The Action
Saffron
755
Shoeless Joe's
Starbucks/Seattle Co.
Tandoori Lane
Tootsies

Pimlico

Blue Jade
Como Lario
Grumbles
Hunan
La Fontana
La Poule au Pot
L'Incontro
Pomegranates
Rhodes in Square
Roussillon

Putney/Richmond

Ask Pizza
Bayee House
Café Flo
Canyon
Cookhouse
Del Buongustaio
El Prado
Emile's
Enoteca Turi
Glasshouse
Jim Thompson's
La Mancha
Le Piaf
Ma Goa
Naked Turtle
Phoenix B&G
Putney Bridge
Redmonds
Terraza
Tootsies

South Kensington

Ask Pizza
Bangkok
Bibendum
Bibendum Oyster
Bistrot 190
Blakes Hotel (SW7)
Bombay Brasserie
Cactus Blue
Cafe Lazeez
Cafe Rouge
Caffè Nero
Collection
Crescent
Daquise
Francofill
Hilaire
Il Falconiere
Joe's
Khan's of Kensington
La Bouchée
La Brasserie
Luigi's Deli
Lundum's
Memories of India
Nam Long Le Shaker
Noor Jahan
190
Pasha (SW7)
Patara
Pelham St.

Pitcher & Piano
Pizza Chelsea
Pizza Express
Rotisserie Jules
Sandrini
Spago
Starbucks/Seattle Co.
Star of India
Texas Lone Star
Tootsies
Tui

Wandsworth

Bayee House
Brady's
Cafe Med
Chez Bruce
Jim Thompson's
Kastoori
Le Gothique
Le Piaf
Nachos
Pitcher & Piano
Pizza Express
Saigon Thuy
San Lorenzo Fuoriporta
Sarkhel's Indian
Smokey Joe's Diner
Tea Rms. des Artistes
Terraza
Tootsies

WEST LONDON

Bayswater

Alounak
Al San Vincenzo
Amandier
Bistro Daniel
Coffee Republic
Fakhreldine Express
Four Seasons Chinese
Halepi
Inaho
I-Thai
Kalamaras Micro
Khan's
L'Accento Italiano
Mandarin Kitchen
Mandola Café
Old Delhi
Poons

Prince Bonaparte
Rodizio Rico
Royal China
Standard Tandoori
T.G.I. Friday's
Veronica's

Chiswick

Ask Pizza
Bedlington Cafe
Cafe Med
Cafe Rouge
Chiswick
Fatboy's Cafe
Grano
La Dordogne
Le Piaf
Mackintosh's
Monsieur Max

Nachos
Pitcher & Piano
Silks & Spice
Texas Lone Star
Tootsies

Hammersmith

Cafe Rouge
Deals
Gate
River Cafe
Tootsies
Vineet Bhatia

Kensington

Abingdon
Arcadia
Ask Pizza
Belvedere
Café Flo
Churchill Arms
Clarke's
Cuba
Dôme
ffiona's
Goolies
Kensington Place
Koi
La Candela
Launceston Place
Maggie Jones's
Memories of China
Novelli W8
Offshore
Phoenicia
Pizza Express
Rain
Spago
Starbucks/Seattle Co.
Sticky Fingers
Stratford's
Sushi Wong
Tenth
Terrace (W8)
Wagamama
Wòdka
Wok Wok

Notting Hill Gate

Alastair Little/Lancaster Rd.
All Bar One
Ask Pizza

Assaggi
bali sugar
Beach Blanket Babylon
Belgo Zuid
Bistrorganic
Books for Cooks
Cafe Med
Cafe Rouge
Calzone
Chez Moi
Coffee Republic
Costa's Grill
Cow Dining Room
Dakota
First Floor
Galicia
Geale's
Japanese Canteen
Julie's
La Brasserie du Marché
L'Altro
Lee Fook
Leith's
Malabar
Mas Café
Mediterraneo
Nachos
New Culture Rev.
192
Orsino
Osteria Basilico
Palio
Pharmacy
Pizza Express
Room/Halcyon
Rotisserie Jules
Thai Kitchen
Tom's Deli
Tootsies
Westbourne
Wine Factory
Wiz
Zucca

Olympia

Alounak
Cibo
Havelock Tavern
Wilson's

Shepherd's Bush

Adams Cafe
Anglesea Arms

Blah! Blah! Blah!
Brackenbury
Cafe Rouge

Chinon
Esarn Kheaw
Snows on Green

IN THE COUNTRY

Amberley Castle, Queens Rm.
Angel
Auberge du Lac
Bear
Beetle & Wedge
Bell Inn
Bishopstrow Hse.
Buckland Manor
Chapter One
Cherwell Boathse.
Chewton Glen Hotel
Cliveden, Waldo's
Compleat Angler
Dining Room
Eastwell Manor
Fat Duck
Fawsley Hall
Feathers Hotel
Flitwick Manor
French Horn
Gravetye Manor
Hambleton Hall
Hartwell House
Horsted Place, Pugin

Hotel du Vin
King's Head
Leaping Hare
Leatherne Bottel
Le Manoir/Quat'Saisons
Le Petit Blanc
Le Talbooth
L'Ortolan
Lucknam Park
Lygon Arms
Mallory Court
Marsh Goose
Old Bridge Hotel
One Paston Place
Orange Balloon
Pennyhill Park, Latymer
Pink Geranium
Royal Oak
Sir Charles Napier
Stapleford Park
Stonor Arms
Three Lions
Waterside Inn

SPECIAL FEATURES AND APPEALS

All-Day Dining

Al Bustan (SW1)
Al Hamra (W1)
All Bar One (multi. loc.)
Alounak (multi. loc.)
Al Sultan (W1)
Aroma (multi. loc.)
Ask Pizza (multi. loc.)
Babe Ruth's (multi. loc.)
Balans (W1)
Barcelona Tapas (multi. loc.)
Belgo Centraal (WC2)
Belgo Noord (NW1)
Bibendum Oyster (SW3)
Big Easy (SW3)
Bistrot 190 (SW7)
Bistrot 2 Riverside (SE1)
Bloom's (NW11)
Browns Rest. (multi. loc.)
Café Delancey (NW1)
Café Flo (multi. loc.)
Cafe Lazeez (multi. loc.)
Cafe Med (multi. loc.)
Café Pacifico (WC2)
Cafe Rouge (multi. loc.)
Caffè Nero (multi. loc.)
Calzone (multi. loc.)
Capital Radio Cafe (multi. loc.)
Casale Franco (N1)
Cheers (W1)
Chelsea Bun (multi. loc.)
Chelsea Kitchen (SW3)
Chicago Rib Shack (SW7)
China City (WC2)
Choys (SW3)
Chuen Cheng Ku (W1)
Coffee Republic (multi. loc.)
Condotti (W1)
Cork & Bottle (WC2)
Côte à Côte (SW11)
Cranks (multi. loc.)
Crescent (SW3)
Cuba (W8)
Cuba Libre (N1)
Dôme (multi. loc.)
Down Mexico Way (W1)
Ed's Easy Diner (multi. loc.)
Efes Kebab Hse. (multi. loc.)
El Metro (SW6)
est (W1)

Fakhreldine (multi. loc.)
Fifth Floor Cafe (SW1)
Food for Thought (WC2)
Fortnum's Fountain (W1)
Foundation (SW1)
Fox & Anchor (EC1)
Fung Shing (WC2)
Golden Dragon (W1)
Green Cottage (NW3)
Harrods (SW1)
Havana (multi. loc.)
Henry J. Bean's (SW3)
Hi Sushi (W1)
Hothouse (E1)
House/Rosslyn Hill (NW3)
Ikkyu (multi. loc.)
Imperial City (EC3)
Istanbul Iskembecisi (N16)
itsu (SW3)
Jade Garden (W1)
Jim Thompson's (multi. loc.)
Joe Allen (WC2)
Joe's Rest. Bar (SW1)
Kettners (W1)
La Bouchée (SW7)
La Brasserie (SW3)
La Delizia (multi. loc.)
La Finca (multi. loc.)
Lahore Kebab Hse. (E1)
La Mancha (SW15)
Langan's Brasserie (W1)
Langan's Coq d'Or (SW5)
La Piragua (N1)
La Rueda (multi. loc.)
Le Bouchon Bordelais (SW11)
Le Bouchon Lyonnais (SW8)
Lee Fook (W2)
Lee Ho Fook (W1)
Le Metro (SW3)
Le Piaf (multi. loc.)
Little Bay (NW6)
Little Havana (WC2)
Little Italy (W1)
Luigi's Deli (SW10)
Luna Nuova (WC2)
Mackintosh's (W4)
Maison Bertaux (W1)
Mandarin Kitchen (W2)
Maroush (multi. loc.)
Maxwell's (multi. loc.)

Melati (W1)
Memories of India (SW7)
Mildreds (W1)
Ming (W1)
Mona Lisa (SW10)
Museum St. Cafe (WC1)
Mustards Smithfield (EC1)
Nachos (multi. loc.)
Navajo Joe (WC2)
New Culture Rev. (multi. loc.)
New World (W1)
Novelli EC1 (EC1)
Oriel (SW1)
Orsino (W11)
Orso (WC2)
Palio (W11)
Paparazzi Lounge (SW3)
Patisserie Valerie (multi. loc.)
Pepper Tree (SW4)
Phoenicia (W8)
Picasso (SW3)
Pitcher & Piano (multi. loc.)
Pizza Express (multi. loc.)
Pizza on the Park (SW1)
Pizza Pomodoro (multi. loc.)
Pizza The Action (SW6)
Pizzeria Castello (SE1)
PJ's Bar & Grill (SW3)
Planet Hollywood (W1)
Porters (WC2)
porters bar/poland st. (W1)
Pucci Pizza (SW3)
Rainforest Cafe (W1)
Randall & Aubin (W1)
Red Fort (W1)
Richoux (multi. loc.)
Rock Garden (WC2)
Rotisserie Jules (multi. loc.)
Royal China (multi. loc.)
Rules (WC2)
Seafresh Fish (SW1)
Seashell (NW1)
Shoeless Joe's (multi. loc.)
Singapura (multi. loc.)
Sofra (multi. loc.)
Soho Spice (W1)
Solly's (NW11)
Southeast W9 (W9)
Spaghetti House (multi. loc.)
Sports Cafe (SW1)
Starbucks/Seattle Co. (multi. loc.)
Sticky Fingers (W8)

Suan Neo (EC2)
Terraza (multi. loc.)
Texas Embassy (SW14)
Texas Lone Star (multi. loc.)
T.G.I. Friday's (multi. loc.)
Toff's (N10)
Tokyo Diner (WC2)
Tom's Deli (W11)
Tootsies (multi. loc.)
Tuttons (WC2)
Vic Naylor (EC1)
Vingt-Quatre (SW10)
Wagamama (multi. loc.)
Wolfe's B&G (WC2)
Wong Kei (W1)
Ye Olde Cheshire (EC4)
Yo! Sushi (multi. loc.)
Zilli Fish (W1)
Zinc B&G (W1)

Breakfast/Brunch

(All hotels and the following
standouts; BR=breakfast;
B=brunch)
Admiral Codrington (SW3) (B)
Avenue (SW1) (B)
Bank (WC2) (BR,B)
Beach Blanket Babylon (W11) (B)
Bistrot 190 (SW7) (BR,B)
Bluebird (SW3) (B)
Brompton Bay (SW3) (B)
Browns Rest. (multi. loc.) (B)
Butlers Wharf (SE1) (B)
Cactus Blue (SW3) (B)
Cafe at Sotheby's (W1) (BR)
Café Delancey (NW1) (BR)
Café Milan (SW3) (BR,B)
Camden Brasserie (NW1) (B)
Cantaloupe B&G (EC2) (B)
Canyon (Richmond) (B)
Chelsea Bun (multi. loc.) (BR,B)
Chelsea Kitchen (SW3) (BR,B)
Christopher's (WC2) (B)
Chutney Mary (SW10) (B)
Coast (W1) (B)
Coq d'Argent (EC2) (BR)
Cow Dining Room (W2) (B)
Crescent (SW3) (BR,B)
Dakota (W11) (B)
Daphne's (SW3) (B)
Ed's Easy Diner (multi. loc.) (BR)
Emporio Armani (SW3) (BR)

Engineer (NW1) (BR,B)
Fifth Floor Cafe (SW1) (BR)
Fortnum's Fountain (W1) (BR)
Fox & Anchor (EC1) (BR)
Giraffe (multi. loc.) (BR,B)
Globe (NW3) (B)
Green's Rest. (SW1) (B)
Grissini (SW1) (BR,B)
Halkin, Stef. Cavallini (SW1) (BR)
Harrods (SW1) (BR,B)
Honest Cabbage (SE1) (B)
Icon (SW3) (B)
Idaho (N6) (B)
Jason's (W9) (B)
Joe Allen (WC2) (B)
Joe's (SW3) (BR,B)
Joe's Brasserie (SW6) (B)
Joe's Rest. Bar (SW1) (BR,B)
Julie's (W11) (B)
La Brasserie (SW3) (BR,B)
Langan's Coq d'Or (SW5) (BR,B)
La Porte des Indes (W1) (B)
Lawn (SE3) (B)
Le Caprice (SW1) (B)
Le Metro (SW3) (BR)
Le Petit Blanc (multi. loc.) (BR)
Le Pont de la Tour (SE1) (B)
Lola's (N1) (B)
Mackintosh's (W4) (BR,B)
Made in Italy (SW3) (B)
Manzi's (WC2) (BR)
Marine Ices (NW3) (BR)
Mas Café (W11) (B)
Mash (W1) (B)
Mezzo (W1) (B)
Min's (SW3) (B)
Mona Lisa (SW10) (BR,B)
Montana (SW6) (B)
Museum St. Cafe (WC1) (BR)
Nicole's (W1) (BR)
Oriel (SW1) (BR)
Osteria Antica Bol. (SW11) (B)
Palio (W11) (B)
Patisserie Val. (multi. loc.) (BR,B)
PJ's Bar & Grill (SW3) (B)
Polygon B&G (SW4) (B)
Rain (W10) (B)
Ransome's Dock (SW11) (B)
Rhodes in Square (SW1) (B)
Riccardo's (SW3) (BR,B)
Richoux (multi. loc.) (BR)
Scotts (W1) (B)

Simpson's/Strand (WC2) (BR)
T.G.I. Friday's (multi. loc.) (B)
Tom's Deli (W11) (BR,B)
Villandry Foodstore (W1) (BR,B)
Vingt-Quatre (SW10) (BR,B)
Vong (SW1) (B)
Waterloo Fire Station (SE1) (B)
Westbourne (W2) (B)
Wiz (W1) (B)

Business Dining

Atrium (SW1)
Avenue (SW1)
Bank (WC2)
Bentley's (W1)
Bibendum (SW3)
Bice (W1)
Blakes Hotel (SW7)
Blue Print Cafe (SE1)
Brown's Hotel, 1837 (W1)
Canteen (SW10)
Capital Rest. (SW3)
Cave (W1)
Caviar Kaspia (W1)
Cecconi's (W1)
Che (SW1)
Chez Nico (W1)
China Jazz (W1)
Christopher's (WC2)
Cibo (W14)
Circus (W1)
City Rhodes (EC4)
Claridge's Rest. (W1)
Clarke's (W8)
Cliveden, Waldo's (Berks)
Club Gascon (EC1)
Connaught Hotel (W1)
Criterion Brasserie (W1)
Dorchester, Grill Rm. (W1)
Dorchester, Oriental (W1)
Elena's L'Etoile (W1)
Fakhreldine (multi. loc.)
Fifth Floor (SW1)
Floriana (SW3)
Four Seasons, Lanes (W1)
Frith Street (W1)
Glasshouse (Kew)
Gordon Ramsay (SW3)
Goring Dining Rm. (SW1)
Gravetye Manor (W. Sus)
Greenhouse (W1)
Green's Rest. (SW1)
Grissini (SW1)

Halkin, Stefano Cavallini (SW1)
Hartwell House (Bucks)
Hilaire (SW7)
I-Thai (W2)
Ivy (WC2)
J. Sheekey (WC2)
Kai (W1)
Landmark, Dining Rm. (NW1)
Lanesborough (SW1)
Langan's Bistro (W1)
Langan's Brasserie (W1)
La Tante Claire (SW1)
Launceston Place (W8)
Le Café du Marché (EC1)
Le Caprice (SW1)
Le Gavroche (W1)
Leith's (W11)
Leith's Soho (W1)
Le Manoir/Quat'Saisons (Oxon)
Le Pont de la Tour (SE1)
Le Soufflé (W1)
L'Incontro (SW1)
L'Odeon (W1)
L'Oranger (SW1)
Manzi's (WC2)
Marquis (W1)
Memories of China (multi. loc.)
Mirabelle (W1)
Mitsukoshi (SW1)
Miyama (W1)
Morton's (W1)
Neal St. (WC2)
Nico Central (W1)
Nobu (W1)
Oak Room MPW (W1)
Odin's (W1)
One-O-One (SW1)
Orrery (W1)
Orso (WC2)
Oxo Tower (SE1)
Park Rest. (SW1)
Pétrus (SW1)
Pied-à-Terre (W1)
Poissonnerie/l'Avenue (SW3)
Princess Garden (W1)
Quaglino's (SW1)
Quo Vadis (W1)
Rib Room (SW1)
Ritz Rest. (W1)
River Cafe (W6)
Room/Halcyon (W11)
Rules (WC2)

Santini (SW1)
Savoy Grill (WC2)
Savoy River Rest. (WC2)
Scotts (W1)
Searcy's/Barbican (EC2)
Shepherd's (SW1)
Shogun (W1)
Square (W1)
Stephen Bull (W1)
Suntory (SW1)
Tamarind (W1)
Tatsuso (EC2)
Terrace (W1) (W1)
Turner's (SW3)
Vong (SW1)
Waterside Inn (Berks)
Wilton's (SW1)
Windows on World (W1)
Zafferano (SW1)
Zen Central (W1)

BYO

Adams Cafe (W12)
Alounak (multi. loc.)
Bedlington Cafe (W4)
Blah! Blah! Blah! (W12)
Books for Cooks (W11)
Chapter One (Kent)
Chelsea Bun (multi. loc.)
Cookhouse (SW15)
El Gaucho (SW3)
Food for Thought (WC2)
Japanese Canteen (W1)
Kalamaras Micro (W2)
Lahore Kebab Hse. (E1)
Mandola Café (W11)
Monsieur Max (Hampton Hill)
Ravi Shankar (EC1)
Smokey Joe's Diner (SW18)
Tom's Deli (W11)
Upper St. Fish Shop (N1)
World Food Café (WC2)

Dancing/Entertainment

(Check days, times and
performers for entertainment;
D=dancing; best of many)
Al Bustan (SW1) (belly dancer)
Archduke (SE1) (jazz)
Arkansas Cafe (E1) (rockabilly)
Atlantic B&G (W1) (D/jazz)
Avenue (SW1) (piano/jazz)
Bar Madrid (W1) (D/band)

Bengal Clipper (SE1) (piano)
Big Easy (SW3) (rock)
Birdcage (W1) (varies)
Bluebird (SW3) (piano)
Blues Bistro (W1) (jazz)
Boardwalk (W1) (D/varies)
Boisdale (SW1) (D/jazz)
Break for the Border (multi. loc.)
  (D/bands/DJ)
Cactus Blue (SW3) (jazz)
Café Boheme (W1) (jazz)
Café Delancey (NW1) (piano)
Cafe de Paris (W1) (D)
Café des Amis du Vin (WC2)
  (jazz)
Cafe Lazeez (SW7) (jazz)
China Blues (NW1) (D/jazz)
China Jazz (W1) (D/jazz)
Chutney Mary (SW10) (jazz)
Claridge's Rest. (W1) (D)
Compleat Angler (Bucks) (piano)
Coq d'Argent (EC2) (piano)
Côte à Côte (SW11) (varies)
Cuba (W8) (D)
Cuba Libre (N1) (D)
Deals (W1) (D/bands)
Don Pepe (NW8) (Spanish)
Dorchester, Bar (W1)
  (jazz/piano)
Dover Street (W1) (D/bands/DJ)
Down Mexico Way (W1)
  (D/bands/DJ)
El Metro (SW6) (Spanish)
El Prado (SW6) (guitar)
Fifth Floor Cafe (SW1) (jazz)
Floriana (SW3) (piano)
Four Seasons, Lanes (W1)
  (piano)
Goring Dining Rm. (SW1) (piano)
Greek Valley (NW8) (D/Greek)
Grissini (SW1) (piano)
Halkin, Stefano Cavallini (SW1)
  (guitar/harp)
Havana (multi. loc.)
  (D/bands/DJ)
Horsted Place, Pugin (E. Sus)
  (piano)
Hothouse (E1) (jazz)
House/Rosslyn Hill (NW3)
  (karaoke)
Idaho (N6) (jazz/piano)
Joe Allen (WC2) (piano)

Lab (W1) (DJ)
La Finca (multi. loc.) (D/salsa)
La Mancha (SW15) (guitar)
Landmark, Dining Rm. (NW1)
  (D/bands)
Lanesborough (SW1)
  (D/jazz/piano)
Langan's Brasserie (W1)
  (band/piano)
La Rueda (multi. loc.) (D)
Le Bouchon Bordelais (SW11)
  (jazz)
Le Bouchon Lyonnais (SW8)
  (jazz)
Le Cafe du Jardin (WC2) (piano)
Le Caprice (SW1) (piano)
Le Pont de la Tour (SE1)
  (jazz/piano)
Le Soufflé (W1) (piano)
Lexington (W1) (piano)
Little Havana (WC2)
  (D/bands/DJ)
L'Odeon (W1) (jazz)
Lola's (N1) (jazz/piano)
Mackintosh's (W4) (jazz)
Maroush (W2)
  (belly dancer/vocals)
Meson Don Felipe (SE1) (guitar)
Mezzo (W1) (D/jazz)
Mirabelle (W1) (piano)
Montana (SW6) (jazz)
Motcomb's (SW1) (D)
Mr. Wing (SW5) (jazz)
Nachos (multi. loc.) (D)
Naked Turtle (SW14)
  (jazz/magician)
Nikita's (SW10) (guitar)
Old Delhi (W2) (harp)
1 Lombard St. (EC3) (band)
Oxo Tower Brasserie (SE1) (jazz)
Palio (W11) (jazz)
Paparazzi Lounge (multi. loc.)
  (D/Italian)
Pelham St. (SW7) (jazz)
Pizza on the Park (SW1)
  (cabaret/jazz)
Princess Garden (W1) (piano)
Purple Sage (W1) (jazz)
Quaglino's (SW1) (jazz)
Rebato's (SW8) (guitar)
Ritz Rest. (W1) (D/piano)
Rock Garden (WC2) (D/bands)

Rodizio Rico (W2) (D)
Saint Bar & Rest. (WC2) (D)
Salsa! (WC2) (D/Latin)
Savoy River Rest. (WC2)
   (D/bands)
Scotts (W1) (piano)
Shoeless Joe's (multi. loc.)
   (D/jazz)
Smollensky's/Strand (WC2)
   (D/varies)
Sofra (multi. loc.) (guitar)
Soho Soho (W1) (piano)
Soho Spice (W1) (D)
Souk (WC2) (music)
Star of India (SW5) (cabaret)
Tea Rms. des Artistes (SW8)
   (jazz)
Tenth (W8) (D)
Terraza (multi. loc.) (jazz)
Texas Lone Star (W4) (country)
T.G.I. Friday's (W1) (magician)
Titanic (W1) (D/DJ)
Townhouse (WC1) (jazz)
Trader Vic's (W1) (Latin)
Troubadour (SW5) (varies)
Voodoo Lounge (WC2) (D/DJ)
Waterloo Fire Station (SE1) (jazz)
Windows on World (W1)
   (D/piano)
Zamoyski (NW3) (Russian)
Zen Garden (W1) (pianist)

Delivers*/Take-away

(D=delivery; T=take-away;
*call to check range and
charges, if any)

Al Bustan (SW1) (D,T)
Al Hamra (W1) (D,T)
Alounak (multi. loc.) (D,T)
Al Sultan (W1) (T)
Ask Pizza (multi. loc.) (T)
Aykoku-Kaku (EC4) (D,T)
Babe Ruth's (multi. loc.) (D,T)
Bangkok (SW7) (T)
Bayee House (multi. loc.) (D,T)
Bedlington Cafe (W4) (T)
Beiteddine (SW1) (D,T)
Bengal Clipper (SE1) (T)
Bengal Trader (E1) (T)
Ben's Thai (WC1) (T)
Big Easy (SW3) (T)
Bloom's (NW11) (D,T)
Blue Elephant (SW6) (T)

Blue Jade (SW1) (T)
Bonjour Vietnam (SW6) (T)
Busabong Tree (SW10) (D,T)
Cafe Lazeez (multi. loc.) (T)
Café Milan (SW3) (T)
Cafe Spice Nam. (multi. loc.) (D,T)
Calzone (multi. loc.) (T)
Chelsea Bun (SW11) (T)
Chelsea Kitchen (SW3) (T)
Cheng-Du (NW1) (D,T)
Chicago Rib Shack (SW7) (T)
China Blues (NW1) (D,T)
China City (WC2) (T)
Chor Bizarre (W1) (D,T)
Chutney Mary (SW10) (D)
Chutney's (NW1) (T)
City Miyama (EC4) (D,T)
Como Lario (SW1) (T)
Condotti (W1) (T)
Cottons Rhum Shop (NW1) (T)
Crescent (SW3) (T)
Deals (multi. loc.) (T)
Defune (W1) (D,T)
DKNY Bar (W1) (T)
Ed's Easy Diner (multi. loc.) (D,T)
Esarn Kheaw (W12) (T)
Fakhreldine (multi. loc.) (D,T)
Four Regions (SE1) (T)
Garbo's (W1) (D)
Good Earth (multi. loc.) (D,T)
Greek Valley (NW8) (D,T)
Gung-Ho (NW6) (D,T)
Halepi (W2) (D,T)
Hard Rock Cafe (W1) (T)
Jenny Lo's (SW1) (D,T)
Kaifeng (NW4) (D,T)
Khun Akorn (SW3) (T)
Koi (W8) (T)
Kulu Kulu Sushi (W1) (T)
La Bersagliera (SW3) (T)
La Delizia (SW3) (T)
Lahore Kebab Hse. (E1) (D,T)
La Porte des Indes (W1) (D,T)
Lee Fook (W2) (T)
Le Muscadet (W1) (D,T)
Luigi's Deli (SW10) (T)
Mackintosh's (W4) (T)
Mandola Café (W11) (T)
Mao Tai (SW6) (T)
Maroush (multi. loc.) (D,T)
Mash (W1) (T)
Melati (W1) (T)

Memories/China (multi. loc.) (T)
Mona Lisa (SW10) (T)
Moshi Moshi (multi. loc.) (D,T)
Mr. Wing (SW5) (D,T)
Nachos (SW10) (D,T)
New Culture (multi. loc.) (D,T)
Noor Jahan (SW5) (T)
Oliveto (SW1) (T)
Osteria Basilico (W11) (T)
Pacific Oriental (EC2) (T)
Patara (multi. loc.) (T)
Pepper Tree (SW4) (T)
Pizza Express (multi. loc.) (D,T)
Pizza Metro (SW11) (T)
Place Below (EC2) (T)
Pollo Bar (W1) (T)
Poons (multi. loc.) (T)
Poons in the City (EC3) (D,T)
Purple Sage (W1) (T)
Randall & Aubin (W1) (T)
Rani (N3) (T)
Red Fort (W1) (T)
Riccardo's (SW3) (D,T)
Richoux (SW3) (T)
Rotisserie Jules (multi. loc.) (D,T)
Royal China (multi. loc.) (T)
Saga (W1) (T)
Salloos (SW1) (D,T)
Sarkhel's Indian (SW1) (T)
Satsuma (W1) (D,T)
Sauce BarOrganic (NW1) (T)
Seafresh Fish (SW1) (D,T)
Seashell (NW1) (T)
Shimla Pinks (EC2) (T)
Singapore Gard. (multi. loc.) (D,T)
Smokey Joe's Diner (SW18) (T)
Soho Spice (W1) (T)
Solly's (NW11) (D,T)
Soup Opera (multi. loc.) (D,T)
Soup Works (multi. loc.) (D,T)
Southeast W9 (W9) (T)
Spighetta (W1) (T)
Star of India (SW5) (T)
Sticky Fingers (W8) (T)
Tamarind (W1) (D,T)
Tandoori Lane (SW6) (D,T)
Tea Rms./ Artistes (SW8) (D,T)
Toff's (N10) (T)
Tui (SW7) (T)
Two Brothers (N3) (T)
Vama (SW10) (T)
Veeraswamy (W1) (D)

Veronica's (W2) (D,T)
Viet Hoa (multi. loc.) (T)
Vineet Bhatia (W6) (T)
Yo! Sushi (multi. loc.) (D,T)
Yum Yum Thai (N16) (T)
Zen Central (W1) (D,T)
Zen Chelsea (SW3) (D,T)
ZeNW3 (NW3) (T)

Dining Alone

(Other than hotels, coffee
shops, sushi bars and places
with counter service)
Benihana (W1)
Bibendum Oyster (SW3)
Books for Cooks (W11)
Cafe at Sotheby's (W1)
Café Flo (multi. loc.)
Cafe Rouge (multi. loc.)
Cave (W1)
Chuen Cheng Ku (W1)
Crescent (SW3)
DKNY Bar (W1)
Dôme (multi. loc.)
Ed's Easy Diner (multi. loc.)
Emporio Armani (SW3)
Fifth Floor Cafe (SW1)
Fortnum's Fountain (W1)
Foundation (SW1)
Harrods (SW1)
Ikeda (W1)
Jenny Lo's (SW1)
Joe's Rest. Bar (SW1)
King's Rd. Cafe (SW3)
La Bouchée (SW7)
Luigi's Deli (SW10)
Matsuri (SW1)
Mezzonine (W1)
Mildreds (W1)
Mon Plaisir (WC2)
New Culture Rev. (NW1)
Nicole's (W1)
Oriel (SW1)
Patisserie Valerie (multi. loc.)
Randall & Aubin (W1)
Richoux (multi. loc.)
Soup Opera (multi. loc.)
Soup Works (multi. loc.)
Tom's Deli (W11)
Villandry Foodstore (W1)
Wagamama (W1)
Wok Wok (multi. loc.)

Fireplaces

Admiral Codrington (SW3)
Angel (Bucks)
Anglesea Arms (W6)
ArdRí/O'Conor Don (W1)
Auberge du Lac (Herts)
Bam-Bou (W1)
Beach Blanket Babylon (W11)
Bear (Oxon)
Beetle & Wedge (Oxon)
Belair House (SE21)
Bell Inn (Bucks)
Bierodrome (N1)
Bishopstrow Hse. (Wilts)
Boisdale (SW1)
Brackenbury (W6)
Brown's Hotel, 1837 (W1)
Buckland Manor (Glos)
Café Delancey (NW1)
Cafe des Arts (NW3)
Cambio de Tercio (SW5)
Camden Brasserie (NW1)
Caviar Kaspia (W1)
Chelsea Ram (SW10)
Chewton Glen Hotel (Hants)
Cicada (EC1)
Cliveden, Waldo's (Berks)
Côte à Côte (SW11)
Cottons Rhum Shop (NW1)
Daphne's (SW3)
Duke of Cambridge (SW11)
Eastwell Manor (Kent)
English Garden (SW3)
English Hse. (SW3)
Fat Duck (Berks)
Fawsley Hall (N'hants)
Flitwick Manor (Beds)
French Horn (Berks)
Glaister's Garden (SW11)
Gravetye Manor (W. Sus)
Grenadier (SW1)
Hambleton Hall (Rut)
Hartwell House (Bucks)
Havelock Tavern (W14)
Horsted Place, Pugin (E. Sus)
I-Thai (W2)
Julie's (W11)
Just Around the Corner (NW2)
King's Head (Bucks)
La Poule au Pot (SW1)
Leaping Hare (Suffolk)
Leatherne Bottel (Berks)

Le Manoir/Quat'Saisons (Oxon)
Lemonia (NW1)
L'Escargot (W1)
Le Talbooth (Essex)
Little Bay (NW6)
Lygon Arms (Wocs)
Mallory Court (Warwks)
Marsh Goose (Glos)
Mediterraneo (W11)
Min's (SW3)
Mon Plaisir (WC2)
Naked Turtle (SW14)
North Pole (SE10)
Old Bridge Hotel (Cambs)
Peasant (EC1)
Pink Geranium (Cambs)
Queens (NW1)
Richard Corrigan (W1)
Royal Oak (Berks)
Salt House (NW8)
Sauce BarOrganicDiner (NW1)
Shimla Pinks (EC2)
Sir Charles Napier (Oxon)
Sonny's (SW13)
Stapleford Park (Leics)
Stonor Arms (Oxon)
Three Lions (Hants)
Vic Naylor (EC1)
Waxy O'Connor's (W1)
Westbourne (W2)
Ye Olde Cheshire (EC4)

Game in Season

(Best of many)
Abingdon (W8)
Andrew Edmunds (W1)
Angel (Bucks)
Anglesea Arms (W6)
Auberge du Lac (Herts)
Beetle & Wedge (Oxon)
Bell Inn (Bucks)
Brackenbury (W6)
Brown's Hotel, 1837 (W1)
Butlers Wharf (SE1)
Capital Rest. (SW3)
Che (SW1)
Cherwell Boathse. (Oxon)
Chewton Glen Hotel (Hants)
Chez Max (SW10)
Chez Nico (W1)
City Rhodes (EC4)
Club Gascon (EC1)
Compleat Angler (Bucks)

Connaught Hotel (W1)
Cookhouse (SW15)
Coq d'Argent (EC2)
Criterion Brasserie (W1)
Dining Room (Surrey)
Dorchester, Grill Rm. (W1)
Eastwell Manor (Kent)
English Garden (SW3)
English Hse. (SW3)
Fawsley Hall (N'hants)
Flitwick Manor (Beds)
French House (W1)
Glasshouse (Kew)
Goring Dining Rm. (SW1)
Gravetye Manor (W. Sus)
Greenhouse (W1)
Green Olive (W9)
Green's Rest. (SW1)
Guinea (W1)
Halkin, Stefano Cavallini (SW1)
Hambleton Hall (Rut)
Hartwell House (Bucks)
Hilaire (SW7)
Horsted Place, Pugin (E. Sus)
Hotel du Vin (multi. loc.)
Hothouse (E1)
Kensington Place (W8)
Lanesborough (SW1)
La Poule au Pot (SW1)
La Tante Claire (SW1)
Launceston Place (W8)
Le Gavroche (W1)
Leith's (W11)
Leith's Soho (W1)
Le Manoir/Quat'Saisons (Oxon)
Le Pont de la Tour (SE1)
Le Soufflé (W1)
Lundum's (SW7)
Marquis (W1)
Marsh Goose (Glos)
Monkeys (SW3)
Monsieur Max (Hampton Hill)
Monza (SW3)
Odette's (NW1)
Orrery (W1)
Pied-à-Terre (W1)
Putney Bridge (SW15)
Ransome's Dock (SW11)
Richard Corrigan (W1)
River Cafe (W6)
Rules (WC2)
Scotts (W1)

Shepherd's (SW1)
Simpson's/The Strand (WC2)
Sir Charles Napier (Oxon)
Square (W1)
Stapleford Park (Leics)
Stephen Bull (multi. loc.)
Stepping Stone (SW8)
St. John (EC1)
Sweetings (EC4)
Teatro (W1)
TECA (W1)
Wilton's (SW1)
Zafferano (SW1)

Historic Interest
(Year opened; *building)
1598 Gravetye Manor (W. Sus)
1640 Compleat Angler (Bucks)
1667 Ye Olde Cheshire (EC4)
1700 Footstool (SW1)
1742 Grenadier (SW1)
1742 Wilton's (SW1)
1759 Simpsons Tavern (EC3)
1777 Home House (W1)
1798 Rules (WC2)
1828 Simpson's/Strand (WC2)
1850 Cliveden, Waldo's (Berks)
1889 Sweetings (EC4)
1897 Connaught Hotel (W1)
1898 Claridge's Rest. (W1)
1906 Ritz Rest. (W1)

Hotel Dining
Amberley Castle
  Queens Rm. (W. Sus)
Angel Inn
  Angel (Bucks)
Bear Hotel
  Bear (Oxon)
Beetle & Wedge Hotel
  Beetle & Wedge (Oxon)
Bell Inn
  Bell Inn (Bucks)
Berkeley Hotel
  La Tante Claire (SW1)
  Vong (SW1)
Bishopstrow House
  Bishopstrow Hse. (Wilts)
Blakes Hotel
  Blakes Hotel (SW7)
Britannia Hotel
  Shogun (W1)

Royal National Hotel
   Poons (WC1)
Royal Oak Hotel
   Royal Oak (Berks)
Savoy Hotel
   Savoy Grill (WC2)
   Savoy River Rest. (WC2)
   Upstairs/The Savoy (WC2)
Sheraton Park Tower
   One-O-One (SW1)
Stapleford Park Hotel
   Stapleford Park (Leics)
St. Martin's Ln. Hotel
   Asia de Cuba (WC2)
Stonor Arms Hotel
   Stonor Arms (Oxon)
Three Lions Hotel
   Three Lions (Hants)
Waterside Inn
   Waterside Inn (Berks)

"In" Places

Admiral Codrington (SW3)
Assaggi (W2)
Atlantic B&G (W1)
Avenue (SW1)
Axis (WC2)
bali sugar (W11)
Bam-Bou (W1)
Bank (WC2)
Belgo Centraal (WC2)
Belgo Noord (NW1)
Belgo Zuid (W1)
Bibendum (SW3)
Bibendum Oyster (SW3)
Bierodrome (N1)
Blakes Hotel (SW7)
Bluebird (SW3)
Cafe at Sotheby's (W1)
Café Milan (SW3)
Canyon (Richmond)
Che (SW1)
Chez Bruce (SW17)
Christopher's (WC2)
Circus (W1)
Claridge's Bar (W1)
Clarke's (W8)
Club Gascon (EC1)
Coast (W1)
Collection (SW3)
Dakota (W11)
Daphne's (SW3)
Elistano (SW3)

Fifth Floor (SW1)
Fifth Floor Cafe (SW1)
Fish! (SE1)
Floriana (SW3)
Frith Street (W1)
Glasshouse (Kew)
Gordon Ramsay (SW3)
Granita (N1)
Halkin, Stefano Cavallini (SW1)
Ivy (WC2)
Joe's (SW3)
J. Sheekey (WC2)
Kensington Place (W8)
Lab (W1)
Langan's Brasserie (W1)
Le Caprice (SW1)
Leith's Soho (W1)
Livebait (multi. loc.)
Lola's (N1)
Maison Novelli (EC1)
Mash (W1)
Mirabelle (W1)
Momo (W1)
Monsieur Max (Hampton Hill)
Montana (SW6)
Nam Long Le Shaker (SW5)
Navajo Joe (WC2)
Nicole's (W1)
Nobu (W1)
Oak Room MPW (W1)
Oliveto (SW1)
Olivo (SW1)
1 Lombard St. (EC3)
Orso (WC2)
Oxo Tower (SE1)
Oxo Tower Brasserie (SE1)
Pasha (SW7)
Pétrus (SW1)
Pharmacy (W11)
PJ's Bar & Grill (SW3)
PJ's Grill (WC2)
Prism (EC3)
Putney Bridge (SW15)
Quo Vadis (W1)
Randall & Aubin (W1)
Richard Corrigan (W1)
Riva (SW13)
River Cafe (W6)
Room/Halcyon (W11)
Saint Bar & Rest. (WC2)
San Lorenzo (SW3)
Sartoria (W1)

Shoreditch Electricity (N1)
Spiga (W1)
Spighetta (W1)
Square (W1)
St. John (EC1)
Sugar Club (W1)
Tajine (W1)
Titanic (W1)
Tom's Deli (W11)
Vingt-Quatre (SW10)
Vong (SW1)
Voodoo Lounge (WC2)
Wagamama (multi. loc.)
Yo! Sushi (multi. loc.)
Zafferano (SW1)
Zaika (SW3)
Zilli Fish (W1)

Late Late – After Midnight

(All hours are AM)
Balans (W1) (3)
Balans West (SW5) (1)
Bar Madrid (W1) (1)
Big Easy (SW3) (12.30)
Boardwalk (W1) (12.50)
Boisdale (SW1) (1)
Browns Rest. (multi. loc.) (12.30)
Café Boheme (W1) (call for hrs.)
Cafe Lazeez (multi. loc.) (12.30)
Cuba (W8) (2)
Denim (WC2) (1.30)
Dover Street (W1) (2)
Hard Rock Cafe (W1) (12.30)
Istanbul Iskembecisi (N16) (5)
Joe Allen (WC2) (12.45)
Little Havana (WC2) (1)
Little Italy (W1) (3)
Maroush (multi. loc.) (3.30)
Mezzonine (W1) (1)
Mr. Kong (WC2) (2.45)
Paparazzi Cafe (multi. loc.) (1)
Planet Hollywood (W1) (1)
Pucci Pizza (SW3) (12.30)
Tea Rms. des Artistes (SW8) (1)
Trader Vic's (W1) (12.30)
Vingt-Quatre (SW10) (24 hrs.)
Voodoo Lounge (WC2) (1)

No Smoking Section

alistair Greig's Grill (W1)
Angel (Bucks)
Apprentice (SE1)
Archduke (SE1)

Arkansas Cafe (E1)
Babe Ruth's (multi. loc.)
Balans Knightsbridge (SW3)
bali sugar (W11)
Beetle & Wedge (Oxon)
Beotys (WC2)
Bertorelli's (WC2)
Bertorelli's Cafe Italian (W1)
Big Easy (SW3)
Birdcage (W1)
Brown's Hotel, 1837 (W1)
Browns Rest. (W1)
Byron's (NW3)
Cactus Blue (SW3)
Cafe des Arts (NW3)
Café Fish (W1)
Café Flo (multi. loc.)
Cafe Lazeez (multi. loc.)
Café Pacifico (WC2)
Cafe Rouge (multi. loc.)
Capital Radio Cafe (WC2)
Casale Franco (N1)
Charco's (SW3)
Cheers (W1)
Chelsea Kitchen (SW3)
Chez Gérard (multi. loc.)
Chicago Rib Shack (SW7)
China Blues (NW1)
China City (WC2)
Chor Bizarre (W1)
Chuen Cheng Ku (W1)
Chutney Mary (SW10)
Claridge's Rest. (W1)
Clarke's (W8)
Compleat Angler (Bucks)
Cookhouse (SW15)
Cork & Bottle (WC2)
Côte à Côte (SW11)
Cottons Rhum Shop (NW1)
Daquise (SW7)
Deals (multi. loc.)
Depot Waterfront (SW14)
Dôme (multi. loc.)
Duke of Cambridge (N1)
East One (EC1)
Eco (SW4)
Ed's Easy Diner (multi. loc.)
El Blason (SW3)
Flitwick Manor (Beds)
Footstool (SW1)
Fortnum's Fountain (W1)

Foundation (SW1)
Four Seasons, Lanes (W1)
Francofill (SW7)
Frederick's (N1)
Futures!! (multi. loc.)
Gresslin's (NW3)
Grissini (SW1)
Hard Rock Cafe (W1)
Harrods (SW1)
Hartwell House (Bucks)
itsu (SW3)
Japanese Canteen (multi. loc.)
Jim Thompson's (SW19)
Joe Allen (WC2)
King's Head (Bucks)
King's Rd. Cafe (SW3)
Kulu Kulu Sushi (W1)
La Cage Imaginaire (NW3)
La Dordogne (W4)
La Famiglia (SW10)
Landmark, Dining Rm. (NW1)
Lanesborough (SW1)
Le Mercury (N1)
Le Petit Blanc (multi. loc.)
L'Estaminet (WC2)
Livebait (multi. loc.)
L'Odeon (W1)
Luna Nuova (WC2)
Mackintosh's (W4)
Maison Bertaux (W1)
Malabar Junction (WC1)
Mao Tai (SW6)
Marine Ices (NW3)
Maxwell's (WC2)
Movenpick Marché (SW1)
Naked Turtle (SW14)
Navajo Joe (WC2)
New Culture Rev. (multi. loc.)
Nicole's (W1)
Nobu (W1)
Offshore (W1)
Old Bridge Hotel (Cambs)
192 (W11)
Orange Balloon (multi. loc.)
Oriel (SW1)
Orsino (W11)
Orso (WC2)
Palm Court (WC2)
Park, The (NW6)
Patara (multi. loc.)
Patisserie Valerie (multi. loc.)
People's Palace (SE1)

Pepper Tree (SW4)
Pescatori (W1)
Planet Hollywood (W1)
Quality Chop Hse. (EC1)
Rasa (multi. loc.)
Rib Room (SW1)
Richoux (multi. loc.)
RK Stanley's (W1)
Royal Oak (Berks)
San Martino (SW3)
Santa Fe (N1)
Savoy River Rest. (WC2)
Scotts (W1)
Searcy's/Barbican (EC2)
Seashell (NW1)
Shoreditch Electricity (N1)
Sir Charles Napier (Oxon)
Smollensky's/Strand (WC2)
Soho Soho (W1)
Soho Spice (W1)
Solly's (NW11)
Sonata (W1)
Soup Works (W1)
Southeast W9 (W9)
Spago (W8)
Spighetta (W1)
Standard Tandoori (W2)
Stephen Bull Smithfield (EC1)
Stepping Stone (SW8)
Stonor Arms (Oxon)
Sugar Club (W1)
Sushi Wong (W8)
Tate Gallery (SW1)
Tenth (W8)
Terraza (Richmond)
T.G.I. Friday's (multi. loc.)
Three Lions (Hants)
Tiger Lil's (multi. loc.)
Tokyo Diner (WC2)
Townhouse (WC1)
Troubadour (SW5)
Tuttons (WC2)
Two Brothers (N3)
Union Cafe (W1)
Uno (SW1)
Vama (SW10)
Verbanella (SW3)
Vinopolis (SE1)
Vong (SW1)
Windows on World (W1)
Wok Wok (SW10)
Yoshino (W1)

Yo! Sushi (W1)
Zamoyski (NW3)
Zoe (W1)

Noteworthy Newcomers (79)
(*Not open yet, but looks promising)
Admiral Codrington (SW3)
Al Duca*
Amandier (W2)
Asia de Cuba (WC2)
Bam-Bou (W1)
Belgo Zuid (W1)
Bierodrome (N1)
Bistro Daniel (W2)
Bistrorganic (W10)
Black Truffle (NW1)
Builders Arms (SW3)
Café Milan (SW3)
Canyon (Richmond)
Chapter Two (SE3)
Che (SW1)
China House*
China Jazz (W1)
Club Gascon (EC1)
Deco (SW10)
Denim (WC2)
Dibbens (EC1)
Fairuz (W1)
FireBird*
Fish! (SE1)
Floriana (SW3)
Four Seasons, Lanes (W1)
Friends (SW10)
Frith Street (W1)
Giraffe (multi. loc.)
Glasshouse (Kew)
Grano (W4)
Great Eastern (EC2)
Gusto*
Home House (W1)
Honest Cabbage (SE1)
Idaho (N6)
Isola*
J. Sheekey (WC2)
La Candela (W8)
latitude (SW3)
Lundum's (SW7)
Maggiore's (WC2)
Mortimer (W1)
Morton's (W1)
North Pole (SE10)

Offshore (W1)
Pacific Oriental (EC2)
Paparazzi Lounge (W1)
Park, The (NW6)
Passione (W1)
Pepe Nero (SW11)
Pétrus (SW1)
porters bar/poland st. (W1)
Prism (EC3)
Purple Sage (W1)
Rasa Samudra (W1)
Real Greek (N1)
Room (SE1)
Salt House (NW8)
Santa Fe (N1)
Satsuma (W1)
Sauce BarOrganicDiner (NW1)
Shimla Pinks (EC2)
Site*
Smith's of Smithfield*
Sonata (W1)
Soup Opera (multi. loc.)
Soup Works (multi. loc.)
Sugar Reef*
Tajine (W1)
Terrace (W1)
Titanic (W1)
Toast (NW3)
Vale (W9)
Vineet Bhatia (W6)
Vinopolis (SE1)
Voodoo Lounge (WC2)
Wiz (W1)
Zaika (SW3)

Noteworthy Closings (42)
Abeno Okonotomi-Yaki
Albero & Grana
Auberge de Provence
Au Jardin des Gourmets
Bahn Thai
Boyd's
Café O
Café Sofa-all
Caspers
Causerie
Chavot
Cy
Football Football
Francesca's
Goode's
Il Faro
Indian Summer

Inn of Happiness
Interlude
La Belle Epoque: L'Orientale
La Ciboulette
La Pomme d'Amour
L'Arte
Les Saveurs
Lozzie's
Mad Dog Bar & Grill
Mange-2
Marabel's
Nam Long Le Buddha Bar
Nippon Tuk
No. 1 Cigar Club
Notre Dame
Pearl of Knightsbridge
San Frediano
Smollensky's Dover Street
Snows by the Pond
33
Tiddy Dols
W11
West Zenders
Wren at St. James's
Zujumas

Offbeat

Alounak (W2)
Anna's Place (N1)
Apprentice (SE1)
Arcadia (W8)
ArdRí/O'Conor Don (W1)
Arkansas Cafe (E1)
Beach Blanket Babylon (W11)
Belgo Centraal (WC2)
Belgo Noord (NW1)
Belgo Zuid (W1)
Bierodrome (N1)
Birdcage (W1)
Blah! Blah! Blah! (W12)
Bloom's (NW11)
Blue Elephant (SW6)
Books for Cooks (W11)
Cave (W1)
Chelsea Kitchen (SW3)
Chinon (W14)
Chor Bizarre (W1)
Club Gascon (EC1)
Cottons Rhum Shop (NW1)
Delfina Studio Cafe (SE1)
Food for Thought (WC2)
Footstool (SW1)
Garlic & Shots (W1)

Hothouse (E1)
Inaho (W2)
itsu (SW3)
Jason's (W9)
Jenny Lo's (SW1)
Jim Thompson's (SW15)
Just Around the Corner (NW2)
Kaifeng (NW4)
Kulu Kulu Sushi (W1)
La Porte des Indes (W1)
Le Gothique (SW18)
Lola's (N1)
Luigi's Deli (SW10)
Maggie Jones's (W8)
Mas Café (W11)
Momo (W1)
Montana (SW6)
Moro (EC1)
Moshi Moshi Sushi (EC2)
Mr. Wing (SW5)
Museum St. Cafe (WC1)
Nancy Lam's Enak Enak (SW11)
Navajo Joe (WC2)
Nikita's (SW10)
Pharmacy (W11)
Picasso (SW3)
Pizza Metro (SW11)
Place Below (EC2)
Polygon B&G (SW4)
Quality Chop Hse. (EC1)
Rainforest Cafe (W1)
Randall & Aubin (W1)
Richard Corrigan (W1)
Sale e Pepe (SW1)
Solly's (NW11)
Souk (WC2)
St. John (EC1)
Sugar Club (W1)
Tate Gallery (SW1)
Tea Rms. des Artistes (SW8)
Tom's Deli (W11)
Troubadour (SW5)
Upper St. Fish Shop (N1)
Villandry Foodstore (W1)
Vinopolis (SE1)
Wagamama (multi. loc.)
Wiz (W1)
Wòdka (W8)
Wok Wok (W1)
Yo! Sushi (multi. loc.)

Outdoor Dining

(G=garden; P=patio; PV=pavement; T=terrace; W=waterside; best of many)

Admiral Codrington (SW3) (G)
Al Hamra (W1) (P)
Amandier (W2) (T)
Angel (Bucks) (T)
Anna's Place (N1) (G)
Aquarium (E1) (T)
Archduke (SE1) (G,P,PV)
Auberge du Lac (Herts) (T,W)
bali sugar (W11) (G)
Bam-Bou (W1) (P)
Beach Blanket Babylon (W11) (P)
Beetle & Wedge (Oxon) (G,T,W)
Belair House (SE21) (T)
Bell Inn (Bucks) (G)
Belvedere (W8) (T)
Birdcage (W1) (P)
Bishopstrow Hse. (Wilts) (G)
Blakes Hotel (SW7) (P,T)
Bleeding Heart (EC1) (T)
Boisdale (SW1) (G,P)
Brackenbury (W6) (P)
Brasserie Rocque (EC2) (T)
Brinkley's (SW10) (G,PV)
Brompton Bay (SW3) (PV)
Buckland Manor (Glos) (G)
Busabong Tree (SW10) (P)
Butlers Wharf (SE1) (T,W)
Café Delancey (NW1) (T)
Cantina del Ponte (SE1) (T,W)
Cantinetta Venegazzu (SW11) (T)
Canyon (Richmond) (G,P,T,W)
Caraffini (SW1) (PV)
Casale Franco (N1) (P)
Cherwell Boathse. (Oxon) (T,W)
Chewton Glen Hotel (Hants) (T)
Chez Max (SW10) (T)
Chinon (W14) (G)
Churchill Arms (W8) (G,P)
Chutney Mary (SW10) (G)
Compleat Angler (Bucks) (T,W)
Coq d'Argent (EC2) (G,T)
Costa's Grill (W8) (G)
Dakota (W11) (PV)
Dan's (SW3) (G)
Daphne's (SW3) (G)
De Cecco (SW6) (T)
Denim (WC2) (P)
Depot Waterfront (SW14) (P)

El Gaucho (SW3) (T)
Elistano (SW3) (PV)
Emile's (multi. loc.) (P)
Engineer (NW1) (G)
Enterprise (SW3) (PV)
Euphorium (N1) (G)
Fat Duck (Berks) (G,T)
Fifth Floor Cafe (SW1) (T)
Film Café (SE1) (P,T)
Flitwick Manor (Beds) (T)
Floriana (SW3) (PV)
Formula Veneta (SW10) (G)
Four Regions (SE1) (T,W)
Gaucho Grill (NW3) (P)
Glaister's Gard. (multi. loc.) (G,PV,T)
Grenadier (SW1) (P)
Hard Rock Cafe (W1) (P)
Henry J. Bean's (SW3) (G)
House/Rosslyn Hill (NW3) (T)
Icon (SW3) (PV)
Idaho (N6) (T)
Jason's (W9) (T,W)
Joe's (SW3) (PV)
Julie's (W11) (G,T)
La Brasserie (SW3) (PV)
La Famiglia (SW10) (G)
Langan's Coq d'Or (SW5) (T)
Lansdowne (NW1) (P)
La Poule au Pot (SW1) (P)
Leaping Hare (Suffolk) (G)
Leatherne Bottel (Berks) (G,T,W)
Le Boudin Blanc (W1) (T)
Le Colombier (SW3) (T)
Le Gothique (SW18) (G)
Le Pont de la Tour (SE1) (T,W)
L'Oranger (SW1) (P)
L'Ortolan (Berks) (T)
Lou Pescadou (SW5) (G,T)
Lucknam Park (Wilts) (G,T)
Luigi's Deli (SW10) (T)
Lundum's (SW7) (P)
Lygon Arms (Wocs) (P)
Mackintosh's (W4) (PV)
Made in Italy (SW3) (T)
Mallory Court (Warwks) (T)
Mirabelle (W1) (G,P)
Montpeliano (SW7) (T)
Monza (SW3) (PV)
Moro (EC1) (PV)
Naked Turtle (SW14) (G,T)
Novelli EC1 (EC1) (PV)
Old Bridge Hotel (Cambs) (P)

Oriel (SW1) (PV)
Orrery (W1) (T)
Oxo Tower (SE1) (T,W)
Oxo Tower Brasserie (SE1) (T,W)
Pennyhill Park, Lat. (Surrey) (T)
Phoenix B&G (SW15) (T)
Picasso (SW3) (PV)
Pink Geranium (Cambs) (G)
PJ's Bar & Grill (SW3) (PV)
PJ's Grill (WC2) (PV)
Putney Bridge (SW15) (T,W)
Queens (NW1) (PV,T)
Ransome's Dock (SW11) (P,T,W)
Riccardo's (SW3) (P)
Ritz Rest. (W1) (G)
Riva (SW13) (PV)
River Cafe (W6) (P,W)
Room/Halcyon (W11) (P)
San Martino (SW3) (G)
Scotts (W1) (T)
Sir Charles Napier (Oxon) (T)
Stapleford Park (Leics) (G,T)
Stonor Arms (Oxon) (G)
TECA (W1) (PV)
Terrace (W8) (W8) (T)
Thai on River (SW10) (P)
Thierry's (SW3) (PV)
Three Lions (Hants) (G,P,T)
Toto's (SW3) (P)
Vama (SW10) (P)
Villandry Foodstore (W1) (PV)
Vine (NW5) (G)
Vineet Bhatia (W6) (PV)
Vingt-Quatre (SW10) (PV)
Wiz (W1) (T)
Zoe (W1) (T)

Outstanding Views

Auberge du Lac (Herts)
Belair House (SE21)
Belvedere (W8)
Bistrot 2 Riverside (SE1)
Blue Print Cafe (SE1)
Butlers Wharf (SE1)
Canteen (SW10)
Cantina del Ponte (SE1)
Canyon (Richmond)
Compleat Angler (Bucks)
Coq d'Argent (EC2)
County Hall (SE1)
Fakhreldine (multi. loc.)
Four Regions (SE1)

Four Seasons, Lanes (W1)
French Horn (Berks)
Gravetye Manor (W. Sus)
Grissini (SW1)
Jason's (W9)
Le Manoir/Quat'Saisons (Oxon)
Le Pont de la Tour (SE1)
Nobu (W1)
Orrery (W1)
Oxo Tower (SE1)
Oxo Tower Brasserie (SE1)
Park Rest. (SW1)
People's Palace (SE1)
Putney Bridge (SW15)
River Cafe (W6)
Savoy River Rest. (WC2)
Tenth (W8)
Terrace (W1) (W1)
Thai on River (SW10)
Waterside Inn (Berks)
Windows on World (W1)

Parties & Private Rooms

(Any nightclub or restaurant
charges less at off-times;
* indicates private rooms
available; best of many)
Alastair Little (W1)*
Alastair Little/Lanc. Rd. (W11)*
Al Bustan (SW1)*
Apprentice (SE1)*
Arkansas Cafe (E1)*
Atlantic B&G (W1)*
Auberge du Lac (Herts)
Babe Ruth's (multi. loc.)*
Bam-Bou (W1)*
Beach Blanket Babylon (W11)*
Belgo Centraal (WC2)*
Belgo Noord (NW1)*
Bell Inn (Bucks)*
Belvedere (W8)*
Benihana (multi. loc.)
Bice (W1)*
Bierodrome (N1)*
Big Easy (SW3)*
Birdcage (W1)*
Bishopstrow Hse. (Wilts)
Bistro Daniel (W2)*
Blakes Hotel (SW7)*
Bluebird (SW3)*
Blue Elephant (SW6)*
Blues Bistro (W1)*

Bombay Bicycle (SW12)*
Bombay Brasserie (SW7)*
Brackenbury (W6)*
Brown's Hotel, 1837 (W1)*
Butlers Wharf (SE1)*
Canteen (SW10)*
Canyon (Richmond)*
Capital Radio Cafe (WC2)*
Capital Rest. (SW3)*
Caraffini (SW1)
Cave (W1)
Caviar Kaspia (W1)*
Che (SW1)
Chewton Glen Hotel (Hants)*
Chez Bruce (SW17)*
Chez Max (SW10)*
Chez Nico (W1)
Chiang Mai (W1)*
Chinon (W14)*
Chor Bizarre (W1)*
Christopher's (WC2)*
Chuen Cheng Ku (W1)
Chutney Mary (SW10)*
Circus (W1)
City Rhodes (EC4)*
Claridge's Rest. (W1)*
Cliveden, Waldo's (Berks)*
Club Gascon (EC1)*
Coast (W1)*
Compleat Angler (Bucks)
Connaught Hotel (W1)
Crescent (SW3)*
Dakota (W11)*
Dan's (SW3)
Daphne's (SW3)*
Delfina Studio Cafe (SE1)*
Dorchester, Oriental (W1)*
Elena's L'Etoile (W1)
English Garden (SW3)*
English Hse. (SW3)
Enoteca Turi (SW15)*
Euphorium (N1)*
Fat Duck (Berks)*
Fawsley Hall (N'hants)*
Flitwick Manor (Beds)
Floriana (SW3)*
Formula Veneta (SW10)*
Four Regions (SE1)*
Four Seasons, Lanes (W1)*
French Horn (Berks)*
French House (W1)*
Garbo's (W1)*
Goring Dining Rm. (SW1)
Grano (W4)*
Gravetye Manor (W. Sus)*
Great Eastern (EC2)*
Greenhouse (W1)
Green's Rest. (SW1)*
Gresslin's (NW3)
Grissini (SW1)*
Guinea (W1)*
Halkin, Stefano Cavallini (SW1)*
Hambleton Hall (Rut)*
Hard Rock Cafe (W1)*
Hartwell House (Bucks)*
Hilaire (SW7)
Ibla (W1)*
Icon (SW3)*
Idaho (N6)*
I-Thai (W2)*
Ivy (WC2)*
Jason's (W9)*
Julie's (W11)
Kensington Place (W8)
La Brasserie du Marché (W10)*
La Famiglia (SW10)*
Lanesborough (SW1)
La Porte des Indes (W1)*
La Poule au Pot (SW1)*
La Tante Claire (SW1)*
Launceston Place (W8)*
Lawn (SE3)
Leatherne Bottel (Berks)*
Le Caprice (SW1)
Le Colombier (SW3)
Le Gavroche (W1)*
Le Gothique (SW18)*
Leith's (W11)*
Leith's Soho (W1)*
Le Manoir/Quat'Saisons (Oxon)*
Lemonia (NW1)*
Le Pont de la Tour (SE1)*
L'Escargot (W1)*
Le Suquet (SW3)*
L'Incontro (SW1)*
L'Oranger (SW1)*
L'Ortolan (Berks)*
Made in Italy (SW3)
Maison Novelli (EC1)*
Mao Tai (SW6)*
Maroush (W2)*
Mas Café (W11)*
Matsuri (SW1)*
Mezzo (W1)*

Mimmo d'Ischia (SW1)*
Min's (SW3)*
Mirabelle (W1)*
Mitsukoshi (SW1)*
Momo (W1)*
Montana (SW6)
Moro (EC1)
Morton's (W1)*
Mr. Chow (SW1)*
Neal St. (WC2)
Nicole's (W1)
Nobu (W1)*
Oak Room MPW (W1)*
1 Lombard St. (EC3)
Orrery (W1)
Orsino (W11)*
Oxo Tower (SE1)
Pasha (SW7) (SW7)*
Pelham St. (SW7)
Pharmacy (W11)
Pied-à-Terre (W1)*
Pink Geranium (Cambs)*
Pizza on the Park (SW1)*
PJ's Bar & Grill (SW3)
PJ's Grill (WC2)
Planet Hollywood (W1)*
Poissonnerie/l'Avenue (SW3)*
Prism (EC3)*
Purple Sage (W1)*
Quaglino's (SW1)*
Quo Vadis (W1)*
Rain (W10)
Rainforest Cafe (W1)
Ransome's Dock (SW11)
Red Fort (W1)*
Red Pepper (W9)*
Richard Corrigan (W1)*
Ritz Rest. (W1)*
Room/Halcyon (W11)*
Roussillon (SW1)*
Royal China (multi. loc.)*
Saga (W1)
Saint Bar & Rest. (WC2)
Sartoria (W1)*
Scotts (W1)*
Shoreditch Electricity (N1)*
Signor Zilli (W1)*
Snows on Green (W6)*
Souk (WC2)*
Sound Republic (W1)*
Spiga (W1)
Spighetta (W1)

Sports Cafe (SW1)*
Square (W1)*
Sugar Club (W1)
Suntory (SW1)*
Tamarind (W1)
Tatsuso (EC2)*
Tentazioni (SE1)
Tenth (W8)
Texas Embassy (SW14)*
Titanic (W1)
Trader Vic's (W1)*
Vama (SW10)*
Vasco & Piero's (W1)*
Veeraswamy (W1)*
Villandry Foodstore (W1)
Vinopolis (SE1)
White Onion (N1)*
Wilton's (SW1)*
Windows on World (W1)
Wiz (W1)*
Wòdka (W8)*
Ye Olde Cheshire (EC4)
Zaika (SW3)

People-Watching

Admiral Codrington (SW3)
Atlantic B&G (W1)
Avenue (SW1)
Bam-Bou (W1)
Bangkok (SW7)
Bank (WC2)
Bibendum (SW3)
Bibendum Oyster (SW3)
Blakes Hotel (SW7)
Bluebird (SW3)
Cafe at Sotheby's (W1)
Cafe de Paris (W1)
Café Milan (SW3)
Canteen (SW10)
Caviar Kaspia (W1)
Che (SW1)
Christopher's (WC2)
Claridge's Bar (W1)
Club Gascon (EC1)
Connaught Hotel (W1)
Dakota (W11)
Daphne's (SW3)
Emporio Armani (SW3)
Fifth Floor (SW1)
Fifth Floor Cafe (SW1)
Fish! (SE1)
Floriana (SW3)
Glasshouse (Kew)

Grissini (SW1)
Ivy (WC2)
Joe's (SW3)
Joe's Rest. Bar (SW1)
J. Sheekey (WC2)
Kensington Place (W8)
Lab (W1)
La Famiglia (SW10)
Langan's Bistro (W1)
Langan's Brasserie (W1)
latitude (SW3)
Le Caprice (SW1)
Le Gavroche (W1)
L'Oranger (SW1)
Mezzo (W1)
Mirabelle (W1)
Momo (W1)
Nicole's (W1)
Nobu (W1)
Orso (WC2)
Pasha (SW7)
Pétrus (SW1)
Pharmacy (W11)
Quaglino's (SW1)
Quo Vadis (W1)
River Cafe (W6)
Room/Halcyon (W11)
San Lorenzo (SW3)
Santini (SW1)
Sartoria (W1)
Savoy Grill (WC2)
Scalini (SW3)
Shoreditch Electricity (N1)
Sugar Club (W1)
Teatro (W1)
Titanic (W1)
Vong (SW1)
Voodoo Lounge (WC2)
Waterside Inn (Berks)
Zafferano (SW1)
Zaika (SW3)
Zilli Fish (W1)

Power Scenes
Atrium (SW1)
Avenue (SW1)
Bank (WC2)
Blue Print Cafe (SE1)
Caviar Kaspia (W1)
Cecconi's (W1)
Che (SW1)
Chez Nico (W1)
City Rhodes (EC4)

Claridge's Rest. (W1)
Club Gascon (EC1)
Connaught Hotel (W1)
Daphne's (SW3)
Dorchester, Grill Rm. (W1)
Dorchester, Oriental (W1)
Four Seasons, Lanes (W1)
Frith Street (W1)
Gordon Ramsay (SW3)
Goring Dining Rm. (SW1)
Greenhouse (W1)
Green's Rest. (SW1)
Ivy (WC2)
J. Sheekey (WC2)
Langan's Brasserie (W1)
Launceston Place (W8)
Le Caprice (SW1)
Le Gavroche (W1)
Leith's (W11)
Le Manoir/Quat'Saisons (Oxon)
Le Soufflé (W1)
L'Incontro (SW1)
Mirabelle (W1)
Mitsukoshi (SW1)
Morton's (W1)
Neal St. (WC2)
Nico Central (W1)
Nobu (W1)
Oak Room MPW (W1)
Odin's (W1)
Pétrus (SW1)
Prism (EC3)
Ritz Rest. (W1)
San Lorenzo (SW3)
Savoy Grill (WC2)
Savoy River Rest. (WC2)
Shepherd's (SW1)
Square (W1)
Wilton's (SW1)
Zafferano (SW1)

Pre-Theatre Dining
(Call to check prices, days
and times)
Al Bustan (SW1)
Alfred (WC2)
Arancia (SW11)
Archduke (SE1)
ArdRi/O'Conor Don (W1)
Avenue (SW1)
Axis (WC2)
Bank (WC2)
Belgo Centraal (WC2)

Belgo Noord (NW1)
Belgo Zuid (W1)
Benihana (multi. loc.)
Bentley's (W1)
Bertorelli's (WC2)
Bice (W1)
Birdcage (W1)
Bistrot 190 (SW7)
Bistrot 2 Riverside (SE1)
Bloom's (NW11)
Bluebird (SW3)
Blues Bistro (W1)
Brasserie St. Quentin (SW3)
Browns Rest. (WC2)
Café dell'Ugo (SE1)
Café des Amis du Vin (WC2)
Café Flo (multi. loc.)
Cafe Rouge (multi. loc.)
Che (SW1)
Cheers (W1)
Chez Gérard (WC2)
China Blues (NW1)
Chor Bizarre (W1)
Christopher's (WC2)
Circus (W1)
City Miyama (EC4)
Connaught Hotel (W1)
County Hall (SE1)
Criterion Brasserie (W1)
Deals (W1)
East One (EC1)
Fakhreldine (multi. loc.)
Food for Thought (WC2)
Footstool (SW1)
Fortnum's Fountain (W1)
Four Regions (SE1)
Frederick's (N1)
French House (W1)
Frith Street (W1)
Goring Dining Rm. (SW1)
Hilaire (SW7)
Home House (W1)
House/Rosslyn Hill (NW3)
Indigo (WC2)
Joe Allen (WC2)
Kavanagh's (N1)
Lanesborough (SW1)
Le Boudin Blanc (W1)
Le Cafe du Jardin (WC2)
Le Caprice (SW1)
Leith's Soho (W1)
Le Pont de la Tour (SE1)

L'Escargot (W1)
L'Estaminet (WC2)
Livebait (multi. loc.)
L'Odeon (W1)
Luigi's/Covent Garden (WC2)
Magno's (WC2)
Maison Novelli (EC1)
Mandeer (WC1)
Manzi's (WC2)
Matsuri (SW1)
Mezzo (W1)
Mezzonine (W1)
Mitsukoshi (SW1)
Mon Plaisir (WC2)
Moro (EC1)
Navajo Joe (WC2)
Oceana (W1)
Offshore (W1)
190 (SW7)
Orsino (W11)
Palm Court (WC2)
Pasha (N1) (N1)
Pescatori (multi. loc.)
PJ's Grill (WC2)
Planet Hollywood (W1)
Polygon B&G (SW4)
Quaglino's (SW1)
Randall & Aubin (W1)
Red Fort (W1)
Reubens (W1)
Richard Corrigan (W1)
Richoux (multi. loc.)
Rowley's (SW1)
Rules (WC2)
San Martino (SW3)
Savoy River Rest. (WC2)
Searcy's/Barbican (EC2)
Signor Zilli (W1)
Simpson's/The Strand (WC2)
Smollensky's/Strand (WC2)
Sofra (multi. loc.)
Soho Soho (W1)
Soho Spice (W1)
Sri Siam (W1)
Stephen Bull (WC2)
Stepping Stone (SW8)
Tamarind (W1)
Tea Rms. des Artistes (SW8)
Teatro (W1)
Tiger Lil's (multi. loc.)
Townhouse (WC1)

Tuttons (WC2)
Uno (SW1)
Upstairs/The Savoy (WC2)
Vama (SW10)
Veeraswamy (W1)
Veronica's (W2)
Vinopolis (SE1)
Vong (SW1)
Waterloo Fire Station (SE1)
Wolfe's B&G (WC2)
Zilli Fish (W1)
Zinc B&G (W1)

Pubs/Sports Bars/ Microbreweries

(*Sports bar)
Admiral Codrington (SW3)
Anglesea Arms (W6)
Archduke (SE1)
ArdRí/O'Conor Don (W1)
Babe Ruth's (E1)*
Blues Bistro (W1)*
Builders Arms (SW3)
Cheers (W1)
Chelsea Ram (SW10)
Churchill Arms (W8)
Cow Dining Room (W2)
Duke of Cambridge (SW11)
Duke of Cambridge (N1)
Eagle (EC1)
Engineer (NW1)
Enterprise (SW3)
Fox & Anchor (EC1)
Freedom Brewing Co. (WC2)
French House (W1)
Grenadier (SW1)
Guinea (W1)
Havelock Tavern (W14)
Honest Cabbage (SE1)
Lansdowne (NW1)
Mash (W1)
North Pole (SE10)
Peasant (EC1)
Prince Bonaparte (W2)
Queens (NW1)
Salt House (NW8)
Shoeless Joe's (SW6)*
Sporting Page (SW10)*
Sports Cafe (SW1)*
Vine (NW5)
Waxy O'Connor's (W1)
Westbourne (W2)
Ye Olde Cheshire (EC4)

Pudding Specialists

Alastair Little (W1)
Aubergine (SW10)
Bibendum (SW3)
Blakes Hotel (SW7)
Capital Rest. (SW3)
Che (SW1)
Chewton Glen Hotel (Hants)
Chez Nico (W1)
City Rhodes (EC4)
Clarke's (W8)
Cliveden, Waldo's (Berks)
Club Gascon (EC1)
Connaught Hotel (W1)
Fifth Floor (SW1)
Floriana (SW3)
Fortnum's Fountain (W1)
Four Seasons, Lanes (W1)
Glasshouse (Kew)
Gordon Ramsay (SW3)
Greenhouse (W1)
Hilaire (SW7)
Lanesborough (SW1)
La Tante Claire (SW1)
Le Gavroche (W1)
Leith's (W11)
Le Manoir/Quat'Saisons (Oxon)
Le Soufflé (W1)
L'Oranger (SW1)
Maison Novelli (EC1)
Mirabelle (W1)
Monkeys (SW3)
Morton's (W1)
Nico Central (W1)
Nobu (W1)
Oak Room MPW (W1)
Orrery (W1)
Patisserie Valerie (multi. loc.)
Pétrus (SW1)
Richard Corrigan (W1)
Richoux (multi. loc.)
Ritz Rest. (W1)
River Cafe (W6)
Room/Halcyon (W11)
Sartoria (W1)
Square (W1)
Sugar Club (W1)
Vong (SW1)
Waterside Inn (Berks)

Quiet Conversation

Al Sultan (W1)
Amandier (W2)

Aubergine (SW10)
Belair House (SE21)
Bengal Clipper (SE1)
Bentley's (W1)
Bice (W1)
Blakes Hotel (SW7)
Brown's Hotel, 1837 (W1)
Capital Rest. (SW3)
Cave (W1)
Chewton Glen Hotel (Hants)
Chez Nico (W1)
Claridge's Rest. (W1)
Cliveden, Waldo's (Berks)
Connaught Hotel (W1)
Dan's (SW3)
Dorchester, Oriental (W1)
English Garden (SW3)
English Hse. (SW3)
Four Seasons, Lanes (W1)
Goring Dining Rm. (SW1)
Green's Rest. (SW1)
Grissini (SW1)
Halkin, Stefano Cavallini (SW1)
Hartwell House (Bucks)
Landmark, Dining Rm. (NW1)
Lanesborough (SW1)
La Tante Claire (SW1)
Launceston Place (W8)
Le Gavroche (W1)
Leith's (W11)
Le Manoir/Quat'Saisons (Oxon)
L'Oranger (SW1)
L'Ortolan (Berks)
Marquis (W1)
Mitsukoshi (SW1)
Monkeys (SW3)
Morton's (W1)
Oak Room MPW (W1)
Odin's (W1)
One-O-One (SW1)
Orrery (W1)
Park Rest. (SW1)
Pétrus (SW1)
Ritz Rest. (W1)
Room/Halcyon (W11)
Roussillon (SW1)
Savoy River Rest. (WC2)
Scotts (W1)
Stonor Arms (Oxon)
Terrace (W1) (W1)
Turner's (SW3)

Waterside Inn (Berks)
Wilton's (SW1)
Windows on World (W1)

Romantic Spots
Amberley Castle, Queens (W. Sus)
Andrew Edmunds (W1)
Belvedere (W8)
Blakes Hotel (SW7)
Blue Elephant (SW6)
Capital Rest. (SW3)
Caviar Kaspia (W1)
Che (SW1)
Chewton Glen Hotel (Hants)
Claridge's Rest. (W1)
Clarke's (W8)
Cliveden, Waldo's (Berks)
Compleat Angler (Bucks)
Connaught Hotel (W1)
Criterion Brasserie (W1)
Daphne's (SW3)
Fifth Floor (SW1)
Floriana (SW3)
Frederick's (N1)
French Horn (Berks)
Gordon Ramsay (SW3)
Graveteye Manor (W. Sus)
Grissini (SW1)
Halkin, Stefano Cavallini (SW1)
Hartwell House (Bucks)
Hilaire (SW7)
Julie's (W11)
La Famiglia (SW10)
Lanesborough (SW1)
La Poule au Pot (SW1)
Launceston Place (W8)
Le Café du Marché (EC1)
Le Caprice (SW1)
Le Gavroche (W1)
Leith's (W11)
Le Manoir/Quat'Saisons (Oxon)
Le Pont de la Tour (SE1)
L'Incontro (SW1)
L'Oranger (SW1)
Lygon Arms (Wocs)
Made in Italy (SW3)
Maggie Jones's (W8)
Mirabelle (W1)
Momo (W1)
Monkeys (SW3)
Morton's (W1)
Mr. Wing (SW5)
Oak Room MPW (W1)

Odette's (NW1)
Odin's (W1)
Orrery (W1)
Park Rest. (SW1)
Pétrus (SW1)
Prism (EC3)
Richard Corrigan (W1)
Ritz Rest. (W1)
River Cafe (W6)
Room/Halcyon (W11)
Roussillon (SW1)
San Lorenzo (SW3)
Savoy River Rest. (WC2)
Snows on Green (W6)
Square (W1)
Stapleford Park (Leics)
Waterside Inn (Berks)
Windows on World (W1)
Zafferano (SW1)

Saturday Dining – Best Bets

(B=brunch; L=lunch; best of many)
Abingdon (W8) (L)
Alastair Little/Lanc. Rd. (W11) (L)
Al Hamra (W1) (L)
Andrew Edmunds (W1) (L)
Anglesea Arms (W6) (L)
Anna's Place (N1) (L)
Arancia (SE16) (L)
Assaggi (W2) (L)
Auberge du Lac (Herts) (L)
Avenue (SW1) (L)
Babe Ruth's (multi. loc.) (L)
bali sugar (W11) (L)
Bam-Bou (W1) (L)
Bank (WC2) (B)
Beach Blanket Babylon (W11) (B)
Beetle & Wedge (Oxon) (L)
Belair House (SE21) (L)
Belgo Centraal (WC2) (L)
Belgo Noord (NW1) (L)
Belgo Zuid (W1) (L)
Bell Inn (Bucks) (L)
Belvedere (W8) (L)
Bentley's (W1) (L)
Bibendum (SW3) (L)
Bibendum Oyster (SW3) (L)
Bice (W1) (L)
Big Easy (SW3) (L)
Bishopstrow Hse. (Wilts) (L)
Bistrorganic (W10) (L)

Bistrot 190 (SW7) (B,L)
Bistrot 2 Riverside (SE1) (L)
Blah! Blah! Blah! (W12) (L)
Blakes Hotel (SW7) (L)
Bluebird (SW3) (B)
Blue Print Cafe (SE1) (L)
Books for Cooks (W11) (L)
Brasserie St. Quentin (SW3) (L)
Brompton Bay (SW3) (L)
Browns Rest. (multi. loc.) (B,L)
Buckland Manor (Glos) (L)
Butlers Wharf (SE1) (B)
Byron's (NW3) (L)
Cactus Blue (SW3) (B)
Cafe Lazeez (multi. loc.) (L)
Cafe Med (multi. loc.) (L)
Café Milan (SW3) (B,L)
Café Pacifico (WC2) (L)
Calzone (multi. loc.) (L)
Cambio de Tercio (SW5) (L)
Camden Brasserie (NW1) (B,L)
Cantina del Ponte (SE1) (L)
Cantinetta Venegazzu (SW11) (L)
Canyon (Richmond) (B)
Capital Radio Cafe (multi. loc.) (L)
Capital Rest. (SW3) (L)
Caraffini (SW1) (L)
Casale Franco (N1) (L)
Cave (W1) (L)
Caviar Kaspia (W1) (L)
Cherwell Boathse. (Oxon) (L)
Chewton Glen Hotel (Hants) (L)
Chez Bruce (SW17) (L)
Chez Gérard (multi. loc.) (L)
Christopher's (WC2) (B)
Chuen Cheng Ku (W1) (L)
Chutney Mary (SW10) (L)
Circus (W1) (L)
Claridge's Rest. (W1) (L)
Coast (W1) (B)
Collection (SW3) (L)
Compleat Angler (Bucks) (L)
Connaught Hotel (W1) (L)
Crescent (SW3) (L)
Criterion Brasserie (W1) (L)
Dakota (W11) (B)
Daphne's (SW3) (L)
DKNY Bar (W1) (B,L)
Dorchester, Bar (W1) (L)
Dorchester, Grill Rm. (W1) (L)
Drones (SW1) (L)

Eagle (EC1) (L)
Eastwell Manor (Kent) (L)
Eco (multi. loc.) (L)
Ed's Easy Diner (multi. loc.) (L)
El Gaucho (SW3) (L)
Elistano (SW3) (L)
Emporio Armani (SW3) (L)
English Garden (SW3) (L)
English Hse. (SW3) (L)
Enterprise (SW3) (L)
est (W1) (L)
Euphorium (N1) (L)
Fat Duck (Berks) (L)
Fawsley Hall (N'hants) (L)
Feathers Hotel (Oxon) (L)
Feng Shang (NW1) (L)
Fifth Floor (SW1) (L)
Fifth Floor Cafe (SW1) (L)
Fish! (SE1) (L)
Flitwick Manor (Beds) (L)
Floriana (SW3) (L)
Formula Veneta (SW10) (L)
Fortnum's Fountain (W1) (L)
Foundation (SW1) (L)
Four Seasons, Lanes (W1) (L)
Foxtrot Oscar (SW3) (L)
Frederick's (N1) (L)
French Horn (Berks) (L)
French House (W1) (L)
Friends (SW10) (L)
Geale's (W8) (L)
Glasshouse (Kew) (L)
Granita (N1) (L)
Gravetye Manor (W. Sus) (L)
Green Olive (W9) (L)
Green's Rest. (SW1) (L)
Grenadier (SW1) (L)
Gresslin's (NW3) (L)
Hambleton Hall (Rut) (L)
Hard Rock Cafe (W1) (L)
Hartwell House (Bucks) (L)
Havelock Tavern (W14) (L)
Henry J. Bean's (SW3) (L)
Horsted Place, Pugin (E. Sus) (L)
Hotel du Vin (multi. loc.) (L)
House/Rosslyn Hill (NW3) (L)
Ibla (W1) (L)
Icon (SW3) (L)
Idaho (N6) (B,L)
Ikkyu (WC1) (L)
Indigo (WC2) (B,L)
I-Thai (W2) (L)

itsu (SW3) (L)
Ivy (WC2) (L)
Jason's (W9) (B,L)
Jenny Lo's (SW1) (L)
Joe Allen (WC2) (B,L)
Joe's (SW3) (B,L)
Joe's Rest. Bar (SW1) (B,L)
J. Sheekey (WC2) (L)
Kai (W1) (L)
Kensington Place (W8) (L)
King's Rd. Cafe (SW3) (L)
Koi (W8) (L)
La Belle Epoque/Bras. (SW3) (B,L)
La Belle Epoque/Salle (SW3) (L)
La Brasserie (SW3) (B,L)
La Brasserie/Marché (W10) (B,L)
La Delizia (SW3) (L)
La Famiglia (SW10) (L)
Lanesborough (SW1) (L)
Langan's Coq d'Or (SW5) (B,L)
La Poule au Pot (SW1) (L)
Lawn (SE3) (B)
Leaping Hare (Suffolk) (L)
Leatherne Bottel (Berks) (L)
Le Caprice (SW1) (L)
Le Colombier (SW3) (L)
Le Manoir/Quat'Sais. (Oxon) (L)
Le Metro (SW3) (L)
Le Palais du Jardin (WC2) (L)
Le Petit Blanc (multi. loc.) (L)
Le Suquet (SW3) (L)
Le Talbooth (Essex) (L)
Livebait (multi. loc.) (L)
L'Odeon (W1) (L)
Lola's (N1) (B)
L'Ortolan (Berks) (L)
Lucknam Park (Wilts) (L)
Luigi's Deli (SW10) (L)
Lundum's (SW7) (L)
Lygon Arms (Wocs) (L)
Mackintosh's (W4) (B,L)
Made in Italy (SW3) (B)
Maggiore's (WC2) (L)
Mallory Court (Warwks) (L)
Maroush (multi. loc.) (L)
Marsh Goose (Glos) (L)
Mas Café (W11) (B)
Mash (W1) (B)
Matsuri (SW1) (L)
Mimmo d'Ischia (SW1) (L)
Ming (W1) (L)
Min's (SW3) (L)

Mirabelle (W1) (L)
Mitsukoshi (SW1) (L)
Montana (SW6) (B)
Montpeliano (SW7) (L)
Monza (SW3) (L)
Museum St. Cafe (WC1) (L)
Neal St. (WC2) (L)
Nicole's (W1) (L)
Novelli EC1 (EC1) (L)
Novelli W8 (W8) (L)
Odette's (NW1) (L)
Offshore (W1) (B,L)
Old Bridge Hotel (Cambs) (L)
Oliveto (SW1) (L)
192 (W11) (L)
One-O-One (SW1) (L)
One Paston Place (W. Sus) (L)
Orange Balloon (multi. loc.) (L)
Oriel (SW1) (L)
Orrery (W1) (L)
Orsino (W11) (L)
Orso (WC2) (L)
Oslo Court (NW8) (L)
Osteria Antica Bol. (SW11) (B,L)
Osteria Basilico (W11) (L)
Oxo Tower (SE1) (L)
Oxo Tower Brasserie (SE1) (L)
Palm Court (WC2) (L)
Paparazzi Lounge (multi. loc.) (L)
Park Rest. (SW1) (L)
Pasha (SW7) (L)
Patara (multi. loc.) (L)
Patisserie Val. (multi. loc.) (B,L)
Pelham St. (SW7) (L)
People's Palace (SE1) (L)
Pharmacy (W11) (L)
Picasso (SW3) (L)
Pink Geranium (Cambs) (L)
Pizza Express (multi. loc.) (L)
Pizza Metro (SW11) (L)
Pizza on the Park (SW1) (L)
PJ's Bar & Grill (SW3) (B,L)
PJ's Grill (WC2) (L)
Planet Hollywood (W1) (L)
Poissonnerie/l'Avenue (SW3) (L)
Porters (WC2) (L)
Purple Sage (W1) (L)
Putney Bridge (SW15) (L)
Quaglino's (SW1) (L)
Rain (W10) (B,L)
Rainforest Cafe (W1) (L)
Randall & Aubin (W1) (B,L)

Ransome's Dock (SW11) (B)
Rasa (multi. loc.) (L)
Ravi Shankar (multi. loc.) (L)
Red Fort (W1) (L)
Redmonds (SW14) (L)
Red Pepper (W9) (L)
Reubens (W1) (L)
Riccardo's (SW3) (B,L)
Richoux (multi. loc.) (B,L)
Ritz Rest. (W1) (L)
River Cafe (W6) (L)
RK Stanley's (W1) (L)
Rodizio Rico (W2) (L)
Roussillon (SW1) (L)
Royal China (multi. loc.) (L)
Royal Oak (Berks) (B,L)
Rules (WC2) (L)
Saga (W1) (L)
Sale e Pepe (SW1) (L)
Salloos (SW1) (L)
Salt House (NW8) (L)
Sambuca (SW3) (L)
Sandrini (SW3) (L)
San Lorenzo (SW3) (L)
San Lorenzo Fuori. (SW19) (L)
San Martino (SW3) (L)
Sarastro (WC2) (L)
Sartoria (W1) (L)
Sauce BarOrganic (NW1) (B,L)
Savoy River Rest. (WC2) (L)
Scalini (SW3) (L)
Scotts (W1) (L)
Seashell (NW1) (L)
Shoeless Joe's (multi. loc.) (L)
Signor Zilli (W1) (L)
Simpson's/The Strand (WC2) (L)
Sir Charles Napier (Oxon) (L)
Smollensky's/Strand (WC2) (L)
Sofra (multi. loc.) (L)
Soho Spice (W1) (L)
Sonny's (SW13) (L)
Sound Republic (W1) (L)
Soup Opera (multi. loc.) (L)
Soup Works (multi. loc.) (B,L)
Spiga (W1) (L)
Stapleford Park (Leics) (L)
Star of India (SW5) (L)
Sticky Fingers (W8) (L)
Stonor Arms (Oxon) (L)
Sugar Club (W1) (L)
Suntory (SW1) (L)
Tate Gallery (SW1) (L)

TECA (W1) (L)
Terraza (multi. loc.) (B,L)
Texas Embassy (SW14) (L)
Texas Lone Star (multi. loc.) (L)
T.G.I. Friday's (multi. loc.) (B,L)
Thierry's (SW3) (L)
Three Lions (Hants) (L)
Tom's Deli (W11) (L)
Toto's (SW3) (L)
Townhouse (WC1) (L)
Tui (SW7) (L)
Two Brothers (N3) (L)
Union Cafe (W1) (B)
Uno (SW1) (L)
Upper St. Fish Shop (N1) (L)
Vama (SW10) (L)
Veeraswamy (W1) (L)
Villandry Foodstore (W1) (B,L)
Vingt-Quatre (SW10) (B,L)
Vong (SW1) (B,L)
Wagamama (multi. loc.) (L)
Waterside Inn (Berks) (L)
White Onion (N1) (L)
Wong Kei (W1) (L)
World Food Café (WC2) (L)
Ye Olde Cheshire (EC4) (L)
Yo! Sushi (multi. loc.) (L)
Yoshino (W1) (L)
Yum Yum Thai (N16) (L)
Zafferano (SW1) (L)
Zen Central (W1) (L)
Zen Chelsea (SW3) (L)
Zen Garden (W1) (L)
ZeNW3 (NW3) (L)
Ziani (SW3) (L)
Zilli Fish (W1) (L)
Zinc B&G (W1) (L)
Zoe (W1) (L)
Zucca (W11) (L)
Zuccato (NW3) (L)

Sunday Dining – Best Bets

(B=brunch; L=lunch;
D=dinner; plus most Asians)
Abingdon (W8) (L,D)
Al Bustan (SW1) (L,D)
Al Hamra (W1) (L,D)
Alounak (multi. loc.) (L,D)
Al Sultan (W1) (L,D)
Andrew Edmunds (W1) (L,D)
Angel (Bucks) (L)
Anglesea Arms (W6) (L,D)

Arkansas Cafe (E1) (L)
Assaggi (W2) (L)
Auberge du Lac (Herts) (L)
Avenue (SW1) (B,L,D)
Babe Ruth's (multi. loc.) (L,D)
bali sugar (W11) (L,D)
Bank (WC2) (B,D)
Beach Blanket Bab. (W11) (B,D)
Beetle & Wedge (Oxon) (L,D)
Beiteddine (SW1) (L,D)
Belair House (SE21) (L,D)
Belgo Centraal (WC2) (L,D)
Belgo Noord (NW1) (L,D)
Belgo Zuid (W1) (L,D)
Bell Inn (Bucks) (L,D)
Belvedere (W8) (L)
Bengal Clipper (SE1) (L,D)
Benihana (multi. loc.) (L,D)
Bentley's (W1) (L,D)
Bibendum (SW3) (L,D)
Bibendum Oyster (SW3) (L,D)
Bierodrome (N1) (L,D)
Big Easy (SW3) (L,D)
Bishopstrow Hse. (Wilts) (L,D)
Bistro Daniel (W2) (L)
Bistrorganic (W10) (L)
Bistrot 190 (SW7) (B,L,D)
Bistrot 2 Riverside (SE1) (B)
Blakes Hotel (SW7) (L,D)
Bloom's (NW11) (L,D)
Bluebird (SW3) (B,D)
Blue Elephant (SW6) (L,D)
Blue Print Cafe (SE1) (L)
Brackenbury (W6) (L)
Brasserie St. Quentin (SW3) (L,D)
Brompton Bay (SW3) (B,L,D)
Browns Rest. (multi. loc.) (B,L,D)
Buckland Manor (Glos) (L,D)
Buona Sera (SW11) (L,D)
Buona Sera/Jam (SW3) (L)
Butlers Wharf (SE1) (B,L)
Byron's (NW3) (L,D)
Cactus Blue (SW3) (B,D)
Café Delancey (NW1) (L,D)
Cafe Lazeez (SW7) (L,D)
Cafe Med (multi. loc.) (L,D)
Café Milan (SW3) (B,L,D)
Café Pacifico (WC2) (L,D)
Calzone (multi. loc.) (L,D)
Cambio de Tercio (SW5) (L,D)
Cantina del Ponte (SE1) (L,D)

Cantinetta Ven. (SW11) (L,D)
Canyon (Richmond) (B,D)
Capital Radio (multi. loc.) (L,D)
Casale Franco (N1) (L,D)
Chapter Two (SE3) (L,D)
Cherwell Boathse. (Oxon) (L)
Chewton Glen Hotel (Hants) (L,D)
Chez Bruce (SW17) (L)
Chez Gérard (multi. loc.) (L,D)
Chicago Rib Shack (SW7) (L,D)
Chiswick (W4) (L)
Christopher's (WC2) (B)
Chuen Cheng Ku (W1) (L,D)
Chutney Mary (SW10) (B)
Cibo (W14) (L)
Claridge's Rest. (W1) (L,D)
Coast (W1) (B,D)
Compleat Angler (Bucks) (L,D)
Connaught Hotel (W1) (L,D)
Coq d'Argent (EC2) (L)
Cottons Rhum Shop (NW1) (L,D)
County Hall (SE1) (L,D)
Cow Dining Room (W2) (B,D)
Crescent (SW3) (B,L,D)
Cucina (NW3) (L)
Dakota (W11) (B,D)
Daphne's (SW3) (B,L,D)
Del Buongustaio (SW15) (L,D)
Denim (WC2) (L,D)
Dorchester, Bar (W1) (L,D)
Dorchester, Grill Rm. (W1) (L,D)
Eagle (EC1) (L)
Eastwell Manor (Kent) (L,D)
Ed's Easy Diner (multi. loc.) (L,D)
El Gaucho (SW3) (L,D)
Engineer (NW1) (B,L,D)
English Garden (SW3) (L,D)
English Hse. (SW3) (L,D)
Enterprise (SW3) (L,D)
est (W1) (L,D)
Euphorium (N1) (B,L,D)
Fairuz (W1) (L,D)
Fakhreldine (multi. loc.) (L,D)
Fat Duck (Berks) (L)
Fawsley Hall (N'hants) (L,D)
Feathers Hotel (Oxon) (L,D)
ffiona's (W8) (L,D)
Fifth Floor (SW1) (L)
Fifth Floor Cafe (SW1) (L)
Film Café (SE1) (L,D)
First Floor (W11) (L,D)
Flitwick Manor (Beds) (L,D)

Foundation (SW1) (L)
Four Seasons, Lanes (W1) (L,D)
Foxtrot Oscar (SW3) (L,D)
Freedom Brewing Co. (WC2) (L,D)
French Horn (Berks) (L,D)
Friends (SW10) (L,D)
Gaucho Grill (multi. loc.) (L,D)
Glasshouse (Kew) (L)
Globe (NW3) (B,L)
Goring Dining Rm. (SW1) (L,D)
Granita (N1) (L,D)
Gravetye Manor (W. Sus) (L,D)
Greenhouse (W1) (L,D)
Green Olive (W9) (L,D)
Green's Rest. (SW1) (B,D)
Grenadier (SW1) (L,D)
Gresslin's (NW3) (L)
Grissini (SW1) (B,L)
Halepi (multi. loc.) (L,D)
Hambleton Hall (Rut) (L,D)
Hard Rock Cafe (W1) (L,D)
Hartwell House (Bucks) (L,D)
Horsted Place, Pug. (E. Sus) (L,D)
Hotel du Vin (multi. loc.) (L,D)
House/Rosslyn Hill (NW3) (L,D)
Icon (SW3) (B,L)
Idaho (N6) (B,L,D)
Indigo (WC2) (B,L,D)
Istanbul Iskembecisi (N16) (L,D)
I-Thai (W2) (L,D)
itsu (SW3) (L,D)
Ivy (WC2) (L,D)
Jason's (W9) (B,L)
Joe Allen (WC2) (B,L,D)
Joe's (SW3) (B,L)
J. Sheekey (WC2) (L,D)
Julie's (W11) (B,L,D)
Kensington Place (W8) (L,D)
King's Head (Bucks) (L)
King's Rd. Cafe (SW3) (B,L)
La Belle Epoque/Bras. (SW3) (B,L,D)
La Belle Epoque/Salle (SW3) (L,D)
La Brasserie (SW3) (B,L,D)
La Brasserie /Marché (W10) (B,L)
La Delizia (SW3) (L,D)
La Famiglia (SW10) (L,D)
Lahore Kebab Hse. (E1) (L,D)
Landmark, Dining Rm. (NW1) (L)
Lanesborough (SW1) (B,L,D)
Langan's Coq d'Or (SW5) (B,L,D)
La Perla B&G (multi. loc.) (B,L,D)
La Porte des Indes (W1) (B,D)

La Poule au Pot (SW1) (L,D)
Launceston Place (W8) (L)
Lavender (multi. loc.) (B,L,D)
Lawn (SE3) (B,L)
Leaping Hare (Suffolk) (L)
Leatherne Bottel (Berks) (L)
Le Caprice (SW1) (B,L,D)
Le Colombier (SW3) (L,D)
Le Manoir/Quat'Sais. (Oxon) (L,D)
Lemonia (NW1) (L)
Le Palais du Jardin (WC2) (L,D)
Le Petit Blanc (multi. loc.) (L,D)
Le Pont de la Tour (SE1) (B,D)
Le Soufflé (W1) (L)
Le Suquet (SW3) (L,D)
Le Talbooth (Essex) (L)
Lola's (N1) (B,D)
L'Ortolan (Berks) (L)
Lucknam Park (Wilts) (L,D)
Lundum's (SW7) (B)
Lygon Arms (Wocs) (L,D)
Mackintosh's (W4) (B,L,D)
Made in Italy (SW3) (B,D)
Mallory Court (Warwks) (L,D)
Maroush (multi. loc.) (L,D)
Marsh Goose (Glos) (L)
Mash (W1) (B)
Mediterraneo (W11) (L,D)
Memories of India (SW7) (L,D)
Mezzo (W1) (B,D)
Min's (SW3) (B)
Mirabelle (W1) (L,D)
Mona Lisa (SW10) (B,L)
Monsieur Max (Hampton Hill) (L,D)
Montana (SW6) (B,D)
Montpeliano (SW7) (L,D)
Monza (SW3) (L,D)
Motcomb's (SW1) (L)
North Pole (SE10) (L,D)
Odette's (NW1) (L)
Offshore (W1) (B,L,D)
Old Bridge Hotel (Cambs) (L,D)
Oliveto (SW1) (L,D)
192 (W11) (L,D)
One-O-One (SW1) (L,D)
Orange Balloon (multi. loc.) (L)
Oriel (SW1) (L,D)
Orrery (W1) (L,D)
Orsino (W11) (L,D)
Orso (WC2) (L,D)
Osteria Antica Bol. (SW11) (B,L,D)
Osteria Basilico (W11) (L,D)

Oxo Tower (SE1) (L,D)
Oxo Tower Brasserie (SE1) (L,D)
Park Rest. (SW1) (L,D)
Patara (multi. loc.) (L,D)
Patisserie Val. (multi. loc.) (B,L,D)
Pelham St. (SW7) (L,D)
People's Palace (SE1) (L,D)
Pharmacy (W11) (L,D)
Phoenix B&G (SW15) (L,D)
Picasso (SW3) (L,D)
Pizza Express (multi. loc.) (L,D)
Pizza Metro (SW11) (L,D)
Pizza on the Park (SW1) (L,D)
PJ's Bar & Grill (SW3) (B,L,D)
PJ's Grill (WC2) (L,D)
Planet Hollywood (W1) (L,D)
Polygon B&G (SW4) (B,L,D)
Porters (WC2) (L,D)
porters bar (WC2) (L,D)
Putney Bridge (SW15) (L,D)
Quaglino's (SW1) (L,D)
Quality Chop Hse. (EC1) (B,D)
Rain (W10) (B,L)
Rainforest Cafe (W1) (L,D)
Randall & Aubin (W1) (B,L,D)
Ransome's Dock (SW11) (B)
Rasa (N16) (L,D)
Red Fort (W1) (L,D)
Redmonds (SW14) (L)
Red Pepper (W9) (L,D)
Reubens (W1) (L,D)
Rhodes in Square (SW1) (B)
Riccardo's (SW3) (B,L,D)
Richoux (multi. loc.) (B,L,D)
Ritz Rest. (W1) (L,D)
Riva (SW13) (L,D)
River Cafe (W6) (L)
Rodizio Rico (W2) (L,D)
Room/Halcyon (W11) (L,D)
Royal China (multi. loc.) (L,D)
Royal Oak (Berks) (B,L,D)
Rules (WC2) (L,D)
Salt House (NW8) (L,D)
Sandrini (SW3) (L,D)
San Lorenzo Fuori. (SW19) (L,D)
Sarkhel's Indian (SW1) (L,D)
Sauce BarOrganic (NW1) (B,L)
Savoy River Rest. (WC2) (L,D)
Scalini (SW3) (L,D)
Scotts (W1) (B,L,D)
Searcy's/Barbican (EC2) (L,D)
Seashell (NW1) (L)

755 (SW6) (L)
Simpson's/Strand (WC2) (L,D)
Sir Charles Napier (Oxon) (L)
Smollensky's/Strand (WC2) (L,D)
Snows on Green (W6) (L)
Sofra (multi. loc.) (L,D)
Solly's (NW11) (L,D)
Sonny's (SW13) (L)
Spiga (W1) (L,D)
Spighetta (W1) (L,D)
Square (W1) (D)
Stapleford Park (Leics) (L,D)
Star of India (SW5) (L,D)
Stepping Stone (SW8) (L)
Sticky Fingers (W8) (L,D)
Stonor Arms (Oxon) (L,D)
Stratford's (W8) (L,D)
Sugar Club (W1) (L,D)
Tamarind (W1) (L,D)
Tandoori of Chelsea (SW3) (L,D)
Terraza (multi. loc.) (B,L,D)
Texas Embassy (SW14) (L,D)
Texas Lone Star (multi. loc.) (L,D)
T.G.I. Friday's (multi. loc.) (B,L,D)
Thai on River (SW10) (L,D)
Thierry's (SW3) (L,D)
Three Lions (Hants) (L)
Tom's Deli (W11) (B)
Toto's (SW3) (L,D)
Townhouse (WC1) (L,D)
Tui (SW7) (L,D)
Turner's (SW3) (L,D)
Vama (SW10) (L,D)
Veeraswamy (W1) (B,D)
Villandry Foodstore (W1) (B)
Vine (NW5) (L,D)
Vingt-Quatre (SW10) (B,L,D)
Vong (SW1) (B,D)
Wagamama (multi. loc.) (L,D)
Waterside Inn (Berks) (L,D)
Westbourne (W2) (B,L,D)
White Onion (N1) (L)
Wilton's (SW1) (L,D)
Windows on World (W1) (B)
Wiz (W1) (B,L,D)
Ye Olde Cheshire (EC4) (L)
Yum Yum Thai (N16) (L,D)
Zen Central (W1) (L,D)
Zen Chelsea (SW3) (L,D)
Zen Garden (W1) (L,D)
ZeNW3 (NW3) (L,D)
Ziani (SW3) (L,D)

Zucca (W11) (L,D)
Zuccato (NW3) (L,D)

Senior Appeal

Belair House (SE21)
Bentley's (W1)
Bloom's (NW11)
Brasserie St. Quentin (SW3)
Cafe at Sotheby's (W1)
Canteen (SW10)
Capital Rest. (SW3)
Caviar Kaspia (W1)
Cecconi's (W1)
Chewton Glen Hotel (Hants)
Chez Nico (W1)
Claridge's Rest. (W1)
Cliveden, Waldo's (Berks)
Compleat Angler (Bucks)
Connaught Hotel (W1)
Dan's (SW3)
Dorchester, Grill Rm. (W1)
Dorchester, Oriental (W1)
Elena's L'Etoile (W1)
English Garden (SW3)
English Hse. (SW3)
Floriana (SW3)
Fortnum's Fountain (W1)
Four Seasons, Lanes (W1)
Glasshouse (Kew)
Gordon Ramsay (SW3)
Goring Dining Rm. (SW1)
Gravetye Manor (W. Sus)
Greenhouse (W1)
Green's Rest. (SW1)
Hartwell House (Bucks)
Hilaire (SW7)
Hotel du Vin (multi. loc.)
Ivy (WC2)
Jason's (W9)
J. Sheekey (WC2)
Kai (W1)
Lanesborough (SW1)
Langan's Bistro (W1)
La Poule au Pot (SW1)
La Tante Claire (SW1)
Launceston Place (W8)
Leatherne Bottel (Berks)
Le Caprice (SW1)
Le Gavroche (W1)
Leith's (W11)
Le Manoir/Quat'Saisons (Oxon)
Le Soufflé (W1)

L'Incontro (SW1)
L'Oranger (SW1)
Lygon Arms (Wocs)
Manzi's (WC2)
Memories of China (SW1)
Mimmo d'Ischia (SW1)
Mirabelle (W1)
Monkeys (SW3)
Morton's (W1)
Motcomb's (SW1)
Neal St. (WC2)
Nico Central (W1)
Oak Room MPW (W1)
Odin's (W1)
One-O-One (SW1)
Orrery (W1)
Park Rest. (SW1)
Patisserie Valerie (SW3)
Pétrus (SW1)
Poissonnerie/l'Avenue (SW3)
Reubens (W1)
Richoux (NW8)
Ritz Rest. (W1)
Room/Halcyon (W11)
Rowley's (SW1)
Rules (WC2)
San Martino (SW3)
Sartoria (W1)
Savoy Grill (WC2)
Savoy River Rest. (WC2)
Scotts (W1)
Shepherd's (SW1)
Simpson's/The Strand (WC2)
Square (W1)
Stonor Arms (Oxon)
Tate Gallery (SW1)
Terrace (W1) (W1)
Trader Vic's (W1)
Turner's (SW3)
Upstairs/The Savoy (WC2)
Waterside Inn (Berks)
Wilton's (SW1)
Zen Central (W1)

Set Price Menus

(Call to check prices, days,
and times; best of many)
Abingdon (W8)
Alastair Little (W1)
Alastair Little/Lanc. Rd. (W11)
alistair Greig's Grill (W1)
Amandier (W2)
Apprentice (SE1)

Aubergine (SW10)
Avenue (SW1)
Bam-Bou (W1)
Belgo Centraal (WC2)
Belgo Noord (NW1)
Belgo Zuid (W1)
Bell Inn (Bucks)
Benihana (multi. loc.)
Bertorelli's (WC2)
Bibendum (SW3)
Bishopstrow Hse. (Wilts)
Bistro Daniel (W2)
Bistrorganic (W10)
Bluebird (SW3)
Blue Elephant (SW6)
Brackenbury (W6)
Brasserie St. Quentin (SW3)
Brown's Hotel, 1837 (W1)
Buckland Manor (Glos)
Butlers Wharf (SE1)
Café Pacifico (WC2)
Canteen (SW10)
Canyon (Richmond)
Capital Rest. (SW3)
Cave (W1)
Caviar Kaspia (W1)
Cherwell Boathse. (Oxon)
Chewton Glen Hotel (Hants)
Chez Bruce (SW17)
Chez Gérard (multi. loc.)
Chez Max (SW10)
Chiswick (W4)
Christopher's (WC2)
Chutney Mary (SW10)
Circus (W1)
Claridge's Rest. (W1)
Clarke's (W8)
Club Gascon (EC1)
Compleat Angler (Bucks)
Connaught Hotel (W1)
Dakota (W11)
Dan's (SW3)
Dorchester, Grill Rm. (W1)
Dorchester, Oriental (W1)
Drones (SW1)
Eastwell Manor (Kent)
Elena's L'Etoile (W1)
Emile's (multi. loc.)
English Garden (SW3)
English Hse. (SW3)
Fat Duck (Berks)

Feathers Hotel (Oxon)
Feng Shang (NW1)
Fifth Floor (SW1)
Floriana (SW3)
Four Seasons, Lanes (W1)
Goring Dining Rm. (SW1)
Granita (N1)
Gravetye Manor (W. Sus)
Greenhouse (W1)
Gresslin's (NW3)
Grissini (SW1)
Halkin, Stefano Cavallini (SW1)
Hambleton Hall (Rut)
Hartwell House (Bucks)
Hilaire (SW7)
Ibla (W1)
Idaho (N6)
Ikeda (W1)
I-Thai (W2)
Ivy (WC2)
Jason's (W9)
Julie's (W11)
Kensington Place (W8)
King's Head (Bucks)
Landmark, Dining Rm. (NW1)
Lanesborough (SW1)
La Poule au Pot (SW1)
Launceston Place (W8)
Lawn (SE3)
Leatherne Bottel (Berks)
Le Colombier (SW3)
Le Gavroche (W1)
Leith's (W11)
Leith's Soho (W1)
Le Manoir/Quat'Saisons (Oxon)
Le Pont de la Tour (SE1)
L'Escargot (W1)
Le Soufflé (W1)
L'Incontro (SW1)
Livebait (multi. loc.)
L'Odeon (W1)
Lola's (N1)
L'Oranger (SW1)
Lundum's (SW7)
Lygon Arms (Wocs)
Marquis (W1)
Marsh Goose (Glos)
Matsuri (SW1)
Mezzo (W1)
Mirabelle (W1)
Mitsukoshi (SW1)
Miyama (W1)

Morton's (W1)
Nico Central (W1)
Nobu (W1)
Novelli W8 (W8)
Oak Room MPW (W1)
Odin's (W1)
Offshore (W1)
Orange Balloon (multi. loc.)
Orrery (W1)
People's Palace (SE1)
Pescatori (multi. loc.)
Pharmacy (W11)
Phoenicia (W8)
Phoenix B&G (SW15)
Pied-à-Terre (W1)
Pink Geranium (Cambs)
Poissonnerie/l'Avenue (SW3)
Pomegranates (SW1)
Putney Bridge (SW15)
Quaglino's (SW1)
Rhodes in Square (SW1)
Richard Corrigan (W1)
Ritz Rest. (W1)
Room/Halcyon (W11)
Royal Oak (Berks)
Rules (WC2)
Sarkhel's Indian (SW1)
Savoy Grill (WC2)
Savoy River Rest. (WC2)
Scotts (W1)
755 (SW6)
Shogun (W1)
Sir Charles Napier (Oxon)
Snows on Green (W6)
Sonny's (SW13)
Square (W1)
Stapleford Park (Leics)
Stephen Bull (multi. loc.)
Suntory (SW1)
Tamarind (W1)
Tate Gallery (SW1)
Teatro (W1)
TECA (W1)
Tenth (W8)
Thierry's (SW3)
Turner's (SW3)
Vama (SW10)
Veeraswamy (W1)
Vong (SW1)
Waterside Inn (Berks)
White Onion (N1)
Wilton's (SW1)
Zafferano (SW1)

Singles Scenes

Admiral Codrington (SW3)
ArdRí/O'Conor Don (W1)
Atlantic B&G (W1)
Avenue (SW1)
Babe Ruth's (E1)
Balans (W1)
Balans West (SW5)
Bank (WC2)
Barcelona Tapas (multi. loc.)
Bar Madrid (W1)
Beach Blanket Babylon (W11)
Belgo Centraal (WC2)
Belgo Noord (NW1)
Belgo Zuid (W1)
Bierodrome (N1)
Big Easy (SW3)
Bistrot 190 (SW7)
Bistrot 2 Riverside (SE1)
Bluebird (SW3)
Blues Bistro (W1)
Brinkley's (SW10)
Brompton Bay (SW3)
Browns Rest. (multi. loc.)
Buona Sera/Jam (SW3)
Cactus Blue (SW3)
Café dell'Ugo (SE1)
Cafe de Paris (W1)
Café Pacifico (WC2)
Cantaloupe B&G (EC2)
Che (SW1)
Cheers (W1)
Chicago Rib Shack (SW7)
Christopher's (WC2)
Circus (W1)
Claridge's Bar (W1)
Coast (W1)
Corney & Barrow (EC3)
Crescent (SW3)
Cuba Libre (N1)
Denim (WC2)
Dorchester, Bar (W1)
Dover Street (W1)
Ebury Wine Bar (SW1)
Engineer (NW1)
Enterprise (SW3)
Euphorium (N1)
Fifth Floor Cafe (SW1)
First Floor (W11)
Foundation (SW1)
Fox & Anchor (EC1)
Freedom Brewing Co. (WC2)

Garlic & Shots (W1)
Havana (multi. loc.)
Henry J. Bean's (SW3)
Hothouse (E1)
Kettners (W1)
Lab (W1)
La Perla B&G (WC2)
latitude (SW3)
Little Havana (WC2)
Maroush (multi. loc.)
Mash (W1)
Mezzo (W1)
Mezzonine (W1)
Min's (SW3)
Momo (W1)
Moro (EC1)
Mortimer (W1)
Motcomb's (SW1)
Nachos (multi. loc.)
Nam Long Le Shaker (SW5)
Nobu (W1)
Oriel (SW1)
Oxo Tower (SE1)
Oxo Tower Brasserie (SE1)
Paparazzi Lounge (multi. loc.)
Pharmacy (W11)
Pitcher & Piano (multi. loc.)
Pizza on the Park (SW1)
PJ's Bar & Grill (SW3)
PJ's Grill (WC2)
Porters (WC2)
Putney Bridge (SW15)
Quaglino's (SW1)
Shoeless Joe's (SW6)
Shoreditch Electricity (N1)
Sound Republic (W1)
Spiga (W1)
Spighetta (W1)
Sports Cafe (SW1)
Sticky Fingers (W8)
Teatro (W1)
Texas Embassy (SW14)
Texas Lone Star (multi. loc.)
Titanic (W1)
Toast (NW3)
Trader Vic's (W1)
Voodoo Lounge (WC2)
Waterloo Fire Station (SE1)
Waxy O'Connor's (W1)
Wine Gallery (SW10)
Zinc B&G (W1)
Zoe (W1)

Sleepers
(Good to excellent food, but little known)

Al Sultan (W1)
Arancia (SE16)
Back to Basics (W1)
Bayee House (multi. loc.)
Bengal Trader (E1)
Bradley's (NW3)
Brady's (SW18)
Byron's (NW3)
Cafe Japan (NW11)
Cave (W1)
Chapter Two (SE3)
Cheng-Du (NW1)
Chez Liline (N4)
Chiang Mai (W1)
Chinon (W14)
City Miyama (EC4)
Cookhouse (SW15)
Defune (W1)
Duke of Cambridge (SW11)
Emile's (multi. loc.)
Enoteca Turi (SW15)
Esarn Kheaw (W12)
ffiona's (W8)
Florians (N8)
Four Seasons Chinese (W2)
Galicia (W10)
Gaudi (EC1)
Gladwins (EC3)
Great Nepalese (NW1)
Gung-Ho (NW6)
Home Bar Lounge (EC2)
Hunan (SW1)
Istanbul Iskembecisi (N16)
I-Thai (W2)
Iznik (N5)
Jen (W1)
Jin Kichi (NW3)
Joy King Lau (WC2)
Kai (W1)
Kaifeng (NW4)
Kastoori (SW17)
Kulu Kulu Sushi (W1)
La Dordogne (W4)
La Fontana (SW1)
Laurent (NW2)
Lee Fook (W2)
Le Soufflé (W1)
Maggiore's (WC2)
Ma Goa (SW15)

Maison Bertaux (W1)
Malabar Junction (WC1)
Matsuri (SW1)
Mesclun (N16)
Mitsukoshi (SW1)
Miyama (W1)
Monsieur Max (Hampton Hill)
Monza (SW3)
Moxon's (SW4)
Mr. Kong (WC2)
Nancy Lam's Enak Enak (SW11)
Nautilus Fish (NW6)
Noto (multi. loc.)
Old Delhi (W2)
One-O-One (SW1)
Park Rest. (SW1)
Pepper Tree (SW4)
Phoenix B&G (SW15)
Pizzeria Castello (SE1)
Place Below (EC2)
Princess Garden (W1)
Quincy's (NW2)
Rebato's (SW8)
Redmonds (SW14)
Roussillon (SW1)
Rudland & Stubbs (EC1)
Saigon (W1)
755 (SW6)
Shepherd's (SW1)
Shogun (W1)
Southeast W9 (W9)
Stratford's (W8)
TECA (W1)
Tentazioni (SE1)
Terrace (W8) (W8)
Toff's (N10)
Tom's Deli (W11)
Veronica's (W2)
Viet Hoa (multi. loc.)
Vrisaki (N22)
Wakaba (NW3)
Wilson's (W14)
Yoshino (W1)
Zen Garden (W1)

Teflons
(Get lots of business, despite so-so food, i.e. they have other attractions that prevent criticism from sticking)

All Bar One (multi. loc.)
Aroma (multi. loc.)
Babe Ruth's (multi. loc.)

Beach Blanket Babylon (W11)
Big Easy (SW3)
Break for the Border (multi. loc.)
Cactus Blue (SW3)
Café Flo (multi. loc.)
Cafe Rouge (multi. loc.)
Capital Radio Cafe (multi. loc.)
Chelsea Kitchen (SW3)
Chicago Rib Shack (SW7)
Coffee Republic (multi. loc.)
Corney & Barrow (multi. loc.)
Dôme (multi. loc.)
Down Mexico Way (W1)
Ed's Easy Diner (multi. loc.)
Henry J. Bean's (SW3)
Kettners (W1)
Pierre Victoire (W1)
Pitcher & Piano (multi. loc.)
Planet Hollywood (W1)
Rainforest Cafe (W1)
Richoux (multi. loc.)
Smollensky's/Strand (WC2)
Spaghetti House (multi. loc.)
Texas Embassy (SW14)
T.G.I. Friday's (multi. loc.)
Wong Kei (W1)
Zinc B&G (W1)

Smoking Prohibited

Amberley Castle, Queens (W. Sus)
Bear (Oxon)
Bedlington Cafe (W4)
Bell Inn (Bucks)
Books for Cooks (W11)
Buckland Manor (Glos)
Cafe at Sotheby's (W1)
Cherwell Boathse. (Oxon)
Chewton Glen Hotel (Hants)
Chez Moi (W11)
Cliveden, Waldo's (Berks)
Dining Room (Surrey)
DKNY Bar (W1)
Eastwell Manor (Kent)
Feathers Hotel (Oxon)
Flitwick Manor (Beds)
Food for Thought (WC2)
Gaudi (EC1)
Giraffe (multi. loc.)
Gravetye Manor (W. Sus)
Hartwell House (Bucks)
Horsted Place, Pugin (E. Sus)
Leaping Hare (Suffolk)
Le Manoir/Quat'Saisons (Oxon)

Lucknam Park (Wilts)
Lygon Arms (Wocs)
Mallory Court (Warwks)
Mandalay (W2)
Mandeer (WC1)
Marsh Goose (Glos)
Mildreds (W1)
Moshi Moshi Sushi (multi. loc.)
Museum St. Cafe (WC1)
Nancy Lam's Enak Enak (SW11)
Pennyhill Park, Latymer (Surrey)
Pink Geranium (Cambs)
Place Below (EC2)
Rainforest Cafe (W1)
Satsuma (W1)
Soup Opera (multi. loc.)
Soup Works (multi. loc.)
Starbucks/Seattle Co. (multi. loc.)
Villandry Foodstore (W1)
Wagamama (multi. loc.)
World Food Café (WC2)
Yo! Sushi (multi. loc.)

Special Occasions

Aubergine (SW10)
Avenue (SW1)
Bibendum (SW3)
Blakes Hotel (SW7)
Blue Elephant (SW6)
Brown's Hotel, 1837 (W1)
Capital Rest. (SW3)
Chewton Glen Hotel (Hants)
Chez Bruce (SW17)
Chez Nico (W1)
Claridge's Rest. (W1)
Clarke's (W8)
Cliveden, Waldo's (Berks)
Club Gascon (EC1)
Compleat Angler (Bucks)
Connaught Hotel (W1)
Criterion Brasserie (W1)
Daphne's (SW3)
Dorchester, Grill Rm. (W1)
Dorchester, Oriental (W1)
Floriana (SW3)
French Horn (Berks)
Frith Street (W1)
Glasshouse (Kew)
Gordon Ramsay (SW3)
Goring Dining Rm. (SW1)
Gravetye Manor (W. Sus)
Halkin, Stefano Cavallini (SW1)
Hartwell House (Bucks)

Hotel du Vin (multi. loc.)
I-Thai (W2)
Ivy (WC2)
J. Sheekey (WC2)
Lanesborough (SW1)
La Tante Claire (SW1)
Launceston Place (W8)
Leatherne Bottel (Berks)
Le Caprice (SW1)
Le Gavroche (W1)
Le Manoir/Quat'Saisons (Oxon)
Le Pont de la Tour (SE1)
Le Soufflé (W1)
L'Oranger (SW1)
L'Ortolan (Berks)
Mirabelle (W1)
Momo (W1)
Morton's (W1)
Neal St. (WC2)
Nobu (W1)
Oak Room MPW (W1)
Orrery (W1)
Pétrus (SW1)
Pied-à-Terre (W1)
Quaglino's (SW1)
Quo Vadis (W1)
Richard Corrigan (W1)
Ritz Rest. (W1)
River Cafe (W6)
San Lorenzo (SW3)
Sartoria (W1)
Savoy River Rest. (WC2)
Square (W1)
Stapleford Park (Leics)
Titanic (W1)
Vong (SW1)
Waterside Inn (Berks)
Windows on World (W1)
Zafferano (SW1)

Specialty Cheeses

Chewton Glen Hotel (Hants)
Chez Bruce (SW17)
Chez Nico (W1)
Claridge's Rest. (W1)
Clarke's (W8)
Connaught Hotel (W1)
Cucina (NW3)
Four Seasons, Lanes (W1)
Gordon Ramsay (SW3)
La Tante Claire (SW1)
Le Gavroche (W1)
Leith's (W11)

Le Manoir/Quat'Saisons (Oxon)
Le Soufflé (W1)
Monkeys (SW3)
Oak Room MPW (W1)
Orrery (W1)
Pétrus (SW1)
Square (W1)
Waterside Inn (Berks)
Windows on World (W1)

Teas

(See also Hotel Dining; the
following are highly touted)
Bell Inn (Bucks)
Berkeley Hotel (SW1)
Brown's Hotel (W1)
Cafe at Sotheby's (W1)
Capital Hotel (SW3)
Chewton Glen Hotel (Hants)
Claridge's (W1)
Compleat Angler (Bucks)
Connaught Hotel (W1)
Dorchester (W1)
Emporio Armani (SW3)
Fifth Floor Cafe (SW1)
Fortnum's Fountain (W1)
Four Seasons Hotel (W1)
Goring Hotel (SW1)
Harrods (SW1)
Hartwell House (Bucks)
Indigo (WC2)
Landmark London (NW1)
Lanesborough Hotel (SW1)
Le Manoir/Quat'Saisons (Oxon)
Le Metro (SW3)
Le Petit Blanc (multi. loc.)
L'Odeon (W1)
Mandarin Oriental/Hyde Pk. (SW1)
One Aldwych (WC2)
Palm Court (WC2)
Patisserie Valerie (multi. loc.)
Richoux (multi. loc.)
Ritz Hotel (W1)
Room/Halcyon (W11)
Savoy Hotel (WC2)
Tate Gallery (SW1)
Terrace (W1)
Upstairs/The Savoy (WC2)

Teen Appeal

Ask Pizza (W1)
Babe Ruth's (E1)
Belgo Centraal (WC2)

Belgo Noord (NW1)
Benihana (multi. loc.)
Big Easy (SW3)
Blue Elephant (SW6)
Break for the Border (multi. loc.)
Browns Rest. (SW3)
Buona Sera/Jam (SW3)
Busabong Too (SW10)
Cafe Lazeez (SW7)
Café Milan (SW3)
Café Pacifico (WC2)
Calzone (multi. loc.)
Cantina del Ponte (SE1)
Canyon (Richmond)
Capital Radio Cafe (WC2)
Casale Franco (N1)
Chelsea Bun (SW10)
Chelsea Kitchen (SW3)
Chelsea Ram (SW10)
Chicago Rib Shack (SW7)
Chuen Cheng Ku (W1)
Chutney Mary (SW10)
Dakota (W11)
Deals (multi. loc.)
DKNY Bar (W1)
Dôme (multi. loc.)
Down Mexico Way (W1)
Ed's Easy Diner (multi. loc.)
Fish! (SE1)
Foxtrot Oscar (multi. loc.)
Giraffe (multi. loc.)
Hard Rock Cafe (W1)
Havana (multi. loc.)
Henry J. Bean's (SW3)
itsu (SW3)
Jason's (W9)
Jenny Lo's (SW1)
Jim Thompson's (multi. loc.)
Joe Allen (WC2)
Kettners (W1)
King's Rd. Cafe (SW3)
La Delizia (multi. loc.)
La Famiglia (SW10)
La Mancha (SW15)
Le Petit Blanc (multi. loc.)
Little Havana (WC2)
Luigi's Deli (SW10)
Marine Ices (NW3)
Mash (W1)
Maxwell's (multi. loc.)
Meson Don Felipe (SE1)
Montana (SW6)

Moshi Moshi Sushi (multi. loc.)
Movenpick Marché (SW1)
Nachos (multi. loc.)
Navajo Joe (WC2)
New Culture Rev. (multi. loc.)
Oliveto (SW1)
Oxo Tower Brasserie (SE1)
Paparazzi Lounge (SW3)
Picasso (SW3)
Pitcher & Piano (multi. loc.)
Pizza Express (multi. loc.)
Pizza Metro (SW11)
Pizza on the Park (SW1)
Pizzeria Castello (SE1)
PJ's Bar & Grill (SW3)
PJ's Grill (WC2)
Planet Hollywood (W1)
Pucci Pizza (SW3)
Rainforest Cafe (W1)
Sauce BarOrganicDiner (NW1)
Shoeless Joe's (SW6)
Smollensky's/Strand (WC2)
Soho Spice (W1)
Sound Republic (W1)
Soup Opera (multi. loc.)
Soup Works (multi. loc.)
Spiga (W1)
Spighetta (W1)
Sports Cafe (SW1)
Sticky Fingers (W8)
Tea Rms. des Artistes (SW8)
Texas Embassy (SW14)
Texas Lone Star (multi. loc.)
T.G.I. Friday's (multi. loc.)
Tiger Lil's (SW10)
Titanic (W1)
Tootsies (multi. loc.)
Uno (SW1)
Vic Naylor (EC1)
Vingt-Quatre (SW10)
Wagamama (W1)
Waterloo Fire Station (SE1)
Wok Wok (multi. loc.)
Wolfe's B&G (WC2)
Yo! Sushi (multi. loc.)

Visitors on Expense Accounts
Bank (WC2)
Belair House (SE21)
Bentley's (W1)
Bibendum (SW3)
Bice (W1)

237

Blakes Hotel (SW7)
Brown's Hotel, 1837 (W1)
Canteen (SW10)
Capital Rest. (SW3)
Cave (W1)
Caviar Kaspia (W1)
Cecconi's (W1)
Che (SW1)
Chez Nico (W1)
City Rhodes (EC4)
Claridge's Rest. (W1)
Clarke's (W8)
Cliveden, Waldo's (Berks)
Club Gascon (EC1)
Connaught Hotel (W1)
Criterion Brasserie (W1)
Daphne's (SW3)
Dorchester, Grill Rm. (W1)
Dorchester, Oriental (W1)
Elena's L'Etoile (W1)
English Garden (SW3)
English Hse. (SW3)
Fifth Floor (SW1)
Floriana (SW3)
Four Seasons, Lanes (W1)
Frith Street (W1)
Glasshouse (Kew)
Gordon Ramsay (SW3)
Gravetye Manor (W. Sus)
Greenhouse (W1)
Green's Rest. (SW1)
Grissini (SW1)
Halkin, Stefano Cavallini (SW1)
I-Thai (W2)
Ivy (WC2)
J. Sheekey (WC2)
Kai (W1)
Lanesborough (SW1)
Langan's Brasserie (W1)
La Tante Claire (SW1)
Launceston Place (W8)
Le Caprice (SW1)
Le Gavroche (W1)
Leith's (W11)
Le Manoir/Quat'Saisons (Oxon)
Le Pont de la Tour (SE1)
L'Incontro (SW1)
L'Odeon (W1)
L'Oranger (SW1)
Maison Novelli (EC1)
Marquis (W1)
Matsuri (SW1)

Mirabelle (W1)
Mitsukoshi (SW1)
Morton's (W1)
Neal St. (WC2)
Nico Central (W1)
Nobu (W1)
Oak Room MPW (W1)
Odin's (W1)
One-O-One (SW1)
Orrery (W1)
Orso (WC2)
Oxo Tower (SE1)
Park Rest. (SW1)
Pétrus (SW1)
Pharmacy (W11)
Pied-à-Terre (W1)
Poissonnerie/l'Avenue (SW3)
Quaglino's (SW1)
Rhodes in Square (SW1)
Ritz Rest. (W1)
River Cafe (W6)
Salloos (SW1)
San Lorenzo (SW3)
Santini (SW1)
Sartoria (W1)
Savoy Grill (WC2)
Savoy River Rest. (WC2)
Scotts (W1)
Shogun (W1)
Square (W1)
Stephen Bull (W1)
Suntory (SW1)
Tamarind (W1)
Tatsuso (EC2)
Turner's (SW3)
Vong (SW1)
Waterside Inn (Berks)
Wilton's (SW1)
Windows on World (W1)
Zafferano (SW1)
Zaika (SW3)
Zen Central (W1)

Water View

Aquarium (E1)
Beetle & Wedge (Oxon)
Bistrot 2 Riverside (SE1)
Blue Print Cafe (SE1)
Butlers Wharf (SE1)
Canteen (SW10)
Cantina del Ponte (SE1)
Canyon (Richmond)
Cherwell Boathse. (Oxon)

Compleat Angler (Bucks)
County Hall (SE1)
Depot Waterfront (SW14)
Feng Shang (NW1)
Four Regions (SE1)
French Horn (Berks)
Hambleton Hall (Rut)
Leatherne Bottel (Berks)
Le Talbooth (Essex)
Oxo Tower (SE1)
Oxo Tower Brasserie (SE1)
People's Palace (SE1)
Putney Bridge (SW15)
River Cafe (W6)
Savoy River Rest. (WC2)
Searcy's/Barbican (EC2)
Stapleford Park (Leics)
Tenth (W8)
Thai on River (SW10)
Waterside Inn (Berks)

Wheelchair Access

(The following have indicated that they have wheelchair access, but it's best to call in advance to confirm)
Abingdon (W8)
Adams Cafe (W12)
Alastair Little (W1)
Alastair Little/Lanc. Rd. (W11)
Alba (EC1)
Alfred (WC2)
Al Hamra (W1)
alistair Greig's Grill (W1)
Al San Vincenzo (W2)
Anglesea Arms (W6)
Anna's Place (N1)
Apprentice (SE1)
Aquarium (E1)
Arancia (SW11)
Arcadia (W8)
Arkansas Cafe (E1)
Asia de Cuba (WC2)
Atlantic B&G (W1)
Atrium (SW1)
Avenue (SW1)
Babe Ruth's (multi. loc.)
Back to Basics (W1)
Balans West (SW5)
Bangkok (SW7)
Bank (WC2)
Bar Bourse (EC4)
Barcelona Tapas (multi. loc.)

Bayee House (SW15)
Bedlington Cafe (W4)
Beetle & Wedge (Oxon)
Belair House (SE21)
Belgo Centraal (WC2)
Belgo Noord (NW1)
Belgo Zuid (W1)
Bell Inn (Bucks)
Belvedere (W8)
Bengal Clipper (SE1)
Bengal Trader (E1)
Bentley's (W1)
Beotys (WC2)
Bierodrome (N1)
Big Chef (E14)
Birdcage (W1)
Bishopstrow Hse. (Wilts)
Bistrot 2 Riverside (SE1)
Blah! Blah! Blah! (W12)
Bloom's (NW11)
Bluebird (SW3)
Blue Elephant (SW6)
Blue Jade (SW1)
Bombay Bicycle (SW12)
Bombay Brasserie (SW7)
Bonjour Vietnam (SW6)
Brasserie Rocque (EC2)
Brinkley's (SW10)
Brown's Hotel, 1837 (W1)
Browns Rest. (W1)
Buchan's (SW11)
Builders Arms (SW3)
Bu-San (N7)
Butlers Wharf (SE1)
Byron's (NW3)
Cafe at Sotheby's (W1)
Café des Amis du Vin (WC2)
Café Fish (W1)
Café Flo (multi. loc.)
Cafe Lazeez (multi. loc.)
Cafe Med (W1)
Cafe Rouge (E14)
Cafe Spice Namaste (multi. loc.)
Caffè Nero (multi. loc.)
Calzone (multi. loc.)
Cambio de Tercio (SW5)
Camden Brasserie (NW1)
Cantaloupe B&G (EC2)
Canteen (SW10)
Canyon (Richmond)
Capital Radio Cafe (WC2)

Capital Rest. (SW3)
Caraffini (SW1)
Caravaggio (EC3)
Casale Franco (N1)
Chapter One (Kent)
Cheers (W1)
Chelsea Kitchen (SW3)
Chelsea Ram (SW10)
Cheng-Du (NW1)
Cherwell Boathse. (Oxon)
Chewton Glen Hotel (Hants)
Chez Gérard (multi. loc.)
Chez Moi (W11)
China Blues (NW1)
China City (WC2)
Chor Bizarre (W1)
Chutney Mary (SW10)
Cicada (EC1)
Cicoria (NW6)
City Rhodes (EC4)
Claridge's Rest. (W1)
Clarke's (W8)
Cliveden, Waldo's (Berks)
Coast (W1)
Como Lario (SW1)
Compleat Angler (Bucks)
Connaught Hotel (W1)
Cookhouse (SW15)
Coq d'Argent (EC2)
Corney & Barrow (multi. loc.)
Côte à Côte (SW11)
Cucina (NW3)
Dakota (W11)
Dan's (SW3)
Daphne (NW1)
Deals (multi. loc.)
De Cecco (SW6)
Del Buongustaio (SW15)
Delfina Studio Cafe (SE1)
dell'Ugo (W1)
Dôme (W8)
Dorchester, Bar (W1)
Dorchester, Grill Rm. (W1)
Down Mexico Way (W1)
Duke of Cambridge (SW11)
East One (EC1)
Eco (SW4)
Ed's Easy Diner (multi. loc.)
El Blason (SW3)
Elistano (SW3)
Emile's (multi. loc.)
Emporio Armani (SW3)

Engineer (NW1)
Enoteca Turi (SW15)
est (W1)
Euphorium (N1)
Fakhreldine Express (W1)
Fifth Floor (SW1)
Fish! (SE1)
Fortnum's Fountain (W1)
Four Seasons, Lanes (W1)
Fox & Anchor (EC1)
Foxtrot Oscar (multi. loc.)
Francofill (SW7)
French Horn (Berks)
Futures!! (EC2)
Galicia (W10)
Garbo's (W1)
Gaucho Grill (NW3)
Gay Hussar (W1)
Gladwins (EC3)
Glaister's Garden (SW11)
Globe (NW3)
Golden Dragon (W1)
Good Earth (SW3)
Gopal's of Soho (W1)
Goring Dining Rm. (SW1)
Granita (N1)
Grano (W4)
Greek Valley (NW8)
Green Cottage (NW3)
Greenhouse (W1)
Green Olive (W9)
Green's Rest. (SW1)
Grissini (SW1)
Halkin, Stefano Cavallini (SW1)
Hambleton Hall (Rut)
Harrods (SW1)
Hartwell House (Bucks)
Ho Ho (W1)
Honest Cabbage (SE1)
Hotel du Vin (multi. loc.)
House/Rosslyn Hill (NW3)
Ibla (W1)
Icon (SW3)
Il Falconiere (SW7)
Imperial City (EC3)
I-Thai (W2)
Ivy (WC2)
Japanese Canteen (multi. loc.)
Jason's (W9)
Jenny Lo's (SW1)
Jim Thompson's (multi. loc.)
J. Sheekey (WC2)

Justin's (W1)
Kai (W1)
Kastoori (SW17)
Kavanagh's (N1)
Kensington Place (W8)
La Belle Epoque/Brasserie (SW3)
La Belle Epoque/La Salle (SW3)
La Bersagliera (SW3)
La Bouchée (SW7)
La Brasserie du Marché (W10)
La Famiglia (SW10)
La Fontana (SW1)
La Mancha (SW15)
Landmark, Dining Rm. (NW1)
Lanesborough (SW1)
Lansdowne (NW1)
La Perla B&G (WC2)
La Porte des Indes (W1)
La Rueda (SW6)
Laurent (NW2)
Lavender (SW11)
Leaping Hare (Suffolk)
Le Bouchon Lyonnais (SW8)
Le Cafe du Jardin (WC2)
Le Caprice (SW1)
Le Colombier (SW3)
Lee Ho Fook (W1)
Leith's (W11)
Leith's Soho (W1)
Le Manoir/Quat'Saisons (Oxon)
Lemonia (NW1)
Le Muscadet (W1)
Le Petit Blanc (multi. loc.)
Le Piaf (multi. loc.)
Le Pont de la Tour (SE1)
Le Soufflé (W1)
L'Estaminet (WC2)
Le Talbooth (Essex)
L'Incontro (SW1)
Livebait (multi. loc.)
Lobster Pot (SE11)
L'Odeon (W1)
L'Ortolan (Berks)
Lou Pescadou (SW5)
Lucknam Park (Wilts)
Luigi's/Covent Garden (WC2)
Luigi's Deli (SW10)
Luna Nuova (WC2)
Lygon Arms (Wocs)
Mackintosh's (W4)
Malabar Junction (WC1)
Mallory Court (Warwks)

Mandarin Kitchen (W2)
Mao Tai (SW6)
Marsh Goose (Glos)
Mash (W1)
Matsuri (SW1)
Maxwell's (multi. loc.)
Mesclun (N16)
Meson Don Felipe (SE1)
Met Bar (W1Y)
Mezzo (W1)
Mezzonine (W1)
Ming (W1)
Momo (W1)
Mona Lisa (SW10)
Mon Plaisir (WC2)
Montana (SW6)
Moro (EC1)
Moshi Moshi Sushi (multi. loc.)
Movenpick Marché (SW1)
Museum St. Cafe (WC1)
Nachos (multi. loc.)
Neal St. (WC2)
New Culture Rev. (W1)
New World (W1)
Nobu (W1)
Noto (EC2)
Oak Room MPW (W1)
Offshore (W1)
Olivo (SW1)
1 Lombard St. (EC3)
192 (W11)
One-O-One (SW1)
One Paston Place (W. Sus)
Orange Balloon (multi. loc.)
Oriel (SW1)
Orrery (W1)
Osteria Antica Bologna (SW11)
Oxo Tower (SE1)
Oxo Tower Brasserie (SE1)
Pacific Oriental (EC2)
Park, The (NW6)
Patisserie Valerie (multi. loc.)
Peasant (EC1)
Pennyhill Park, Latymer (Surrey)
Pepper Tree (SW4)
Phoenicia (W8)
Phoenix B&G (SW15)
Pied-à-Terre (W1)
Pitcher & Piano (multi. loc.)
Pizza Express (multi. loc.)
Pizza The Action (SW6)
Pizzeria Castello (SE1)

PJ's Grill (WC2)
Planet Hollywood (W1)
Polygon B&G (SW4)
Pomegranates (SW1)
Poons (multi. loc.)
Poons in the City (EC3)
Porters (WC2)
Prism (EC3)
Purple Sage (W1)
Putney Bridge (SW15)
Quaglino's (SW1)
Quincy's (NW2)
Ransome's Dock (SW11)
Rasa (multi. loc.)
Redmonds (SW14)
Red Pepper (W9)
Rhodes in Square (SW1)
Rib Room (SW1)
Riccardo's (SW3)
Richoux (multi. loc.)
Riva (SW13)
River Cafe (W6)
RK Stanley's (W1)
Rodizio Rico (W2)
Rotisserie Jules (W11)
Rowley's (SW1)
Royal Oak (Berks)
Rudland & Stubbs (EC1)
Saigon Thuy (SW18)
Saint Bar & Rest. (WC2)
San Martino (SW3)
Santa Fe (N1)
Santini (SW1)
Sartoria (W1)
Satsuma (W1)
Scotts (W1)
Seafresh Fish (SW1)
Searcy's/Barbican (EC2)
755 (SW6)
Shoeless Joe's (multi. loc.)
Shoreditch Electricity (N1)
Simply Nico (EC1)
Simpson's/The Strand (WC2)
Singapura (multi. loc.)
Sir Charles Napier (Oxon)
Sofra (WC2)
Soho Soho (W1)
Soho Spice (W1)
Sonata (W1)
Sound Republic (W1)
Soup Opera (multi. loc.)
Soup Works (multi. loc.)

Spaghetti House (WC2)
Spago (W8)
Spiga (W1)
Sporting Page (SW10)
Sports Cafe (SW1)
Sri Siam City (EC2)
Stapleford Park (Leics)
Stephen Bull (multi. loc.)
Stephen Bull Smithfield (EC1)
Stepping Stone (SW8)
St. John (EC1)
Stonor Arms (Oxon)
Suntory (SW1)
Tajine (W1)
Tate Gallery (SW1)
Teatro (W1)
TECA (W1)
10 (EC2)
Tenth (W8)
Terraza (multi. loc.)
Texas Embassy (SW14)
Texas Lone Star (W4)
T.G.I. Friday's (multi. loc.)
Thai on River (SW10)
Three Lions (Hants)
Tiger Lil's (multi. loc.)
Tootsies (multi. loc.)
Townhouse (WC1)
Tui (SW7)
Union Cafe (W1)
Uno (SW1)
Vama (SW10)
Vasco & Piero's (W1)
Veronica's (W2)
Viet Hoa (E2)
Vinopolis (SE1)
Vong (SW1)
Voodoo Lounge (WC2)
Wagamama (multi. loc.)
Wòdka (W8)
Wok Wok (multi. loc.)
Wolfe's B&G (WC2)
Zafferano (SW1)
Zamoyski (NW3)
Zen Central (W1)
Zen Garden (W1)
Ziani (SW3)
Zinc B&G (W1)

Wine/Beer Only

Bloom's (NW11)
Brackenbury (W6)
Chelsea Kitchen (SW3)

Cork & Bottle (WC2)
Cranks (multi. loc.)
DKNY Bar (W1)
Eco (SW4)
Ed's Easy Diner (multi. loc.)
Fatboy's Cafe (W4)
Gate (W6)
Japanese Canteen (EC1)
Jenny Lo's (SW1)
Joe's Rest. Bar (SW1)
King's Rd. Cafe (SW3)
La Delizia (multi. loc.)
Mildreds (W1)
Moshi Moshi Sushi (EC4)
Noor Jahan (SW5)
Patisserie Valerie (multi. loc.)
Pepper Tree (SW4)
Randall & Aubin (W1)
Rasa (N16)
Rotisserie Jules (multi. loc.)
Troubadour (SW5)
Viet Hoa (E2)
Wong Kei (W1)

Winning Wine Lists

Auberge du Lac (Herts)
Aubergine (SW10)
Bibendum (SW3)
Brown's Hotel, 1837 (W1)
Cafe at Sotheby's (W1)
Capital Rest. (SW3)
Che (SW1)
Chewton Glen Hotel (Hants)
Chez Bruce (SW17)
Chez Nico (W1)
Christopher's (WC2)
Claridge's Rest. (W1)
Clarke's (W8)
Cliveden, Waldo's (Berks)
Connaught Hotel (W1)
Cork & Bottle (WC2)
Corney & Barrow (EC3)
Crescent (SW3)
Criterion Brasserie (W1)
Dorchester, Grill Rm. (W1)
Ebury Wine Bar (SW1)
Enoteca Turi (SW15)
Fifth Floor (SW1)
Four Seasons, Lanes (W1)
Glasshouse (Kew)
Gordon Ramsay (SW3)
Gravetye Manor (W. Sus)
Halkin, Stefano Cavallini (SW1)

Hilaire (SW7)
Hotel du Vin (multi. loc.)
La Dordogne (W4)
Lanesborough (SW1)
Langan's Bistro (W1)
La Tante Claire (SW1)
Le Gavroche (W1)
Leith's (W11)
Le Manoir/Quat'Saisons (Oxon)
Le Metro (SW3)
Le Pont de la Tour (SE1)
L'Escargot (W1)
Le Soufflé (W1)
L'Incontro (SW1)
L'Oranger (SW1)
L'Ortolan (Berks)
Mirabelle (W1)
Monkeys (SW3)
Nicole's (W1)
Oak Room MPW (W1)
Odette's (NW1)
Orrery (W1)
Park Rest. (SW1)
Pétrus (SW1)
Pied-à-Terre (W1)
Reynier Wine Library (EC3)
Richard Corrigan (W1)
Ritz Rest. (W1)
Room (SE1)
RSJ (SE1)
Sartoria (W1)
Savoy Grill (WC2)
Savoy River Rest. (WC2)
Square (W1)
Tate Gallery (SW1)
TECA (W1)
Turner's (SW3)
Vinopolis (SE1)
Waterside Inn (Berks)
Wilton's (SW1)
Windows on World (W1)
Zafferano (SW1)

Young Children
(Besides the normal fast-food
places; * indicates children's
menu available)
Abingdon (W8)*
Al Bustan (SW1)*
Al Hamra (W1)*
Angel (Bucks)*
Anglesea Arms (W6)*
Ask Pizza (multi. loc.)

Babe Ruth's (multi. loc.)*   Flitwick Manor (Beds)*
Back to Basics (W1)*   Florians (N8)*
Bank (WC2)*   Footstool (SW1)*
Bear (Oxon)*   Fortnum's Fountain (W1)*
Belair House (SE21)*   Four Seasons, Lanes (W1)*
Belgo Centraal (WC2)*   Frederick's (N1)*
Belgo Noord (NW1)*   Gaucho Grill (NW3)*
Belgo Zuid (W1)*   Hambleton Hall (Rut)*
Benihana (multi. loc.)*   Hard Rock Cafe (W1)*
Big Easy (SW3)*   Harrods (SW1)*
Bishopstrow Hse. (Wilts)*   House/Rosslyn Hill (NW3)*
Bistrot 2 Riverside (SE1)*   Idaho (N6)*
Bloom's (NW11)*   Istanbul Iskembecisi (N16)*
Bluebird (SW3)*   itsu (SW3)
Bombay Bicycle (SW12)*   Jim Thompson's (SW19)*
Brady's (SW18)*   Julie's (W11)*
Browns Rest. (multi. loc.)*   Kettners (W1)
Buona Sera (SW11)*   King's Rd. Cafe (SW3)*
Busabong Tree (SW10)*   Koi (W8)*
Café Fish (W1)*   La Delizia (multi. loc.)
Café Flo (multi. loc.)*   La Famiglia (SW10)
Café Milan (SW3)   Landmark, Dining Rm. (NW1)*
Café Pacifico (WC2)*   Lanesborough (SW1)*
Cafe Rouge (multi. loc.)*   La Porte des Indes (W1)*
Calzone (multi. loc.)*   Laurent (NW2)*
Cantina del Ponte (SE1)*   Lawn (SE3)*
Canyon (Richmond)*   Le Bouchon Bordelais (SW11)*
Capital Radio Cafe (WC2)*   Le Bouchon Lyonnais (SW8)*
Chelsea Bun (SW10)*   Le Manoir/Quat'Saisons (Oxon)*
Chelsea Kitchen (SW3)*   Le Petit Blanc (multi. loc.)*
Cherwell Boathse. (Oxon)*   Little Havana (WC2)*
Chicago Rib Shack (SW7)*   Livebait (WC2)*
Christopher's (WC2)*   Lola's (N1)*
Chuen Cheng Ku (W1)   Lou Pescadou (SW5)*
Chutney Mary (SW10)*   Luna Nuova (WC2)*
Cicoria (NW6)*   Lygon Arms (Wocs)*
City Miyama (EC4)*   Mackintosh's (W4)*
Como Lario (SW1)*   Maggiore's (WC2)*
Compleat Angler (Bucks)*   Mandalay (W2)*
Cuba Libre (N1)*   Marine Ices (NW3)
Dakota (W11)*   Matsuri (SW1)
Deals (multi. loc.)*   Maxwell's (multi. loc.)*
Del Buongustaio (SW15)*   Mitsukoshi (SW1)*
Depot Waterfront (SW14)*   Mona Lisa (SW10)*
Dôme (multi. loc.)*   Monsieur Max (Hampton Hill)*
Don Pepe (NW8)*   Montana (SW6)*
Dorchester, Grill Rm. (W1)*   Nachos (multi. loc.)*
Down Mexico Way (W1)*   Naked Turtle (SW14)*
Ed's Easy Diner (multi. loc.)*   Nautilus Fish (NW6)*
El Metro (SW6)*   Navajo Joe (WC2)*
Fifth Floor Cafe (SW1)   New Culture Rev. (multi. loc.)
Fish! (SE1)   Offshore (W1)*

244

Old Bridge Hotel (Cambs)*
Oliveto (SW1)*
Orange Balloon (multi. loc.)*
Oxo Tower (SE1)*
Oxo Tower Brasserie (SE1)*
Pelham St. (SW7)*
People's Palace (SE1)*
Phoenix B&G (SW15)*
Picasso (SW3)*
Pizza Express (WC2)*
Pizza Metro (SW11)
Pizza on the Park (SW1)
PJ's Bar & Grill (SW3)*
PJ's Grill (WC2)*
Planet Hollywood (W1)*
Putney Bridge (SW15)*
Quaglino's (SW1)*
Rainforest Cafe (W1)*
Redmonds (SW14)*
Red Pepper (W9)*
Reubens (W1)*
Riccardo's (SW3)*
Richoux (NW8)*
RK Stanley's (W1)*
Rock Garden (WC2)*
Rotisserie Jules (multi. loc.)*
Royal Oak (Berks)*
Sauce BarOrganicDiner (NW1)*

Seafresh Fish (SW1)*
Seashell (NW1)*
Shoeless Joe's (SW6)*
Smollensky's/Strand (WC2)*
Spaghetti House (SW1)*
Spiga (W1)
Spighetta (W1)
Sports Cafe (SW1)*
Stapleford Park (Leics)*
Sticky Fingers (W8)*
Tate Gallery (SW1)*
Tea Rms. des Artistes (SW8)*
Texas Embassy (SW14)*
Texas Lone Star (multi. loc.)*
T.G.I. Friday's (W2)*
Three Lions (Hants)*
Tiger Lil's (multi. loc.)*
Toff's (N10)*
Tootsies (multi. loc.)*
Townhouse (WC1)*
Veeraswamy (W1)*
Veronica's (W2)*
Vinopolis (SE1)*
Wagamama (multi. loc.)
Waterloo Fire Station (SE1)*
Wok Wok (SW11)*
Wolfe's B&G (WC2)*
Yo! Sushi (multi. loc.)

Rating Sheets

To aid in your participation in our next *Survey*

F | D | S | C

⌐⌐⌐⌐

Restaurant Name _____
Tel _____
Comments _____
_____
_____

⌐⌐⌐⌐

Restaurant Name _____
Tel _____
Comments _____
_____
_____

⌐⌐⌐⌐

Restaurant Name _____
Tel _____
Comments _____
_____
_____

⌐⌐⌐⌐

Restaurant Name _____
Tel _____
Comments _____
_____
_____

⌐⌐⌐⌐

Restaurant Name _____
Tel _____
Comments _____
_____
_____

⌐⌐⌐⌐

Restaurant Name _____
Tel _____
Comments _____
_____
_____

F | D | S | C |

⌐⌐⌐⌐

Restaurant Name _____
Tel _____
Comments _____
_____
_____
_____

⌐⌐⌐⌐

Restaurant Name _____
Tel _____
Comments _____
_____
_____
_____

⌐⌐⌐⌐

Restaurant Name _____
Tel _____
Comments _____
_____
_____
_____

⌐⌐⌐⌐

Restaurant Name _____
Tel _____
Comments _____
_____
_____
_____

⌐⌐⌐⌐

Restaurant Name _____
Tel _____
Comments _____
_____
_____
_____

⌐⌐⌐⌐

Restaurant Name _____
Tel _____
Comments _____
_____
_____
_____

F | D | S | C

⌐⌐⌐⌐

Restaurant Name _____
Tel _____
Comments _____
_____
_____

⌐⌐⌐⌐

Restaurant Name _____
Tel _____
Comments _____
_____
_____

⌐⌐⌐⌐

Restaurant Name _____
Tel _____
Comments _____
_____
_____

⌐⌐⌐⌐

Restaurant Name _____
Tel _____
Comments _____
_____
_____

⌐⌐⌐⌐

Restaurant Name _____
Tel _____
Comments _____
_____
_____

⌐⌐⌐⌐

Restaurant Name _____
Tel _____
Comments _____
_____
_____

┘┘┘┘

Restaurant Name _____
Tel _____
Comments _____
_____
_____

┘┘┘┘

Restaurant Name _____
Tel _____
Comments _____
_____
_____

┘┘┘┘

Restaurant Name _____
Tel _____
Comments _____
_____
_____

┘┘┘┘

Restaurant Name _____
Tel _____
Comments _____
_____
_____

┘┘┘┘

Restaurant Name _____
Tel _____
Comments _____
_____
_____

┘┘┘┘

Restaurant Name _____
Tel _____
Comments _____
_____
_____

Wine Vintage Chart 1985-1997

This chart is designed to help you select wine to go with your meal. It is based on the same 0 to 30 scale used throughout this *Survey*. The ratings (prepared by oenophile **Howard Stravitz**) reflect both the quality of the vintage and the wine's readiness for present consumption. Thus, if a wine is not fully mature or is over the hill, its rating has been reduced. We do not include 1987 or 1991 vintages because, with the exception of cabernets and '91 Northern Rhônes, those vintages are not especially recommended.

	'85	'86	'88	'89	'90	'92	'93	'94	'95	'96	'97
WHITES											
French:											
Burgundy	24	25	20	29	24	24	–	23	28	27	26
Loire Valley	–	–	–	26	25	19	22	23	24	25	23
Champagne	28	25	24	26	28	–	24	–	25	26	–
Sauternes	22	28	29	25	26	–	–	18	22	24	23
California:											
Chardonnay	–	–	–	–	–	25	24	23	26	23	22
REDS											
French:											
Bordeaux	26	27	25	28	29	19	22	24	25	24	22
Burgundy	25	–	24	27	29	23	25	22	24	25	24
Rhône	26	20	26	28	27	16	23*	23	24	22	–
Beaujolais	–	–	–	–	–	–	20	21	24	22	23
California:											
Cab./Merlot	26	26	–	21	28	26	25	27	23	24	22
Zinfandel	–	–	–	–	–	21	21	23	20	21	23
Italian:											
Tuscany	27	16	24	–	26	–	21	20	25	19	–
Piedmont	26	–	25	27	27	–	19	–	24	25	–

*Rating is only for Southern Rhône wine.

Bargain sippers take note: Some wines are reliable year in, year out, and are reasonably priced as well. These wines are best bought in the most recent vintages. They include: Alsatian Pinot Blancs, Côtes du Rhône, Muscadet, Bardolino, Valpolicella and inexpensive Spanish Rioja and California Zinfandel.